★ *lifestyle* │ 时尚生活

我在美国做妈妈

耶鲁法学院教授的育儿经

[美] 蔡美儿◎著　张新华◎译

Battle Hymn
of
the Tiger
Mother

中信出版社

CHINA CITIC PRESS

图书在版编目（CIP）数据

我在美国做妈妈：耶鲁法学院教授的育儿经/（美）蔡美儿著；张新华译.
—北京：中信出版社，2011.1
书名原文：Battle Hymn of the Tiger Mother
ISBN 978–7–5086–2611–6

I. 我… II. ①蔡… ②张… III. 家庭教育 IV. G78

中国版本图书馆 CIP 数据核字（2010）第 245825 号

我在美国做妈妈——耶鲁法学院教授的育儿经
WOZAI MEIGUO ZUOMAMA

著　　者：[美] 蔡美儿

译　　者：张新华

策划推广：中信出版社（China CITIC Press）

出版发行：中信出版集团股份有限公司（北京市朝阳区惠新东街甲4号富盛大厦2座　邮编　100029）
　　　　　（CITIC Publishing Group）

承 印 者：北京诚信伟业印刷有限公司

开　　本：787mm×1092mm　1/16　　　印　张：18　　　字　数：161千字

版　　次：2011 年 1 月第 1 版　　　　　印　次：2011 年 6 月第 8 次印刷

京权图字：01–2010–6623

书　　号：ISBN 978–7–5086–2611–6/G·648

定　　价：32.00 元

谨以本书献给索菲娅、路易莎和美文。

目录
Content

个"长着天使面孔的野丫头"。

———— *Part Two* ————

第二部分

倾巢出动，驾车9个小时，带着花大价钱请来的辅导老师及其男友、受伤后拄着双拐的索菲娅，还有我们的狗……

杰德永远不会明白，为什么我和露露前一分钟还扯着大嗓门儿朝死里地相互威胁，而后一分钟就见我们嘻嘻哈哈地躺在床上，一起海阔天空地谈琴聊书，笑声不断。

杨教授把手掌和手指拢成杯状、拱成帐篷之形，那些琴键似乎变成了一群孩子，他的手指"哄"着他们发出美妙的声音。而他的手指既刚劲有力又柔美优雅，就像芭蕾舞演员修长美丽的腿。

中国人为教育孩子所付出的努力大大超过西方人。作为母亲，我就是不会让自己停下来，喘口气，轻松一下。我知道，那些我们曾经害怕去尝试的事情，其实才是最有价值的。

从练习的准备到登台演出，为观众表演就像是在为他们"献血"，它掏空了你的情感，让你感到有一点儿轻飘飘的。这首曲子把欢乐带给观众，而与你朝夕相伴、耳鬓厮磨的音乐，就不再仅仅属于你……

热情豪放、慷慨宽厚的匈牙利人三次全场起立，把长时间雷鸣般的掌声，送给了这对美国的"音乐神童小姐妹"。可他们哪里知道，演出前的排练却是如此的一波三折……

—— *Part Three* ——

第三部分

本书讲述了一个故事——关于一位母亲、两个女儿和两条狗，关于莫扎特、门德尔松、钢琴和小提琴，以及我们是怎样荣登卡内基音乐圣殿。

你或许以为，这个故事想告诉读者——在教育和培养孩子方面，中国父母比西方父母更优秀。

可实际上，本书却聚焦了激烈的文化冲突、展现了如过眼烟云般掠过的赞美和荣耀，以及一位生活在美国的中国妈妈，是如何在一个13岁的孩子面前变得谦卑……

"中国式妈妈" → "美国式成功"

我是本书的翻译，也是一个生活在北京的中国妈妈。在繁忙的工作之余，我有幸赶在众多读者之前，走近了本书作者蔡美儿。

一页页地感受美儿教育孩子的真实和真情，一遍遍地惊叹美儿的投入和执著，一次次地体验美儿的超凡和绝然，一步步地走进美儿的喜怒和哀乐……美儿的鲜活形象越来越栩栩如生地展现在我的面前。

不经意间，我就被美儿深深地吸引了，打动了。

我不得不说，做母亲做到美儿这份儿上，真的很震撼！

引发竞价大战的猜想

毫无疑问，出生在美国、生活在美国的美儿，当然是一位"美国妈妈"。可在本书中，美儿却总是骄傲地称自己为"中国妈妈"。而在美国人的眼里，她却是两位"音乐神童小姐妹"的母亲，充满传奇色彩，并散发着几分东方的神秘。

美儿有两个女儿——索菲娅和路易莎，姐姐17岁，妹妹13岁。从跨进学校大门的第一个学期开始，她们就保持着门门功课皆"A"的全优纪录。姐妹俩差不多从3岁开始练琴。姐姐索菲娅14岁就把钢琴弹到了世界音乐的圣殿——著名的卡内基音乐大厅；妹妹路易莎在12岁那年，就坐上了耶鲁青年管弦乐团首席小提琴手的头把交椅。大庭广众之下，她们的举手投足更是彬彬有礼、可爱迷人，被羡慕不已的美国妈妈看做同龄人的楷模。

在美国这个竞争激烈的社会，这对姐妹的出类拔萃令美国父母惊叹："中国式妈妈"是怎样获得了他们极难企及的"美国式成功"？

或许，这正是本书在美国尚未出版，就引发竞价大战的一个重要原因。

在经济全球化的今天，中国的崛起和中国的成功越来越令世界刮目相看。"中国方式"不再是一个仅仅与落后为伍、与保守同类的贬义词。尤其是2010年12月，由世界经合组织（OECD）公布的、有34个国家参赛的国际学生评估项目（PISA）测试中，上海学生一举夺得阅读、数学、科学的冠军，使得中国的教育也进一步吸引了世界人民的眼球。而中国家庭教育孩子的方式，是不是也将在今后得到更多的关注呢？

2010年10月，我随先生在美国待了一个月，并去了好几个城市拜访朋友。谈起这本尚未在美国出版的书，我的美国朋友依然感觉这位中国式妈妈教育孩子的做法相当"另类"，这本书很可能会引起西方社会的争议。其实，在我们中国人眼里，她的做法甚至也非同寻常！也许，正因为"另类"

或非同寻常，人们才值得走近后看个究竟。①

对"不努力"说"No"

美儿在美国西方文化的包围中坚持做"中国妈妈"，绝不是海外华人追根寻祖的情感使然，而是在经历中西方文化的激烈冲突和认真比较后，她清醒而坚定地认同并选择了中国人教育孩子的方式。

美国人特别强调对孩子的尊重，他们常常把选择的权利交给孩子。结果孩子很轻易地就选择了放弃，因为没有什么人天生就喜欢努力，孩子们也宁愿张开双臂去拥抱轻松。美儿认为，西方父母对孩子的自尊担忧过多，但是作为父母，最不利于保护孩子自尊心的行为，就是你眼看着他们在困难面前放弃努力而不作为。

时间对每个人都是公平的，做每件事情都会有机会成本。因此我们所作出的每个选择，其实都意味着与此同时的某些放弃。而美儿的选择，是在一开始就不给孩子选择"不努力"的机会。我们看到，这其实是最好的一种选择。至于你是让孩子去弹钢琴还是拉小提琴，是玩吉他还是吹长笛，是画画还是游泳……让孩子选择任何有价值、有意义的事情，然后专心致志、全力以赴、坚持不懈地去做。孩子自然就会体验到，要做好一件事情，他需要怎样去做、要努力到何等程度。其实这个过程本身，就会让孩子在

---

① 本书的中文版与英文版几乎将同时在2011年1月面市。——译者注

举一反三中受益终身。

"青春"不会永远"反叛"

我们从第31章美儿的"泪洒红场",看到她与小女儿露露长期以来的对立和冲突,由一粒小小的鱼子酱而激起轩然大波。青春期叛逆的波涛,冲毁了美儿多年来构筑的坝堤……

然而,美儿在美国做妈妈的成功,并不会因露露的青春期反叛而黯然失色,也不会因女儿辞去青年交响乐团首席小提琴手的职务而前功尽弃,虽然这令美儿在每一秒钟都感到撕心裂肺的痛。

实际上,当露露活跃在网球场上,从刚开始参赛时被人"剃光头",到打败新英格兰种子选手;当露露主动延长训练时间、狂练反手球,并要求妈妈为她申请额外的网球训练课程;当我们听到露露的网球教练感叹:"她是那种不付出110%的努力,就绝不会善罢甘休的小姑娘。"我们清楚地看到,美儿已经把追求卓越的优秀品质,深深地种在了女儿的心里;让自信、执著的基因,成为了流淌在孩子血液中的红细胞;更别说高难度的小提琴带给灵魂的洗礼、情操的熏陶,以及赋予女孩的那份优雅和美丽!而那些曾经魂牵梦绕的旋律,难道会轻飘飘地悄然远去或消失吗?

当越来越多的中国父母将目光投向国外,寻求和接受西方先进的教育理念和方法,并开始反思我们自己甚至摈弃中国传统的养育思想之时,蔡美儿——这个"中国式妈妈"获得"美国式成功"的故事,值得我们回味和深思……

最后，请允许我对毕明建、江燕、晶晶、朱莉（Julie）、艾丽珂（Erica）和珍妮弗（Jennifer）表示诚挚的感谢。感谢你们帮助我解读本书的音乐专业术语和难点，才让我得以把这本书生动地呈现给千千万万个读者和母亲。

张新华

2010 年 12 月 20 日于北京

BATTLE HYMN
OF THE TIGER MOTHER

Part One
第一部分

老虎——力量与权力最为鲜明的象征。让人畏惧，
也令人肃然起敬。

1 中国妈妈

在学习上对孩子施加压力是否有害？怎样要求才算"严格"？学习上的生动有趣是第一位的吗？生活在美国的中国妈妈Vs.西方妈妈。

全家福（1996年）

许许多多的美国人，都对中国父母如何能够成功地培养出不同凡响的优秀孩子备感惊讶。他们想知道——"制造"众多的数学精英和音乐奇才，中国父母到底做了什么；他们家庭内部的结构是什么样子；中国父母的成功又能不能被他们所复制。

好吧，让我来揭开这个谜底，因为我就是一个这样的中国妈妈。

不过，在揭开谜底之前，我们最好还是先来看看下面这些我从来就不允许女儿索菲娅和路易莎涉足的事情：

- 在外面过夜
- 参加玩伴聚会
- 参加学校的戏剧表演
- 抱怨没有参加学校的戏剧表演
- 看电视或玩电脑游戏
- 选择自己喜欢的课外活动
- 任何一门功课的学习成绩低于"A"
- 除了体育和戏剧，其他科目不是第一
- 练习除了钢琴和小提琴以外的乐器
- 不拉小提琴或不弹钢琴

我总是宽泛地看待"中国妈妈"这个称谓。最近，我遇到一位超级成功的美国白人小伙子，他来自南达科他州（美国读者应该在电视上见过他）。在比较了我们各自家庭的"清规戒律"后，我们发现，他的蓝领爸爸，俨然就是一位"中国妈妈"。我还认识一些来自韩国、印度、牙买加、爱尔兰和加纳的父母，他们也完全拥有中国父母的品质。相反，我所认识的一些出生在西方国家但有着中国血统的妈妈，她们自觉或不自觉地，却并没有成为真正的"中国妈妈"。

我也宽泛地使用"西方父母"这个称谓。西方父母们林林总总、风格各异。事实上，我只要走出家门就会敏感地发现，与中国父母相比，西方父母教育孩子的方式迥然不同：有的严厉，有的宽松。父母们的类型也五花八门：同性恋的，信奉正统犹太教的，单亲的，前嬉皮士的，在投资银行工作的和出身于军人家庭的……显然，没有一对西方父母对教育孩子拥有相同的看法。因此，当我使用"西方父母"这个称谓时，并不是指所有的西方父母，正如我提到的"中国妈妈"，也不能代表每一位中国母亲一样。

尽管西方父母认为他们要求孩子已足够严格，但他们严格的尺度通常很难接近中国妈妈的标准。例如，我的西方朋友们要求孩子弹奏乐器，每天半小时，最多一小时，他们认为这已经严厉有加了。然而，对中国妈妈来说，孩子们进行弹奏的第一个小时，就像是轻松愉快的热身，而不停地弹上两三个小时，那才算得上是"练习"，才具有一定的难度。

尽管我们对文化差异的老生常谈已提不起兴趣，但在养育孩子方面，的确有无数研究有理有据地证实了中西文化之间存在着明显差异。

一份对50位西方妈妈和48位中国妈妈的调查研究显示，70%的西方妈妈认为，"在学习上对孩子施加压力的做法是有害的"，"父母应本着让学习变得生动有趣的思路来培养孩子"。可是与此相反的是，没有一个中国妈妈赞成这样的想法。大多数的中国妈妈确信她们的孩子可以在学校里出类拔萃，她们认为"孩子在学业上的成就反映了家长教子有方"；如果孩子不能在学校里如鱼得水，那就"有问题"了，就说明做父母的"严重失职"。此外，还有一些研究发现，中国妈妈每天督促孩子进行学习的时间，大约是西方妈妈的10倍。而西方的孩子，则更热衷于在学校运动队的活动中抛头露面、展示才华。

观察这些现象让我找到了问题的关键。或许有人认为美国的"运动妈妈"与中国的"功课妈妈"没什么两样，那他们可就大错特错了。与按照日程表监督孩子参加训练的西方"足球妈妈"相比，中国妈妈相信：（1）完成学业总是第一位的；（2）考试中的"A–"是不合格的；（3）必须要在数学上比同班同学领先两个学年；（4）绝不能在公共场合夸奖孩子；（5）如果孩子与老师或教练发生冲突，做家长的必须坚定地站在老师或教练一边；（6）父母唯一允许孩子参加的课外活动，是那些他们能赢得奖牌的项目；（7）而且必须是金牌！

2　索菲娅

　　在我们这个"华裔＋犹太＝美国"的家庭，她18个月就认识字母表，3岁阅读《小妇人》简写本并开始学弹钢琴。

索菲娅
(Susan Bradley Photography)

索菲娅是我的第一个女儿。我丈夫杰德是个美籍犹太人，而我是个华裔。这样，我们的孩子就成了"华裔—犹太—美国"人，属于一个似乎颇具异国风情的人群。确切地说，在某些社交圈子里，这类人的数量还不少，尤其是在大学城里。

在英语里，索菲娅的名字代表"智慧"，而这个词的发音，很像是我母亲给孙女取的中国名字——思慧。

从索菲娅呱呱落地起，她就显示出极为理性的禀赋和特别专注的能力，而这些品质得益于她的父亲。当时，尚在襁褓之中的索菲娅总是乖乖地入睡，整个夜晚都不吵不闹；偶尔啼哭，也有着格外明确的目的。那时，我正在撰写一篇有关法律的文章（从我供职的华尔街一家法律事务所休产假后，我拼命地想找到一个大学里的教职——这样我就不必再重返华尔街了），仅仅两个月大的索菲娅对此似乎十分理解。在她1岁之前，她都是那么安然而沉静，只是睡觉、吃东西，并瞪着一双纯净无邪的大眼睛，看着时常文思枯竭、大脑短路的我。

索菲娅的智力发育比较早，她在18个月时就认识字母表。我们的小儿科医生从神经学的意义上否认这种可能性，他坚持说，这只是小孩子的牙牙学语。为了证明这一点，他拿出一张由蛇和独角兽等小动物乔装打扮的大大的字母彩图。医生看看图片，瞧瞧索菲娅，然后再把目光转向图片。他狡黠地眨眨眼睛，指着一只披着睡袍、戴着贝雷帽的蟾蜍所代表的字母。

"Q！"索菲娅用稚气的嗓门尖声地叫道。

"无师自通……"医生惊讶地咕哝着。

我在一旁为医生的非正式测验暗暗紧张。终于到了最后一个字母，那是一条飞吐着数根血红舌头的九头蛇。"I。"索菲娅依然准确无误地读出了它。

索菲娅在上幼儿园时就非常出众，尤其是在数学方面。当其他孩子还在用创造性的美国式方法，以小棒、珠子和锥形物体等道具学习从1数到10的时候，我已经在用死记硬背的中国式方法，教索菲娅加、减、乘、除，以及分数和小数，而它们是很难用小棒、珠子和锥形物体来演示正确答案的。

杰德和我结婚的时候曾达成协议，要让我们的孩子说中国的普通话，但遵从犹太人成长的礼节。（我虽然是在信奉天主教的家庭里长大的，但对宗教信仰并不十分执著，因为天主教在我的家庭里并没有扎下多深的根，是到了后来才有了更多的影响。）回想起来，这真是一个可笑的协议。因为我的家乡在中国福建，我自己并不会说普通话，而杰德压根儿就不信教。我雇了位能不断和索菲娅说普通话的中国保姆。在索菲娅两个月大的时候，我们也第一次欢庆了犹太人的"光明节"（Hanukkah）。

待索菲娅长大一点点，我们发现她似乎吸纳了两种文化中最优秀的部分。她秉承了犹太人永无止境地追求和刨根问底的精神，也从我这里学会了各种各样的技能。我并不是指任何天生就拥有的技能，而是指那些以中国人的方式培养出的勤奋、自律和自信，并让这些素质不断拓展的技能。

刚刚3岁，索菲娅就能够阅读《小妇人》（*Little Women*）的简写本，能够进行简单的归纳，并用中文写出100个字的短文，还不包括其中的数字。当我看到美国的父母试图用一次又一次的表扬，来鼓励孩子完成那些诸如画出一条歪歪扭扭的线条或学会挥舞小棒这样极其简单的任务时，我发现中国父母有两件事超越了美国的父母：（1）他们在孩子身上寄予了更高的期望、更美的梦想；（2）他们更在意自己的孩子在人生路上到底能"走"多远、能"跳"多高。

　　我也渴望看到索菲娅能够吸收美国社会最优秀的文化，不希望她像很多亚洲孩子那样，最后成为机器人似的怪胎——有的孩子从父母那里感受到难以承受的压力，甚至仅仅因为在国家公务员考试中得了第二名就会去自杀！我盼望她多才多艺、全面发展，有自己醉心的业余爱好和着迷的活动，但不是任何小兴趣（比如"手工劳动"这种努力方向不明确的活动；或者更糟，去练习敲鼓，最后可能染上吸毒的恶习），而是更有意义、更难掌握、更能发展高深的艺术造诣、提高自身潜能的爱好。

　　基于以上的想法，我为女儿选中了钢琴。

　　1996年，就在索菲娅3岁的时候，她张开稚嫩的双臂，迎来了生活中的两件新鲜事儿：第一次钢琴课，还有她可爱的小妹妹。

3 路易莎

叫她向东，她偏要向西——我的小女儿就是这样一个"长着天使面孔的野丫头"。

路易莎

有一首乡村歌曲这样唱道，"她是一个长着天使面孔的野丫头"，说的就是我的小女儿露露。说到她，我就不由得想到如何才能驯服一匹狂野奔放的马。甚至在我怀孕的时候，小露露就经常在我的子宫里大展拳脚，并在我的肚皮上留下清晰可见的"霹雳脚"。露露的大名叫路易莎，意思是"闻名天下的武士"。嗨，我也纳闷，我们为何在她如此年幼之时就为她取了这么个八面威风的名字。

露露的中国名字叫"思珊"，即指"珊瑚"，隐含着精美绝伦之意。对露露来说，这个名字真是再贴切不过了。从出生的那天起，露露就有着非凡的味觉。她不喜欢专为婴儿配制的奶粉，对儿科医生建议我们喂她的豆奶也十分抗拒，因此常常饿肚皮。与圣雄甘地无私无畏并配合冥思静养的绝食斗争迥然不同，腹中饥饿的露露每天夜里都挥舞着小手放声啼哭。每当我们的中国保姆格蕾丝及时赶来"营救"时，杰德和我都是一副头戴耳塞、手忙脚乱的狼狈样。格蕾丝用一种带有淡淡的鲍鱼和香菇味道的调味汁，烹制出一款口味绵滑的豆腐脑，竟然令露露止住了哭闹，咂巴着小嘴吃得津津有味。

很难用语言来描述我与露露的关系，说我们母女间的对阵犹如打一场"全面升级的核战争"并不能一语中的。然而，颇具讽刺意味的是，露露和我非常相似：她秉承了我火暴的脾气、伶俐的口齿和从不记仇的个性。

说到人的个性，我并不相信什么占星术（我认为每个人都不可能回避自己人生道路上的难题），但是中国传统的十二生肖却对索菲娅和露露的个性作出了完美的解释。索菲娅出生在中国的猴年，属猴之人通常好奇、聪明，没有什么事情能够难住他们。生在猪年的人则比较任性、倔犟，其火暴脾气常常"一点就着"，但却从不把怨恨留在心里；他们全然是诚实可靠、拥有一副火热心肠的人。而这——正是露露的生动写照。

出生在虎年的我并不想沾沾自喜、自吹自擂，但是属虎的人一般气质高贵、勇敢无畏，他们强壮有力、仪态威严，并具有天生的号召力。他们也是一些被命运垂青的宠儿，贝多芬、孙中山，皆是属虎之人。

我与露露的第一次冲突发生在她3岁那年。

康涅狄格州纽黑文市，冬日里一个北风凛冽的下午——那年最寒冷的一天。在耶鲁法学院担任教授的杰德忙着工作，而索菲娅正在上幼儿园。我期待着让露露第一次接触钢琴、走进音乐的神奇天地，而那天下午正是一个绝佳的机会。

一头褐色的卷发、一双圆圆的眼睛，还有一张中国式的娃娃脸，露露看起来真是可爱极了。我非常兴奋地将她抱起来放到覆盖着柔软坐垫的琴凳上。舒舒服服地落座后，我教她怎样用一根手指头在钢琴上弹出一个音符。我示范了三次，并要求她跟着我做。可是露露却拒绝学做这个简单的动作，她宁愿伸出双手，用两个巴掌在琴键上胡乱拍击。钢琴发出恐怖的怪叫声。我让露露"住手"，可她却拍打得越来越重、越来越快、越来越起劲儿。我想将她从琴凳上抱下来，结果她连蹬带踹、又哭又闹地不肯撒手。

15分钟过去了，她依然号叫着、哭泣着、蹬踢着。终于，我忍无可忍。躲避着她的拳打脚踢，我把这个尖叫的小魔鬼拖到后门，直接扔到了室外的门廊里。

刺骨的寒风在-6℃的低温中扑面而来，短短几秒钟，我就感觉到像刀一样锋利的北风似乎刮伤了我的脸。但是，如果孩子桀骜不驯、难以管教，我宁愿要一个听话的中国孩子。在西方的文化里，顺从只与狗和森严的等级联系在一起；而在中国文化中，它却是一种高尚的美德。

"如果你不听妈妈的话，你就不能待在屋子里。"我严厉地对露露说，"那么现在，你想做个好女孩，还是要待在外面？"

听了我的话，露露竟然自己走到院子里。她扬起头来看着我，一脸的挑衅。

我开始有些担心，因为露露只穿着毛衣、紧身裤和饰有皱褶花边的小裙子。她不再哭喊，事实上，她安静得让人害怕。

"好吧，你想做个乖孩子，"我赶紧为她搭了个台阶，说，"那么现在，你可以进来了。"

可露露却摇了摇头。

"露露，别傻了。外面冰天雪地，你会冻坏的，赶快进来吧！"

瑟瑟的寒风中，露露冻得牙齿打战，但她依然摇着头，用倔犟的神情拼写出一个无言的"No"。将此情此景看得真真切切的我发现自己低估了露露。她到底是用什么材料做的——小小的她宁愿站在雪地里冻死，也不愿意屈服！

我不得不迅速改变战术，我知道——在这场战争中，针尖对麦芒，我赢不了！我的脑子飞快地转动着，于是掉转头来，乞求、哄骗加贿赂，终于把露露拉回了屋里。当杰德和索菲娅回家的时候，他们看见露露浸泡在热气腾腾的浴缸里，正就着带蜜饯的核仁巧克力饼，惬意地享用着一杯香甜浓郁的热可可。

而露露也低估了我——刚刚打了败仗的我正在重新武装自己。

战场已然铺开，可露露对此却一无所知。

4 蔡氏家族

展开我们的"美国梦"——父亲拿到了麻省理工学院的博士学位，我们三个姐妹也相继走进哈佛法学院、耶鲁大学和哈佛大学，捧回硕士和博士学位……

我姓"蔡"(Chua)——普通话的汉语拼音是"Cài"，我喜欢自己的姓氏。我的家乡在中国南方的福建省，一个盛产学者和科学家的地方。

明朝神宗年间，我父亲的家族里，有一位直系的先祖蔡武能在朝廷做天文学家，他同时也是个哲学家和诗人。1644年，当时的明朝正面临着满清入关的危境。因为技艺全面、学识渊博，武能被皇帝御封为朝廷的兵部重臣。家族中最珍视的传家之宝（事实上，也是我们唯一的祖传遗物），是由武能手书的长达2 000页的专著，该书阐述了中国最古老的经典之作《易经》。这本牛皮封面上写着一个"蔡"字的传家之宝，如今就醒目地摆放在我家起居室的咖啡桌上。

我所有的祖辈都出生于福建。在20世纪二三十年代，他们先后乘船前往菲律宾，据说那里有更多的机会、更好的生活。

我姥爷原本是一位儒雅、慈祥的教书匠，为了维持生计，他不得不放下教鞭去卖大米。姥爷不信教，尤其不擅长经商。而姥姥是一位非常美丽而虔诚的佛教徒，尽管她所信奉的观音菩萨并不看重物质的享受，可她还是希望丈夫的生意更加红火、兴旺。

我爷爷经营鱼酱的生意，他是个好脾气的商人。和姥爷一样，既不信教，也无缘于经商。我精明能干的奶奶在第二次世界大战后做塑料制品的买卖（主要是为强生公司生产塑料容器）赚了许多钱，然后，她把盈余都换成了金条和钻石。变得富有之后，她在马尼拉最具声望的社区买了座华丽的豪宅。后来，奶奶和我的叔叔开始在火奴鲁鲁收藏蒂法尼玻璃制品（Tiffany glass）、玛丽·卡萨特（Mary Cassatt）和布拉克斯（Braques）的画作，并在火奴鲁鲁拥有了独立产权的公寓。同时，他们皈依了新教，并在饭桌上用西式的叉子和汤勺代替了中式的筷子，活得越来越像美国人。

我母亲1936年出生于中国，与父母举家迁往菲律宾时，她才两岁。后来日本人占领了菲律宾。在那个兵荒马乱的年月，她失去了尚在襁褓之中的小弟弟。我也绝不会忘记母亲曾经向我描述的那幅恐怖画面：一群日本兵抓住了舅舅，他们掐住他的脖子迫使他张大嘴巴，然后一边拼命地给他灌水，一边残忍地狞笑着，想要看看可怜的舅舅会不会像只充气过度的气球那样砰然爆炸。

1945年，道格拉斯·麦克阿瑟将军领导的美国军队解放了菲律宾。母亲清楚地记得美军吉普车驶过街头的情景，在士兵们向人群不停地抛掷火腿罐头时，当时还仅仅是个小女孩的她，追着军车一路上欢呼雀跃。

战争结束后，母亲到一所修道士开办的中学读书。在那里，她改信了天主教。后来，她以全班第一的优异成绩毕业于圣托马斯大学，并获得了化学工程学位。

我的父亲对移民美国总是充满向往。颇有数学天分、酷爱天文学和哲学的他，对在唯利是图、尔虞我诈的生意场上周旋的家族生意深恶痛绝，本能地反抗家人为他作出的每个安排。甚至在他还是个小男孩的时候，就拼命地寻找去美国的机会。后来，马萨诸塞州的麻省理工学院批准了他的入学申请，他终于"好梦成真"。

父亲在1961年正式向母亲求婚，同年的晚些时候，他们就双双来到波士顿。当时并不知道，这个地方正是美国的灵魂所在。他们用微薄的奖学金维持日常的开销，甚至无法负担冬季的取暖费。在他们初到波士顿的那两个冬天，常常要裹着毯子来保暖。可是不到两年，父亲就拿到了博士学位，并在印第安纳州西拉斐特的普渡大学担任助教。

在美国中西部长大，我和三个妹妹时时感受到我们与别人的不同。

我们每天都要用保温盒将中式午餐带到学校，而我是多么渴望像其他同学那样吃到一块夹着腊肠的三明治！父母要求我们在家里说中国话，如果一不留神说漏了嘴，在言语间夹杂着一两个英语单词，立刻就会为此受到惩罚：用筷子打手板，而且是被狠狠地打。每天下午，我们都得演算数学、练习钢琴，父母从不允许我们到朋友家过夜。父亲每天晚上下班回到家，我都要恭恭敬敬地为他脱下皮鞋和袜子，递上拖鞋。

我们的成绩通知单一定要完美无缺——我们的朋友也许会因好几门功课得到"B"而获得家长的奖励，可我们哪怕是在全"A"中仅有一个"A-"，都会令父母感到难堪。记得八年级那年，我在一次历史考试中得了第二名，学生和家长都参加了颁奖仪式。有位同学因为全优的成绩获得基瓦尼斯奖，还在会上受到特别褒奖。颁奖仪式结束后，记得父亲只对我说了一句话：
"千万、千万不要再让我像这样丢脸了！"

我的朋友听到这个故事之后，他们通常以为我的童年恐怖无比，可这并
不是事实。实际上，在这个让外人感到怪异的家庭里，我汲取了奋发向上
的力量和信心。在刚开始步入美国社会的时候，我们完全就像一些局外人；
但逐步地，我们融入了美国社会，成为美国人。

记得父亲每天晚上都工作到凌晨 3 点。他是那样的专注，甚至常常无法
察觉我们走进了房间。我至今还记得他兴奋地向我们推荐墨西哥玉米面豆
卷、邋遢乔辣汁肉末三明治①、奶品皇后等各种风味美食，以及可以敞开肚
皮吃个够的自助餐，更别提那些带我们去坐雪橇、滑雪、捉螃蟹和野营的
开心时光了。

记得上小学的时候，有个美国男孩嘲笑我将饭店的单词"restaurant"
发成了"restOWrant"，他一边做着鄙视的手势并模仿我的口音，一边狂笑
不止。就在那一刻，我发誓要彻底摆脱我的中国口音。参加女童子军、玩
呼啦圈、进行诗词竞赛、到公共图书馆看书、在"美国革命的女儿征文比赛"
获奖，以及为父母加入美国籍而自豪的情形，都给我留下了极深刻的印象，
至今都感觉历历在目。

1971 年，父亲接到去加利福尼亚大学任教的聘书，于是，我们全家打
点行装来到美国西部城市伯克利。在那里，父亲留长发，穿着带有"和平"
印记的夹克衫。后来，他对收集葡萄酒产生了浓厚的兴趣，并建造了一个
能容纳上千瓶葡萄酒的酒窖。在他因自己的混沌理论而成为国际知名学者

① 邋遢乔辣汁肉末三明治（sloppy Joes），一种将酸辣汁烹饪的牛肉末夹在碗状三明治中的美
国风味食品。——译者注

时，我们开始在世界各地旅行。我的高中二年级先后在英国的伦敦、德国的慕尼黑和瑞士的洛桑就读。在父亲的带领下，我们甚至把足迹留在了遥远的北极。

然而，我父亲仍然是个中国式的家长。

到了该选择并申请大学的时候，他坚持让我就读加州大学伯克利分校（当时我已经被这所大学录取），并且要住在家里。这就是说，我要面对一种全然没有校园生活的学习——这样的选择令我极其痛苦。我开始违抗父命，一如当年他对家庭的反叛。我伪造他的签字，悄悄地申请了我听人们谈及的一所位于东海岸的学校。当我公开自己的秘密行动，告诉父亲我已被哈佛大学录取时，他的反应真令我大跌眼镜——从大发雷霆逐渐转变成为女儿骄傲，他折腾了整整一宿。

尽管在女儿离家时会有一丝淡淡的哀伤在他心里挥之不去，但父亲后来享受到了很多的自豪时刻——我从哈佛法学院毕业；他的二女儿美夏怀揣毕业证书走出耶鲁大学和耶鲁法学院；而他最开心的，是他的三女儿美文也上了哈佛大学，并在那儿拿到了硕士和博士学位。

美国改变着生活在那里的人们。

我4岁的时候，父亲曾经对我说过——"你将来嫁人一定要嫁给华裔。嫁给非华裔男人？哼，只要我还在喘气儿，就绝对没门儿！"但是最后，我却嫁给了杰德，一个有着犹太血统的美国人。如今，我的丈夫和父亲居然成为了最好的朋友。

在我很小的时候，我父母对残疾人并无特别的同情心。即便是在今天，许多亚洲人也将身患残疾看做是令人羞愧之事。因此，在我最小的妹妹美音带着唐氏综合征①的先天残疾来到这个世界时，母亲经常为可怜的小女儿伤心落泪，一些亲戚也劝我们赶快把她送到菲律宾的慈善机构去。可母亲并没有这样做，她拜访了对残疾人进行特殊教育的老师，联络了不少拥有残疾孩子的父母。很快，她就开始不厌其烦地花费大量的时间，和美音一起玩拼图，并教她画画。当美音该上小学的时候，母亲就教她读书，和她一起练习乘法口诀。如今，美音已在国际特殊奥林匹克运动会游泳项目上先后夺得过两枚金牌。

担心数千年灿烂的华夏文明在我这里不能得以延续，对没有嫁给中国人我似乎有那么一点点惋惜。但对我来说，更多的是对美国给我们提供的自由天地和机会心怀深深的感激。我的女儿生活在美国已不再有异国他乡之感（我有时候还会有），而对我来说，那丝淡淡的乡愁并不是一种负担，而更像是一种殊荣。

---

① 唐氏综合征（Down's Syndrome），又称为先天愚型，是最常见的严重的出生缺陷疾病之一。1959年，研究人员证实唐氏综合征是由染色体异常（多了一条21号染色体）而导致的。患者绝大多数为严重智能障碍并伴有多种脏器的异常，如先天性心脏病、白血病、消化道畸形等。——译者注

5 一代不如一代？

打破"富不过三代"的魔咒，是我坚持让孩子们学习古典音乐的原因。因为弹钢琴、拉小提琴不会让人在溺爱中走向堕落、懒惰和粗鲁。

勇敢无畏的父母和刚刚出生的我（摄于他们来美国的一年后）

我最大的恐惧是家族的没落。中国有一句魔咒般的俗语——"富不过三代。"如果有人对两代人的成就进行一项纵向的调查研究，我确信，他们会在那些最近50年来以大学毕业生或技术工人的身份幸运地来到美国的中国移民中，发现一种共同的生存模式。这种模式大致如下：

- **移民的一代**（就像我的父母）总是拼命工作，许多人刚来美国时几乎是一贫如洗。他们起早贪黑、没完没了地干活，直到功成名就，成为工程师、科学家、医生、学者或商人。身为父母，他们是超级严厉的长辈和省吃俭用的节俭狂——"不许倒掉剩菜剩饭！""你为什么用这么多的洗洁剂？""你不需要进美容院，我的理发技术比他们更棒。"他们很少喝酒，会把节约的钱用于房地产投资。他们所做的每一件事情、所挣的每一分钱，通通都是为了孩子们的教育，并虔诚地期待他们拥有与自己不一样的未来。

- **第二代移民**（就像我）是出生在美国的第一代，他们中的典型人物颇有建树。他们通常弹钢琴、拉小提琴，进常春藤盟校；成为专门的人才——律师、医生、银行家、电视主持人。他们的收入大大超越父母，一方面是由于自己挣得多，一方面是缘于父母在他们身上进行了巨大的投资。不像父母那样节俭，他们喜欢喝鸡尾酒。女性通常会嫁给白人；不管是男性还是女性，他们对待自己的孩子再也不会像父辈那样严厉。

- **第三代移民**（就像索菲娅和路易莎）是那些让我们躺在床上彻夜难眠、烦扰不断的人。由于他们的父母和祖父、祖母付出了艰苦的努力，第三代人出生在生活条件极为舒适的中上层家庭。在孩提时代，他们就拥有许多精装本的书籍（在第一代移民——我们的父母眼里，那简直奢侈得近乎于犯罪）；有一些富裕的、成绩为"B+"的朋友。不管进不进私立学校，他们都渴望穿昂贵的名牌服装。最后，也最成问题的是，他们认为个人的权利受到美国宪法的保护，因而很不情愿顺从自己父母的意志、听从父母对他们的职业劝告。简而言之，所有的现象都表明，第三代人正在走下坡路。

虽然孩子们的路要靠他们自己来走，但索菲娅一出生，我还是希望她聪明伶俐、自尊自重；我告诫自己，绝不能让"富不过三代"的魔咒在我的家里应验，绝不能养育一个没有真才实学又狂妄自大的孩子，绝不能让我的家族走向穷途末路。

这也是我为什么坚持要索菲娅和露露学习古典音乐的原因。我知道，我无法让她们因为生在贫苦的移民家庭而发奋努力。我不能改变生活的现状——我们居住在一所老式的大房子里；有两辆体面的汽车；出门度假时，住在高档的宾馆里。但我确信无疑的是，与我和我的父母相比，索菲娅和露露能接受到更好的教育且更具可塑性。而古典音乐不会让人堕落、不会令人懒惰、不会教人粗鲁，也不会宠坏孩子。相反，它会鞭策我的孩子达成我未能企及的目标，而它与我们祖先光宗耀祖的文化传统紧密相连。

我的"反堕落运动"还有其他的组成部分。像我的父母一样，我也要求索菲娅和露露能说一口流利的中国话，在学校里成为成绩全优的学生。"每次考试答题后都要记得检查3遍，"我告诫她们，"学习时，要查证每一个你不认识的字，要准确地记住它们的定义。"为了确信她们不会像罗马人一样在帝国的陨落中过着饱食终日、骄奢淫逸的生活，我也坚持要求她们干一些体力活。

我不止一次地告诉女儿："14岁的时候，我用锄头和铁锹挖了一个游泳池。"这事儿可是一点儿不假。我在靠近太浩湖①那座我父亲买下的小木屋旁建造的这个游泳池，只有3英尺深、10英尺见方，但"麻雀虽小，五脏俱全"。

我也喜欢向女儿们念叨："每个星期六的早晨，我都用吸尘器打扫房间，我负责一半的面积，妹妹完成另一半。我还要清洗卫生间，在院子里除草、伐木。我还曾经为父亲修建了一座带假山的花园，为此不得不搬运50多磅的大石头。这也是我之所以如此强壮、强硬的原因。"

我希望女儿有尽可能多的时间提高琴艺，所以没有要求她们去伐木头或挖池子。但我也尽量让她们携带重物，比如，抱着装得满满当当的盛衣筐楼上、楼下地跑，星期天要负责扔垃圾，在外出旅游的时候提箱子。有趣的是，怜香惜玉的杰德对此却有着本能的反感，他看不惯让女孩子们拿重物、干重活，总是担心伤到她们稚嫩的背。

在向孩子们传授经验时，我不断地回忆起父母曾经对我说过的那些话。"要虚心，要谦卑，要朴素。"母亲总是告诫我们，"最后就是最前。"我认为她真正想说的是——"确保你名列前茅，这样你才拥有谦虚的本钱。"而父亲的基本原则则是——"绝对不要怨天尤人或寻找借口。如果在学校发生的事情看起来对你不太公平，你就要用加倍的努力获得加倍的成就来证明你自己！"我也试图将这些做人和做事的信条灌输给索菲娅和露露。

像我的父母一样，我还试图从索菲娅和露露那里得到更多的尊重。然

---

① 太浩湖（Lake Tahoe），著名的避暑胜地，位于美国加利福尼亚州和内华达州之间，是北加州旧金山湾区人们度假的首选之地。——译者注

而这却是我最不成功的一点。在我成长的过程中，我害怕父母的反对，可索菲娅不怕，露露就更加满不在乎了。在我们生活的社会，美国人要传达给孩子的东西与中国的文化背道而驰。在中国的文化中，孩子质疑父母的想法、不服从爹妈的管教，或与长辈顶嘴，都是不被允许的。而在美国的文化中，图书、电视节目和电影，都在频频地为孩子敏捷的反驳、独立的个性特征拍手叫好。尤其是一些美国的父母，似乎需要由孩子们来给他们上一堂鲜活的人生课。

6 良性循环

为什么索菲娅3岁开始练钢琴，7岁获奖？在千难万难的"开头"，许多西方父母都会选择放弃。然而中国父母却会在一开始，就不给孩子选择"不努力"的机会。

索菲娅的前三个钢琴教师，都不太适合她。

第一位老师是个俄罗斯老太太，她叫埃莉娜，是我们的邻居。她穿着样式老旧的裙子，过膝的长筒袜；在授课时，从头至尾都面无表情，好像她把整个世界的悲哀都一肩扛了。她来我家做家庭教师，仿佛就是为了自己练习一个小时钢琴，而索菲娅和我只是傻傻地坐在长沙发上听她弹奏，并感受莫名的苦闷和折磨。第一次课结束时，我觉得自己很崩溃，而索菲娅则一直在玩她的纸娃娃。我不敢告诉埃莉娜她无法胜任钢琴教师的工作，担心她会伤心流泪。我只是告诉她，我们盼望着她下一次的钢琴课，到时候我会跟她联络。

我们尝试的第二位钢琴老师，是一个奇怪的小个子。此人一头短发，戴着圆圆的金边眼镜，曾经在军队里服役，名为"MJ"。MJ总是穿着西装、打着领结，从外表你很难判断其性别，而我却喜欢这种朴实的风格。头一次见面，MJ就告诉我们，索菲娅天生就是块学音乐的料。然而不幸的是，三个星期后的一天，我们像往常一样到MJ的家里去上课，而MJ却人间蒸发了。我们只看到那所房子里摆着截然不同的家具，住着完全陌生的人。

第三位教师理查德是个说话轻声细语、臀部丰满、好玩爵士乐的男人。他说他有个两岁的女儿。首次谋面，他就大侃特侃活在当下的重要性以及如何及时行乐，给索菲娅和我好好地上了一课。不像其他比较传统的老师会按部就班地授课，他说他不屑于使用别人撰写的教材；他强调即兴的发挥和自我的表现。理查德认为音乐里没有什么法则需要遵循，只要跟着感觉走，就无人有权对你作出评判；而那些商业化的运作和你死我活的所谓竞赛，已经毁灭了钢琴的世界。

可怜的家伙——我猜他根本就没有做钢琴教师的能力。

作为中国移民家的大女儿，我没有时间来临时拼凑或编造自己的法则。我要维护家庭的名誉，要为一天天衰老的父母赢得骄傲和自尊。我喜欢明确的目标，看到通向成功的确定无疑的路！

正是因为这个原因，我十分欣赏铃木钢琴教学法。它有7本书，每个人都必须从第一册开始入门；每本书都有10至15首曲子，练习者要循序渐进地逐一练习。而孩子们刻苦地投入练习，为的是每星期都能学习新的曲子。如果一首曲子就要练好几个星期，甚至好几个月，他们就会感到厌烦而放弃练习。不管怎么说，至少有一些孩子通过学习铃木的教材，琴艺就是提高得比别人更快——孩子们如果勤学苦练，就会4岁的比6岁的厉害，6岁的比16岁的更牛。

制造"音乐神童"，铃木教学系统名声在外。

发生在索菲娅身上的故事，验证了铃木钢琴教学法的传奇。那时候，索菲娅才5岁，师从铃木钢琴教学法知名教师米歇尔。米歇尔在纽黑文一个被称为社区音乐学校的地方，拥有一间庞大的钢琴工作室。在那里，她以极大的耐心和敏锐的慧眼，发现了索菲娅。她不仅赞赏索菲娅在音乐方面的天赋，而且让索菲娅爱上了钢琴。

铃木钢琴教学法简直就像是为索菲娅量身定做的。她学得很快，并能够自觉地在课后留下来，专心致志地延长练习的时间，这说明索菲娅已经从中国文化在教育孩子方面的优势中获益。而学校里大多数西方学生的父母，都对孩子们来这里练琴抱着宽松和放纵的态度。我记得有个叫奥布里的女孩，长期以来，她每天竟然只练习一分钟，而那时她已经7岁了。有的孩子练琴是有偿的——大杯的圣代冰激凌，或者大盒的乐高牌拼装玩具。许多学生还以种种借口逃避练习，即便是在授课的日子里也常常缺席。

铃木钢琴教学法最显著的特征，是希望家长也能旁听每一次的音乐课，这样才有利于督促孩子们平时在家里的练习。这就是说，索菲娅上钢琴课，从头至尾我都得"陪读"。于是，我也受到了音乐的熏陶。小时候，我也要上钢琴课，但是我的父母没有钱聘请优秀的老师，因此，我只能接受一位邻居的指导。授课期间，他还要时不时地主持特百惠家用塑料制品公司的聚会。跟着索菲娅的老师，我得以恶补了许多音乐的理论和相关的历史知识。

因为我的陪伴，索菲娅每天至少练琴90分钟，周末也不间断。在那些上课的日子里，我们练习的时间就会翻倍。我帮助索菲娅记住了她学过的所有东西，甚至包括那些老师不曾传授的内容。而我，没有给过索菲娅一分钱的奖励。我想，这也是我们之所以能够沿着铃木钢琴教学法的阶梯拾级而上的根本原因。

其他学生的父母将练习目标定为一年完成一本书，而我们从第一册——星星变奏曲（Twinkle Variations）入门；3个月后，索菲娅就开始弹奏第二册——舒曼钢琴曲（Schumann）；6个月后，她进阶第三册——由克莱门特创作的小奏鸣曲（Sonatina）。而我依然感觉进度缓慢。

现在，我该把自己心知肚明的事实挑明了。我知道，有我这样的母亲，其实索菲娅常常并不开心。在我督促索菲娅练琴的日子里，她记得我有3句口头禅：

1. 天哪，你怎么弹得越来越糟糕！

2. 快点儿，我数三下，你就得找准音调！

3. 如果下次你再弹错一个音符，我就要把你所有的毛茸玩具扔到火里化为灰烬！

现在回想起来，这些"杀气腾腾"的督战方式似乎有点儿过激，但它们的确十分奏效。索菲娅和我，真是一对天生默契的母女组合。我意志坚定、认准的事情会"一根筋走到头"，而索菲娅则显得成熟、耐心，富有同理心——这些我本应具有却一直缺失的优秀品质。她相信妈妈知道，对她来说什么是最好的选择。即便我有时大发雷霆或出口伤人，她也会原谅我。

7岁那年，索菲娅在当地的钢琴比赛中，以一曲由挪威作曲家爱德华·格里格创作的《蝴蝶》（Butterfly），赢得了她的第一块奖牌。《蝴蝶》是格里格66首抒情乐曲中的一首，其中每个细小的片段，都意在唤起听众独特别致的心绪和海阔天空的想象，表现出蝴蝶轻盈的翩翩之态和欢快舒畅的情趣。只有花费大量的时间、进行刻苦的演练，才有可能达到如此美丽的意境。

中国父母深知这样的道理：成为行家里手的过程，其实毫无乐趣可言。要掌握任何高超的技艺，必须付出艰苦的努力。而孩子们从本性来讲，绝不会爱好努力。因此，一开始就不给他们选择"不努力"的机会，便显得至关重要。

孩子的反抗对父母的韧性提出了很高的要求。万事总是开头难，在千难万难的"开头"，许多西方父母都会选择放弃。然而，如果应用得当，中国父母的教子策略会带来良性循环。要想走向卓越，就得坚持不懈地练习、练习、再练习；而美国父母则不欣赏机械的重复。其实，不管是弹奏钢琴还是演算数学，一旦孩子展现了杰出的天赋，就会得到赞扬、钦佩和满足。这将为他们的人生奠定自信的基石，并令艰苦卓绝、了无情趣的活动变得充满乐趣。这样的良性循环，使父母更容易引导孩子们登上更加努力的新台阶。

在获奖者的音乐会上，当我看着索菲娅灵巧的手指，像蝴蝶的翅膀一样在琴键上上下翻飞、跃动，我克制住内心的自豪、欢欣和憧憬。我迫不及待地期待着明天的来临——明天，我要和索菲娅一起，加倍地努力，朝着音乐的广阔天地大踏步迈进……

7 "虎"运当头

　　我在哈佛法学院成绩优异，是因为我近乎发疯般的努力。我的文章甚至发表在竞争激烈的《哈佛法律评论》上。正是在那儿，我撞见了我未来的丈夫杰德，我自己也成为那里的责任编辑。

我和杰德——摄于婚礼当天
（Bachrach Photography）

　　与那些接近30岁的亚裔美国女性一样，我也曾经想过，要就母女关系这个主题，以我自己家族的故事为梗概，创作一部贯穿几代人的史诗般的小说。早在索菲娅出生之前，我在纽约为一家华尔街律师事务所工作时，这个想法就已经萌发了。

　　感谢上帝，我是个被命运眷顾的宠儿。因为时至今日，我生活中所作出的重大决定，皆为"歪打正着"。我在哈佛大学开始学习应用数学，是因为我认为这样做会讨好父母；而我后来放弃了它，却是因为我父亲眼睁睁地看着我被一个数学难题折磨了整整一个寒假，他说我这样下去会毁了自己的脑子，于是，把我从数字的游戏中拯救出来。可是我又机械地转向经济学，以为它大概比较像一门科学。我以"双职工家庭的通勤模式"为题撰写了自己的毕业论文，其间的枯燥乏味使得我干脆记不住我得出了怎样的结论。

　　我上哈佛法学院，主要是因为我不想进医学院。我在法学院成绩优异，是因为我近乎发疯般的努力。我的文章甚至发表在竞争激烈的《哈佛法律评论》(*Harvard Law Review*) 上。正是在那儿，我遇见了我未来的丈夫杰德，我自己也成为那里的责任编辑。总是担心法律不是我真的要终生侍奉的天职，我并不像其他人那样关心罪犯的权利，无论教授何时就此向我发问，我的脑子都像结了冰一样僵硬。我不是一个天生好质疑、爱提问的人，我只想记下教授讲述的一切内容，然后死记硬背。

　　毕业后我之所以到一家华尔街律师事务所工作，是因为这样做无须费劲、顺理成章。由于不喜欢替人打官司，我选择了公司法律业务。我工作得很出色，我擅长与人打交道，了解客户的需求，并把它们变成法律的文件。然而，整整3年的公司生活，我感觉自己一直都披着那身滑稽的套装在装腔作势。我通宵达旦地和投资银行家一同起草法律文件，在人人都为亿万美元生意的细枝末节而心力交瘁、血脉贲张之时，我发现自己不由自主地想着晚餐，无法集中精力面对正在进行的谈话。

然而，杰德却十分热爱法律，这种差异真是让我相形见绌。

尤其是在20世纪80年代，公司并购的热潮风起云涌，杰德醉心于为法律事务所写辩护状、进行法律诉讼，并大获成功。后来，他在美国检察长办公室工作，起诉几个黑手党成员，同样是乐此不疲。他以极大的兴趣就"隐私权"的主题撰写了一篇文章，洋洋洒洒长达100页，而他竟一气呵成，并刊登在我们做学生时就曾合作过一把的《哈佛法律评论》（这本刊物几乎清一色地只发表教授撰写的文章）。

此后，耶鲁法学院院长邀请杰德去任教，尽管我是那么渴望像父亲那样在大学里工作，可是这个令人羡慕的殊荣还是首先落到了丈夫身上。在索菲娅出生之前，他就得到了耶鲁法学院终身教授的职务，这是杰德梦寐以求的工作。他也是该院教职员工中唯一一位资历最浅的教授，如金童一般，被一堆同样盯着教授之职的才华横溢的同僚们簇拥着。

我总以为自己是那种点子多多、想象力丰富的人，可是在杰德的同事面前，我的想法似乎一文不值。我们刚刚搬到纽黑文的时候，我正怀着索菲娅。杰德告诉几位在法学院任职的朋友，说我也"很想在法学院做个教授"。但是，当他们谈起我感兴趣的法律问题时，我却像个中风病人一样无法思考、难以开口，这令我感到万分沮丧。我强迫自己加入对话，却思维混乱、词不达意、言不由衷。

正当我决定要写一部史诗般的小说之时，不幸被杰德看到了我的手稿，他那副欲言又止、差点儿没笑出声来的滑稽模样好像在告诉我，我似乎不具备这样的才华。此外，还有马克辛·红·金斯顿[①]、艾米·谭[②]和张戎[③]，已然以她们创作的《女战士》（*Woman Warrior：memoirs of a girlhood among ghosts*）、《喜福会》（*The Joy Luck Club*）和《鸿》（*Wild Swans*），成功地捷足先登。一开始，我备受打击、怨气十足，但是很快，我就有了重新定位自己的想法。考虑我攻读法律学的专长和移民家庭的背景，我打算在发展中国家的法律与种族的领域开辟属于自己的天地。而种族问题，是我无论何时何地都百说不厌的话题。那时候，亦很少有人研究法律和发展，而这恰好是我的专长。

幸运之星似乎就在头顶上闪亮。

索菲娅出生之后，我撰写了一篇文章，内容是关于拉丁美洲和东南亚的私有化、国有化和种族特色，并发表在《哥伦比亚法律评论》（*Columbia Law Review*）上。有这篇力作垫底，我向全美各地的相关学校发出了法律教职的申请，并斗胆应耶鲁法学院聘任委员会的邀请前往面试。

在耶鲁大学看起来有几分恐怖的莫里（Mory's）餐厅里，我与聘任委

---

① 马克辛·红·金斯顿（Maxine Hong Kingston），又名汤婷婷，美籍华人作家，祖籍广东新会，1940年出生于加利福尼亚州蒙士得顿市。她以海外华人在国外发财致富的传奇式经历创作了三部传记性长篇小说，因而蜚声美国和欧洲文坛。她的第一部作品《女战士》于1976年出版后获得业内多项大奖。——译者注

② 艾米·谭（Amy Tan），又名谭恩美，美国华裔作家，1952年出生于加利福尼亚州奥克兰。曾就读医学院，后取得语言学硕士学位。她因处女作《喜福会》而一举成名，成为当代美国的畅销书作家。——译者注

③ 张戎（Jung Chang），1952年出生于四川宜宾。"文革"中做过农民、赤脚医生、翻砂工和电工。1973年就读于四川大学外文系，毕业后留校当助教。1978年留学英国，1982年获博士学位。1991年，其自传体著作《鸿》（或译为《野天鹅》）出版，成为英国出版史上非小说类最畅销的书籍，全球销售量高达1 000多万册。——译者注

员会的教授共进午餐、边吃边聊。令我大为吃惊的是，两位教授借故提前离席，留下法学院院长在后面的两个小时里，与我就纽黑文市意大利风格的建筑海阔天空地好一通神侃。

我没有得到耶鲁全职的教师工作，这就是说，我把午餐面试搞砸了，被杰德所在的学校拒绝了。这可不太妙呀——它使我的社交活动变得有点儿尴尬。

不过，这也让我好好地轻松了一阵。索菲娅两岁的时候，杜克大学法学院给我发来聘书，我大喜过望，迫不及待地接受了，并搬到了北卡罗来纳州的达勒姆。

8 露露的乐器

露露对音乐有着近乎完美的感受力。然而不幸的是，她讨厌训练，练习时经常走神——不是议论窗外的鸟儿，就是……

露露和她的第一把小提琴

达勒姆——我喜欢这个地方。

我的同事们慷慨大方、和蔼可亲、聪明睿智，我在那儿结交了不少密友。生活中唯一的不爽就是，我的丈夫杰德依然在500英里之外的耶鲁大学任教。不过，我们轮流往返于达勒姆和纽黑文之间，还是挺过了那段两地分居的日子。

1999年，在索菲娅已经7岁、路易莎也满4岁时，纽约大学法学院邀请我去做访问学者，时间是6个月。我不想离开达勒姆，但是纽约距离纽黑文可是近了不少。因此，我打点行装去了曼哈顿。

那6个月的压力可真大呀！

在法律教学的世界里，"访问"意味着加入教学的行列，真刀真枪地干。差不多整整一个学期，你既要给那里的每个人留下聪明能干的好印象，同时还要拍他们的马屁。[例如："本尼迪克特，我想直截了当地问问你，你与众不同的新思维模式，是不是比你所预想的具有更加深远的意义？""在你撰写的《法律与拉康①》（*Law and Lacan*）一文的注释81中，你陈述的观点非常危险，我不能确信我是否被你说服了。你是否介意我把它拿到我任教的课堂上去讨论？"]

在考虑让索菲娅进哪所学校读书的时候，我们发现曼哈顿果然"名不虚传"。杰德和我被引进了三年级小学生的世界，我们发现那些小家伙们在信托基金一套又一套培训方案的鼓动下，要为美国高中毕业生进入大学前

---

① 拉康·雅克（Lacan Jacaueo, 1901~1983），法国心理学家。第二次世界大战后最具独立见解而又最具争议的欧洲精神分析学家，被称为"法国的弗洛伊德"。——译者注

的标准考试SAT^①作准备，这就像一个蹒跚学步的小孩子，却硬要去追赶成年人的大步流星一样滑稽。我们最终决定将索菲娅送到纽约第三公立学校去读书，而且学校很近，就在我们租住公寓的街对面。而露露则要在经过一系列测验后，去上学前班。

我非常希望露露能进一所教堂开办的学前班。教堂很美，五颜六色的玻璃窗在阳光下闪耀着迷人的光彩。露露单独进了测验室。短短5分钟，招生办公室主管就领着露露走了出来。小测试一切正常，并没有什么事情不对劲，她只是想跟我确认一下，露露是不是不会数数。

"哦，天哪，她当然会数数！"我吃惊地解释道，"请给我一点点时间。"

我把女儿拉到一旁。"露露！"我压低嗓门，"你想干吗？这可不是在开玩笑呀！"

露露皱了皱眉，"我只在心里数数。"她说。

"你不能只是心里有'数'，你必须大声地说出来，让这位女士知道你能够数数！她正在测试你呐。如果你不能数给她看，你就进不了这所学校！"

"我不想上这所学校！"

正如我前面所提到的，我不认为对孩子的贿赂、纵容会对他们的成长有任何好处。联合国和经济合作与发展组织所通行的国际公约都严禁贿赂；而且，即便要行使贿赂，那也该是由孩子们来贿赂父母。但是在那会儿，我真是被逼无奈、铤而走险了。

"露露，"我悄悄地说，"如果你好好数数，我就给你一个棒棒糖，还要

---

① SAT（Scholastic Assessment Test，学术水平测验考试），是由ETS（Educational Testing Service，美国教育考试服务中心）组织的，其成绩被美国3 600余所大学和加拿大全部大学认可，是决定录取和评定奖学金发放的重要参考指标。——译者注

带你去逛书店。"

然后，我把露露拽了回来。"她现在准备好了。"我爽快地说。

这一次，招生办主管允许我陪着露露走进测验室。落座后，她把4块石头放到桌上，然后让露露数一数。

露露瞟了一眼桌上的石子儿，然后说："11、6、10、4。"

那一刻，我气得浑身冰凉，真想拽着露露找个地缝钻进去。可是招生办主管却异常平静地加上另外4块石头，"现在是几块呀，露露，你能数出来吗？"

这一次，露露盯着石子儿多看了一会儿，"6、4、1、3、0、12、2、8。"

我忍无可忍："露露，停下来，别胡闹了！"

"不，不……请等一下。"招生办主管举起双手，一种饶有兴致的表情浮现在她脸上。她转向露露："路易莎，我知道你想按照自己的方式来数数，对吗？"

露露偷偷地看了我一眼（她知道妈妈已经失望至极），然后，轻轻地点了点头。

"这里的确有8块石头，"招生办主管以随和亲切的口吻对露露说，"虽然你的回答与众不同，但你是对的。你用自己的方式来回答，这是一件值得赞扬的事情，正好也是我们这所学校要大力提倡的精神。"

我发现这位女士喜欢露露，终于喘了口大气。实际上，很多人都喜欢露露，被她那种从不逢迎讨好的个性所吸引。"感谢上帝，我们生活在美国"，我暗自庆幸，因为革命、造反的精神在美国毫无疑问地得到肯定。

好玩的是，露露后来竟然爱上了她的新学校，而索菲娅的校园生活却并不那么惬意，她在学校里总是有那么一点点腼腆。在家长会上，索菲娅的老师告诉我们，她从来没有教过像索菲娅这么优秀的学生，但同时也对索菲娅的社交感到担心，因为她在午餐和课间休息时间总是独来独往，还经常抱着一本书兀自在校园里漫步、闲逛。杰德和我对此万分惊讶，可是当我们追问索菲娅"在学校过得怎样"时，她的回答总是——"不错，挺好玩儿的。"

那个待在纽约的学期真是漫长而难熬。我甚至试图接受纽约大学的聘任，然而，生活的步伐并没有像我们所预料的那样往前迈进。我就发展中国家的民主与民族，发表了一篇法律评述的文章。由于该文在决策圈反响热烈，耶鲁法学院终于向我敞开了久违的大门，聘请我担任终身教授。7年后的那一天，不用再去经历午餐面试，我接受了这个职位，欣喜中夹杂着一丝自嘲的苦涩。我们家的游牧生活终于结束了——杰德不用再在两个城市间长途跋涉、疲于奔命，索菲娅和露露也在纽黑文上了小学。

那时候，露露也开始跟着索菲娅在社区音乐学校的钢琴老师米歇尔练习弹琴。而我，则一头扎进了某种两副重担一肩挑的生活。我清晨5点就得起床，用半天时间写作，像耶鲁的法律教授那样做事做人。然后飞奔回家，完成照顾两个女儿的"家庭作业"，而在管教难缠的露露时，总少不了相互的威胁、要挟和"勒索"。

事实证明，露露是一个天生的音乐家，对音乐有着几乎完美的感受力。然而不幸的是，她讨厌训练，练习时经常走神——不是议论窗外的鸟儿，就是关注我脸上的斑点。尽管如此，通过铃木钢琴教材的学习，她还是进步得飞快。在音乐演奏会上，她从来不像姐姐那样表现得无可挑剔，但是，对在技术精益求精方面的不足，她会以突出的风格和个性来弥补。

在那段时间里，我想到露露应该开始学习新的乐器。

有些朋友的孩子都长大了，他们以"过来人"的口吻告诫我，在音乐方面，两个女儿最好有各自不同的兴趣，这样可以将姐妹间的竞争降至最低。这个建议给了我很大的启发，因为索菲娅的钢琴当时已弹得相当不错，在当地频频获奖、小有名气，并经常应邀前往学校、教堂和社区组织进行演奏。我们所到的每一个地方，露露都不得不坐在台下，感受人们赞美姐姐的扑面热浪。

那么，什么样的新乐器适合露露呢？

我的公公、婆婆，这一对自由的犹太知识分子对此有着鲜明的倾向。他们深知露露桀骜不驯的性格，也领教过小孙女在练习钢琴时的高声尖叫，他们力劝我选个容易一点儿的乐器，放孙女一马。

"选择竖笛怎么样？"公公赛（Sy）建议说。赛是一位身材魁梧的男人，看起来颇像希腊神话中的众神之王——威风凛凛的宙斯。他曾经在华盛顿特区从事了多年心理学临床治疗工作，有着丰富的实践经验。他浑身上下充满音乐细胞，还有一副洪亮、低沉的好嗓子。事实上，杰德的姐姐也拥有美妙圆润的嗓音。看起来，索菲娅和露露较好地秉承了家族中的音乐基因。

"学竖笛？"我婆婆弗洛伦斯听了赛的提议，一副难以置信的表情。"多么无聊乏味呀！"她说。

弗洛伦斯是一位艺术评论家，住在纽约城里。最近，她刚刚出版了在业内颇具争议的现代艺术评论家克莱门特·格林伯格的传记。格林伯格及时地发现了杰克逊·波洛克[①]和美国抽象表现主义。弗洛伦斯和赛已经离婚20多年了，无论赛发表什么意见，她总是会大唱反调。"何不学点儿更让人

---

① 杰克逊·波洛克（Jackson Pollock，1912~1956），是20世纪美国富有影响力的抽象绘画奠基人之一，也是抽象派表现主义运动的主要推动者。他的艺术被视为"二战"后新美国绘画的象征。——译者注

兴奋的乐器，比如加麦兰[①]？或敲击的锣鼓？"

弗洛伦斯是一位十分优雅的女人，喜欢冒险、四海为家。许多年前，她就踏上了印度尼西亚之旅。在那儿，她被爪哇人的加麦兰迷住了：那是由15至20名乐手组成的小型乐团，盘腿坐在地板上，摆弄像平锣（kempul，一组由不同音调组成的挂锣）、铜片琴（saron，一种很大的金属木琴）或者铜鼓（bonang，用鼓槌敲击、听起来像编钟的双排铜鼓）这样的敲击乐器。

有趣的是，和我婆婆一样，法国作曲家克劳德·德布西[②]对加麦兰敲击乐也有着同样的好感，并认为加麦兰体现了一种革命。1895年，德布西在写给朋友的信中称加麦兰音乐"能够表达每一种晦涩的含义，甚至包括那些非常阴郁的色调"。后来，他还发表了一篇文章，将爪哇人描述为"奇妙的人种"，称他们"掌握音乐的技巧就像学会呼吸一样自然、轻松。律动的海浪、穿过树叶的轻风，以及其他数不清的来自大自然的呢喃，组成了爪哇人学习音乐的天堂；他们用心去倾听，没有参考过任何一篇难以自圆其说的学术论文"。

在我看来，那时候的德布西正在经历一个迷恋异国风情的人生阶段。同样的事情也发生在他的法国同伴亨利·卢梭和保罗·高更的身上，波利尼亚土著一直是他们画布上的主角。而在现代的加利福尼亚，我们还能找到这种不肯谢世的遗风：对亚洲女性情有独钟的男人只与亚洲女人约会，有时甚至一连与十几个女人约会，而不管她是亚洲何方人氏、相貌有多丑陋。可

---

① 加麦兰（gamelan），一组印尼的民族管弦乐器。——译者注

② 克劳德·德布西（Claude Debussy, 1862~1918），杰出的法国作曲家，钢琴创作贯穿了他的一生。早期的《阿拉伯斯克》、《贝加摩组曲》接近浪漫主义风格，《版面》、《欢乐岛》、《意象集》和《24首前奏曲》则为印象主义的精品。1918年，他身患癌症在巴黎去世。他的印象主义乐风，对欧美各国的音乐产生了深远影响。——译者注

能因为这样的情况，杰德在我之前没有约会过任何亚洲女性。

或许，我之所以无法欣赏1992年我们游览印度尼西亚时听到的加麦兰音乐，是因为我对困难与成就的内在关系近乎盲目的崇拜。

不知道我曾经对露露高声嚷嚷过多少次："人世间所有意义非凡、值得去追求的事情，都充满了艰辛！你知道，为了得到我今天在耶鲁大学的工作，我付出了多少努力、走过了多少崎岖不平的路？"而加麦兰音乐之所以迷人，是因为它如此简洁、古朴，无雕琢、多重复。相反，德布西创作的那些炫目、美妙的曲子，却反映了复杂的、雄心勃勃的、精巧的构思，以及在意识上对和谐的刻意追求。当然，也反映了加麦兰音乐对作曲家的影响，这种浸淫至少清晰地呈现在了他的一部分曲子里。这就像辉煌的凡尔赛宫和清新的乡间竹屋，有着迥然不同的美。

我曾经吹过竖笛，可无论如何，我都不能让露露去敲锣打鼓！我的直觉与公公、婆婆正好相反。我坚信，要摆脱姐姐大获成功的"阴影"，露露只能去练习更为困难、技艺更加精湛的乐器。

这样的乐器，非小提琴莫属！

没有征求露露的意见，抛开身边所有人的建议、忠告，从那天起，我作出了这个铁板上钉钉的决定。

9 小提琴

小提琴一到了露露手里，就显示出它与露露似乎有着八辈子的缘分。然而，督促她练琴却常常令我们母女俩像丛林中的老虎和野猪般"血战一场"。

在公开场合拿自己的孩子与他人的孩子作比较，这恐怕是许多中国人做得最糟糕的事情。

小时候我对此浑然不觉，因为在这种比较中我总是把别人比下去的一方。只有长大后，我才意识到公开比较的弊端。在我父亲看来，我们家的"龙夫人"——我的祖母过着优裕的生活。她对我异乎寻常的宠爱，大大超过我所有的姐妹。在家庭聚会上，她会指着某个兄弟姐妹，说："瞧你那扁平的鼻子，哪像我们美儿，鼻梁又高又挺，美儿才像我们蔡家的后代。你呀，一定是继承了你妈那一族血脉，长得像只猴子。"

不可否认，我祖母是个极端的例子，但是，许多中国人总是一而再再而三地做着同样的事情。

最近，我去了一家中药店，店主告诉我，他有两个孩子——6岁的女儿和5岁的儿子。"我女儿，"他说，"她可聪明了，唯一的麻烦是精力不太集中。我儿子笨笨的，不像我女儿那么机灵。"

还有一次，在网球比赛的观众席上，我的朋友凯瑟琳与一位来看女儿比赛的中国母亲闲聊起来。这位中国母亲告诉凯瑟琳，她女儿是布朗大学的学生，她就要输掉这场比赛了。"我这个闺女柔弱无能，"她说，并摇了摇头，"她姐姐上了哈佛大学，比她可强多了。"

我知道，既然父母的偏爱百害而无一利，但是站在中国人的立场，我还是想强调两点。

首先，在任何一种文化里，我们都能找到父母对孩子的偏爱。在旧约圣经第一卷《创世记》（*Genesis*）里，亚伯拉罕之子以撒（Isaac）偏爱儿子以扫（Esau），而利百加（Rebekah）则更喜欢雅各布（Jacob）。①格林兄弟的童话故事中也有三个兄弟，他们从来就不曾被父母平等对待过。相反，并不是所有的中国父母都是偏心眼。在《中国五兄弟》（*The Five Chinese Brothers*）②中，我们看不出中国妈妈更偏爱一口气喝干海水的儿子，还是更青睐脖子坚硬似铁的儿子。

其次，我不相信父母对孩子的所有比较都是有害的。杰德一直在批评我对索菲娅和露露的比较。不错，我是对露露说过——"我让索菲娅做什么事，她立刻就答应了，这就是她为什么会进步神速的原因。"西方人会误

---

① 以扫（哥哥）和雅各布（弟弟）为以撒和妻子利百加的双胞胎儿子。——译者注

② 这是根据中国民间故事《刘家五兄弟》改编的英文儿童读物，曾荣获美国刘易斯书卷奖。讲的是刘家妈妈生了5个长得一模一样、神通广大的儿子。老大能把海水喝光，老二刀砍不死，老三有通天长腿，老四火烧不焦，老五则听得懂鸟兽之语。由于兄弟们各有所长，最后斗败官府，过上了太平日子。——译者注

读我的本意——其实我并没有偏爱索菲娅，恰恰相反，我表达的是对露露的信心。我相信，她能做索菲娅能做的任何事情，而露露自身的强势也足以保证她能应对我指出的事实。我也知道，露露总是在心里和姐姐进行比较的。这也是我有时对露露特别严厉的原因，我不想让她沉溺于自己内心的疑虑中。

正因为如此，送露露去上第一堂小提琴课的那天早晨，在她要见自己的新老师之前，我对她说："露露，你已经6岁了。索菲娅在7岁半的时候，就赢得了音乐学校表演奖，我认为你的获奖时间甚至会更早。"

露露的反应十分恶劣："我讨厌比赛，也不想去学什么小提琴！"她干脆拒绝去上小提琴课。我威胁说要打她的小屁股，而且不许吃晚饭（在那个时候，这一招还算管用）。好一通威逼哄骗，终于把露露带到了社区音乐学校。在那里，露露的铃木小提琴老师卡尔·舒加特接待了我们。

50岁的舒加特先生有一头稀疏的金发和学生般的脸庞。他是那种特别善于和孩子打交道的人，和家长在一起，则显出几分冷淡和尴尬，而且很少直视我们的眼睛。他是个与孩子相处的天才，孩子们令他释放出轻松、诙谐、灵感和快乐。他就像社区音乐学校的"花衣吹笛人"①，后面紧紧地跟着30来个学练小提琴的孩子，露露也在其中。

舒加特先生教学的秘密武器，是他将拉小提琴的每一个技巧，都转变成孩子们能够理解的生动故事或大胆想象。他没有直接讲授连音、断音、渐快等音乐术语，而是谈到轻轻地抚摸喵喵叫的猫咪、如军队般列队行进

---

① 花衣吹笛人（Pied Piper），源自德国的一个民间故事，讲的是一个花衣吹笛人应邀用魔笛将小镇哈默林泛滥成灾的老鼠引入河中淹死，但该镇官员却违约拒付酬金。于是他一怒之下再次吹响魔笛，全镇的孩子们便跟着他一去不复返，消失在附近的山洞中。——译者注

的蚂蚁，以及骑独轮车的老鼠骨碌碌滚下山坡……

他教露露理解德沃夏克①著名的幽默曲第7号的方式，也着实令我惊叹不已。这首幽默曲有着朗朗上口的主旋律，不管你来自世界的什么地方，即便你从来就没有聆听过这首曲子，当音乐响起的时候，你也会随之低声吟唱。这首乐曲还有着过于多愁善感的第二主题曲，意在将悲喜交加的、夸张的感伤杂陈其间。那么现在，该怎样将如此复杂的含义告诉一个年仅6岁的孩子呢？

舒加特先生告诉露露，第二主题曲是悲哀的，但还不像有什么人就要离开我们那么令人哀恸。而接下来他让露露想象：如果她每天自己整理床铺并坚持一周，妈妈就答应给她买一个双球的冰激凌卷。露露真的这样做了，但是到了周末，妈妈却说话不算话。这还不算，她竟然给什么都没干的姐姐买了冰激凌卷。老师的这番话果真引起了露露的共鸣，她拉的幽默曲充满酸楚，好像这首曲子就是为她而写的。直到今天，当我听到这首幽默曲（你可以在网上的Youtube观看伊扎克·帕尔曼②和马友友的演奏）时，耳边就仿佛响起由舒加特先生填词的曲子：

"我想……要我的冰激凌，喔，把我的冰激凌给我，你答应给我的冰激凌到底在……在……哪里……"

有意思的是，虽然是我拿主意为露露选择了小提琴，但小提琴一到了

---

① 安托宁·德沃夏克（Antonin Dvorák，1841~1904），19世纪捷克最伟大的作曲家之一，民族乐派的主要代表人物。——译者注

② 伊扎克·帕尔曼（Itzhak Perlman），当今世界最引人注目的小提琴家，出生于以色列的特拉维夫，5岁开始学琴，13岁时在美国电视节目中演奏《野蜂飞舞》而一举成名，随后移居美国。他制作了许多著名的小提琴专辑，获无数大奖，并在斯皮尔博格导演的影片《辛德勒的名单》中担任小提琴的独奏。——译者注

露露手里，就显示出它与露露似乎有着八辈子的缘分。在她刚刚开始练习的时候，人们就不断地为她拨动琴弦、拉动琴弓的自然、流畅和灵活而震惊，为她似乎真的理解和感知了自己演奏的音乐而感叹。

在舒加特先生为学生组织的独奏会上，露露经常闪亮登场，一展"小荷尖尖角"。其他孩子的父母会羡慕地问我，"你们是不是音乐世家呀？""打算培养露露成为技艺精湛的小提琴家吗？"可他们哪里知道，为了让露露回家后完成练习任务，我们母女俩会像丛林中的野兽般"血战一场"——那是老虎 Vs.野猪之战，她越是反抗，我越是强硬。

每个星期六都是我生活中的重中之重。

整个上午，我们都待在社区音乐学校，紧张得就像你在20种乐器的伴奏声中全力以赴。露露不仅要上舒加特先生的小提琴课，还要在课后和老师一起直奔另一个教室，接着上一堂小提琴和钢琴合班讲授的铃木教学课。（露露在每个星期五的钢琴课我们也从不缺席。）

回家以后，尽管上午三四个小时的课程已让我们筋疲力尽，我还是常常想方设法地给露露增加课后练习——绝不会让她无所事事，舒舒服服地只等着上下个星期的课！

到了晚上，疲劳的露露已进入梦乡，我还会在灯下阅读有关小提琴的专业文章，听艾萨克·斯特恩①、伊扎克·帕尔曼或日本小提琴家美岛莉的CD，努力地去体会他们精湛的技艺，捕捉那些在琴弦中跃动的音符和那些抑扬顿挫的小精灵。

---

① 艾萨克·斯特恩（Isaac Stern，1920~2001），美国著名的小提琴大师，出生于乌克兰。他在卡内基音乐厅举办过175场音乐会，共录制过100多张唱片；在事业的巅峰时期，曾创下一年演出200多场的纪录。——译者注

我承认，这样的日程表的确过于紧张，但我总感觉在与时间赛跑。要知道，中国的孩子每天要练琴10个小时。萨拉·张在纽约交响乐团为祖宾·梅塔试音时年仅8岁。每一年，一些7岁的孩子都会在拉脱维亚或克罗地亚脱颖而出，以演奏高难度的柴可夫斯基小提琴协奏曲而将国际竞赛的奖杯揽入怀中。我希望露露也能站在那样的领奖台上。说实话，我真的有些等不及了。

此外，在教育和培养孩子方面，我在家里并不占优势。因为，我有一位美国丈夫，他认为孩子的童年应该拥抱欢乐。杰德经常喜欢和孩子们一起下棋或打迷你高尔夫球；最过分的是，驾车带着两个丫头大老远地跑到水上公园去玩危险的水上滑道。而我最喜欢的活动，是读书给孩子们听。每天晚上，我们一家四口都会坐在一起读书，那是每个人都感到开心的惬意时光。

拉小提琴真的很难，在我看来，它比弹钢琴难多了。

首先，你得保持负重的状态，而钢琴就没有这样的要求。与人们的理解和想象完全不同，小提琴并不是依靠左臂来握持的。著名的小提琴教师卡尔·弗莱什在他撰写的《小提琴演奏的艺术》（*The Art of Violin Playing*）一书中指出，小提琴是"放在锁骨上"，并"始终由左下颚来固定的"。这样，才能保证左手自由、灵活地移动。

假如你认为用锁骨和左下颚来夹住什么东西一定会很不舒服，那你就说对了。将一块木制的腮托和金属的夹具嵌入脖肩之间，大多数小提琴艺术家和小提琴演奏者，都会在下巴处形成一片粗糙、经常疼痛的红色斑块，他们甚至将这块"小提琴压痕"看做荣誉的徽章呢！

其次是"音调"，即你用什么调子来演奏。这是我认为拉小提琴比弹钢琴要难得多的另一个原因。弹钢琴时，你只要用手指按下琴键，就知道你选择的是哪一个音符。而拉小提琴时，你必须把你的手指头准确无误地以准确的接触部位放到那个准确的"点"上，否则，仅仅一个毫米的误差，你拉的曲子就会"跑调"。虽然小提琴只有4根琴弦，但它可以由半音增量而产生53个不同的音符；点按不同的琴弦、利用不同的运弓技巧，可以演绎五彩斑斓、变幻无穷的音调。所以人们常说，小提琴能捕捉人类的每一种情感，它是最接近人类声音的一种乐器。

弹钢琴和拉小提琴有一点是相通的（许多运动项目也是这样），那就是：只有彻底地放松自己，你才能表现完美。在网球场上，如果你不能保持手臂的放松，就无法大力扣杀；在棒球比赛中，如果你手臂僵硬，就无法掷出又快又狠的"好球"；拉小提琴时，如果你握弓太紧，或把太大的压力放在琴弦上，就只会产生很大的噪音，而无法拉出优美的琴声。

"把你自己想象成一个布娃娃，"舒加特先生会这样启发露露，"软软的，松松的，什么事都不必在意。你的手臂是如此的放松，你只感觉到它自己的重量……把一切都交给地心引力……不错，露露，嗯，很好！"

"放松！"我也在家里大声地提醒露露，"注意舒加特先生所说的'布娃娃'！"我总是尽自己的最大努力来强调舒加特先生的教学要点，但在露露这儿，事情可没那么简单，我的话常常令她紧张、急躁。

有一次，练习已进行到一半，她突然暴怒地大喊："别说了，妈妈，你别说了！"

"露露，我什么也没有说，我一个字也没有说啊！"我强调说。

"你在心里不停地说，"露露说，"我知道你在想什么。"

"我什么也没有想！"我假装愤愤不平地说。实际上，露露说得没错，我一直在琢磨露露拉琴时右肘抬得太高，用力不对，她需要养成更好的表达音乐的习惯。

"别再胡思乱想！"露露命令道，"我不练了，除非你不再瞎琢磨！"

露露常常试图激怒我，挑起我们之间的争吵是她争取停止练习的"阴谋诡计"。可这一次，我没有上当。"那好，"我冷静地说，"那你想让我怎么做？"有时候，把控制权交给露露，会化解她的小脾气。

露露想了想说："捏住你的鼻子5秒钟。"

不错，是个美妙的暂停。我照做了，练习继续进行。那是我们俩都很快活的一天。

露露和我有着既难以调和又无法割舍的关系。当孩子们很小的时候，我就在电脑上建了一个文档，用以逐字地、随时地记录我们之间值得关注的交流情况。在露露7岁时，我们之间有一段对话被记录在案：

> 美儿：露露，我们是非常好的朋友，以一种不可思议的方式友好相处。
>
> 露露：是呀——一种怪异的方式、恐怖的方式。
>
> 美儿：!!（呈愕然状。）
>
> 露露：开个玩笑嘛！（给了妈妈一个拥抱。）
>
> 美儿：我要把你说的写下来。
>
> 露露：别，别写！听起来太过分了！
>
> 美儿：我要把这个拥抱也加在旁边。

我对孩子比较极端的教养方式有一个可爱的副产品，那就是索菲娅和露露的关系非常亲近：因为她们得团结起来，手挽手地对抗专横而狂热的妈妈。

"她真是神经错乱！"我听到她们一边窃窃私语，一边偷着乐。但是我一点儿也不在乎，我不像有些西方父母那样脆弱。我常常对女孩们说："我的目标，是做一个为你们的未来着想的妈妈，不是要讨你们的喜欢。"

有一年春天，社区音乐学校的校长邀请索菲娅和露露两姐妹在一次特别的庆典中登台表演，这次活动是为了庆祝女高音歌手杰西·诺曼因在威尔第作曲的著名歌剧《阿依达》（Aida）中的精彩表演赢得格莱美奖而举办的。凑巧的是，我父亲特别喜欢歌剧《阿依达》，而杰德和我，正是踏着《阿依达》的"凯旋进行曲"走进了婚姻的神圣殿堂。于是，我邀请了我的父母从加利福尼亚赶来观看孙女的演出。

穿上合体的长裙，两个小美女用小提琴和钢琴一块儿演奏了莫扎特的E小调奏鸣曲。在我看来，这首曲子要表达的成熟意境超越了她们的年龄——音乐在小提琴和钢琴来来回回的变换中，显得不是那么默契、那么像两种乐器间的窃窃私语。但是似乎没人在意这个美中不足，两个女孩的表演大获成功。

后来，杰西·诺曼对我说："你的女儿真是一对天才——你太幸运了！"

幸运的我深知，这是经历了无数场战斗才赢得的结果。

硝烟散去，我体验到了生命中那些最美好的时光。

10　泡泡和牙印

　　我目不转睛地看着索菲娅在台上演奏。小小的她看起来是那么瘦弱，但却在庞大的钢琴前奋力地表现着莫扎特的激情澎湃——那一刻，我的心感受到一种难以名状的痛……

　　中国父母在教育孩子的事情上比较超脱，而西方父母则难以做到这一点。

　　小时候，有一次（或许不止一次），我对母亲非常不尊重，父亲愤怒地用我们家乡的闽南话斥责我，说我是"垃圾"。这句话说得很重，我对自己的所作所为深感羞耻，但这并没有打击我的自尊或任何其他的自我认知，我不会真的认为我就像一堆垃圾那样一文不值。

　　作为成年人，当索菲娅的行为对我构成极大的不恭时，我也曾经用英语对她说过同样的话——你，像堆垃圾！而且是在一次和朋友聚会的晚餐上。记得当时的我立刻就遭到了大家的排斥，一位叫马西的客人为此深感不安，她甚至流下了眼泪，早早地离席而去。我的朋友，女主人苏珊极力挽留我继续和客人们待在一起。

"喔，亲爱的——这只是个误会，美儿只是在进行比喻，对吧，美儿？你的意思并不是真的说索菲娅是垃圾。"

"不错，是这样，我说了，但是这句话是有文化背景的。"我想作点解释，"这是中国移民的事情。"

"可你并不是一个中国移民。"有人指出我其实是出生在美国这个事实。

"说到点子上了，"我承认，"所以我这么说对索菲娅不起作用，也就不足为奇了。"

我当时是在极力息事宁人，而我清楚，这句话其实让索菲娅颇为震动。

在教育孩子方面，中国父母可以做出西方父母似乎难以想象的事情，甚至在法律上采取行动。中国妈妈可以直截了当地对女儿说，"嗨，小胖子——减减体重吧！"相反，西方父母只能小心翼翼地围绕这个同样的话题，可能从"健康"入手"旁敲侧击"，绝不会提到半个"胖"字。而他们的孩子最后依然会陷入饮食混乱的反复调理和负面的自我形象中难以自拔。（我也曾经听一位父亲用"美丽而难以置信的能力"来盛赞已经长大成人的女儿。可这个女儿后来告诉我，在她看来，这些话空洞干瘪得如同垃圾。）

中国父母会要求孩子照着自己说的话去做，而西方父母只会要求孩子尽自己的最大努力去做。中国父母可以说"大懒虫，所有的同学都比你棒"，而西方父母会在自己内心的矛盾冲突中痛苦地挣扎，极力去挖掘孩子的点滴成就，努力说服自己不要为孩子眼前的失利而失望。

中国父母为什么能够对自己直言不讳的行为感到心安理得，对此，我思考了很久、很多。我认为中国父母与西方父母在心态上有三个显著的不同。

第一，我注意到西方父母非常在意他们孩子的自尊。假如孩子做某事失败了，他们非常担忧孩子的自我感受，会不断地安慰孩子，启发他们肯定自己的长处，即使他们在考试或表演中表现平平。这就是说，西方父母特别在意孩子的心理感受；中国父母则不同，他们相信孩子的力量，相信他们没有那么脆弱。

对待孩子自尊心的不同态度，导致中西方父母在教育孩子的行为上出现了差异。

例如，一个孩子带着在考试中得到的"A-"回到家里，西方父母很可能为此赞美孩子，而中国妈妈的脸上会现出恐怖的惊讶："这是怎么回事？"如果孩子在考试中得了"B"，一些西方父母仍然会表扬孩子，另一些西方父母则会和孩子面对面地坐下来表达他们的不满，但他们不会让孩子感觉到自己的不足或不安全，也绝对不使用"愚蠢"、"无用"或"丢脸"这样的词汇。

可在我看来，西方父母的做法也可能失当。孩子为什么没有考好，是在某个科目上能力有问题，还是课程的安排或整个学校有什么问题，这些因素都应该被考虑到。假如孩子的成绩总是得不到提高，父母还可以约见校长，质疑某个科目的教学方法或教师的资质问题。

孩子要是在考试中得到"B"（恐怕这样的事情发生在华裔家庭的概率较小），中国父母立刻就会大发雷霆。为此震惊不已的中国妈妈会让孩子练习十多道甚至上百道测验题，直到孩子在考试中重新得到"A"。

中国父母要求孩子的考试成绩门门优秀，是因为他们相信自己的孩子有能力做到。如果孩子没有取得最优异的成绩，那么，一定是孩子不够用功。这也是中国父母为什么总是对孩子们不合格的表现会进行严厉指责、惩罚，让孩子感到羞耻的原因。

中国父母还认为他们的孩子有足够的坚强，来承担蒙受的耻辱并拿出实际行动重新改进。事实上，当中国孩子在行动上争取优秀时，有许多西方父母却正在家里滥用令孩子自我膨胀的表扬。

第二，中国父母认为孩子就是他们的一切。其原因似乎不那么一目了然，但这或许是源于孔夫子的孝道和中国父母自我牺牲的精神，他们为孩子的确付出了太多。中国妈妈亲自参与教学，投入大量的时间，充当家庭教师、教练，监督和教导孩子的一言一行——这就是他们与孩子相处的真实画面。而中国孩子听从父母的管教，努力在自己的一生中成为令父母骄傲的后代，就是对父母最好的理解和报答。

相反，我不认为西方人对孩子与父母这种永久性的知恩图报会有相同的看法。实际上，杰德对此就有着截然不同的观点。他曾经对我说："孩子无法选择他们的父母，甚至也无法选择自己是否要来到这个世界。是父母，把生命强加给了孩子。因此，父母有责任抚养孩子，而孩子对父母没有任何的亏欠，他们的责任是抚养他们自己的孩子。"

这个说法让我对西方父母与孩子的可怕关系留下极为深刻的印象。

第三，中国父母认为自己知道怎样做对孩子最好，因此，他们会管理孩子所有的欲望和爱好。这也是中国孩子不能参加在外过夜的野营和中国的女孩在高中没有男朋友的原因。同样，也没有中国孩子敢对父母说："我在学校的演出中扮演了一个角色！我是第6号营地的成员；每天下午3点至7点，我得在放学后留下来参加排练；每个周末我都需要用车。"

哦，天哪，中国孩子怎么能够提出这样无理的要求！

别误解我的意思：这不是中国父母不关心自己的孩子，恰恰相反，他们为了孩子可以放弃自己的一切！这只是一种迥然不同的养育模式。我用中国人的思维方式来看待这种方式，我也知道不少其他国家的父母——通常来自韩国、印度，或巴基斯坦，他们与中国父母有着非常相似的心态。因此，这些想法也许带着移民的特征，或者是某些移民和某种文化相结合的特征。

杰德提出了一个非常不同的教育模式，而他的父母都不是移民。赛和弗洛伦斯出身于宾夕法尼亚州靠近斯克兰顿市的严格的东正教犹太家庭，并在那里长大成人。他们俩都幼年丧母，度过了压抑的、不愉快的童年。他们结婚后，尽可能快地离开了宾夕法尼亚州，最终定居华盛顿特区，杰德和哥哥、姐姐都在那里长大。作为他们的父母，赛和弗洛伦斯决定要把自己童年时被剥夺的空间和自由交给孩子，他们相信个人的选择和独立的价值，提倡发展创造性才能、敢于质疑权威。

我的父母和杰德的父母生活在完全不同的世界。

杰德的父母把儿子看做有头脑的人类的一员，将去不去上小提琴课的选择权交给了他（结果儿子就轻轻松松地放弃了，而现在却为此感到后悔）。我的父母没给我任何的选择，也从未就任何事情来询问我的看法。每年的整个夏季，杰德的父母都让他和兄弟姐妹们到一个被称为水晶湖的田园诗般的地方，去尽情地玩乐嬉戏；杰德说，那是他一生中最开心的时光，我们也要尽可能地带索菲娅和露露去水晶湖度假。而我，总是带着电脑前往那里，因此我似乎讨厌夏天。（比我小7岁、与我性情相投的妹妹美文也是一样。这位计算机编程的高手，一边阅读语法书，一边用图表来进行句法分析，并以此来消磨时间。）

杰德的父母有着良好的艺术品位，并爱好艺术品的收藏，而我的父母不是搞艺术的。杰德的父母为他支付一定的教育经费，但不是全部；而我的父母为我们工作前的一切付费，他们渴望在老年的时候全然得到子女的尊敬和热爱。杰德的父母却从来没有这样的奢望。

杰德的父母通常会离开孩子出门去度假，他们和朋友到过一些危险的地方。在危地马拉，他们差点儿被人绑架；在津巴布韦，他们参加狩猎远征；在印度尼西亚的婆罗浮屠，他们听到了天籁般的加麦兰音乐。

我的父母从不会丢下4个孩子去度假，这意味着我们这一大家子出门旅行时，不得不在相当便宜的汽车旅馆过夜。此外，在发展中国家长大成人。如果有人付费，我的父母也不会去危地马拉、津巴布韦或婆罗浮屠；而会带我们去欧洲，那儿是有政府管理的、适合旅游的地方。

尽管我和杰德没有对养育孩子的问题进行明确、透彻的讨论，但我们基本上认为，要在我们家采用中国式的培养模式。这样做有几个原因。

首先，像许多母亲一样，我承担了大部分的抚养工作，因此，我的养育方式应该被优先考虑。虽然杰德和我在耶鲁法学院有着同样忙碌的工作，可是在家里，我还是那个盯着女孩们做家庭作业，上中文家教课、练习钢琴和小提琴的人。

其次，完全撇开我教育孩子的观点，杰德依然倾向于严格的培养方法。他经常批评那些在家里从来不对孩子说"No"的父母（其实更糟糕的是，说完"No"但从不执行）。而杰德善于对女孩们说"No"，但不擅长为她们提供一个积极的方案。他从不会强迫孩子做什么事情，就像不会强迫孩子练习钢琴和小提琴一样。他没有绝对的自信，来为孩子们作出正确的选择。而我，正好弥补了他的缺憾。

在用中国模式培养孩子的过程中，也许最重要的经验是万事开头难，那时我们也经历了争吵不断的困扰。其他的父母不断地追问我们培养孩子的秘诀，因为索菲娅和露露的举手投足，就像是孩子们成长的模特。她们在公共场合表现得彬彬有礼、可爱风趣、助人为乐，而且口才出众；她们在学校里是成绩全优的学生，索菲娅在数学方面领先于她所在班级的同学两个学年；她们还能讲一口流利的普通话；所有的人都为她们演奏古典音乐的高超技艺惊叹不已。

简而言之，她们其实就像是中国的孩子。不过，还是有一些不同。

1999年，我们带着孩子们第一次去中国旅行。索菲娅和露露都有着褐色的头发、褐色的眼睛和亚洲人的长相特征；她们俩都说中国话。索菲娅能吃各种各样的动物内脏和肉类食物——鸭蹼、猪耳朵、海参，这是另一个辨别中国人的关键特征。

在中国，我们每到一个地方，包括国际大都市上海，我的女儿都会吸引当地人的目光。他们在一旁看着、笑着、比画着，称她们是"两个会说中国话的小老外"。在四川省成都市的大熊猫饲养中心，我们看到了大块头的新生的熊猫宝宝，它们粉粉的、肉肉的，像幼虫般局促不安地蠕动着，听说很难养活。当索菲娅和露露在给熊猫宝宝拍照时，那些中国的旅行者也在给她们姐俩拍照哩！

回到纽黑文的几个月后，我与人聊天，不经意间在言语中提到索菲娅是中国人。此时她打断我说："妈妈，我不是中国人。"

"你是中国人。"

"不是的，妈妈，你是唯一一个这样想的人。在中国，没有人认为我是中国人。在美国，也没有人把我看做中国人。"

这个说法让我颇为不爽，我只是一个劲儿地说："这么说，他们都错了，你就是中国人！"

2003年，10岁的索菲娅在纽黑文钢琴协奏曲大赛上获奖，并作为钢琴独奏选手获得了在耶鲁大学的巴特尔礼堂与纽黑文青年管弦乐队同台演出的殊荣。

她迎来了人生中第一个音乐的盛大节日，我为此欣喜若狂。

我在地方报纸发表了介绍索菲娅的文章，并附上了照片；我邀请了100多人前来欣赏音乐会，并计划在会后举办一个大型聚会；我为索菲娅置办了闪亮的行头，买了第一件长裙曳地的漂亮礼服和崭新的皮鞋。4位长辈——爷爷、奶奶，姥爷、姥姥都来了。

在演出的前一天，我母亲在厨房里做了上百个中国的珍珠丸子（猪肉馅儿的，外面裹着白色的糯米）；杰德的妈妈弗洛伦斯烹饪了10磅渍鲑鱼片（用盐、黑胡椒、小茴香、酒等腌制而成）。

与此同时，我们紧锣密鼓地投入了表演前的排练，累得几乎筋疲力尽。索菲娅要在演出中弹奏莫扎特的钢琴回旋曲，管弦乐队则是D大调，那是作曲家创作的最令人振奋的乐曲之一。

在业界，莫扎特乐曲的高难度是众所周知的。他的音乐可以说是五光十色、灿烂炫目，既让人激情澎湃，又给人轻盈愉悦的感官享受，深深地打动了众多的音乐家。业界也流传着"只有年轻人和老年人能更好地诠释莫扎特"的说法。因为年轻人是一张白纸，无所顾忌，而老年人已不在意给人留下什么印象，因而能够更自由地发挥。索菲娅弹奏的回旋曲是莫扎特的经典之作。索菲娅的钢琴老师米歇尔告诉她："你在表现滑音（runs）和颤音（trills）时，想想香槟酒或意大利汽水，在开启瓶盖的那一刹那，无数的泡泡都争先恐后地冒出来……"

索菲娅是个优秀的学生，能面对任何挑战。她还是一个令人难以置信的快手，以闪电般敏捷的指法，掠过一个又一个新的曲子。而最让我开心的是，她听我的。

在那个特别的时段，我成了组织预演的首席指挥官。我把莫扎特的回旋曲拆分开来，有时根据分段，有时根据练习中的主要目标。我们会花一个小时，只注意发音（清晰、准确的音调）；然后，在下一个小时，聚焦于节拍（与节拍器的协调配合）；接下来的一个小时，主攻弹奏力度的变化（大声、柔和、渐强、渐弱）；最后一个小时，再主要解决乐句的问题，以塑造音乐的旋律。

我们每天都练习到很晚，坚持了好几个星期。我不吝啬我严厉的话语，甚至在索菲娅眼里已充满泪水的时候更加变本加厉。

演出的日子终于临近，我忽然感觉浑身瘫软。看来，我永远也做不了一个真正的演员，而索菲娅则显得异常兴奋。在巴特尔礼堂，当她款款地走上舞台，向观众优雅地弯腰鞠躬，她的脸上绽放出灿烂的笑容。我知道，她现在是多么快活。在以深色橡木装饰的宏伟大厅，我目不转睛地看着她在台上演奏。小小的她看起来是那么瘦弱，但却在庞大的钢琴前奋力地表现着莫扎特的激情澎湃——那一刻，我的心感受到一种难以名状的痛……

演出结束后，朋友们和陌生的观众都涌上前来向杰德和我祝贺。

"索菲娅的演奏太精彩了！"他们说，"她弹得如此美妙、如此优雅，真让人难以置信。"

"索菲娅显然是一个莫扎特音乐人。"笑容满面的米歇尔老师告诉我们，称她还从来没有听到有人能将回旋曲弹得如此清风扑面、繁星闪烁。

"看起来，她真是沉浸在那美好的音乐里了。"社区音乐学校校长拉里兴高采烈地对我说，"从音乐里找不到乐趣，就不会表现出音乐的美妙。"

拉里的评论让我想起了好些年前一个意外的故事。

那时索菲娅才刚刚开始学弹钢琴，而我已经给了她很大的压力。一天，杰德在钢琴中央C①的木质部分发现了一些有趣的印记。当他问索菲娅"这是怎么回事"时，索菲娅的眼里滑过一丝内疚，"你说什么？"她支支吾吾地明知故问。

杰德俯下身子，仔细地检查那些印记。"索菲娅，"他慢悠悠地说，"这些印记是不是你的牙印？"

真相不幸大白。

一番询问之后，那时大概才6岁的索菲娅承认，她常常啃咬钢琴。杰德告诉她，钢琴是我们家最贵重的物件，索菲娅答应以后再也不啃了。而我不知道，为什么拉里的评论会把我带回这个有趣的插曲。

---

① 钢琴中央C（Middle C），即钢琴弹奏C大调时中音"Do"的部位，是小字一组的C¹。——译者注

11　小白驴

西方父母对孩子的自尊担忧颇多，但是作为父母，最不利于保护孩子自尊心的行为，就是你眼看着他们在困难面前放弃努力而不作为。

有一个故事，是关于中国式的强制。

那时，露露大约7岁，依然在学练钢琴和小提琴这两种乐器。她正在练习一支被称为"小白驴"的钢琴曲。这首曲子是由法国作曲家雅克·艾伯特创作的，曲调相当可爱——你可以想象一匹小白驴迈着轻松欢快的步子，与自己的主人一起沿着乡间小路乐颠颠地向前跑去。可是对于年幼的弹奏者来说，它也有着不可思议的难度，因为它要求两只手精神分裂般地保持不同的节奏。

露露无法做到。

我们不间断地练习了一个星期，一遍又一遍刻苦地分别训练她的左手和右手，可是当我们试图把两只手的动作合到一起时，一只手常常会被另一只手同化。一时间，所有的努力都化为泡影。

在露露要去上钢琴课的前一天，她终于忍无可忍地暴发了："我不练了！"她决意放弃，站起来便摔门而去。

"回到钢琴前来，露露！"我命令道。

"你不能逼我。"

"我当然能。"

让她重新回到钢琴前，露露把我折腾得够呛。她好一通拳打脚踢，并抓住乐谱把它撕成碎片。我将乐谱拼凑起来装进塑料套封里，这样，她就再也无法对乐谱"施暴"了。然后，我把露露的玩具屋拖出去放到车上，告诉她："如果你在明天之内不把'小白驴'练得滚瓜烂熟，我就要把你的玩具一个接一个地捐献给救世军二手货商店。"

"我看你该去商店了，干吗还待在那儿呀？"露露故意气我。

我威胁她不准吃午饭和晚饭，甭想要圣诞节和犹太光明节礼物，更别说生日礼物——两年、三年、四年，压根儿就别再惦记什么礼物！

……

后来，露露好不容易坐到了钢琴前，两只手仍然出错。我说她是故意让自己抓狂，因为她暗自担心自己做不好。我要她告别懒惰，克服懦弱，别再自我放纵，让悲哀见鬼去！

这时候，杰德把我拉到一旁。他要我别再侮辱露露（其实我根本就没这个意思，我只是想刺激刺激她，让她好好练琴），他说他不认为威胁露露对她会有什么帮助。他还说，或许露露真的无法掌握这个技术，可能她不具备这种双手配合的协调能力。最后，他还一本正经地问我："你能不能哪怕是考虑一下这样的可能性？"

"你其实就是不相信露露。"我谴责他。

"这太可笑了,"杰德轻蔑地说,"我当然相信她。"

"索菲娅在露露这个年龄,就能弹这首曲子。"

"可露露和索菲娅是两个不同的个体。"杰德指出。

"噢,不,不是在这件事上。"我转了转眼珠盯着他。"每个人都以他们独特的方式成为独特的人,"我以嘲讽的口吻模仿说,"即便是失败者也以他们独特的方式成为独特的失败者。好吧,不用担忧,这事儿一点儿都不用你插手。我宁愿一竿子插到底,我乐意做那个被孩子憎恨的恶人。你为她们摊薄饼、带她们去玩美国佬的游戏,你可以成为那个被她们崇拜的大善人!"

我卷起袖子回到露露身边,用尽了我能想到的每一种"武器"和"诡计"。我们没有吃晚饭,一直练到晚上。我没有让露露从琴凳上站起来,没有喝水,甚至没有去卫生间,我们的琴房俨然成为一片没有硝烟的战场。我喊得嗓子嘶哑,口干舌燥,露露的琴技不但没有提高,甚至只是在倒退——终于,我快要挺不住了,信念的堡垒不再坚不可摧……

然而,就在那个摇摇欲坠的时刻,奇迹发生了——露露的双手开始"紧急集合",左手和右手各司其职、协调配合,出色地完成着各自不同的任务。

哈哈,事情原本就应该这样!

露露在同一时间意识到了这一点。我在一旁屏住呼吸,她怀着忐忑的心情又试了一次。然后,她越弹越自信、越弹越快,并保持着她刚刚找到的节奏。一会儿,她开心地笑了:"妈妈,你看,这一点儿也不难!"她坐在钢琴前,一遍又一遍地、兴致勃勃地弹奏着那首可爱无比的"小白驴"。

那天夜里睡觉的时候,她钻到我的被窝里。我们俩挤在一起相互依偎着、打闹着。最后的胜利让白天的不快消失得无影无踪。

几个星期之后，露露在社区音乐学校的独奏会上演奏了这首"小白驴"。一些家长跑过来对我说："这首曲子简直是为露露写的——听起来是那么生气勃勃，其实露露就是那匹小白驴呀！"

这一回，就连杰德也心悦诚服，对我大加赞扬。

西方父母对孩子的自尊担忧颇多，但是作为父母，最不利于保护孩子自尊心的行为，就是你眼看着他们在困难面前放弃努力而不作为。此外，明明知道自己能行却以为自己不行，对构筑自信心毫无帮助。

所有新近出版的书籍，都将亚洲母亲描述成诡计多端、冷酷无情、超速运转的人，她们对孩子真正的兴趣漠不关心。另一方面，许多中国人又暗自确信，与放任孩子变坏却心安理得的西方人相比，他们更关心自己的孩子，愿意为孩子作出更多的牺牲。我认为如果这样看待中西方的父母，这对双方都是一种误解。所有文明的、体面的父母，都愿意做对孩子最有益的事情，而中国父母只是对怎样做最有益的事情，有着完全不同的想法。

西方父母竭力去尊重孩子的个性，鼓励他们追求自己真正的激情，支持他们自我的选择，给他们提供积极的肯定和成长的环境。而中国父母确信，保护孩子的最佳方式，就是帮助他们为未来作好准备，让他们看到自己的能力，用实用的技术、工作的好习惯和内在的、没人能够带走的自信来武装他们。

12 华彩段

　　如果露露心情好、精力集中，她就能够抓住滑动于指尖的这个小精灵；如果她情绪不佳、心烦意乱，华彩段就会不"华彩"，最终流于平淡。最糟糕的是，我从来就无法控制她的心情。

旅途中，露露和严厉的妈妈在宾馆里练习小提琴

露露叹了口气，她正在为学校的下一个活动发愁。

我驾车带着两个女儿从学校回家，我的心情也比较阴郁。索菲娅刚刚提醒我，她六年级的中世纪节（Medieval Festival）就要到了。我非常讨厌这些节日，以及那些私立学校才盛行的种种特殊项目。因为学校不是让学生通过书本来学习，而是不断地组织让学习看起来生动有趣的活动来给家长增加额外负担。

为了露露的"周游世界"项目（Passport-Around-the-World project），我得准备一份厄瓜多尔的菜肴（将一种美洲热带树木的种子捣碎，与鸡肉放在一起炖4个小时，再与油炸香蕉一起盛盘奉上），一个厄瓜多尔的艺术品（一匹产自玻利维亚的雕刻的骆驼，天知道和其他地方的骆驼有何不同），一个真的厄瓜多尔人供露露采访（我好不容易"挖掘"到一个厄瓜多尔留学生）。而露露要做的，就是制作护照：将一张纸折叠成1/4大小，写上"护照"两个字，然后带着它出席学校组织的国际风味食品节。在那里，上百个国家的特色食品摆放得琳琅满目，每一种都是由各种各样的学生家长烹饪的。

这样的活动我还算可以应付，可参加六年级精彩纷呈的中世纪节，就有些难准备了。每位学生都要穿中世纪的服装去参加活动，既不能悄悄地去租借，也不能搞得过于华丽昂贵，还要带去一种中世纪菜肴，保证是按照实实在在的中世纪方式烹饪的。最后，每个学生都得完成一项手工劳动，即制作一所中世纪风格的房屋模型。

那一天，我始终处于一种抓狂的状态，绞尽脑汁地琢磨哪位建筑家可以被我雇用，当然还得确保他不是另一位学生的父母。

就在我忙得四脚朝天的时候，露露却深深地叹了口气。

"我的朋友珠珠可幸运了，"她满脸羡慕地说，"她有好多宠物——两只鹦鹉，一条狗和一尾金鱼。"

我没有吭声儿。类似的话，我听索菲娅说过多次了。

"还有两头几内亚猪。"

"也许这就是她的小提琴才学到第一册的原因，"我说，"因为她尽忙着照顾宠物了。"

"我真想有个宠物。"

"你已经有了一个，"我忽然说道，"小提琴就是你的宠物。"

我从来就不是一个喜欢动物的人，小时候我也没有养过宠物。虽然没有作过调查研究，但在美国，我估计大多数中国移民的家庭都没有养宠物。中国父母忙于照顾孩子，没有余力去喂养宠物。他们在经济上也通常并不宽裕（我父亲那双去上班的鞋，他整整穿了8年），饲养宠物无疑是一种奢侈。此外，中国人对动物有着不同的看法，尤其是对狗。

在西方世界，长期以来狗都被看做忠实的伴侣；而在中国，它们会出现在菜单上。这么说或许让人很是不安，感觉就像是在进行种族的诋毁，但不幸的是，这是真实的情况。在中国，狗肉（尤其是小狗的肉）是一种美味佳肴，在韩国更是这样。我从来没有吃过狗肉，因为我爱莱西①。此外，卡迪·伍德朗聪明、忠实的狗狗尼罗，帮助他找到从波士顿返回威斯康星的路，也是我最喜欢的文学形象之一。然而，食用狗肉和拥有一条狗之间有很大的区别，我从来没想过在家里养一条狗，我就是不觉得有这个必要。

---

① 莱西 (Lassie)，一条牧羊犬的名字，是影片《灵犬莱西》(*Lassie Come Home*) 中的主人公。故事发生在大萧条时期的英国约克郡，说的是一个家庭在困境中被迫卖掉了他们心爱的狗狗莱西。莱西在远离老家几百英里处逃出来，一路历尽艰辛，最后终于回到小主人的身旁。——译者注

我希望露露喜欢她的"小提琴宠物"。然而，督促露露在弹钢琴的同时也练习小提琴，这个任务变得越来越艰巨。有一天，她对我喊道："别在我面前晃来晃去的，你让我想起伏地魔①。你贴着我站在旁边，我就没法拉了！"

自己被孩子比喻成伏地魔，我并不像西方父母那样感觉受到了刺激，我还是坚持集中全力达到自己的目的。"为我做件小事好吗？露露。"我得把话说得更容易接受，"一件小事：再把这一节拉一遍，但这次要很好地注意保持颤音的连贯，保证从第一个指位平滑地变换到第三个。还要记住，要用上全弓，因为这是最强音，最后运弓时要加一点儿速度。此外，别忘了保持右手拇指和左手小指的弯曲。来吧——开始！"

对我的"全方位指导"，露露的反应是"拒不执行"，好像我什么都没说。把我激怒后，她则装傻说："抱歉，你想让我再做什么来着？"

在另外一些时候，露露则是像弹五弦琴那样把小提琴琴弦拨得震天响，来抗拒我提出的练习要求。更过分的是，她抓住小提琴琴把像拿着套马绳一样在头顶挥舞，直到我惊恐地大叫起来才罢手。当我提醒她挺直腰板，把小提琴拿高一点儿，她有时干脆像摊烂泥一般倒在地板上，伸出舌头，假装已劳累致死。而且常常还会一边练习，一边没完没了地唠叨："我们练完了吗？我们练完了吗……"

也有一些时候，露露好像很喜欢小提琴。在我们一起练习后，她还要再练一会儿。当美妙悠扬的琴声在房间里回荡，她甚至会忘记了时间的流逝。她偶尔会要求把小提琴带到学校去为同学们演奏，放学回家时则难掩

---

① 伏地魔（Lord Voldemort），《哈利·波特》中黑暗势力的魔头。——译者注

一脸的兴奋和快乐。或者在回家后飞快地冲到我的电脑桌旁，说："妈妈，猜猜我最喜欢巴赫的哪一段曲子！"于是，我开始尽力去猜，基本上是70%的命中率。而露露就会说，"你怎么知道的"，或者是"不，是这一段——它是不是很美呀"。

假如不是为了让孩子们成功地站在舞台上，我也许会放弃，也许不会。就像对索菲娅和她的钢琴艺术充满希望一样，我对露露和她的小提琴也寄予厚望。我渴望她能赢得纽黑文协奏曲比赛的大奖，这样，她就能作为小提琴独奏演员在耶鲁大学的巴特尔礼堂演出。我渴望她成为青年管弦乐团最棒的首席小提琴手、成为美国最好的小提琴家——而她现在才刚刚开始上路。我知道那是唯一真正能让露露感受快乐的路，因此，她浪费的时间越多——在练习时跟我软磨硬泡、三心二意、装神弄鬼，我就要求她补习的时间越长。

"我们今天得把这首曲子练好，"我对露露说，"要花多少时间，这完全取决于你。如果有必要，我们可以在这儿磨蹭到半夜。"有些时候，我们真的练到满天星斗、万籁俱静。

有一天下午，露露对我说："我的朋友达妮埃拉对我练习小提琴的时间非常吃惊。我告诉她我一天练6个小时，她简直不敢相信……"说到这儿，露露模仿达妮埃拉的表情，拼命地张大嘴巴。

"露露，你不应该说6个小时，达妮埃拉会误解的。因为在6个小时里你就浪费了5个小时。"我说。

露露对我的调侃并不介意，她说："达妮埃拉非常同情我，她问我还有没有时间做别的事情，我告诉她我真的没有更多的时间来找乐，因为我是华裔孩子。"

我沉默着，什么也没说。露露经常为自己寻找盟友、拉帮结派组织小团伙，对此，我并不在乎。哪怕全美国的人总是站在她那一边，我也不会让这种压力影响我。有几件我曾经做过的事情，至今都很后悔。

比如，有一次，我破例允许索菲娅去参加在外面过夜的同学聚会。小时候，我妈妈就常常对我说："你为什么要到别人家去过夜？你家里出什么问题了吗？"当我也做了妈妈，我也会这样想。但是那一次，索菲娅央求我说，这是她"最好的朋友的生日聚会"，我最后心一软，就答应了。可是第二天早晨看到她回到家里，不仅筋疲力尽（无法顺利地进行钢琴练习），而且脾气暴躁、心绪不宁，我就后悔不迭。

其实，在外过夜的聚会对大多数孩子来说，毫无乐趣可言——它对那些放纵孩子却浑然不觉的父母，完全是一种惩罚。

在对索菲娅盘问一番后，我知道了那天晚上A、B、C同学串通一气在排斥D同学；当B同学在另一间屋子里时，她恶毒地诋毁E同学；而12岁的F同学，整晚都在喋喋不休地谈论她对性的神秘尝试。看来索菲娅完全没有必要把自己扔到西方社会的糟粕里去"经风雨、见世面"；我也不会让诸如"孩子需要去探索外面的世界"或"他们有必要从自己的错误中学习"之类的陈词滥调来误导我。

在许多方面，中国人与西方人的做法都截然不同。例如，关于怎样对待做不做考试加分题。一次，露露从学校回到家，说她刚刚参加了一个数学测验，完成得非常好，所以感觉没必要再做加分题。

我一时不知道说什么才好，她的做法我难以理解。

"为什么？"我追问，"为什么你没有做？"

"我不想错过课间休息时间。"

可我认为中国人的基本原则，是在任何时候都要尽力完成加分的测试题。

"为什么？"在我向露露解释这个基本原则时，她反问道。

对我来说，这就好像在问我为什么要呼吸。

"我的朋友中，没有一个人会这么做。"露露补充说。

"这不是事实，"我说，"我百分之百地肯定，艾米和朱诺做过加分题。"艾米和朱诺是露露班上的亚裔孩子。露露承认我说的没错。

"拉沙德和伊恩也做了加分题，可他们不是亚裔孩子。"她强辩道。

"啊哈，你有这么多朋友都做过加分题！可我并没有说只有亚裔孩子才做加分题，任何有着良好的家庭教育的孩子，都知道做加分题是天经地义的。露露，我对你的说法和做法感到震惊。老师会怎么看你？你为了课间休息而放弃做加分题？"

说到这里，我的眼泪都快流下来了。

"额外的分数并不是额外的，它就是实实在在的分数。正是这些分数，将优秀的学生和平庸的学生区别开来！"

"可是，课间休息实在是太好玩儿了。"露露还在作最后的突围。不过，她只是嘴硬而已。从那以后，露露像索菲娅一样，再也没有放弃过加分题。有时候，她们得到的加分甚至比测验本身的分数还要多——这种荒谬的"倒挂"在中国就永远不会发生。在美国，是加分令亚裔孩子得到众所周知的好成绩。

死记硬背的训练是另外一个例子。

索菲娅的五年级老师在每个星期五都会进行乘法速算测试。一次，索菲娅输给了一个韩国男孩，获得第二名。接下来的那个星期，我让索菲娅每天晚上做20张试卷（每个都包括100道速算题），而我则在一旁掐着秒表计时。一周的强化训练之后，索菲娅就次次稳拿第一。

比别人练习得更多，也是亚裔孩子能在音乐学校名列前茅的重要原因。正因为更加刻苦，露露神速的进步在每个星期六都会给舒加特先生留下深刻印象。他经常对露露说："你这么快就掌握了新学的内容，将来一定会成为杰出的小提琴家。"

2005年秋天，露露9岁了。

舒加特先生说："露露，我想你已经可以开始练习协奏曲了。我们把循序渐进的铃木教材先放一放，你说好不好？"他希望露露学练维奥蒂的23号G大调协奏曲。"如果你真的刻苦训练，我保证你能为冬季音乐会准备好第一乐章，唯一的问题是……"他意味深长地补充道，"乐曲中的华彩乐段非常难。"

舒加特先生真是老谋深算，他了解露露。华彩乐段是一个独特的部分，通常靠近协奏曲的尾声，需要无伴奏独奏。"它也是一个展示自己琴艺的机会，"舒加特先生说，"但它真的又长又难，像你这个年龄的孩子很难完成它。"

"它有多长呀？"露露的兴趣似乎被调动起来了。

"你问协奏曲吗？"舒加特先生说，"噢，很长，差不多有一页。"

"我想我能行。"露露说。她看起来信心十足——只要不是我逼她去做的事，她其实还是热爱挑战的。

身陷"维奥蒂"，我们之间的战争不断升级。"嘿，安静点儿吧，妈妈。"露露会暴怒地冲我嚷嚷，"你又变得歇斯底里、语无伦次了，我们还有一个月练习时间。"而我考虑的是未来的规划。尽管完成这个协奏曲不是什么大不了的事，但维奥蒂的协奏曲可以将露露的小提琴水平拔高一大节。在华彩乐段里，有很多非常快的琴弦跳动和不少像钢琴一样的双音和三音和弦，对小提琴而言，做到音准是非常困难的。

我期待着露露对华彩段的美丽演绎，几乎要走火入魔。而维奥蒂协奏曲的其他部分则比较一般，有的还略带学究气。舒加特先生所言极是，是华彩段令整个曲子大放异彩、价值倍增。

还有一周，音乐会就要如期举行了。我发现露露有潜力将华彩段表现得淋漓尽致，她能让旋律"唱响"优美的"歌"。对她来说，那是某种直觉。这部分的技术含量很高，尤其是结尾的那一长串非常炫耀的双音，很难做到完美无缺。练习时，这些美妙的技巧经常会因为一些因素被影响：如果露露心情好、精力集中，她就能够抓住滑动于指尖的这个小精灵；如果她情绪不佳、心烦意乱，华彩段就会不"华彩"，最终流于平淡。最糟糕的是，我从来就无法控制她的心情。

然而，我那天忽然有了一个灵感。"露露，"我说，"我有个主意……"

"哦，不……你还是打住吧。"露露发出呻吟。

"这可是个好主意，露露，你会喜欢的。"

"你说什么——练习两个小时？然后在饭前可以免去摆桌子的任务？不，谢谢了，妈妈。"

"露露，给我一秒钟，你听我说嘛。如果下个星期六你真的很好地完成了华彩段——就是说，超水平发挥，我要送你一件难以置信的礼物，我知道你会喜欢得发狂的。"

"你是说一份小甜点？或者是玩5分钟电脑游戏？"露露的口吻带着嘲讽。

我摇摇头，说："它是如此令人惊讶，它的诱惑力甚至你根本就无法抗拒。"

"允许我参加一次玩伴聚会？"

我又摇了摇头。

"给我一大盒巧克力？"

我继续摇头。这回，该我来点儿嘲讽了。"你以为一盒巧克力你就难以抗拒？我比你还了解你自己，露露。我想送你的那样东西你永远也猜不到。"

正如我所说的那样，露露猜来猜去，压根儿就不着边际。这或许是因为这种想法是如此疯狂，大大超出了她的想象。

最后，我揭开了谜底。"是宠物，一条狗。如果下个星期六你能完美地表现华彩段，我就给咱家买一条狗。"

露露平生第一次被惊呆了。"一条……狗？"她重复道，"一条活蹦乱跳的……狗？"她满腹狐疑地强调说。

"是呀，一条小狗。要什么样的，你和索菲娅随便挑。"

想出这个主意的我，真是个天才呀！它永远永远地改变了我们的生活。

BATTLE HYMN
OF THE TIGER MOTHER

Part Two

第二部分

　　属虎之人总是高度警觉、雷厉风行。他们信心十足，或许有时过于自信。他们喜欢被别人服从而不是服从他人。适合属虎之人的职业包括：广告经理人、办公室经理、旅行社代办、演员、作家、飞行员、空中乘务人员、音乐家、喜剧演员和司机。

13 可可

我们家有一条不会好好散步、出门就狂奔的萨摩耶犬。

可可是我们家的狗，我的第一只宠物。

它不是杰德的第一只宠物，在他还是个小男孩的时候，他就有过一条叫做弗里克的狗。在杰德一家外出度假之时，总喜欢高声狂吠的弗里克被一些坏心肠的邻居给弄死了。至少，杰德是这样怀疑的。其实，或许弗里克只是走丢了，或是被一个住在华盛顿市里的极富爱心的家庭收养了。

严格地说，可可也不是索菲娅和露露的第一只宠物。

很久以前，我们曾经有过一段令人难堪的日子，好在它并没有折磨我们太久。在孩子们都还很小的时候，杰德给她们带回一对宠物兔——惠吉和托里。

我第一眼看到这对兔崽子就没什么好感，后来也没怎么管它们。它们看起来笨笨的，什么也做不了。宠物商店的人告诉杰德，它们是侏儒兔，长不大，总保持着娇小玲珑的乖巧样。结果，事实证明这完全是一派谎言。

短短几个星期后，它们就不再"袖珍"，而是长得膘肥体壮，走起路来，晃晃悠悠地带着日本相扑选手的步态，6平方英尺大小的笼子根本就不够它们折腾。尽管这对兔宝宝都是公的，但它们总想待在一起，把到处都搞得乱七八糟，让杰德很是头疼。

"爸爸，它们在干吗呀？"两个小女孩总是在问杰德。终于有一天，两只小肥兔神秘地失踪了。

可可是一条萨摩耶犬，一身雪白松软的毛发，有西伯利亚哈士奇狗那么大，长着一对深褐色的杏仁形状的眼睛。萨摩耶犬这一品种因拥有经典的笑脸和蓬松华美、卷曲到后背的尾巴而声名远扬。可可就有着这样一张讨人喜欢的笑脸和迷人的纯白色皮毛。不知为何，可可的尾巴长得不够张扬，有点儿短小。当它把尾巴立起来的时候，看起来就像举着一朵毛茸茸的球，可它的漂亮依然令人惊叹。

据说萨摩耶犬继承了狼的血统，但是它们的个性却与狼迥然不同。它们可爱、温顺、友好，喜欢其他的小动物，因而是很不尽职的看家狗。在它们的原产地西伯利亚，白天它们拉雪橇，晚上它们像被褥一样为主人保暖。在寒冷的冬天，可可就是这样为我们带来温暖。此外，萨摩耶犬还有另外一个大优点——它们没有狗的臭味。闻闻我家可可吧，它简直就像一件干干净净的皮大衣！

可可出生于2006年1月26日，是狗妈妈产下的那窝幼崽中最小的一个，因此总显得胆小羞怯。我们把可可带回家时它才3个月大，浑身颤抖着，就像一朵长着白色绒毛的马勃菌。（萨摩耶犬的幼崽看起来酷似刚刚生下来的北极熊，呆头呆脑的，与娇小可爱根本就不沾边。）

在我们开车回家的路上，可可蜷缩在板条箱里不停地哆嗦。回到家后它胆小如鼠，小心翼翼地不敢吃任何东西。直到今天，比起大多数萨摩耶犬，它的个头差不多也要小1/10，顶多算是个"小号"的萨摩耶犬。它惧怕电闪雷鸣、人们愤怒时的大嗓门儿，害怕喵喵叫的猫、体形矮小的恶狗，也不敢从我家狭窄的后梯下楼。也就是说，可可在它的族群里差不多就是个倒数第一的主儿。

　　然而，尽管我对怎样养狗一无所知，却本能地要用中国式的饲养方法来照顾可可。狗狗的饲养员告诉我们，萨摩耶犬非常聪明。过去，我也听说狗可以做算术，用哈姆立克急救法①救治呼吸道异物堵塞的主人，我还听过许多著名的萨摩耶犬的故事。凯法斯和萨格吉是两条萨摩耶犬，它们曾在著名的探险家南森②1895年的北极之行中，担当领头犬的重任。1911年，一条名叫"Etah"的萨摩耶领头犬随人类第一支探险队成功抵达南极。

　　我惊讶地发现可可动作灵活、身手敏捷，我敢肯定它一定身怀绝技、深藏不露。而杰德越是轻描淡写地说可可还不具备超然的长相（over-achieving personality），认为既然是养宠物就没必要为它们设定那么高的目标，我越是确信可可拥有惊人的、尚未开发的潜能。

　　于是，我开始进行广泛的研究，并购买了大量相关的书籍，尤其是新精舍（New Skete）僧侣们撰写的《饲养幼犬的艺术》（*The Art of Raising a Puppy*）这类的书。我和养狗的邻居交朋友，了解了不少关于怎样遛狗、让

---

　　①　哈姆立克急救法（the Heimlich maneuver），指在发生呼吸道异物堵塞时，及时进行腹部的快速按压，通过挤压患者肺部的空气，异物会像瓶子的软木塞一般被推出。曾经有狗在主人呼吸道异物堵塞时将其扑倒，并在主人胸口跳上跳下施行哈姆立克急救法，而将主人从窒息的生命危险中解救出来。——译者注

　　②　南森（Fridtjof Nansen，1861~1930），挪威北极探险家、博物学家及外交家，曾荣获1922年诺贝尔和平奖。——译者注

狗与同伴一起玩耍以及带狗参加户外活动的实用知识。我发现有个地方讲授饲养小狗的基本知识和方法，后面还有一系列更为高级的课程，立刻就兴致勃勃地报了名。

开始时，我们对可可进行了非常基础的训练，比如教它养成日常生活的好习惯。结果，其难度超乎想象。实际上，教会可可一个简单的动作，就要花费我们好几个月的时间。而当我们终于成功地训练它跑到门口表示它想外出时，那简直就像是个奇迹！

令人难以置信的是，在那些日子里，我的家人对怎样训练可可却发生了分歧。

杰德、索菲娅和露露似乎认为可可已经得到了足够的训练——尽管它掌握的唯一技能，是不能再到卫生间的小地毯上去撒尿。他们只想抱着可可、哄它开心，在院子里和它一块儿玩耍。在我对这一切颇为不满时，杰德则告诉我，可可还会听话地坐下，去拿东西，而且非常善于玩飞盘。

不幸的是，可可就只有屈指可数的这点儿本事。如果你说"过来"，它压根儿就不答理你。最让人窝火的是，在它忙着叼铅笔、咬影碟、啃我最心爱的鞋子时，把我们说的"No"全当耳旁风；它居然只听杰德的招呼，这令他的大男子主义得以在这个家初露端倪。

无论我们何时在家里举办晚宴，可可都会先在厨房里趴着假装睡觉，然后在我们把开胃食品准备就绪、和盘托出时猛然"醒来"。接着，它会火速地冲到客厅里，叼起一整个蔬菜肉卷，飞快地在房间里转圈儿。一边跑，一边狼吞虎咽。蔬菜肉卷在它的嘴边拍打着、飞舞着，越变越小。几个圈儿跑下来，蔬菜肉卷已不见踪迹。

对可可的突然袭击，我们真的是防不胜防。

带可可出门时，它根本就不打算跟着你慢慢地"遛"，只会以最快的速度疯跑。这对我来说，麻烦可就大了。我看见所有的狗狗都在和主人一块儿闲庭信步，可我们的可可却以每小时50英里的速度拽着我一路狂奔。为了追赶一只稍纵即逝的小松鼠，它常常会直接冲向一棵大树，或是别人家的车库。每次外出都把我累得筋疲力尽。当我把这个难题提交其他家庭成员时，却没有人肯接这个茬儿。

"我没有时间……我得练琴。"索菲娅咕哝着。

"可可为什么需要出门去遛弯呀？"露露则反问道。

有一次，我带可可"遛弯"后回到家，胳膊肘擦伤了，膝盖也被锋利的草割破了。见我如此狼狈，杰德说："这是萨摩耶犬的天性使然。它把你当做雪橇，只想拉着你朝前飞跑。"他进一步调侃说："别再想着教它遛弯了，为什么不搞个带轱辘的小车，你只需要坐在里面，就可以让可可拉着你满世界转了？"

可我并不想在我们社区里成为一部"战车"的驾驭者，我也不愿放弃教它好好散步的想法。假如别人的狗都能彬彬有礼地散步，为什么我们的狗就做不到呢？于是，面对这个难题，我开始独挑。

我从书本上学习了一些方法，我让可可绕着我们房子前的车道转圈儿。如果它做到亦步亦趋，没有拉着我往前冲，我就奖励它切碎的小块牛排，并在它反抗时低声提醒它，在它听话时高声鼓励它。由于在走的过程中，我不得不停下来以打消它飞跑的念头。每次我都要从1数到30，并拉紧系在它脖子上的皮带。

我们仅仅走了半个街区，可那段路漫长得好似没有尽头。

后来，在经过了种种失败之后，我去拜访了一位饲养萨摩耶犬的朋友，并买了一副在可可朝前用力时，可以紧贴它胸部的精致皮带。

在那段艰苦训练的日子里，我的两位好朋友——魅力十足的亚历克西斯和乔丹从波士顿来拜访我，还带来了他们举止优雅的狗狗——黑貂色的米利亚和巴夏，一对澳大利亚的牧羊犬姐妹。米利亚和巴夏与可可年纪相仿，但体形看起来更小，油亮的皮毛散发着迷人的光泽。

米利亚和巴夏对玩球兴致勃勃，它们的牧羊犬性格在游戏中表露无遗。它们俩就像一个共同努力的团队，而可可仿佛就是一只绵羊。米利亚和巴夏一直在试图控制可可的活动范围，寻找有利的角度来驱赶可可。这对牧羊犬姐妹还能自己开门、自己打开意大利细面条的盒子——要完成这类高难度的动作，可可简直是望尘莫及！

一天晚上，我们坐下来一边喝饮料一边聊天。我对亚历克西斯说："我真不敢相信，米利亚和巴夏居然能自个儿打开花园里浇水的管子来喝水，这简直太不可思议了！"

"澳大利亚的牧羊犬就像边境猎犬一样，"亚历克西斯回答说，"也许因为它们肩负重任，所以就变得格外聪明、机灵，至少有些网站是这样介绍的。网站还为牧羊犬分级哩，搞得我都不知道我到底该买什么样的狗。"

"分级？什么样的级别呀？"我给自己又斟上了一杯红酒，"萨摩耶犬是怎样分级的？"

"嗯……我不记得了，"亚历克西斯有些抱歉地说，"我想，给狗狗分级主要是根据它们的智力，不过，这么做有些愚蠢，我是不会在意的。"

在亚历克西斯和乔丹离开我家后，我急忙冲到电脑前，上网搜索"狗的智力级别"。搜索的结果大多出自不列颠哥伦比亚大学神经心理学博士斯坦利·科恩撰写的"10种最亮丽的狗"。我快速地浏览目录，拼命地寻找

"萨摩耶犬"，并发现了一个扩展目录。那里有79种狗，萨摩耶犬排在第33位，不是最笨的（倒数第一的"殊荣"给了阿富汗猎犬），但也属于中不溜儿的等级。

这个结果真让我作呕。于是我作了深入的、更有针对性的研究，让我终于松了一口气的是，我发现这样评估萨摩耶犬的智力完全是个错误！

在每一个关于萨摩耶犬的网站，专家们都说萨摩耶犬的智力水平极高。萨摩耶犬之所以在IQ测试中表现不佳，是因为所有的测试都是基于狗的可训练性。而众所周知的是，萨摩耶犬恰恰是那种很难训导的狗。为什么呢？这正好是因为萨摩耶犬格外引人注目，它们因此会变得高傲倔犟。米歇尔·D·琼斯对此作出了十分清晰的解释：

> 萨摩耶犬的聪明和极为独立的天性，使人类对它们的训练充满挑战。例如，金毛猎犬可以"为"主人工作，而萨摩耶犬却是"和"主人一起工作，或根本就不服管、不工作。令萨摩耶犬保持对主人的尊敬，是训练它们的先决条件。它们可以学得很快，其中的诀窍就在于，训教狗狗时不要超越它们感到乏味的极限。这就是征服萨摩耶犬——这种被称为"非传统地服从人类之狗"的鲜明特征。

我的研究还有一些新的发现。著名的挪威探险家、诺贝尔和平奖的获得者南森，总是带着萨摩耶犬去北极探险。在他1895年远征北极之前，就对狗进行了广泛的比较和研究，并由此得出结论："在果断、专注、耐力以及在任何情况下都能本能地坚持工作方面，萨摩耶犬超越了其他种类的狗。"

这就是说，与斯坦利·科恩博士"研究"的结果相反，萨摩耶犬实际上异常聪明，它们比其他种类的狗能更为专注、坚定地拼命工作。我不禁为此精神振奋。我认为，萨摩耶犬的各种优秀品质放在一起真是一种完美的组合。假如唯一的问题是它们顽固、不驯服的个性，那事情就好办了。

一天晚上，在音乐的伴奏声中，我与两个女儿的争吵好似一场高音比赛。之后，又和杰德发生了争论。尽管他在家里总是以各种方式支持我，但还是担心我要求太高、太强硬，制造了太多的紧张气氛，以至于让家庭生活缺乏自由呼吸的空间。而我，则指责他自私自利，只为自己着想。

"你脑子里只有你正在写作的书和你自己的未来，"我抨击他，"你对索菲娅的未来有什么梦想？对露露又抱着怎样的期望？你曾经想过吗？还有我们的狗狗——可可的未来，你有什么梦想吗？"

听了我的话，杰德的脸上浮现出一种滑稽的表情。停顿了一下，他突然大笑起来。走过来，他亲吻了一下我的额头。"对可可的梦想——这太可笑了，美儿。"接着，他又带着体贴的口吻对我说，"别担心，我们会找到解决办法的。"

我不明白这有什么好笑的，但令我高兴的是，我们之间的战斗结束了。

14 伦敦、雅典、巴塞罗那和孟买

我们非常喜欢带着孩子去旅行。在大女儿12岁、小女儿9岁那年，她们就已经把自己天真烂漫的脚印，留在了世界各地的39座城市和岛屿上。

我想，我可能有一点儿热衷于布道的倾向。像许多传教士那样，我喜欢将自己感兴趣的话题翻来覆去地讲。比如，我的"反地方主义系列讲座"（Anti-Provincialism Lecture Series）就是其中之一。只要想起这个话题，差不多就会令我气血上涌。

无论何时，我只要听到索菲娅和露露在讥笑一个有着外国名字的美国人——不管是"Freek de Groot"，还是"Kwok Gum"，我都会勃然大怒。

"你们知不知道这么说有多么愚昧和陈腐？"我生气地质问道，"'Jasminder'和'Parminder'在印度是很普通的名字，来自这些家庭的人，难道就不光彩，就带着耻辱的印记吗？我妈妈的爸爸名叫'Go Ga Yong'，你们认为这个名字很可笑吗？那么，我是不是也可以认为'Brittany'和'Shelby'这两个名字很愚蠢，只有失败者才会取这样的名字呢？永远不要

根据名字来对人作出判断！”

我不相信我的女儿会取笑别人说英语的外国口音，但如果我不是有言在先，她们或许会这样做。不谙世事的孩子有时会极其残忍无理。“绝不能拿别人的外国口音开玩笑，”我在许多场合都告诫过她们，“你们知道外国口音代表着什么吗？那是勇敢的象征！这些人远渡重洋才来到这个国家。我父母说英语有口音，我也有口音。我被送到幼儿园的时候，一个英语单词都不会，甚至在小学三年级，有些同学还在嘲笑我的外国口音。可是你知道他们现在在干什么吗？看大门儿。”

索菲娅惊奇地睁大了眼睛。

“索菲娅，假如有一天你移居中国，你要问问自己，你会是什么样子，你以为你说中国话的腔调会有多么完美吗？我认为这样的换位思考对你来说非常重要，我不希望你成为一个褊狭的美国人。你知道美国人中的超重者胖得有多离谱吗？那么，在做了3 000年的苗条美女和挺拔俊男后，中国人忽然间也肥胖起来，因为他们一直在吃美国的肯德基。”

“等一等，”索菲娅说，“你不是说你小时候很胖，商店里买不到你能穿的衣服，你妈妈不得不自己动手为你做衣服吗？”

“没错。”

“而你之所以这么胖，是因为你用妈妈烹饪的面条和饺子来填满肚子。”索菲娅继续问道，“你是不是曾经一口气吃了45个烧麦？”

“是啊，”我回答，“我爸爸很是为我骄傲。这个数字可是他的10倍，是我妹妹、骨感美人美夏的3倍。”

“这么说，吃中国食品也能让你肥胖啰。”索菲娅咄咄逼人地说。

或许我说话的逻辑不够严密，但我有自己要强调的重点。我珍视世界大同、五湖四海的理念，确信女孩子要接受不同文化的熏陶。因此，杰德和我总是抓住我们外出旅行的一切机会，带她们去看世界，甚至在女儿还很年幼的时候，我们就有意识地这么做了。有时候，为了省钱，我们全家人会挤在一张床上睡觉。于是，在大女儿12岁、小女儿9岁那年，她们就已经把自己天真烂漫的脚印，留在了伦敦、巴黎、尼斯（法国南部港市）、罗马、威尼斯、米兰、阿姆斯特丹、海牙（荷兰城市）、巴塞罗那、马德里、马拉加（西班牙港口城市）、利希滕斯坦城堡（位于德国境内）、摩纳哥、慕尼黑、柏林、布鲁塞尔、布鲁日（比利时西北部城市）、斯特拉斯堡（法国东北部城市）、北京、上海、东京、香港、马尼拉、伊斯坦布尔、墨西哥城、墨西哥坎昆岛、布宜诺斯艾利斯（阿根廷首都）、圣迭哥（智利首都）、里约热内卢、圣保罗（巴西圣保罗州首府）、拉巴斯（玻利维亚实际的首都，政府和议会所在地）、苏克雷（玻利维亚法定的首都，最高法院所在地）、科恰班巴（玻利维亚中西部城市）、牙买加、丹吉尔（摩纳哥北部古城）、非斯（摩纳哥北部历史名都）、约翰内斯堡（南非城市）、开普敦（南非法定首都）、直布罗陀岩（位于伊比利亚半岛）。

　　我们一家四口在整个一年中都在期盼着我们的假期。

　　通常，我们会将旅行时间的安排与我父母和小妹妹美音的出国游玩计划协调起来，7个人租借一辆大面包车，由杰德负责驾驶。我们把欢笑洒满旅途，路旁的行人目不转睛地盯着我们，对眼前这个奇怪的、不同人种的联合体颇为诧异。也许他们在想：那个男人（杰德）是不是这个亚洲家庭收养的白人儿子？或者那个男人是个不法分子，要将其他6人贩卖为奴？索菲娅和露露则非常喜欢姥姥和姥爷。两位老人对孙女表现出由衷的溺爱和荒谬的放纵，与当年他们管教我的方式相比，完全是天壤之别。

女孩们对我父亲——她们的姥爷非常着迷，他的确不像她们曾经认识的任何一个人。在我们外出游玩的时候，他经常消失在闹市的巷子里，然后怀抱着各种各样诸如上海蒸饺或比利时薄煎饼这样的地方特产，忽然间出现在大家面前。（我父亲总喜欢尝试一切，在西方的饭店里，他常常会点两种特色的正餐来品尝。）与此同时，我则表演"爬行动物模仿秀"（我有一张非同寻常的、弹性十足的脸），逗得全家人哈哈大笑。我们一起走过了妙趣横生的旅途，难忘的点点滴滴融入我们每个人的心里，成为一份永久的珍藏。

人在旅途中，一切都是那样圆满，唯一的缺憾是孩子们无法坚持练琴。

在家时，她们没有一天不练钢琴和小提琴，即便是在她们的生日里（开心之余——坚持），或者病了（服用阿德维尔止痛药——坚持），或刚刚去牙科医生那儿拔了牙（服用含有可待因的泰诺–3——坚持）。我没有看到在旅行时就应该中断练习的理由，可我父母却极力反对让孩子们在旅行时练琴。

"这也太离谱了！"他们摇着头说，"让孩子们好好地享受假期吧，停练几天时间，不会对琴艺带来什么影响。"

然而，严肃认真对待艺术的音乐家可不这么看。

露露的小提琴老师舒加特先生认为，"一天不练手生，一天不练就会退步"。我也向女儿们挑明："当我们去旅行的时候，你们知道金家的孩子们在做什么吗？练习！他们没有去旅行。难道你们会眼看着他们超过我们吗？"

对露露来说，携带小提琴比较容易，她可以把它直接带上飞机，然后放进头顶的行李仓。对索菲娅来说，事情就没有那么简单了。如果我们只是在美国国内旅行，通常几个长途电话就能把练习的钢琴搞定。美国的宾馆里，总是流淌着钢琴悦耳的旋律。在一楼的大堂酒吧，一般都会摆放钢琴。此外，至少还有两架钢琴放在不同的会议接待室。我会提前打电话给芝加哥万豪国际酒店，预订在大宴会厅早晨6点至8点练习钢琴的时间，或提前预订帕萨迪纳朗廷酒店晚上10点至午夜的练琴时段。

在这个过程中，偶尔也会发生一些小插曲。

在毛伊岛①的维雷亚大酒店，服务员把索菲娅带到了火山酒吧的电子琴前。但是，电子琴的键盘只有两个8度音阶，无法弹奏肖邦的波兰舞曲升C小调。而且，旁边还有一堂让人分心的潜水课同时在酒吧里讲授。因此，索菲娅只好转移到地下室的储藏间练琴。在那里，我们看到服务员正在拂去酒店婴儿钢琴上的灰尘。

到国外去旅行时，要为索菲娅找到练习的钢琴就更加困难了。这常常需要我们发挥创造力来破解难题。

我们曾经寻遍伦敦所有的地方，发现找到可供练习的钢琴，简直比登天还难。那一年，因为杰德撰写的《谋杀的解析》（*The Interpretation of Murder*）一书获奖，我们在伦敦待了4天。杰德的书描写了一桩历史上发生的恐怖疑案，由西格蒙德·弗洛伊德1909年唯一一次访美之行而展开。当时，杰德的这本书在英国荣登图书销量的榜首，他也被当做名人受到热捧，可这对我在音乐的"前线"督促孩子们练琴毫无帮助。

在我们下榻的切尔西酒店，我问服务员能不能让我的女儿找个时间在他们图书馆里练习钢琴，她听了我的话显得非常惶恐，好像我在要求把酒

---

① 毛伊岛（Maui），美国夏威夷群岛的第二大岛，位于夏威夷岛西北41公里处。——译者注

店变成老挝难民营。

"图书馆？喔——天哪，不，我想这不可能！"

就在那天的晚些时候，显然是由于一位宾馆的服务员将露露在房间里练习小提琴的事儿报告了上级，露露的练习马上就被禁止了。幸运的是，我通过互联网发现伦敦有个地方可以租借练习钢琴的房间，按小时付费，而且并不贵。

每天，当杰德在接受电台和电视台采访时，我和女儿们就离开我们下榻的酒店，搭乘公交车，前往那个被夹在两个三明治店之间、设计装修得就像殡仪馆似的商店。90分钟的练习后，我们再坐公交车返回酒店。

我们一直想方设法地在旅行中坚持练习。在比利时的勒芬①，我们在一家曾经是修道院的地方练琴；在另一个城市（我已不太记得地名了），我们发现一家拥有钢琴的西班牙餐馆，他们允许索菲娅在员工打扫完卫生、准备好晚餐的桌子后，从下午3点至5点在那里进行练习。

偶尔，杰德会为我把假期搞得这么紧张而不开心。"那么，我们今天下午是去看看罗马圆形大剧场，"他带着几分嘲讽的口吻问道，"还是再次光顾那家钢琴商店？"

索菲娅对我也极为愤怒。当我向酒店的人介绍，说她是一位"音乐会的钢琴演奏家"时，她都颇为不悦。"你可别这么说！这不是真的，太不好意思了！"

我则全然不赞成她的说法。"你当然是个钢琴演奏家，索菲娅。你在为音乐会演奏，就是音乐会的钢琴演奏家啦。"

---

① 勒芬（Leuven），比利时第九大城市，靠近首都布鲁塞尔。——译者注

我与露露还常常会陷入乏味冗长的、不断升级的争吵——浪费了太多的假日时光，错过了博物馆的开放时间，或不得不取消某个餐馆的预订……

然而，所有的放弃和牺牲都是值得的！

每当我们回到纽黑文，索菲娅和露露在假期中的进步，总是让她们的音乐老师感到震惊。

我们到达中国西安不久，索菲娅就已在黎明前练习了两个小时的钢琴。然后，我们才去参观了由 8 000 个如真人般大小的秦朝士兵组成的兵马俑，那是秦始皇——中国的第一位皇帝为自己在另一个世界准备的军队。也正是在中国西安，索菲娅第二次在协奏曲大赛上获奖。这次，她弹奏了莫扎特的降 B 大调第 15 钢琴协奏曲。与此同时，露露也作为首席小提琴手，应邀参加了各种三重奏和四重奏的演出。一时间，我发现露露受到其他小提琴老师的关注和青睐，而他们则正在寻找年轻的音乐天才，为自己的音乐世界锦上添花。

不过，我也不得不承认，在旅途中坚持练习有时真的是困难重重。

记得有一次我们在希腊度假，我父母也与我们同行。游览雅典时，就是在参观雅典的卫城和海王的波塞冬神殿之间，我们还见缝插针地进行了练习。之后，我们搭乘一架小飞机前往克里特岛。下午 3 点钟到达提供住宿和早餐的旅店后，我父亲迫不及待地要带着女孩子们去看克诺索斯宫。在希腊的神话传说中，在那里，克里特的米诺斯国王曾经将一个人身牛头的怪物囚禁在地下的迷宫里。

"好吧，爸爸，你可以带她们去。"我说，"但是露露和我只需要 10 分钟练练小提琴。"

听了我的话，在场的每个人都流露出惊讶的神情。"能不能晚饭后再练？"我母亲建议道。

"不行，妈妈。"我坚定地回答，"露露答应今天加练10分钟，因为她昨天练琴时提前结束了。假如她说话算话，我们真的只需要耽搁10分钟，就能轻松愉快地出门了。"

天哪，我真不希望任何人再经受这样的折磨。

那天下午，杰德、索菲娅、露露和我被困在一间差不多要让人患上幽闭恐惧症的小屋子里。杰德躺在床上，手里拿着一份《国际先驱论坛报》（*International Herald Tribune*），一脸严肃地试图将注意力集中到阅读上；索菲娅躲到卫生间里看书；我父母在旅店大堂里焦急地等候着，他们既不想打扰我们，又担心其他客人会听到露露与我之间的唇枪舌剑、高音比赛和相互攻击——"那个音符又降调了，露露。""实际上，它是太高了。妈妈，你根本就不懂！"

10分钟过去了，露露拒绝再好好地哪怕是拉动一下琴弓。显然，我们不能就这样收尾……最后，当我们终于完事儿后——露露愤愤不平、泪流满面；杰德双唇紧闭、郁闷至极；我父母则等得疲劳过度、昏昏欲睡；而我们要参观的克诺索斯宫，则到了该关门谢客的时间……

我不知道20年以后，我的女儿们会怎样回忆起妈妈逼着她们苦苦练琴的这些岁月、这些故事。她们会不会告诉自己的孩子，"我妈妈是一架操控他人的机器，我们即便在印度游览孟买和新德里之前都得练琴"？或者，她们也会拥有一些柔美的记忆？

或许，露露会忆起在印度的北部城市阿格拉，她第一次完美流畅地演奏布鲁赫小提琴协奏曲的情景——就在那个透过明亮的窗户，就能将美丽的泰姬陵尽收眼底的拱形酒店前，景美，人美，琴声更美。那一天，我们母女俩没有"拉开战场",也许是因为时差的折磨,让我们"斗志"尽失。

索菲娅会不会想起那个令人心酸的地方——巴塞罗那,我曾经在钢琴前给过她一巴掌,只因她弹琴时手指不够刚劲有力? 如果她没有忘记这件事,我希望她还记得在法国的洛克布鲁娜——那个栖息在悬崖上的村庄。在那里,旅店经理听到索菲娅练习的琴声很是惊讶,当即便邀请她晚上为饭店所有的宾客演奏。

小小的音乐会在一间可以俯瞰地中海迷人风光的玻璃屋里举行,索菲娅弹奏了圣桑①第二协奏曲的第二乐章,博得满堂喝彩。客人们团团围住索菲娅,给了她真诚的祝福和热情的拥抱。

---

① 圣桑 (Saint-Saën),法国著名作曲家、电影配乐家,主要作品有《约翰·威廉斯》、《侏罗纪公园》、《辛德勒名单》、《大白鲨》等。——译者注

15 婆婆

　　我的西方婆婆坚信，孩子们的童年就应该是一幅用顺其自然的随意、自由自在的天性、充满好奇的发现和丰富多彩的体验泼墨挥就的美丽画卷，而我从来不会把整整一天变成女儿们随心所欲的"开心秀"。

弗洛伦斯

2006年1月，我婆婆弗洛伦斯从她居住的曼哈顿公寓打来电话。"我刚刚接到医生从办公室打来的电话，"她的声音听起来怪怪的，还带着些许恼怒，"他们告诉我，说我得了急性白血病。"

早在两个月前，弗洛伦斯就被诊断出早期乳腺癌。个性坚强的她经历了手术和放疗，没有呻吟，没有抱怨。我最近听说她身体康复得很好，已经重返她在纽约的艺术舞台，并正在着手写作她的第二本书。

听了弗洛伦斯的坏消息，我的胃感到一阵痉挛。75岁的她看起来就像60岁的人，她怎么会……"这怎么可能？弗洛伦斯，医生一定是搞错了。"我笨拙地高声说道，"我马上给杰德打个电话，他会去问个究竟。别担心，一切都会好起来的！"

可是遗憾的是，这一切并没有好起来。

在我们通话的一周后，弗洛伦斯就在纽约长老会医院得到确诊，并开始进行化疗。经过数小时痛苦而艰难的研究，以及对其他治疗方案的权衡，杰德帮助弗洛伦斯选择了一个不那么严酷、不会让她过于恶心的以砷①为基础成分的化疗方案。

弗洛伦斯总是珍视杰德的意见，她乐意让索菲娅和露露知道，从杰德当年早产一个月来到人世间的那一刻起，她就对这个幼小的生命满心欢喜。"他当时因新生儿黄疸浑身发黄，看起来就像一个皱皱巴巴的小老头。"说到这个细节，她总是禁不住开怀大笑，"可我却认为他是那么完美。"杰德有许多地方都酷似弗洛伦斯，他遗传了母亲对美的感受力，有着与母亲一样匀称、好看的眼睛。人人都说杰德和母亲"简直是一个模子里刻出来的"，

---

① 砷（arsenic），是一种有效治疗急性早期幼细胞白血病的新药。——译者注

这话总是透着由衷的赞美。

我婆婆年轻的时候光彩照人。在她的大学毕业纪念册里，她看起来像极了美国著名影星丽塔·海沃思。即便已经50岁了，可她在聚会上依然以卓尔不群的魅力吸引着众人的目光；我也正是在那一年认识了她。

弗洛伦斯机智而迷人，有着非同寻常的判断力。你可以经常听到她的独特见解——什么样的衣服透着俗气，哪里的菜肴琳琅满目，哪国的人们对生活充满渴望。有一次，我穿着一套新衣服从楼上款款而下，令弗洛伦斯眼前一亮。"你看起来真是太棒了，美儿！"她热情地赞美说，"你近来的装扮集中地体现了你所有的优点！"

弗洛伦斯是一个不可思议的结合体。她常常着迷于一些怪诞离奇的事物，总说她艺术生涯中亲密接触的那些"美丽"事物让她感到乏味、产生审美疲劳。她以令人惊讶的独到眼光，在19世纪70年代投资了一批包括罗伯特·阿尼森和萨姆·吉列姆在内的当时相对还不太知名的现代艺术家的作品，当这些艺术家被人们一一地发掘出来，随着艺术的新星冉冉升起时，弗洛伦斯买下的画作一时间便价格飞涨，于是她大赚了一笔。

从来就不眼红任何人的弗洛伦斯，对人们对她的嫉妒毫无感觉，也并不在意自己的孑然一身；她喜欢自己独立自在的生活，拒绝了许多富裕而成功的男士对她提出的第二次结婚的请求。尽管她热衷于参加时髦服饰和艺术画廊的开幕式，但是这个世界上她最最乐此不疲的事情，是在水晶湖里游泳（她像个孩子一样，在那里度过了每一个旖旎的夏日时光），亲手为老朋友们准备丰盛的晚餐。当然，她最开心的事情，要数和她的孙女索菲娅和露露待在一起。"婆婆"——孙女们总是这样亲热地称呼她，这可是孩子们对弗洛伦斯奶奶的爱称。

6个星期的化疗后，弗洛伦斯的病情在3月份得到缓解。那时候，虚弱的阴影笼罩着她。我记得去医院看望她的那一幕：她背靠白色的枕头坐在病床上，看起来是那么瘦小，就像她自己被缩小了25%后的"影印本"。不过，她的头发都还"健在"，胃口相当不错，轻松愉快的个性也丝毫未变——她正为自己的"刑满释放"而心花怒放。

而杰德和我知道，她病情的缓解只是暂时的。医生一再警醒我们，弗洛伦斯病情的预后不容乐观。白血病来势凶猛，极具攻击性，在半年至一年之内，复发的可能性极大。由于她已是75岁的耄耋之人，已无可能做脊髓移植手术——简而言之，就是已经没有治愈的可能。然而，弗洛伦斯对自己的病情并不全然了解，对治疗前景到底有多么令人绝望也似乎一无所知。杰德几次试着将这个严酷的现实解释给她听，但在人生的灾难面前，弗洛伦斯还是表现出她一贯的不屈不挠和乐观。在她眼里，事情并没有那么糟。

"噢，亲爱的——等我出院以后，我得将大把的时间花在健身房了。"她令人惊异地说，"你瞧，我肌肉的张力都快丧失殆尽了。"

而对我们来说，最要紧的，是要对弗洛伦斯下一步该怎么办作出决定。她已经虚弱得无法走路，还得定期到医院输血，要延续过去那种过着"独行侠"般的生活已绝无可能。弗洛伦斯也不能求助于其他的家庭成员。她很少与前夫联系，还有个女儿，也住在遥远的外地。

我建议弗洛伦斯到纽黑文来与我们同住。在我幼小的时候，我妈妈年迈的双亲就和我们一起住在印第安纳州。我爸爸的母亲和叔叔生活在芝加哥，直到她87岁那年去世。我也总在想，必要时我是会把父母接过来照顾他们的。

这就是中国人对待父母的方式。

令我惊讶的是，杰德对我的建议表现得比较迟疑。这并不是意味着他不爱自己的母亲，而是担心我过去就与弗洛伦斯常起争执，甚至搞得不开心。在教育孩子方面，弗洛伦斯和我有着截然不同的看法，而我们俩的个性都非常强。我知道，即便是身患绝症，弗洛伦斯也不会放弃她的观点。杰德要我试想一下，倘若露露和我摆开战场、剑拔弩张，而弗洛伦斯感觉有必要加入战斗，并和孙女成为同一条战壕的"战友"……

当然，杰德的担心是有道理的。

弗洛伦斯多年来和我相处得很好——是她，把我领进了现代艺术的神圣殿堂，我一直都特别喜欢和她一起参加博物馆和画廊的各种活动。可是，在索菲娅出生之后，我们之间就开始发生冲突。事实上，正是由于与弗洛伦斯的矛盾冲突，才让我第一次认识到中西方文化在养育孩子方面存在着如此明显、深刻的差异。

首先，弗洛伦斯很有品位，她是一位艺术、食品和红酒的鉴赏家。她喜欢华丽张扬的面料，喜欢有益于健康的黑巧克力。无论何时我们旅游归来，她都要向孙女们问起她们在外面看到的色彩、闻到的气息、尝到的美味。对孩子们该怎样度过童年，弗洛伦斯绝对是自有主张。她坚信，童年就应该是一幅用顺其自然的随意、自由自在的天性、充满好奇的发现和丰富多彩的体验泼墨挥就的美丽画卷。

在水晶湖，弗洛伦斯认为她的孙女应该学会游泳、远足，并勇于探索她们感兴趣的地方。而我却告诉她们，假如你们独自走出这所房子的前廊，绑架儿童的坏蛋很可能正在暗处虎视眈眈！我还提醒女孩们，水晶湖的深处有凶猛残忍的食人鱼。我的做法或许看起来有些过分，但我认为貌似尊重的"信任"就意味着不负责任的"放手"。

有一次在湖边度假，弗洛伦斯在住地帮我们照看孩子。我回去时，发现两岁的索菲娅独自在外面跑来跑去，手里还拖着把园丁用的大剪刀，而那把剪刀的"个头"和小小的她差不多一样高。

我当时的第一反应是一把夺过大剪刀扔到一边。

"她想用这把剪子剪野花儿呐！"弗洛伦斯却天真地说。

事实上，我不是很会享受生活。我想做的事情总是排着长长的队伍，等待着我的亲历亲为。我讨厌花时间去作按摩，我不喜欢去加勒比海度假。弗洛伦斯把童年看做逝去就永不再来的欢乐，我把它看做一个进行基础训练、塑造个性和为未来投资的阶段。弗洛伦斯常常希望能有整整一天的时间，可以和孙女待在一起。她曾经这样要求过，可我从来不会把整整一天变成她们随心所欲的"开心秀"。如果满足了这样的要求，她们就没有时间完成作业、学说中国话、练习钢琴和小提琴。

弗洛伦斯赞赏叛逆的精神，乐于探究道德两难的哲学含义，也喜欢研究心理的复杂性。我也有这样的爱好，但不会将它们运用到孩子们身上。

"索菲娅对她的新妹妹太嫉妒了，"在露露出生不久，弗洛伦斯曾经咯咯地笑着说，"她只想划着小船把露露送回她降临人间的地方。"

"不，她不会的！"我回应道，"索菲娅喜欢她的新妹妹。"我感觉弗洛伦斯似乎正在虚构手足同胞相互竞争的例证。西方人有多种心理失调的现象，而亚洲人则很少有这样的问题。我们认识的中国人中，有几个人会因注意力无法集中而导致混乱？

作为中国人，我几乎从不与弗洛伦斯发生公开的争论。我在前面所说的"矛盾冲突"，指的是背地里在杰德面前对弗洛伦斯的批评和指责。对弗洛伦斯的诸多建议，我总是表现出包容和表面上的好脾气。因此，我们应该为杰德加分，特别是由于中西方文化发生冲突时，他成为了首当其冲的受害者。

然而，所有的问题都不成问题，因为弗洛伦斯是杰德的母亲。在中国人看来，既然他们是你的父母，就没有什么好商量的。父母就是父母，他们的地位不可质疑。要知道，是他们把你带到这个世界上来，你一辈子都欠着他们一份情（即便你并不这么想），你要为他们做一切你应该做的事情（即使这样做会毁了你自己的生活）。

4月初，杰德从医院里将弗洛伦斯带回了我们在纽黑文的家，并把母亲背上了二楼。刚刚出院的弗洛伦斯表现出难以置信的兴奋和快乐，仿佛我们一家人又齐聚到了某个度假胜地。我们把她安顿在一间客房里，紧挨着孙女们的卧室；从我们的主卧走到客厅，就会经过弗洛伦斯的卧室。我们雇了位看护，负责照看弗洛伦斯的衣食住行；理疗医师也常常来为她进行身体的检测和护理。

几乎在每个夜晚，杰德、孩子们和我都与弗洛伦斯一起吃晚饭；在最初的几个星期，晚餐经常安排在她的房间里，因为她下楼不太方便。我也曾经邀请过她的几位好友前来共进晚餐。我们在她的房间里打开红酒、摆上奶酪，好好地热闹了一番。

那天，弗洛伦斯一看到我挑选的那些奶酪就貌似大惊失色，并要我去买一些不同的奶酪回来。我没有恼怒，反而为弗洛伦斯的"依然固我"感到高兴。她的好品位已然随着血脉的传承，植入了我女儿们的基因中，我也因此知道了哪些奶酪不能再买。

那时候，杰德要送弗洛伦斯到纽黑文的医院进行检查和治疗，每周至少两次。尽管凶多吉少的阴霾始终笼罩着我们，可弗洛伦斯的病情在我们家里竟然奇迹般显示出好转的迹象。

5月3日是她的生日，我们全家倾巢出动，到一家非常不错的饭店为她庆贺，我们的朋友亨利和玛丽娜也参加了聚会。他们吃惊地看到，眼前的弗洛伦斯与6个星期前在医院里见到的那个她，简直是判若两人！身着一件高领的、不对称裁剪的"三宅一生"①短上衣，她迷人的魅力再次大放光彩，看起来一点儿也不像个病人。

可是仅仅在几天后的5月7日清晨，弗洛伦斯突然病情恶化，杰德匆匆忙忙地将她送往医院进行紧急的输血救治。及时的抢救把她从死亡的边缘拉了回来，当8位客人前来看望她时，她看起来气色不错。

就是在那一天，索菲娅在家里接受了犹太女孩的成年礼②。

万里无云、天幕湛蓝的晴空下，我们摆好桌子，在花瓶里插上了洁白的郁金香。在索菲娅的成人仪式结束后，我们在一起享用了黄澄澄的法国土司、红艳艳的草莓和香喷喷的中国广式点心。所有的菜肴、瓜果、糕点，都是索菲娅和露露安排的。杰德和我有幸做了回"甩手掌柜"，对生活能将如此简单、朴实的幸福呈现在我们的面前，感到万分惊讶。

一个星期后，弗洛伦斯感觉自己已经有足够的体力在看护的陪伴下返回她在纽约的公寓，于是她回到了自己的"老窝"。5月21日，弗洛伦斯在

---

① 三宅一生（Issey Miyake），日本著名的国际顶尖服装设计大师三宅一生创造的时尚品牌。——译者注

② 犹太女孩的成年礼（Bat Mitzvah），是犹太女孩在13岁时接受的成人仪式，这意味着她从这个时刻已开始承担宗教义务。——译者注

公寓里由于突发中风去世，而她当天晚上本来计划要外出和朋友一块儿喝酒，对冥冥中自己生命的"大限"一无所知……

葬礼上，索菲娅和露露朗读了自己撰写的简短悼词。下面的话选自露露的悼词：

在婆婆过去住在我们家的一个多月里，我有许多时间和她待在一起——不管是一块儿吃午饭、玩牌，还是聊天。有两个夜晚，我们单独相处，互相照顾。尽管抱病在身的她无法像正常人那样行走，可是和她在一起我一点儿也不害怕。她是个非常坚强的人。只要想起婆婆，我就会想到她的欢快和笑声。她对快乐的热爱让我也强烈地感受到快乐的拥抱。

我真的会非常想你的——婆婆！

索菲娅则说：

婆婆从未停止过对人生的思考，她总是渴望做一个知性达人，以全方位地体验幸福，到达生命的极限，活出不一样的人生。我想她已经如愿以偿了，因为直到生命的最后一刻，她都没有放弃自己的追求。

希望有一天，我也能像婆婆一样，找到属于自己的精彩。

听了索菲娅和露露的肺腑之言，我不禁万分感慨地想到，杰德和我以中国人对待父母的方式将弗洛伦斯接到家里与我们同住，让孩子们亲眼看到我们是如何对待生病的老人，这样做令我感到骄傲和开心。

在这个过程中，索菲娅和露露也帮助我们照顾了弗洛伦斯，对此，我同样深感欣慰。"对快乐的钟爱"，"全方位地体验幸福"，孩子们的话一直在我的耳旁回响。我在想，如果哪一天我们忽然也病倒了，女儿们也会把我们接到家里，像我们照顾奶奶那样照顾我们吗？或者，她们会选择自己的"幸福"和"自由"？

我想进一步阐明的是，幸福不是一个空洞的概念，中国父母在教育孩子的时候，并不会刻意把幸福挂在嘴边。中西方父母面对幸福的理解差异常常让我感到忧虑。当我的目光缓缓扫过我家的钢琴、小提琴，看到孩子们纤细、稚嫩的手指因为长期练琴而磨出的老茧，或者是那些留在钢琴上赫然可见的牙印……有时候，我真的会怀疑自己，这么做是否值得。

然而举目四望，我看到的事实却是，无数的西方家庭在崩溃——无数个长大成人的儿子和女儿并没有出现在父母的身旁，甚至是最起码的口头上的关心都没有。那么，我很难相信，西方父母的养育方式在把孩子们引向幸福人生时能做得更好。

有趣的是，我遇见过许多西方父母，他们常常会摇摇头，失望而沮丧地说："作为父母，在孩子面前你永远都是个失败者。无论你曾经为孩子们做了什么、付出多少，他们长大以后都只会怨恨你。"

而许许多多亚洲孩子的情况却与此相反。我接触过很多这样的孩子，他们承认自己在成长过程中承受过父母极为苛刻甚至是严酷的要求，但是他们在描述自己对父母的尊敬、爱戴以及难以表达的感激时，依然情真意切。

在他们身上，你找不到痛苦和怨恨的踪迹。

　　我真的不知道事情怎么会是这样。他们被"洗脑"了？或是患上了斯德哥尔摩综合征①？但是有一件事情却是确定无疑的，那就是：西方的孩子肯定不比中国的孩子更幸福!

---

　　① 斯德哥尔摩综合征（Stockholm syndrome），又称为人质情结、人质综合征，是指被害者（人质）对于犯罪者产生一种心理上的依赖感，甚至反过来帮助犯罪者的一种情结。——译者注

16　生日卡

作为一位中国妈妈，我只做正确的事儿，并不在乎怎样讨孩子们喜欢。

所有参加弗洛伦斯葬礼的人，都为索菲娅和露露的悼词而动容。

"如果弗洛伦斯在天有灵，"她生前最好的朋友西尔维亚后来伤感地说，"再没有比听到这样纯洁真挚的话语更让她快乐的了。"而有些朋友则惊讶，这对13岁和10岁的女孩，怎么能够如此准确而生动地抓住弗洛伦斯的风格特点呢？

这里还有一个不为人知的小故事。

那是在很久以前，两个女孩还很年幼，大概也就是姐姐7岁、妹妹4岁的时候。那一天，是我的生日。因为杰德事先忘记预订好一点儿的饭店，我们一家四口临时决定在一家稀松平常的意大利餐馆为我过生日。

显然，杰德为此感到内疚，他试图在晚餐前制造一点儿轻松气氛，便煞有介事地道出开场白："现在，我们在这里为妈妈举行一个美好盛大的生日晚宴！你们说好不好呀，宝贝们？你们每个人都会给妈妈一个小小的惊喜，对吧？"

餐桌上，我正在把一些已不新鲜的意式薄饼浸泡在餐馆服务员送上的一小碟橄榄油里。在杰德的催促下，露露把她的那份儿"惊喜"递给了我——那是一张生日贺卡。更准确地说，那只是被草草对折的一张纸。正面画着一个大大的笑脸，打开后，里面是另一张笑脸，上面用蜡笔歪歪扭扭地写着："生日快乐，妈咪！爱你的露露。"我猜想，制作这样的生日卡，恐怕露露只需20秒钟就能搞定。

我也知道，杰德会说"哇塞，太棒了，谢谢你，宝贝儿"，然后，再照着露露的额头来个匆忙而生硬的吻。然后他或许说他不太饿，他只想来碗汤，或者是面包和水也行。于是，除了他，我们剩下的人可以点任何我们想要点的东西。

我把卡片还给了露露。"我不想要这个，"我说，"我想要好一点儿的——就是说，你在制作它的时候，得把自己的想法和努力融入其中。我有一个特别的盒子，我会用它来存放你和索菲娅送给我的所有贺卡。而这一张，根本就没资格被放进去。"

"你说什么？"露露疑惑地问道。那一刻，我看见杰德的额头上渗出豆大的汗珠。

我抓住卡片，将它翻过来放在桌上。从我的提包里抽出一支笔，然后在纸上快速潦草地写下"生日快乐，祝露露乐翻天"几个字，再画上一个大大的不开心的脸。

"露露，如果我在你的生日时送给你这个，你会喜欢吗？我从来就没有像这样做过，而我送你的魔法师和巨型滑梯，可是花掉了我好几百美元；我为你预订了硕大的企鹅冰激凌蛋糕；我用自己月工资一半的'巨资'，来购买那些无聊的不干胶图片和形状各异的橡皮擦，而参加聚会的孩子们玩过之后就满地乱扔。我如此用心良苦，就是为了给你一个美好的生日！那么，今天是我的生日，我想我应该得到比这个更好的生日礼物。因此，这个——我拒收。"

"能不能给我一点点时间？"索菲娅轻声地问道，"我得再……"

"索菲娅，递过来让我看一看吧。"我说。

索菲娅惊恐地睁大了眼睛，她慢吞吞地拿出了她制作的生日卡。这张用红色卡纸制作的卡片比露露的要大一些，表面上似乎更加热情洋溢，但同样显得空洞。她在卡片上画了一些花儿，在旁边写着："我爱你！祝世界上最好的'No.1妈妈'生日快乐！"

"还不错，索菲娅，"我口气平淡地说，"但也不够好。我在你这个年纪，已经会写诗来祝贺妈妈生日快乐了。还会起个大早，打扫房间，为妈妈做好早餐。我总是努力让自己的祝贺富有创意，比如送给妈妈一些优惠券，上面写着'免费洗车一次'。"

"我也想做得好一些，可你总让我练习弹琴，我哪有空闲的时间呀！"索菲娅生气地抗议说。

"你应该早一点儿起床。"我回答说。

那天晚上睡觉之前，我收到了两张漂亮的、翻然改进的生日贺卡，我很喜欢，并珍藏至今。

此后不久，我向弗洛伦斯描述过这个关于生日卡的小故事。她听后一脸讶异，然后便大笑不止。而让我更加吃惊的是，她不赞成我的做法。"也许我应该试着用同样的方法来对待我的孩子，"她若有所思地说，"可事情总是这样，假如你刻意去要求别人做什么事情，或许这件事会变得一钱不值。"

"指望孩子们自然而然地做正确的事儿，我想这不免过于理想化了。"我说，"此外，如果孩子们按照你的要求来做事儿，你就不会和他们生气了。"

"可是孩子们却要生你的气。"弗洛伦斯指出。

事隔多年，在弗洛伦斯的葬礼上，我想起了我们之间曾经的这段交流。根据犹太人的习惯，人去世后必须尽快安葬，最好是在24小时之内。弗洛伦斯的突然离世令我们措手不及，在一天之内，杰德就得确定墓地、邀请拉比①、联系殡仪馆、张罗各种相关的丧葬服务。杰德一如既往地、迅速高效地掌控着一切，而把他自己的悲哀藏在心里。可我知道，他的身体已经摇摇欲坠，他内心的悲痛沉重得几乎就要把他压垮了。

那天早晨我去了女儿的卧室，发现她们神色惶惑地蜷缩在一起，眼里装满了震惊和恐惧。对于年幼的她们来说，还是第一次经历身边如此亲密的人永远地离去。她们也从来没有参加过什么人的葬礼；而她们喜欢的婆婆在一个星期前，还在隔壁的房间里发出爽朗的笑声。

我告诉女儿，她们每人都得为婆婆下午的安葬仪式准备一个简短的悼词。

"不，妈妈，求你了，别让我做这件事，"索菲娅含着眼泪对我说，"我真的不想这么做。"

"我也没法去说什么，"露露抽泣着，"你走吧。"

"你别无选择。"我带着命令的口吻说，"你们俩都得'上场'！要知道，婆婆在天堂里张望着你们、期待着你们。"

---

① 拉比（rabbi），是犹太人中的一个特别阶层，多为有学问的学者、老师。拉比在犹太社会中功能广泛，他们通常在宗教活动和仪式中担任主持，扮演主要角色。——译者注

索菲娅的第一份草稿简直没法儿看，既杂乱无章，又肤浅平淡。露露的也半斤八两，好不到哪儿去。而我对大女儿的要求则更高，也许我真的在难为我自己。

"你怎么能这样？索菲娅！"我毫不客气地打击她，"你写的草稿糟透了！没有思想，没有深度，它就像一块了无生气、空洞死板的路牌——那正是婆婆深恶痛绝的东西。你太自私了，想想婆婆生前如此疼爱你们……还有你，露露，你居然将一份儿本该充满感情的悼词写成——这样？"

索菲娅再也无法控制自己夺眶而出的眼泪，她愤怒地向我还击，着实令我大吃一惊。索菲娅的性格不像露露，也不像我，而酷似她的父亲。她通常会将愤怒锁在心底，很少大发雷霆。但是现在，她说："你没有权利说什么婆婆在期待我们！你甚至并不喜欢婆婆——你有着中国人的价值观，保持着对老年人的尊敬，但是你总是在嘲笑她，即便是她所做的很小的事情——比如做蒸丸子这道菜。这反映了你存在某种可怕的道德缺陷。你为什么如此像一个摩尼教①徒？为什么你眼里的事物非黑即白？"

我愤怒地想："我哪里嘲笑过她？"我只是在保护自己的孩子不要落入某种浪漫的、理想化抚养模式的窠臼，而那种不切实际的方式是注定要失败的。此外，是我邀请弗洛伦斯来家里居住，让她能够每天都看到孙女，是我为她带来了感受幸福的源泉——美丽可爱的、懂礼貌的、小有成就的、令她无比骄傲的小孙女！如此聪明甚至知道"摩尼教"这个词的索菲娅，怎么就看不到这些，却反而来攻击我呢？！

---

　　①　摩尼教（Manichaean），又称牟尼教或明教，源自古代波斯宗教袄教，为西元3世纪中叶波斯人摩尼（Mani）所创立。这是一种将基督教与伊朗马兹达教义混合而成的哲学体系。其教义认为，在世界本源时，存在着两种相互对立的世界，即光明与黑暗。——译者注

表面上，我没有计较索菲娅的暴怒，而是就在悼词里她应该怎样提及弗洛伦斯，提出了一些修改的建议。比如谈谈与弗洛伦斯在水晶湖度假、参观博物馆的美好时光。

索菲娅对我的建议置之不理。在我走开后，她砰的一声关上门，把自己锁在卧室里闭门造车。她拒绝将修改后的悼词让我过目，甚至在她平静下来，换上黑色紧身衣和黑色礼服时，也没有抬头看我一眼。而我却看到，在安葬仪式上发表悼词时，索菲娅一脸肃穆和平静。我的心在倾听，没有遗漏她所说的每一行字：

> 婆婆是一位追求真实的人：一番不诚实的对话，一部不忠实于原著的电影，在情感上表现出的一丝丝虚假，都不会博得她的赞许。婆婆也不会允许别人通过她的口说出他们想说的话。

好一段精彩的演讲！露露的发言也改写得很不错，呈现了一个10岁小女孩非凡的洞察力和风采。我猜想，弗洛伦斯九泉之下，一定会笑容满面地说："我实在是太开心了！"

除此之外我还想到，弗洛伦斯所言极是：孩子们肯定会生我的气。然而作为一位中国妈妈，我并不在乎这个。

17 "大篷车"奔向肖托夸

为了带露露拜见一位世界顶尖的小提琴老师，我们倾巢出动，驾车9个小时，带着花大价钱请来的辅导老师及其男友、受伤后拄着双拐的索菲娅，还有我们的狗……

弗洛伦斯离开我们后的那个夏天是那样的难熬。

开始，是我压伤了索菲娅的脚。当时，她从我的车上跳下去捡地上的网球拍，而我还在倒车。她的左踝关节被前轮挤压，我们俩都快被吓晕了。索菲娅被紧急送往医院，在全身麻醉的情况下，两枚大个儿的螺丝钉被嵌入踝关节进行固定和修复。此后，在整个漫长的夏季，索菲娅都得穿着硕大的靴子，依靠腋下双拐才能艰难地挪动。这令她郁闷至极，但也因祸得福地有了大把的时间进行钢琴练习。

不过，在我们的生活中，还是有一个让人开心的小东西，那就是我们的爱犬可可，随着时间的流逝，它长得越发秀美可爱了。它对我们一家四口有着同样神奇的效用：只要看它一眼，你的心情就会云开雾散、阳光明媚。尽管我寄托在它身上的所有期许，不过是某种一相情愿，但只要它用充满恳求的巧克力色杏仁眼含情脉脉地看着我——我就会不由自主地满足它所有的愿望。通常是带它出门去跑步，每次4英里，无论是细雨霏霏、风雪交加，还是晴空万里。而它则用自己的同情心来回报我——我知道，它不喜欢我对女儿们大喊大叫，但是它从不对我妄加评判；它懂得，我一直都在努力地做一个好妈妈。

降低了对可可的期望并没有让我感到沮丧，因为我只想让它感到快乐。我也最终认识到，可可只是一种动物，它内在的潜力远远比不上索菲娅和露露。虽然在真实的世界里，有些狗参加了炸弹搜寻组或缉毒队，而大多数的狗并没有经过专业训练，甚至不具备一技之长，其实这样也无可挑剔。

就在那段时间，我与彼得这位才华出众的朋友兼同事，进行了一次谈话，令我们的生活发生了变化。彼得会说6个国家的语言，能阅读11个国家的文字，包括梵文和古希腊文。他还是一位天才的钢琴家，早在青少年时代就在纽约这个国际化的大都市崭露头角。在我们的社区音乐学校，彼得参加了一次索菲娅的钢琴独奏音乐会。

后来，彼得告诉我，他认为索菲娅在钢琴演奏方面极具天赋。然后，他又补充说："我并不想干涉你们对未来的构想，但是你有没有想过让索菲娅上耶鲁音乐学院？"

"你是说……为她换老师？"我说道，同时我的脑子也在飞快地转动。要知道，近10年来，社区音乐学校已成为我最为青睐的地方。

"是的。"彼得说，"我相信社区音乐学校是个非常不错的地方，但是和其他在那儿学习音乐的孩子相比，索菲娅已达到了一个非同寻常的境界。当然，一切都取决于你们学习音乐的目的是什么，或许你们觉得好玩儿，只想从中不断地体验音乐世界的美妙和乐趣。"

彼得的一番话让我感到震惊。很少有人说我做这一切是为了"好玩儿",只是我碰巧接到过另一位朋友打来的电话,对露露练习小提琴提出过同样的问题。

那天晚上,我发出了两封至关重要的电子邮件。第一封给最近从耶鲁大学音乐学院毕业的小提琴手基旺·纳姆,我偶尔会邀请她来帮助露露练琴。第二封是给杨伟毅教授的,这位最新加盟耶鲁的杰出钢琴教师,是位曾经轰动音乐界的、众所周知的钢琴神童。

事情进展的速度比我预想的还要快。无比幸运的是,杨教授知道索菲娅;他曾经在一次基金募集的演奏会上听索菲娅弹奏过莫扎特钢琴四重奏,并且印象深刻。我们约好了待他从夏季演出返回后的8月下旬,在一起吃午饭。

同样令人兴奋的事情也发生在露露身上。基旺——这位12岁就在林肯中心(纽约市最大的艺术表演中心)登台亮相、进行小提琴独奏表演的艺术家,慷慨地向自己以前的老师阿尔迈塔·瓦莫斯推荐了露露。

瓦莫斯夫人和丈夫罗兰都是当今世界顶尖的小提琴教师,他们曾经6次获得由美国白宫颁发的奖项。他们教出的学生中有不少像雷切尔·巴顿这样知名的独奏表演艺术家,以及众多声名鹊起的国际大奖赛得主。他们把教学的大本营设在芝加哥,只招收才华出众的学生,大部分都是亚洲人。

我们等待着瓦莫斯夫人的约见,焦急得如坐针毡。一个星期后,电子邮件如期而至。瓦莫斯夫人邀请露露前往位于纽约州北部的肖托夸学会(the Chautauqua Institution)演示小提琴。那年夏天,瓦莫斯夫人就住在那里。会见的时间定在仅仅三个星期后的7月29日。

在接下来的20天里,露露把全部精力都投入了苦练小提琴。为了尽可能地在短时间内提高琴艺，我付钱请基旺老师一天两次，甚至三次，前来指导露露练琴。

杰德看到我们支付学费的现金支票时，惊讶得目瞪口呆。我向他允诺，我会以整个夏天都不外出吃晚餐（意味着我得动手做晚饭）和不买新衣服，来弥补这个家庭财政的缺口。

"此外，"我满怀希望地说，"你不是刚刚得到你写的小说的预付金吗？"

"嗯，我现在得赶快着手把结局写完。"杰德痛下决心。

"把钱花在孩子身上，再没有比这更好的投资了！"我说。

很快，杰德就陷入了另一个让他不开心的意外。

开始，我以为去肖托夸拜访瓦莫斯夫人，开车3至4小时就足矣，并事先告诉了杰德。就在我们准备动身之前，杰德登录网络地图想确认一下，他说："再给我说说，这个地方在哪里呀？"

非常不幸的是，我不知道纽约州的地盘竟如此辽阔，肖托夸居然位于伊利湖附近，差不多快到加拿大了。

"美儿，我们驾车去那儿要9个小时，不是你说的3个小时。"杰德有点儿恼怒，他问，"那么，我们还得在那儿待多久？"

"就一个晚上。索菲娅去听计算机动画课，我为她报了名。这个课程星期一开始，这是在她还挂着双拐时就期盼的事情。我想，我们能够将车程缩短到7个小时……"

"那可可怎么办呢？"杰德打断我说。我们训练可可不再随地大小便才两个月，它还从来没有出门旅行过呐！

"我想，带着它去旅行一定很好玩儿，这将是我们在一起度过的第一个假期呀！"我说。

"在两天内驾车18个小时，这可不是真正意义上的度假。"杰德挑明这一点，因为他得负责开车。"嗯，有一点点自私。"我暗想，"索菲娅受伤的脚怎么办？我们不在她身边的时候，她能保持把腿抬高吗？我们全家老小都挤进车里，倾巢出动又怎么样呢？"

对了，我们可以驾驶一辆老式切诺基吉普车。我建议索菲娅在后座上躺下，把头枕在露露的腿上，她的腿则用枕头垫高。可可一路上可以待在车尾的一个箱子里，和小提琴放在一块儿（不过，不止一把小提琴哦！这一点我会再解释的）。

"还有一件事情，"我补充道，"我已问过基旺，假如她愿意和我们一块儿去见她的老师瓦莫斯夫人，我会按小时付费，路上耽误的时间也计算在内。"

"什么？"杰德吃惊得下巴都快掉下来了，"这会花掉3 000美元哪！我们的车已经满员，难道把她和可可一起塞进吉普车车尾？"

"她可以开自己的车——我已告诉她，汽油费由我来支付。其实，她真的不想跟我们去，这可是一次长途跋涉。再说，她还得取消按小时收费的小提琴课才能成行。为了说服她，我还邀请了她的现任男友亚伦一同前往，并负责支付他们俩在那儿待上三个夜晚、下榻在高档宾馆的费用。我找到一个叫做威廉·苏厄德的好地方，为他们预订了豪华的套间。"

"三个晚上？"杰德说，"你在开玩笑吧！"

"如果你愿意，我们俩可以入住便宜的宾馆，好省点儿钱。"我说。

"我才不愿意呐。"

"亚伦可是一个相当不错的小伙子，"我继续花言巧语地说服杰德，"你会喜欢他的。他是一位法国的管乐器吹奏艺术家，他可喜欢小狗了！当我们与瓦莫斯夫人在一起的时候，他可以帮我们在室外照看可可。"

那一天，我们的大队人马在黎明时分就开拔了。基旺和亚伦开着一辆白色的本田，紧紧跟着我们的白色吉普。这似乎不是一趟开心之旅。杰德以自己的大男子主义气概，坚持全程驾驶，这让我感到不安。索菲娅一路都在叫疼，说她的脚胀痛得好像血液都快凝固了。

"真想再和你们理论一下——为什么一定要我跟你们出这次远门？"她天真无辜地问道。

"因为一家人总是要待在一起。"我回答，"再说，这对露露未来的发展非常重要，你得为妹妹助阵才是。"

吉普车在公路上飞驰。

整整9个小时，我在副驾驶座上跷着让我浑身紧张的"二郎腿"，可可毛茸茸的睡垫侵占了我本来应该放脚的地方；索菲娅的双拐横置在我头后的靠垫处，而双拐的另一头则伸向另一侧，紧贴着挡风玻璃。

与此同时，露露一路上的表现就好似这个世界上没人去关心她、安慰她。而我知道，她紧锣密鼓苦练20天，为的是在瓦莫斯夫人面前好好表现一下。而现在，她却不由得为即将到来的那一刻感到紧张和恐惧……

18 深水潭

杰德永远不会明白，为什么我和露露前一分钟还扯着大嗓门儿朝死里地相互威胁，而后一分钟就见我们嘻嘻哈哈地躺在床上，一起海阔天空地谈琴聊书，笑声不断。

"你说什么？"杰德问道，"但愿你没有说过这句话。"他惊讶地看着我，又加上了这一句。我们的争论发生在去肖托夸的一个月前。

"不幸的是，我说了。我正在考虑兑现我的养老基金，不是全部，而只是从克里利那儿支取的部分。"克里利、戈特利布、斯蒂恩和汉密尔顿，都是华尔街律师事务所创始合伙人的名字，我在生索菲娅之前曾在那里工作。

"在我看来，你这么做毫无意义。"杰德说，"首先，你得支付高额的税费和一半金额的罚金。更重要的是，我们需要存下这笔钱，将来退休后的生活才会有保障。这正是建立退休基金的目的，也体现了社会的进步和文明。"

"可是我想买一样东西。"我说。

"什么东西？美儿。"杰德问道，"如果有什么东西你非要不可，我会另想办法的。"

在爱情生活中，我好像是中了彩票。

我的丈夫杰德不仅英俊潇洒、幽默风趣、睿智机灵，而且对我的粗俗和花钱大手大脚的倾向极为宽容。生活中，我其实并不会为自己买什么东西。我不喜欢逛商店，不去美容或修指甲，也不买珠宝首饰。但是，常常会有一些东西让我失去自制力、迫不及待地想要得到它——比如，从中国买一匹重达1 500磅的陶土制作的马。这份奢侈令我们在接下来的整个冬天都捉襟见肘。

杰德总是尽可能地满足我的奢求。这一次，一种强烈的冲动令我备受折磨——我想为露露买一把真正高品质的小提琴！

我接触过一些业内知名的小提琴商人（有两个在纽约，一个在波士顿，还有一个在费城），他们向我推荐优质的小提琴。我要求每位商人都递送三把在某个价位范围内的小提琴，来让露露亲自感觉一下。结果，商人们常常会送上四把。其中，三把的价格在特定的范围内，另一把"会比你设定的价格范围稍稍贵一些"——他们婉转地对我说。然而，实际上他们的"稍稍贵一些"却是价格翻番——"但是我还是决定随其他的小提琴送给你看看，因为这是一把极为特别的精品，或许它正是你正在找寻的梦想之物。"就像乌兹别克斯坦的地毯商，小提琴商人也会以同样的方式来推销产品。

当我们中意的小提琴价格不断攀升至新的价格高地，我都试图说服杰德认同："就像投资艺术品或房地产，买到一把品质上乘的小提琴是最好的一种投资。"

"这么一来，我们实际上挣钱的速度总是赶不上花钱的脚步啰？"他会如此这般干巴巴地回敬我。

与此同时，我与露露则忙得不亦乐乎。

每当收到由UPS（United Parcel Service，美国邮件联合服务公司）寄送的硕大包裹，我们都会迫不及待地、几乎是粗暴地撕开它的包装，以尽快"一饱眼福，二饱手福，三饱耳福"。逐一拉响不同的小提琴，仔细欣赏它们异样的木质、静心比较它们不同的音调、认真阅读它们不同的历史渊源、尽力搜集它们呈现的各色特质，真是一件幸福无边的乐事。

我们尝试的小提琴中，少量是新近制作的，多数是一些20世纪30年代或历史更加久远的珍品。我们试用了产自英格兰、法国和德国的小提琴，但更多的是意大利制造的，通常出自克雷莫纳、热那亚或那不勒斯艺术工匠之手。

我和露露把全家人都召集在一起进行"盲听"测试。即在不能眼见小提琴的情况下，看看我们只用耳朵听，能否将琴声和琴对号入座，而我们偏爱的小提琴是不是奏出了听起来最美妙的旋律。

这项工作真是太伟大了！它将曾经水火不相容的露露与我，紧密、真实地联系在一起。过去，我们可以快活、忘情地在一起度过开心时光，也会互相伤害，而且伤得很深。我们常常知道对方在想什么，彼此也都承受了某种心理上的折磨，而我们俩对此皆无可奈何、无法解脱。遇到矛盾，我们可能会首先挽起袖子，真刀真枪地对着干。当鸣金收兵后，我们又会重归于好、亲密无间。

杰德永远不会明白，为什么我们俩前一分钟还扯着大嗓门儿朝死里地威胁对方，而后一分钟就见我们嘻嘻哈哈地躺在床上，露露亲热地搂着我，我们一起海阔天空地神侃，谈琴聊书、笑声不断。

　　说到这里，让我们再把镜头切换到肖托夸之行。其实，当我们到达瓦莫斯夫人在肖托夸学会的音乐工作室时，我们携带的小提琴可不止一把，而是三把。说实话，我们挑来选去，还是没能作出最后的决定。于是，就把这个难题带到了肖托夸。

　　"酷毙了！"瓦莫斯夫人说，"太有趣了，我特别喜欢试用小提琴。"瓦莫斯夫人有着脚踏实地、一针见血的作风，还带有某种怪异的幽默感。她直言不讳——我讨厌维奥蒂第23号小提琴协奏曲，简直是平庸乏味！她浑身上下透着威严，而且让人印象深刻。她也格外喜欢和孩子们在一起，至少对露露是这样，她似乎立刻就接受了露露。瓦莫斯夫人和杰德也非常谈得来。我认为，她唯一不那么喜欢的人是我。我有一种感觉，也许她接触过千百个来自亚洲的妈妈，却发现我缺乏美感。

　　露露为瓦莫斯夫人演奏的第一支曲子，是莫扎特的第3号协奏曲。琴声停止后，瓦莫斯夫人告诉露露，她的乐感非常棒。瓦莫斯夫人问露露："你是不是非常喜欢拉小提琴？"

　　我紧张得屏住呼吸，说真的，我不知道这个小丫头在这种场合会不会犯傻。还好，她回答"是的"。然后，瓦莫斯夫人对露露说："人世间有些事情是不能被别人教会的。尽管你有浑然天成的乐感，但是你的技巧却不够娴熟。"她问露露是不是练习过音阶（"是的，她练过一点点"）和琶音①（"这是什么东东"）。

　　瓦莫斯夫人告诉露露，假如她真的想成为一名优秀的小提琴家，那么，

---

　　① 琶音（原文中的études是法文，英文写做arpeggio），指一串和弦音从低到高或从高到低依次连续奏出，可视为分解和弦的一种。通常作为一种专门的技巧训练用于练习曲中，有时作为短小的连接句或经过句出现在乐曲旋律声部中。——译者注

就要努力改变现状。她需要通过海量的音阶和琶音的练习，来发展无可挑剔的技巧、肌肉运动的记忆力，以及完美无缺的音调。瓦莫斯夫人认为露露训练的进展过于缓慢，花上整整6个月练习一首协奏曲的一个乐章，这并不恰当。"我的学生在你这个年龄，已经能在两个星期内将整支协奏曲练得滚瓜烂熟了——我想，你也应该能做到。"

然后，就在我的眼前，瓦莫斯夫人手把手地、一行接一行地指点露露练习莫扎特协奏曲。她真是位风格独特的老师：既严格要求又不失诙谐风趣，敢于批评又善于鼓舞士气。一个小时飞也似的过去了，五六个学生走了进来，抱着自己的乐器坐在地板上等候。瓦莫斯夫人给了露露一些要自己练习的内容，还告诉我们她非常乐意在第二天再见到露露。

我简直不敢相信自己的耳朵——瓦莫斯夫人愿意再次见到露露！

我几乎高兴得差点儿从我坐的椅子上跳起来。是的，如果不是这样，我就无法看到我们的爱犬可可在窗外纵身跃过，而亚伦拽着它脖子上的绳索正跌跌撞撞地紧跟其后。

"那是什么？"瓦莫斯夫人问道。

"我们的狗狗，它叫可可。"露露解释说。

"我也喜欢狗狗，你们的可可真是太机灵可爱了！"接着可可制造的小插曲，这位大名鼎鼎的小提琴教师把话题拉回小提琴："我们明天来看看这些小提琴能拉出什么样的声音。我喜欢意大利人制作的小提琴，不过，或许法国的能工巧匠也会给我们一个大大的惊喜。"

回到宾馆，我依然兴奋得微微颤抖。多么难得的机会啊！我迫不及待地要和露露马上投入练习。我知道，瓦莫斯夫人的身边围绕着不少野心勃勃、雷厉风行的亚洲人，而我是他们中铁了心要令她大吃一惊的人，我要让她真实地触摸到我们做人的质地。

我从行李中抽出莫扎特的乐谱时，正好瞥见露露把自己扔在一把舒适惬意的沙发里。"啊……呵！"她心满意足地发出一声叹息，将头斜靠在椅背上，"今天真是个好日子呀，我们去吃晚饭吧！"

"晚饭？"我不敢相信我的耳朵，"露露，瓦莫斯夫人不是给你布置了作业吗？她想看看你通过练习，提高的速度到底会有多快。这可是超级重要啊——绝不是闹着玩的！快来，让我们开始练习。"

"你说什么？妈妈，我已经拉了5个小时的琴了。"

千真万确！在拜见瓦莫斯夫人之前，露露整个上午都在基旺的指导下练琴。

"我得歇会儿了，不能再练了。再说，现在已经5点半了，该吃晚饭了。"

"5点半还不是晚餐时间。应该先练习，然后再奖励我们自己吃晚饭。我已经在一家意大利餐厅预订了美食——那是你的最爱。"

"哦……不！"露露发出呻吟，"你是说真的吗？什么时间？"

"什么'什么时间'？"

"你预订的晚餐是什么时间？"

"哦，是9点钟。"我回答，话音刚落就悔不该说。

"9点……你说什么？9点？妈，你有没有搞错喔！我不干，我坚决不干！"

"露露，那么，我把时间改到……"

"我绝对不同意！我现在没法儿再练了，我不会这么做！"

我不用添油加醋地重现当时的情景，说说最后的两个事实就足够了。第一，我们的确没有在9点之前吃晚饭。第二，我们也没有练习。回忆往事，我真不知道我哪儿来的那么股力量，强硬地与露露对阵。我只记得，那个夜晚让我感到筋疲力尽。

第二天，露露起了个大早，独自去找基旺练琴，因此，她又把失去的时间补上了。杰德给了我一个最为奇怪的建议，于是我带着可可去跑步。那是一次长跑，我们跑出去很远很远。中午，我们又返回来在基旺的陪同下去见瓦莫斯夫人。后来的事情进展得很顺利。

我满怀希望，盼着瓦莫斯夫人会说："我很愿意收露露为徒，你们能每月一次，飞到芝加哥来上课吗？"至于我的回答，那肯定是"yes"啦！可是，瓦莫斯夫人却建议露露在接下来的一年先拜基旺为师，进行强化训练。

"你们恐怕找不到比基旺技术更好的老师了。"瓦莫斯夫人对她从前的得意门生微笑着说道，"而露露，你还有许多不足之处需要改进、提高，但是在一年左右的时间里，你可以考虑争取到朱利亚音乐学院去上预科。基旺，你不就是这么做的吗？入学的竞争将异常激烈，你如果非常刻苦，露露，我敢肯定你能如愿以偿。当然，我也希望你回去以后还能在明年夏天来看我。"

在动身返回纽黑文之前，杰德、女儿们和我驾车直奔一处自然保护区。在那儿，我们发现了一个美丽的可供游泳的深水潭，掩映在山毛榉树的葱葱绿荫中，还有一些小型的瀑布点缀其间。旅店老板告诉我们，在当地，那真是一块隐藏在大自然中的瑰宝。

可可害怕下水，因为它从来没有机会去游泳。杰德把它轻轻地拖到深水潭的中央，然后放开它。我担心可可会溺水，杰德却相信它不会。果然，可可"秀"出它经典的、无师自通的狗刨式安全地返回岸边，博得"全体人民"热烈的掌声和欢呼声。我们用毛巾为它擦干身子，并拥抱了这个勇敢的小家伙。

后来，有一天我忽然想到狗与女儿的不同。狗可以做它的同类能做的任何事情——比如，狗刨式游泳，我们为它骄傲、为它高兴、为它鼓掌。倘若我们的女儿做点儿什么事情也像狗这么简单，那该多么轻松呀！遗憾的是，我们不能像对待狗一样地对待女儿，不能粗心大意。

我不得不集中精力紧盯目标。瓦莫斯夫人的指令如水晶般清晰无误，我们该认认真真地做点儿事情了。

19 梦想的舞步

　　杨教授把手掌和手指拢成杯状、拱成帐篷之形，那些琴键似乎变成了一群孩子，他的手指"哄"着他们发出美妙的声音。而他的手指既刚劲有力又柔美优雅，就像芭蕾舞演员修长美丽的腿。

索菲娅和她的"监工"，以及在一旁欣赏音乐的姥爷

我的心在下沉。

眼前这张乐谱的内容看起来单薄得令人失望，没有密集的音符和起伏跌宕的音调，几个断断续续的音符，散落在只有短短6页的破旧的影印纸上。

索菲娅和我来到耶鲁音乐学院杨伟毅教授的钢琴工作室。

宽敞的长方形房间里，并排摆放着两架油黑的斯坦威小型钢琴，一架是老师的，另一架是为学生准备的。我的目光落在"少女朱丽叶"的乐谱上，这首曲子选自谢尔盖·普罗科菲耶夫①的《罗密欧与朱丽叶》(*Romeo and Juliet*)。伟毅教授建议索菲娅以这首曲子，去参加即将举行的国际钢琴比赛。

在我与伟毅第一次见面时，他告诉我他从来没有教过像索菲娅这么小的、年仅14岁的学生。他的门生主要是耶鲁钢琴专业的研究生和少数才华出众的在校生。听了索菲娅的演奏后，他愿意收下这个小姑娘，但有一个条件：她不能因自己年幼就提出任何需要特殊对待的要求。我向他保证，这绝对不成问题。

我喜欢对索菲娅的未来想入非非。她内在的力量甚至比我更强大，面对排斥、责难、羞辱和孤独，她都能够春风化雨、举重若轻。

然而，严峻的考验在等待着她。

与瓦莫斯夫人一样，伟毅对索菲娅的预期也大大超过了她过去练习的水准。索菲娅的第一次课甚至让我都大跌眼镜——伟毅交给索菲娅一大堆要完成的教学和训练任务：6支巴赫的创意曲，一本莫斯科夫斯基的钢琴练

---

① 谢尔盖·普罗科菲耶夫 (Sergei Prokofiev, 1891~1953)，前苏联著名作曲家、钢琴家。——译者注

习曲，一首贝多芬的奏鸣曲，哈恰图良①创作的一曲托卡塔，还有勃拉姆斯②的G小调狂想曲！他解释说，索菲娅还要补练许多的内容，技术基础还不够扎实，熟练掌握的曲目尚存在巨大的缺口。

而更加咄咄逼人的是，他毫不客气地对索菲娅说："别用跑调的乐曲来浪费我的时间。按照你目前的水准，没有任何借口犯这样的错误。找准音调——这是你应该做好的。做好你该做的事情，我们才能在上课时把注意力集中到应该解决的问题上。"

两个月后，当杨伟毅教授建议索菲娅练习《罗密欧和朱丽叶》组曲时，我却不以为然。我认为普罗科菲耶夫的曲子看起来并不难——它并没有给索菲娅能够竞赛夺奖的冲击力。为什么要选普罗科菲耶夫？我对他音乐的唯一印象是那首《彼得和狼》（*Peter and the Wolf*）。为什么不选难一点儿的，比如俄裔作曲家拉赫曼尼诺夫的曲子？

想到这些，于是我高声地对杨伟毅教授说："哦，那首曲子呀，索菲娅过去的钢琴老师认为，对索菲娅来说这太容易了。"这不完全是真的，实际上，这样说甚至大部分都不是事实。我不想让伟毅认为是我在挑战他的判断力。

"容易？"伟毅轻蔑地低声说道。

杨伟毅教授有一副低沉的男中音，这与他浅色的、有几分孩子气的眼镜框不太搭调。30出头、有着中国和日本血统的他，在伦敦和俄罗斯接受教育并长大成人。

---

① 哈恰图良（Khachaturian，1903~1978），前苏联作曲家、指挥家、音乐教育家。——译者注
② 约翰奈斯·勃拉姆斯（Johannes Brahms，1833~1897），德国作曲家。——译者注

"普罗科菲耶夫的协奏曲享誉整个乐坛，其中没有任何一个曲目是容易的。我敢说，任何人要想将它完美地呈现出来，都不是——'容易'的！"

我乐意听到这样的声音，我喜欢权威的描述，我崇敬专家（这与杰德截然相反，他讨厌权威，认为大多数所谓"专家"都是江湖骗子）。而更重要的是，普罗科菲耶夫的曲子并不容易！杨伟毅教授——这位音乐的专家如此这般地告诉我们。

我开始兴奋起来。

在这次比赛中拔得头筹的选手，将获得到卡内基音乐厅进行独奏演出的殊荣。迄今为止，索菲娅还只是在地方性比赛中获奖。当索菲娅在顿谷交响乐音乐会（乐手都是志愿者）上进行独奏表演时，我的感觉糟透了。从业余的舞台要晋级到国际化的赛场，其艰难可想而知。但这是一个荣登卡内基音乐圣殿的好机会——它绝对值得我们去梦想、去期待。

接下来的几个月让索菲娅和我了解到，大师级的钢琴课究竟是什么样子。看杨教授指导索菲娅练习"少女朱丽叶"这首曲子，真是让我有一种叹为观止和深感惭愧的全新体验。他帮助索菲娅将生命的活力注入指尖、渗透到每个音符，一层一层、掰开揉碎地使每个细节都变得有血有肉……

我只是不由得感叹：这个男人真是一位货真价实的天才，而我是一个野蛮人；普罗科菲耶夫是一位奇才，而我是一个白痴；伟毅和普罗科菲耶夫都很伟大，而我是个食人的生番……总之是一个天上、一个地下，让我无地自容！

很快，去上伟毅的课就成为我最最痴迷、时时期盼的事。每一堂课我都在笔记本上虔诚地记下授课要点，不同的音阶如飞流的瀑布一般在我的眼前掠过。偶尔，我会感觉他讲授的内容过于深奥。比如，什么是三和弦？

何为三全音？怎样得到音乐的和谐感？为什么索菲娅能迅速地理解并掌握它们？有时，我关注索菲娅上课时可能会疏忽的细节——我像鹰一般盯着伟毅的演示，时不时地在笔记本上以绘画或素描来形象化地捕捉那些宝贵的点点滴滴。

回到家后，索菲娅和我则通过一种新的方式，来共同努力地消化、吸收伟毅在课上传授的内容，体会他对音乐的真知灼见。我不再对索菲娅大喊大叫，或为她的钢琴练习而"拔刀亮剑"。因为一个饱含刺激和新奇的音乐世界，不仅呈现在她的面前，也令我这个"陪练的小伙伴"全身心地沉迷其间……

主旋律打造了"少女朱丽叶"的脊梁，是普罗科菲耶夫创作的这首曲子中最难的一部分。后来，索菲娅在学校写了一篇题为《征服朱丽叶》的作文，她写道：

> 在教授位于地下室的钢琴工作间，我按下"少女朱丽叶"的最后一个音符，然后，便是死一般的沉寂。杨教授目不转睛地看着我，我死死地盯着脚下的地毯，而妈妈则在我们的钢琴笔记本上奋笔疾书。

> 这首曲子在我的脑海里回旋、环绕。是音阶的滑行，还是音符的跳跃？我得死死地锁定它们。要注意力度的变化，还是要留意速度和节奏？我须顺从每一个渐强和渐弱。那么，杨教授和妈妈到底是怎么了，他们还希望我做什么？我只要把这些问题搞明白，我的表现就会无可挑剔。

> 终于，杨教授打破了沉默："索菲娅，你知道这首曲子沉浸在什么样的'温度'里么？"

"温度？"我张口结舌，不知道该怎样回答。

"这是个脑筋急转弯的问题，我来告诉你它有多容易。想想曲子的中间部分，它是什么颜色的？"

我回过神来，知道我得说出答案："蓝色，是淡蓝色？"

"那么，淡蓝色的温度是什么样的？"

这个不难——"淡蓝色是冷色调的。"

"那么，就让那段音乐降温、变冷吧！"

这是什么样的训练指令呀？

钢琴是一种需要用手指去弹奏的乐器，温度似乎与它风马牛不相及。此时，精美的旋律在我的脑子里萦绕——好好想想，索菲娅！我知道，这是朱丽叶的主旋律。可是，谁是朱丽叶？她到底有多"冷"？我想起杨教授一个星期前曾经提到，朱丽叶就像我一样，是个14岁的小女孩。如果一个英俊潇洒的大男孩突然站在我面前，宣称他爱我——直到永远，我会怎么办呢？好吧，让我来假设一下：朱丽叶已经知道自己对罗密欧充满磁力，但是她也有些受宠若惊、局促不安。她被罗密欧迷住了，同时又感到羞怯，对罗密欧的急切期待不知所措。这就是我能够理解的那抹"冷"色。

我做了个深呼吸，然后开始……

令人吃惊的是，杨教授笑了。"嗯，好多了！现在再来一次。这次要让朱丽叶回到你的手上，而不是挂在你的脸上。看着，你要这样……"他坐到我的琴凳上作了演示。

我绝不会忘记，他是怎样在我面前自如地变幻出那些微妙的旋律。他表现出了我心中的那个朱丽叶：迷人、脆弱，还带着些许疲惫。我开始理解了其中的窍门，就是用手来展现这首曲子的独特。杨教授把手掌和手指拢成杯状、拱成帐篷之形，那些琴键似乎变成了一群孩子，他的手指"哄"着他们发出美妙的声音。而他的手指既刚劲有力又柔美优雅，就像芭蕾舞演员修长美丽的腿。

"现在，该你了。"他命令道。

可惜，这首曲子中仅有一半的篇章在刻画朱丽叶。翻到下一页，则呈现出不一样的曲风：罗密欧相思成疾，在雄性激素的燃烧中受尽煎熬。他准备迎接完全不同的挑战，他发出的声音饱满而有力，而朱丽叶的嗓音则空灵而纤细。当然，杨教授提出了许多的问题要我去思考和回答。

"索菲娅，你的罗密欧和朱丽叶怎么听起来没有区别呀？如果他们也弹奏乐器，他们各自会选择什么样的乐器？"

我不知道怎样回答。"嗯，大概是钢琴？"我暗自思忖。

杨教授继续道："索菲娅，这首芭蕾舞曲是为整个乐团而创作的。作为一个钢琴演奏者，你必须复制每一种乐器的声音。那么，什么是朱丽叶的，什么又是罗密欧的？"

我被难住了。我琢磨着每个主旋律的第一个小节。"朱丽叶是……长笛，而罗密欧是……大提琴？"

可杨教授说朱丽叶是低音管，而罗密欧——我说对了，是大提琴。在普罗科菲耶夫最初的设想中，他的主旋律真的是由大提琴来演奏的。我不敢确定，为什么我常常比较容易理解罗密欧的特点，而这种灵感肯定不是来自我真实生活的体验。或许，我对他就是没有好印象。显然，他命中注定与朱丽叶有缘没分，但却毫无希望地痴迷于朱丽叶。朱丽叶主旋律最隐晦的线索，是罗密欧跪下来向她求爱。

朱丽叶让我困惑了好长时间，而我总是知道怎样抓住罗密欧，表现他的忧郁需要运用大量不同的弹奏技巧。有时候，他声音洪亮、信心十足；而仅仅几小节之后，他又会变得绝望和悲悯。我试图训练我的双手像杨教授要求的那样随心所欲，但既要展示朱丽叶的女高音，又得把握她在芭蕾舞中担纲主要角色的感觉，则相当困难。而现在，我得用钢琴弹出大提琴的感觉来。

请允许我将索菲娅这篇作文的尾声留到后面的章节。

索菲娅准备参加的比赛向全世界年轻的钢琴选手敞开大门，每一个尚未成为专业音乐家的年轻人都可以在比赛中展示自己。有点儿非同寻常的是，此种比赛的参选人并不需要亲临现场。每位参选者只需呈上一张15分钟未经修饰、剪辑的录音光盘，并自由选择录音曲目。伟毅强调，我们的这张光盘要将索菲娅弹奏的"少女朱丽叶"排在第一，另一首选自《罗密欧与朱丽叶》的短曲"街上渐渐活跃起来"紧随其后。伟毅就像一个艺术展览馆的馆长，悉心地挑选其他要展示的作品——李斯特的匈牙利狂想曲、贝多芬中年时期的奏鸣曲，他确定了这张光盘的全部内容。

让人筋疲力尽的8个星期过去了。伟毅终于对索菲娅说："你已经准备好了。"

接下来那个星期二的晚上，在索菲娅完成了当天的家庭作业和钢琴练习后，我们驾车来到专业音响工程师伊斯特万的录音室，为索菲娅录制参赛的光盘。那个过程真让人备受折磨。开始，我不太了解这件事儿的难度，以为只是小菜一碟，很容易搞定。而且，即便有什么问题，我们也可以重复录制多次，直到满意地得到那个完美无缺的版本。

事实证明，我错了，而且错得很离谱！

我没有料到的是：(1) 钢琴弹奏者的双手不是机器，它们会产生疲劳；(2) 在没有观众，同时又知道每个音符都会被录下来的情况下，要想奏出美妙的音乐是极其困难的；(3) 索菲娅眼泪汪汪地告诉我，她弹得越多，在一遍又一遍的重复中越是努力地倾注自己的感情，她的音乐听起来便越显得空洞、乏味。

而最后那一页（有时是最后那一行）总是最为艰巨的。这就像在赛场边，眼看着心仪的奥林匹克花样滑冰选手只要在最后一跳稳稳落地就能赢得金牌一样，你紧张得难以自持。那个场景可能是这样的：她前面都滑得很好，你以为，这一次应该不错。可是在完成最后的三周半跳时却"马失前蹄"，她突然狠狠地摔了出去，在一片叹息声中四仰八叉地倒在冰面上。

类似的事情也发生在索菲娅弹奏贝多芬奏鸣曲的时候，无论她怎么努力都做不好。第三次录音时，索菲娅在接近尾声处遗漏了整整两行。伊斯特万温和地建议我出去透透气。

伊斯特万的扮相看起来很酷——黑色的皮夹克、黑色的滑雪帽，外加黑色的克拉克·肯特眼镜。酷酷的伊斯特万对我说："这条街有一家咖啡馆，或许你可以给索菲娅要杯热可可，给我来点儿咖啡。"

15分钟后，当我端着饮品回到录音室，伊斯特万已经在收拾东西，而索菲娅满面笑容地告诉我，他们搞定了贝多芬，录音效果很棒——既没有出错，又非常流畅。我终于松了口气，没有提任何问题。

我们把这盘每一曲都饱含着索菲娅千辛万苦的原声CD，呈送伟毅教授进行最后的排序。他确定："普罗科菲耶夫的两首曲子排第一和第

二，第三是李斯特，最后是贝多芬。"然后，伊斯特万制作了正式的 CD
参赛版，我们随即快递给了这次比赛的组委会。

接下来，我们只能耐心等待了。

20　卡内基音乐圣殿

　　中国人为教育孩子所付出的努力大大超过西方人。作为母亲，我就是不会让自己停下来，喘口气，轻松一下。我知道，那些我们曾经害怕去尝试的事情，其实才是最有价值的。

　　该把镜头转向露露了！

　　做个中国妈妈是没有喘息之机的——没有时间去为自己再次充电，没有可能和朋友们一起飞到加利福尼亚的泥泉潇洒几天。就在静候索菲娅参赛佳音之时，我把注意力转向了露露。那时，她已经11岁了。而我的脑子里冒出个绝妙的想法：纽约朱利亚音乐学院的预科向7至18岁才华出众的孩子们敞开怀抱，露露可以去试一试。基旺还不敢肯定，露露已经作好了琴艺上的准备，但我对我们的超速追赶则信心满满。

　　而杰德却持反对意见，并一直在试图让我改变主意。朱利亚音乐学院的预科班声名卓著。每一年，来自世界各地（尤其是亚洲，最近是俄罗斯、东欧）的数千个能耐了得的音乐神童都汇聚到这里，竞争那屈指可数的几个名额。孩子们踊跃申请的原因有三：一是他们自己梦想成为一个职业的音乐家；二是他们的父母希望自己的孩子成为职业的音乐家；三是他们的父母真真切切地认为，能进入朱利亚音乐学院，实际上是一块叩开常春藤盟校之门的敲门砖。少数的幸运者可以参加朱利亚音乐学院的培训班，每周在星期六举办，训练9至10个小时。

杰德并不为每个星期六披星戴月地开车送露露到纽约参加训练的主意而发狂（我说过，这件事包在我身上），他真正担忧的是朱利亚音乐学院出了名的高压氛围，以及有时达到自相残杀程度的竞争环境。他不敢肯定这有益于露露的成长，而露露自己，也和父亲一样心里没谱。实际上，她一直在说她不想去试音，即便是被录取了也不想去。露露从来就不会听从我的建议去做什么事情，那么，她的意见只好被我忽略不计了。

还有另外一个原因，促使杰德无法确信让露露去朱利亚音乐学院训练究竟是不是一个好主意。

许多年前，他实际上就曾经是那里的一名学生。当时他从普林斯顿大学毕业后，就被朱利亚音乐学院的戏剧系录取了。该学院的戏剧系比享有盛誉的音乐系还要出名。因此，杰德到纽约城学习表演艺术。他的同班同学中有《壮志凌云》（*Top Gun*）的女主角凯利·麦吉利斯（Kelly McGillis），有《蝙蝠侠》（*Batman*）中的瓦尔·基尔默（Val Kilmer），还有《绝望主妇》（*Desperate Housewives*）里的马西娅·克罗斯（Marcia Cross）。那时候，他约见芭蕾舞演员，学习放松和控制形体的亚历山大技巧（Alexander Technique），在《李尔王》（*King Lear*）中担任主角。

后来，杰德因为"不听指挥"而被赶出了戏剧系。

事情是这样的：他当时在契诃夫的《樱桃园》（*The Cherry Orchard*）一

剧中扮演商人罗伯兴（Lopakhin），怎样诠释这个角色，他与导演有不同的看法。几周后，在一次排练中，导演忽然对杰德大发雷霆，狠狠地折断了手中的铅笔。她宣称："我再也无法和一个只会站在那儿讥笑我，对我说的每个字都品头论足的人一起工作了！"

两天以后，他就被戏剧系主任告之，他恐怕得自己"另谋生路"了。事情为什么会是这样？原来非常凑巧又非常不幸的是，杰德得罪的这位导演，正好是戏剧系主任的夫人！在纽约待了一年后，杰德终于昂首挺胸地走进了哈佛法学院。

也许因为我把它看做歪打正着的喜剧性结局（假如杰德一直待在朱利亚音乐学院，我和他恐怕就会擦肩而过、形同陌路了），我在不同的聚会上，把这个好玩儿的故事添油加醋、不厌其烦地讲了一遍又一遍，每次都令听众反响强烈。我似乎能从人们的眼神里读到：一位法学教授曾经到朱利亚音乐学院去学表演，并且认识凯文·斯贝西①，简直是酷毙了！而美国人对敢于反抗和被迫出局之类的事情，也似乎情有独钟、充满同情。

可是，当我把这个故事讲给我的父母听，他们却没有表示出丝毫的肯定和赞赏。那时候，我还没有与杰德结婚。实际上，他们也刚刚才知道我的生活圈子中有杰德这么个人。我们之间的恋情一直处于地下状态。两年之后，我终于正式地告诉父母，我与杰德在谈恋爱，这个消息让他们大跌眼镜。而我妈妈在吃惊之余，还备感伤心。

在我还是个小女孩的时候，关于怎样找到一位好丈夫，母亲就给过我

---

① 凯文·斯佩西（Kevin Spacey），好莱坞著名演员，参与演出无数大片，曾凭借1995年的《非常嫌疑犯》（*The Usual Suspects*）荣获奥斯卡最佳男配角奖，又凭借2000年的《美国丽人》（*American Beauty*）荣获奥斯卡最佳男主角奖。——译者注

一箩筐的忠告。"别嫁给一表人才的帅哥——这太危险了！良好的品德和健康的身体才是最重要的；如果你嫁给一个病快快的男人，那等待你的，将是痛苦和悲惨的生活。"而在她的心目中，那个健壮如牛的女婿一定是个华裔，最好还是位有着中国闽南血统的医学博士。

可我让她失望了，因为我选择了杰德——犹太血统的美国白人！听说杰德曾经就读于戏剧学校，我的父母对他的这段经历均无好感。

"啊，演戏？"母亲坐在沙发上，面无表情地说。同样错愕的父亲和她并排坐着，他看着杰德："你想做个演员？"

提到瓦尔·基尔默和凯利·麦吉利斯等这些如雷贯耳的名字，对我的父母来说似乎毫无意义，他们坐在那里就像两尊石像不为所动。当杰德的故事讲到他被赶出校园，不得不去端盘子、洗碗，在餐厅做了6个月的服务员时，母亲惊讶得说不出话来。

"被开除了？"她说着，并满脸痛苦地看了一眼我父亲。

"这件事情会不会被记录在案？"父亲则严厉地问道。

"爸，别担心！"我笑着安慰他，"杰德其实是因祸得福，他最后上了法学院，他热爱法律，这只是一个让人忍俊不禁的故事。"

"但是你说他现在在为政府工作。"父亲仍然板着一张脸严肃地说。我知道，关于杰德，他脑子里已有一张图画，以为他的工作就像那些坐在窗口为人们办理驾照的公职人员一样无趣。

我于是第三次耐心地向父母解释，由于杰德对某些与社会公共利益相关的事情感兴趣，他已经离开华尔街律师事务所，并以联邦检察官的身份，在为位于纽约南区的美国联邦检察官办公室工作。"这个机构非常有名，"我解释说，"得到这个工作职务实属不易，杰德的收入甚至比过去降低了

80%。"

"80%！"母亲提高了嗓门儿。

"妈，只是短短的3个月。"我有些烦躁地说完便赶快打住。在我们西方朋友的圈子里说杰德宁愿降低薪酬去做公共服务性的工作，他们多半会拍着你的肩膀，说："这对你真是件大好事儿呀！"

"即便不图别的，它至少也是很难得的人生经历。杰德喜欢参与诉讼，他以后没准儿想做一个出庭辩护的律师。"我说。

"为什么？"妈妈带着几分苦涩地说，"他就为了做个演员？"她冲口而出的最后一句话，仿佛携带着某种道德的污点。

然而，斗转星移、今非昔比。回忆往事，看看我父母究竟改变了多少，真是一件有趣的事情！到我开始考虑让露露去朱利亚音乐学院学习时，他们对杰德已是崇拜有加、宠爱至极。他们对朱利亚音乐学院的名气也一清二楚，知道马友友就是从那里升起的一颗璀璨之星。让露露去那里完成大学预科的学习——与杰德一样，他们也不能理解我为什么会有这样的想法。

"你该不会期望露露将来成为一个专业的小提琴手吧？你真的这样想吗？"一头雾水的父亲不解地问。

我没有立刻为父亲答疑解惑，但却没有放弃我最初的想法。就在我向钢琴竞赛组委会递交了索菲娅的参赛光盘的那段时间，我也向朱利亚音乐学院呈上了露露的入学申请。

我在前面说过，中国人为教育孩子所付出的努力大大超过西方人。作为母亲，我就是不会让自己停下来，喘口气，轻松一下。就像我数着钟点，用两个月的时间为索菲娅进行参赛准备一样，现在，我得把注意力转向露露，为她付出同样的努力。

朱利亚音乐学院预科班试音的安排充满了人为的压力。与露露年纪相仿的申请人要准备演奏3个8度的小调音阶和琶音，一首练习曲，另外还要一个对比强烈的快板和慢板协奏曲乐章，外加一首不同风格的小曲。试音时当然没有乐谱可看，你得将它们通通烂熟于心。实际试音时也没有父母的陪伴，孩子们要独自进入一个房间，在大约由5至10名预科班教师构成的专家评审组面前，展示自己以及自己的音乐。这些严阵以待的老师们，可以要求申请人按照任意的顺序、从任意一个段落开始演奏任意一首曲目，并随时可以让你停下来。

预科班的小提琴老师包括大名鼎鼎的伊扎克·帕尔曼①、纽约爱乐乐团的首席小提琴手格伦·迪特洛，以及一些才华横溢、蜚声世界乐坛的年轻小提琴教师。我们看好的教师有田中直子，她就像瓦莫斯夫人一样抢手，来自世界各地的学生总是千方百计、打破脑袋也要挤进她的音乐工作室。我们知道直子小姐，因为基旺在17岁师从瓦莫斯夫人之前，曾经与她在悠悠琴声中同窗整整9年。

帮助露露准备应试尤其艰难，因为她依然坚称："哪怕再过一万年也不会去试音！"她不分青红皂白地痛恨从基旺那里听到的任何事情。她知道，一些朱利亚音乐学院预科班的申请者从中国、韩国和印度等国家飞到这里，就是为了参加试音。而他们通通是有备而来，为了这个"愚蠢"的时刻已经准备了许多许多年。有的人甚至已不是头一次应试，他们被拒绝了两次

---

① 伊扎克·帕尔曼（Itzhak Perlman），以色列小提琴家，生于特拉维夫。4岁患小儿麻痹症下肢瘫痪，5岁开始学琴，13岁到纽约朱利亚音乐学院，师从著名小提琴教授加拉米安。1963年在卡内基大厅举行首次职业性演出，大获成功，此后开始了他辉煌的演奏生涯。自海菲兹70年代退休以来，帕尔曼或许要算世界小提琴乐坛最风光的人物了。——译者注

或三次，但就是不肯放弃。还有人在预科班老师的指导下受训，俨然已私下吃过"小灶"。

于是，我放低姿态与露露商量。"露露，最后的主意你得自己拿。"我很有策略地说，"我们可以作好去试音的准备，如果到最后你真的不想去，那就不去好了。"在另外一个场合，我则严肃地告诫她——"绝不要因为畏惧而放弃自己的尝试。"我告诉她："在我过去所做过的事情中，那些我曾经害怕去尝试的事情，其实才是最有价值的。"

为了提高准备的效率，我不仅雇用基旺每天数小时前来指导露露练习，而且还请了一位耶鲁大学在校的本科生来陪练。这个可爱的女孩叫莱克西，露露很喜欢她。虽然莱克西在音乐上的专业技能无法与基旺媲美，但她是耶鲁管弦乐队的成员，青春的血液里流淌着对音乐的酷爱。她头脑聪慧并富有哲理，喜欢思考问题，她将对露露产生绝妙的影响。莱克西和露露会在一起谈论她们青睐的作曲家、协奏曲、成就卓然的小提琴家，并且就怎样理解和诠释露露正在练习的曲子进行交流。在两个小姑娘的谈话之后，露露总是能更加兴致勃勃地投入练习。

在帮助露露"备战"的过程中，我一刻也没闲着。我依然在耶鲁大学当教师，并完成了第二本书的写作（这本书的内容是关于美国这个伟大帝国的历史和走向成功的秘密）。与此同时，我一直在各地旅行，就民主与种族冲突举办讲座。

有一天，我正在机场等候，准备乘班机返回纽黑文。我从手机上查看邮件，看到一封来自索菲娅钢琴比赛组委会的回复。有那么几分钟，我害怕得到坏消息，竟然捧着手机呆住了。最后，我实在是想早点儿知道结果，才点击了打开的图标……

让我释然的是，索菲娅获奖了，而且是一等奖！

这就是说——卡内基音乐厅这个神圣的音乐殿堂，在等待着她闪亮登场！

可能唯一有点儿麻烦的是，索菲娅去卡内基音乐厅演奏的时间，正好是露露参加朱利亚音乐学院试音的前一个晚上。

21 首演和试音

从练习的准备到登台演出，为观众表演就像是在为他们"献血"，它掏空了你的情感，让你感到有一点儿轻飘飘的。这首曲子把欢乐带给观众，而与你朝夕相伴、耳鬓厮磨的音乐，就不再仅仅属于你……

索菲娅在卡内基音乐大厅演出（2007年）

　　索菲娅走进卡内基音乐大厅登台演出的那一天，真是个大喜的日子！而我，也简直是到了欣喜若狂的地步。

　　我对杰德说，我们今年放弃冬季度假的计划吧，因为我已准备为这个美好的日子一掷千金。我从豪华高档的巴尼斯纽约精品店为索菲娅的演出定做了一身墨绿色绸缎的曳地长裙，并精心准备了演出后的欢庆招待会。我在纽约圣瑞吉斯酒店预订了枫丹白露厅，那里有两个房间，可以热闹两个晚上；备有寿司、蟹饼、饺子、油炸玉米粉饼，一个食用生蚝的吧台，用银质冰碗盛装的大虾，我还订下了优质牛肉和北京烤鸭餐台。搞定这一切的最后一分钟，我又加上了法式的格鲁耶尔奶油巧克力小圆酥饼、西西里岛的野生蘑菇饭团，还有一个巨大的甜食餐台。当然，我也印制了精美的请柬，把它送给每一位我们想邀请的人。

　　在那段疯狂的日子里，每当新的账单不期而至，杰德都会挑挑眉毛，对我说："呃呵，我们的夏季度假游又泡汤了。"而我母亲对我的极度奢侈也颇感震惊，因为在我们成长的岁月里，我们全家外出旅行也只是栖身在6美元汽车连锁旅馆①或假日酒店这类价廉物美的地方。可是，到卡内基音乐大厅去演出恐怕是一个千载难逢的机会，我要让它成为被我们珍藏一生的记忆！

　　为了清晰地剖析我自己，我或许应该介绍一下自己的某些行为特征——比如，我有喜欢炫耀、夸大的倾向，而这些特征并不是大部分中国妈妈所具有的。我从父亲身上继承了这些缺点，而且还有着一副隔着八丈远就能听到的大嗓门儿，喜欢热闹而盛大的聚会，并酷爱红色。甚至在我

---

　　①　6美元汽车连锁旅馆（Motel 6），1962年创建于美国加利福尼亚州圣塔巴巴拉市，因初创时的房价每人每夜仅收6美元而命名。——译者注

一天天长大时，我那处事淡定、端庄谦虚的母亲，也会摇着头说："从遗传学来看，美儿真是一个古怪之人的复制品。"她说的"古怪之人"，就是我父亲。而在那时，我常常把他当做自己崇拜的偶像，却是千真万确。

我在圣瑞吉斯酒店安排的一切，还包括我们可以有权使用一架钢琴。在独奏演出的前一天，索菲娅和我在那儿断断续续地练习了一整天。杰德担心我做过头了，反而练坏了索菲娅的手指。伟毅教授则告诉我，索菲娅里里外外、彻头彻尾地了解自己要演奏的曲子，保持镇定和专注比什么都重要。但我还是想确认一下，索菲娅的表演是否完美无缺，她不能忽略伟毅传授给我们的每一个非凡而精致的细微差别。

与每个人给予我们的忠告背道而驰。在独奏演出的前一天，我们一直练习到差不多凌晨1点。在练习结束时，我对索菲娅说："你一定会非常出色的！在你付出了如此巨大的努力之后，你知道自己无所不能，无论发生什么事情，你都会举重若轻的。"

第二天，当那个伟大的时刻朝我们一步步走来——紧张得喘不过气来的我，死死地抓住座位的扶手，活像一具僵尸。索菲娅的独奏发挥得太棒了，她令整个卡内基音乐厅喜气洋洋。美妙的琴声在大厅里回荡，而坐在观众席上的我，对这曲调中的每一个音符、每一处起伏、每一组机智诙谐的弹奏，皆了如指掌。

我知道——哪些是她容易出错的地方，但索菲娅如轻风般一一掠过，没有留下一丝瑕疵。

我了解——哪些是她特别喜爱的部分，成为最为出神入化的转换。

我明白——该在什么地方感谢上帝，因为她在处理时没有表现出慌张和匆忙。

其实确切地说，早在她把独奏曲子带回家里，即兴地、充满感情地沉浸其间时，我就知道她已经走在了通向胜利的大道上……

演出结束时，当每个人都赶来祝贺她、拥抱她，我退到了人群的后面。在这个我不需要凑热闹的时刻，我看到索菲娅在人群中搜寻我的身影。我只是远远地望着我美丽可爱的、正在长大成熟的小女孩，和她的朋友们一起开心地笑着，忙着接过一束又一束绚丽芬芳的花儿。

在后来的岁月中，每当我感到绝望的时候，我都会逼着自己重温这个难忘的时刻。

对于我们家来说，这个聚会真是盛况空前。当时，我父母和妹妹们来了，杰德的父亲和他的新任太太哈里特以及许多朋友和同事也来了。伟毅从纽黑文专程赶来观看索菲娅的演出，他显然为自己这个年轻的学生颇感欣慰。而对索菲娅来说，这是她一生中最最幸福的一天。音乐会后，我不仅邀请了她所在八年级班级的全体同学（共25个），而且还租了辆面包车往返于纽黑文和纽约之间接送他们。将一群让人眼晕的唧唧喳喳的八年级学生放羊般"赶"到纽约，他们的掌声和那个热乎劲儿无人能比——当然，他们在圣瑞吉斯酒店自助餐厅吃掉的基围虾也"打遍全酒店无敌手"！

下面，我将兑现我在前面作出的承诺，将索菲娅的作文《征服朱丽叶》的尾声呈现给你们：

演出的那一天，我还没有完全回过神来，就发现自己已经呆呆地、惊恐地站在即将演出的后台，浑身发抖，双手冰凉，脑子里一片空白，甚至不记得我要弹奏的曲子该怎样开头。我眼前那面古老的镜子，清晰地映照出我苍白的面颊和深色衣裙的反差。而且我还在猜想，有多少音乐家也在同时注视着这面镜子。

卡内基音乐厅，它并不像一个我应该努力的目标。它似乎无法企及，就像一个虚假的希望，引诱我将自己整个的一生都投入钢琴练习——永无止境。是的，在这里，我只是一个八年级的学生，却要为众多翘首盼望的观众弹奏"少女朱丽叶"。

为了这个时刻我是如此努力。罗密欧和朱丽叶在曲子里并不是唯一的一对人物，陪伴在朱丽叶身旁的保姆发出甜蜜的、反复的喃喃低语；喧闹的和弦是罗密欧那些喜欢恶作剧的朋友。在一首曲子里，用一种或另一种方法，我要刻画众多的人物形象、展现他们的喜怒哀乐。在这个时刻，我才发现我是多么喜欢这首曲子。

上台表演真不容易——事实上，它是一件让人心碎八瓣的事情。你用数月或数年的时间去练习、掌握一首曲子，你就会慢慢地被它融化，最终成为这首曲子的一部分。从练习的准备到登台演出，为观众表演就像是在为他们"献血"，它掏空了你的情感，让你感到有一点儿轻飘飘的。这首曲子把欢乐带给观众，而与你朝夕相伴、耳鬓厮磨的音乐，就不再仅仅属于你……

那个期待已久的时刻到了。

我缓缓地从钢琴前起身，向观众鞠躬。只有舞台明亮如昼，我看不清台下观众的脸。我对我心中的罗密欧和朱丽叶轻轻地说了声"再见"，然后，就把他们放逐到了深邃的黑暗中。

索菲娅的成功激励我孕育着新的梦想。

索菲娅登台演出的威尔演奏厅位于卡内基音乐厅的三楼，它并不太大。

我久久地凝视着那些反映第一次世界大战前，法国一派歌舞升平美好景象的拱门，它们有着对称的比例，看起来非常迷人。我曾经从电视上得知，在卡内基音乐厅更大、更重要的演奏厅里，世界上一些最优秀的音乐家为大约3 000名观众表演。这个大厅被称为"伊萨克斯特恩礼堂"。我暗想，我们在将来的什么时候，应该争取到这个大厅里去演奏。

那一天，我们在无尽的欢乐中也感受到几丝忧郁。弗洛伦斯的缺席留下了一个无法弥补的遗憾；索菲娅的钢琴老教师米歇尔没能前来观看也让我们心里不安，尽管我们极力维持我们之间的友谊，但索菲娅转到伟毅教授门下学习也对她造成了一定的伤害。而最为糟糕的是，露露在姐姐独奏演出那天食物中毒。

那天上午，她一直都和基旺在一起练习要试音的曲目，之后去了一家熟食店吃午饭。20分钟后，露露感到恶心，它的胃开始翻江倒海，疼痛得抽搐不已。她勉强坚持到索菲娅在独奏会上按下最后一个音符，然后便摇摇晃晃地走出卡内基音乐厅，基旺叫出租车把她送回了我们下榻的酒店。露露错过了整个欢庆的招待会，我和杰德在聚会中轮流抽身赶回酒店去看望她。整个晚上，露露都在不停地呕吐，好在有我母亲在她身边照料。

第二天早晨，虚弱不堪的露露脸上没有一丝血色，惨白如纸，几乎没有力气行走，我们把她送到了朱利亚音乐学院。她穿着黄白相间的连衣裙，头上扎了个大大的蝴蝶结，这令她的脸色看起来更加憔悴。我也曾想过取消这次试音，可我们已经投入了这么多的时间和精力来进行准备，就连露露都不忍心放弃。

在等待应试的地方，我们看见到处都是亚洲父母的面孔，他们焦急地来回踱步，或神色凝重，或目不斜视，显得是那样的呆板、拘谨。我不由得在想，他们有可能热爱音乐吗？然后，我发现几乎所有的父母都是外国人或移民，音乐对他们来说似乎就是一张进入美国的入场券。

"下一位，路易莎！"听到点名，露露勇敢地独自走进了试音室。

我的心几乎要碎了——就在那一刻，我甚至差点儿就退缩了，想放弃了。

杰德拉着我把耳朵紧紧地贴在门上，我们听到她在演奏莫扎特的第三协奏曲和加布里埃尔·弗莱的《摇篮曲》（*Berceuse*）。我们俩都被感动得就好似从来没有听过露露的琴声。后来，露露告诉我们，著名的小提琴教师伊扎克·帕尔曼和田中直子也在那间屋子里担任试音评判人。

一个月后，我们收到了邮件。杰德和我从那个薄薄的信封上，立刻就掂出了我们得到的坏消息。那时，露露还在学校里。阅读了仅有两行文字、措辞正式的拒绝信函，杰德没有对我说一句话，就厌恶地转身走开了。而我从他的沉默中读出的是："美儿，现在你开心了吧？我看你怎么收场！"

露露回家了。

我尽量装出一副愉快的样子对她说："嗨，露露，甜心宝贝，猜猜看，我们从朱利亚音乐学院得到了什么消息？他们没有录取你，但这没什么关系——我们其实并不期望在今年就进预科班。许多人都不是在第一次就如愿以偿，而现在，我们知道下一次该怎么努力了。"

我真不忍心看着露露吃惊的面孔。有那么一两秒钟，我以为露露会放声大哭，但马上就明白，她从来不会这么做。天哪，我怎么能把她拉进如此令人沮丧的境地？我们投入了难以计量的时间，可是得到的结果却为我们的记忆蒙上了一块巨大的阴影。而以后，我又将怎样让她再次投入练习呢？

我不禁暗自神伤……

"我很高兴我没能被录取。"露露的话打断了我的忧思。现在,她看起来有点儿愤怒了。

"露露,你爸和我是如此为你感到骄……"

"嘿,别说了!"露露打断我。"我说过了——我不在乎。是你逼着我去试音的,我讨厌朱利亚音乐学院。没有去那里读预科,我真是开心极了。"她再次强调说。

第二天,我接到了一大堆电话。我真的不知道,如果没有从电话里听到田中直子的声音,我究竟会是怎样的六神无主。直子小姐对我说,她认为露露在试音时表现得非常出色,充分显示了她非凡的音乐天赋。她自己已为露露投了赞成票。但是她解释说,今年预科班已作出决定,缩小小提琴专业的招生规模。因此,人数空前众多的申请者来竞争空前稀少的几个名额,就无形中加大了被录取的难度。出乎我预料的是,田中直子愿意接受露露,到她的私人音乐工作室接受指导,成为她的"关门弟子"。

我惊呆了。

直子小姐的私人音乐工作室太有名了——几乎很难挤进去。我一下子兴奋起来,立刻想到,我折腾半天,不就是想为露露找个最好的小提琴老师吗?跟最棒的老师练琴,我不在乎露露能不能进朱利亚音乐学院的预科班。我也知道,"拜直子小姐为师",这同时也意味着我每个周末都得驾车送露露去纽约。而露露对此会作何反应,我还不得而知。

可我立刻就代表露露接受了田中直子老师的提议。

22　走红布达佩斯

　　热情豪放、慷慨宽厚的匈牙利人三次全场起立，把长时间雷鸣般的掌声，送给了这对美国的"音乐神童小姐妹"。可他们哪里知道，演出前的排练却是如此的一波三折……

索菲娅和露露在旧李斯特学院的舞台上谢幕

　　为参加朱利亚音乐学院的试音，露露进行了长时间的艰苦准备；接着是遭受食物中毒的突然袭击；然后又收到被拒绝的"最后通牒"。经历了一连串的折磨和打击，你可能认为我应该让露露喘口气了。也许我真的应该这么做，可是这些事发生在两年以前，那时似乎还"很年轻"的我并没有这么做。

　　降低对露露的要求，实际上就是在低估露露。这么做毫不费力，很像是西方人的行为方式。我不仅没有这么做，反而还加大了压力。这种做法让我开始付出真实的代价，但它与我最后付出的代价相比，真是小巫见大巫。

　　在索菲娅卡内基音乐厅独奏会后的招待会上，我们迎来了两位最重要的贵客——奥斯卡和克里斯蒂娜·蒲甘。他们是我父母的老朋友，碰巧那时到访纽约。奥斯卡是一位著名的物理学家，我父亲的密友。他的妻子克里斯蒂娜则是一位知名的职业钢琴演奏家，目前正热心于布达佩斯音乐节的组织活动。

　　索菲娅的表演刚刚结束，克里斯蒂娜就立刻挤到我们身边，对索菲娅的表演大加赞赏。她尤其喜欢索菲娅弹奏的"少女朱丽叶"这首曲子，还夸奖索菲娅灵气十足。

　　我们从克里斯蒂娜那里得知，在布达佩斯，"博物馆之夜"的庆典很快就要拉开帷幕。届时，坐落于这个城市各处的博物馆将组织各种演讲、表演和音乐会；购买一张联票，人们就可以选择不同的博物馆，从早晨参观到夜晚。作为"博物馆之夜"的一部分，李斯特音乐学院将出席许多音乐会。克里斯蒂娜认为这将是"美国钢琴神童"索菲娅大展才艺的绝佳机会。

　　这真是一个令人振奋的邀请。

布达佩斯是世界闻名的音乐之都，那里不仅诞生了李斯特，还是匈牙利作曲家贝拉·巴托克和佐尔坦·柯达伊的家乡。其令人叹为观止的国家歌剧院，据说在音响设备方面仅次于米兰的斯卡拉歌剧院。

克里斯蒂娜建议索菲娅到老音乐学院（the Old Music Academy）去演出，那是一栋优雅的三层楼房，建于新文艺复兴时期，曾经是该学院创建人和院长李斯特办公的地方。老音乐学院于1970年被位于几条街之遥的新音乐学院所取代。现在，老音乐学院院址已成为一处博物馆，里面陈列着李斯特使用过的各种乐器、家具和手写的乐谱原稿。

克里斯蒂娜告诉索菲娅，她将使用一架李斯特的私人钢琴来进行表演！而且，会有许多人来观看演出——这更是索菲娅第一次面对付费的观众。

可我心里还有个疑问：继索菲娅在卡内基音乐厅辉煌一场之后，这么快就在另一个重大场合再掀高潮、成为观众瞩目的人物，露露会怎样想呢？

露露欣然接受了田中直子的提议，而且答应得很干脆，这多少让我有些吃惊。但这只能微微地减轻由朱利亚音乐学院试音失败而导致的失望和刺激。而更加糟糕的是，数月以来，露露不得不频频应付人们的询问——"你得到朱利亚音乐学院试音的结果了吗？我敢肯定你没问题。"我不认为一直保守露露试音失败的秘密是个好主意。

中国父母在教育孩子时不善于面对挫折，无法容忍失败的可能性。从另外一个角度来看，他们的教育模式倾向于获得成功，这也是他们能使"自信满满、拼命努力、从成功走向更大的成功"形成良性循环的原因。我知道，我得确信露露也能和索菲娅一样，获得同样水准的成功，而现在努力还不算晚。

很快，我就有了个想法，并说服母亲客串了一把我的经纪人。我请求她给她的老朋友克里斯蒂娜打电话，将露露练习小提琴的情况一五一十地介绍给老朋友，包括：她怎样师从杰西·诺曼，然后在著名的小提琴教师瓦莫斯夫人门下学艺；两位高人都看好露露惊人的音乐天赋。最后，还要强调露露怎样刚刚被世界知名的朱利亚音乐学院的世界重量级老师慧眼识中，收为私人弟子。我告诉母亲，去试探一下有无让露露与索菲娅组成一个姐妹组合在布达佩斯登台表演的可能性——即便只是合作一首曲子。或许，还可以建议姐妹俩用钢琴和小提琴合奏巴托克创作的罗马尼亚民间舞曲，她们最近表演过这首舞曲，而且我知道克里斯蒂娜会感兴趣的。李斯特和巴托克是匈牙利最为著名的作曲家，巴托克的民间舞曲一定会感动并取悦观众。

幸运之星在我们面前散发出炫目的光彩！

克里斯蒂娜会见了露露，她立刻就被露露激情燃烧的个性吸引了。她告诉我母亲，让索菲娅与小妹妹合奏罗马尼亚民间舞曲——她爱死了这个绝妙的主意！在整个的演出中，这将是一个完美至极的附加节目。克里斯蒂娜说她会安排演出的一切事宜，甚至还包揽了关于推介"两个美国音乐神童小姐妹"的所有费用。

姐妹俩的音乐会将在6月23日举行，只有短短一个月的准备时间了。我再一次斗志昂扬、全力以赴地面对许许多多必须完成的准备工作。我夸大其词地告诉母亲，女孩们最近在一起表演过罗马尼亚民间舞曲，可是这个"最近"其实已是一年半载之前的事情了。

这首舞曲分为6个部分，有3个部分极富挑战。要再次学习和磨合这首舞曲，女孩们和我得进行连轴转的突击。而与此同时，索菲娅还得狂练伟毅教授为她选择的另外4首钢琴曲，它们是：伯拉斯姆的G小调狂想曲、一位中国女作曲家创作的一首曲子、普罗科菲耶夫的《罗密欧与朱丽叶》，当然也少不了李斯特著名的匈牙利狂想曲。

虽然索菲娅要准备的节目也有难度，但我真正担心的是露露。为了让她像姐姐那样耀眼、绚丽，我愿付出自己全部的心血。

我的父母也会出席那场音乐会；非常凑巧的是，整个6月份他们都会待在布达佩斯，因为我父亲正好应邀为匈牙利科学院做事。我当然也不想让克里斯蒂娜失望。最为重要的是，我希望露露能有机会展露自己的音乐天赋。我想，这一点是她目前最最需要的。如果她发挥得好，这会给她带来足够的自信和骄傲。我知道，我首先得解决来自露露的抗拒。因为我之前曾答应，不管试音结果如何，我都会给她放个"假"，喘口大气。可是现在，我得将"说过的话"这盆"泼出去的水"再收回来，其难度可想而知。可是我铁了心要做好这件事，我知道冲突不可避免，并准备在事态发展到忍无可忍之时，再雇用基旺和莱克西做我的坚强后盾。

我经常面对这样的疑问："美儿，我能不能问你一个问题，你给自己这么大的压力，在高压之下做了这么多的事情，都是为了……你的女儿？"听话听音，其实他们的话通常还拖着条真正想表达的"尾巴"——"还是为了你自己？"我发现这样的问题"很西化"，因为按照中国人的思维方式，孩子就是我们的作品——我们自我的延伸，这对我们是非常重要的。

我的回答相当肯定：毫不含糊地说，我所做的一切，百分之百都是为了我的女儿！

我与索菲娅和露露在一起所做的那么多事情，真是费心劳神、历尽艰辛，对我来说完全谈不上什么乐趣，这就是一个明证。让孩子们做她们不想做的事情，这并不轻松；在这个让人筋疲力尽的过程中，眼看着你自己

的青春年华就这样悄然流逝，这并不开心；在孩子们（也许是你自己）对
要达成的目标充满恐惧时，要说服她们（包括我自己）建立信心，这并不
容易。

"你们是否知道，这么些年来，我在你们身上耗费了多少宝贵的生命时
光？"我经常会这样问女儿，"假如我厚厚实实、福气多多的大耳垂预示着
长寿，那真是你们俩的幸运呀！"

说实在的，我有时也寻思，如果也拿"你这样做究竟是为了什么"的
问题，去问以另一种方式对待孩子的西方父母，他们又会怎样回答？

有时候我会在清晨醒来，对我不得不做的事情平生忧虑，心想，要是
对孩子说"没问题，露露，我们今天可以不练小提琴了，歇歇吧"，那该是
多么轻松惬意、皆大欢喜！可是，我却永远不会像我的西方朋友那样对孩
子说："我只需要让孩子听从内心的呼唤、作出他们自己的选择——这是世
界上最为艰巨的事情，而我尽量克制自己不去帮助他们作决定。"然后，他
们便为自己斟上一杯红葡萄酒——干杯，接着动身去健身房练习瑜伽。而
我，却不得不待在家里，对孩子们大喊大叫，让她们讨厌我、恨我……

在动身去布达佩斯的几天前，我给克里斯蒂娜发了封邮件，问她是否认
识什么经验丰富的音乐老师，既能辅导女孩们彩排罗马尼亚民间舞曲，又能
对恰如其分地表演匈牙利作曲家的作品指点迷津。

克里斯蒂娜的回复带来了好消息。

一位杰出的东欧小提琴教师考津齐夫人慨然应允与姐妹俩见面。考津齐
夫人最近刚刚退休，现在她只教那些极具天赋、才华横溢的小提琴手。在
我们到达布达佩斯的那一天，她只有一点点空余的时间，我们必须见缝插
针。

在音乐会举行的前一天，我们在上午10点到达了我们在布达佩斯下榻的酒店，而此时却是纽黑文的凌晨4点。我们一家子睡眼惺忪，像喝醉酒似的东倒西歪，杰德和露露还感到头疼。女孩子们只想睡觉，我也无精打采。然而不幸的是，与考津齐夫人约定的上课时间到了。这时，我们也收到了两条手机短信，一条来自我的父母，一条是克里斯蒂娜发来的，他们询问在哪里见面。我们4人急急忙忙地把自己塞进一辆出租车，几分钟后，就赶到了新音乐学院。

那是一幢面向李斯特广场、占据了几乎半条街的新艺术派建筑，庄严的圆柱托起音乐人的梦想，看起来宏伟壮丽。在楼上的一个大房间里，我们见到了考津齐夫人。我父母和满面笑容的克里斯蒂娜也已经到达那里，正坐在靠墙的一排椅子上。房间里有一架古典的老式钢琴，克里斯蒂娜把索菲娅领到钢琴前落座。

怎样描述考津齐夫人呢？说得客气一点儿，她神经紧张、容易激动。她的表情看上去就像她丈夫刚刚为了一个年轻女人离开了她，并在出走前将他所有的财产转移到了国外的账户一样。考津齐夫人在一所管理严格的俄罗斯音乐学校任教，她性情暴躁、待人苛刻，无法忍受她认为错误的一切事物。

露露拉响了第一个音符。

"不！"只听考津齐夫人大喊一声。

"你为什么这样拿着琴弓呀？"她不以为然地问道。

当姐妹俩开始练习的时候，她差不多每隔两个音符就要露露停下来纠错，重复前面的曲调。她指手画脚，动作十分夸张。在她看来，露露的指法不合章法，而且错得离谱。尽管第二天就要登台表演了，她也要她马上改正。她还不断地转向钢琴责备索菲娅，忘了她的主要注意力应该放在露露身上……

我的感觉一落千丈。

我在一旁已经明显察觉到露露的情绪，她认为考津齐夫人的要求不合理，她的谴责不公正。露露对此越恼怒，她的动作便越生硬，越不能集中精力练琴。渐渐地，露露的节奏开始错乱，越拉越不成调。

噢，不！我最最担忧的事情就要发生了。

没错，我清楚地看到一种忍无可忍的表情飞速地掠过露露的脸庞。她不再好好拉琴，也不听考津齐夫人在说什么。与此同时，考津齐夫人却越发激动了。她气血上涌，嗓音尖利，不断用匈牙利语与克里斯蒂娜说着什么。更加令人担忧的是，她走近露露，面对面地批评露露，用手指戳着露露的肩。就在愤怒的干柴已经在冒着青烟的当口，考津齐夫人用手中的铅笔敲了敲露露正在弄弦的手指头。

我看到，露露的愤怒被点着了。要是在家里，她会立刻发作。但在这里，她强压怒火，继续拉琴。遗憾的是，考津齐夫人挥舞铅笔，又点了她一下。两分钟后，一段乐曲刚练到一半，露露停下来说她要上卫生间，便头也不回地跑了出去，我赶快起身追了上去。露露怒气冲冲地走到大厅的角落，泪流满面。

"我不会再回到那儿了！"她咬牙切齿地说，"你不能逼我，那个女人简直就是个疯子——我讨厌她，我恨她！"

一时间，我真不知道如何是好。考津齐夫人是克里斯蒂娜的好朋友，我父母现在还坐在那间屋子里，而这堂辅导课只剩下最后的30分钟。每个人都在翘首盼望露露回到那里，继续将就要登台表演的节目练得滚瓜烂熟。

我试图找到说服露露的理由。

我提醒她："考津齐夫人也说你拥有令人难以置信的天赋，这也是她为什么要向你提出那么多要求的原因呀！"（"我不在乎！"）

我承认："考津齐夫人不太善于与人沟通，可我认为她的出发点是很好的。露露，你就不能再给她一个尝试的机会？"（"没门儿！"）

劝告无效，我开始指责露露："你不认为你对克里斯蒂娜负有责任吗？她不嫌麻烦，不辞辛苦地安排了所有的事情。还有你的姥姥和姥爷，如果你不回去接着练习，他们会为你的行为而震惊。露露，就这次表演来说，你不是唯一的当事人，你应该坚强一些，找到做好这件事情的方法。我们各自都承担了许多责任，露露——你能够做到的！"

我的苦口婆心好似对牛弹琴，露露依然拒绝回去练琴。尽管考津齐夫人的做法有失公允，但她毕竟是一位老师，一个业界公认的权威人物。而中国人做人的第一要义，就是要尊敬长辈、老师和专家，无论如何，你都不能与他们顶嘴。

我不得不独自回到房间，一再地去道歉、解释，善意地谎称露露在生我的气。然后，我让既没有与考津齐夫人发生冲突，又不是小提琴手的索菲娅，接着上完了剩下的课，从表面上得到了一些关于怎样表演好二重奏的小贴士。

回到酒店后，我生气地冲露露嚷嚷，也和杰德发生了争吵。他说他不认为露露的离开应该受到责备，面对矛盾冲突，兴许回避是更好的解决方式。他为女儿辩护说，露露在刚刚结束的朱利亚音乐学院的试音准备中累得要命，今天又因时差的缘故感觉筋疲力尽，然后还要被一个陌生人品头论足地好一通折腾。"考津齐夫人在音乐会举办的前一天，试图在短短几十分钟内改变露露练了多年的指法，你不觉得有点儿奇怪吗？我知道你不会赞成她这么做。"他说,"或许你应该努力地多给露露一点儿怜悯之情。我明白你到底想干什么,但是假如你不注意提防,小心弄巧成拙!"

我部分地承认杰德是对的,但是我却不能这么想,我不得不把精力集中到演出上。第二天,在新音乐学院,我紧紧地盯着姐妹俩,在她们练习的屋子间来回穿梭、跑前跑后。

然而,不幸的是,露露对考津齐夫人的恼怒在一夜之间有增无减。我知道那些不愉快的镜头在她的脑海里"放电影",让她更加怒火中烧、心烦意乱。在我要她练一段乐曲时,露露突然大发脾气:"她(考津齐夫人)根本就不知道自己在说什么——她建议的指法简直是太荒谬了!你难道没有注意到,她一直在用自己的'矛'戳自己的'盾'?"或者嚷嚷:"我不认为她真的理解巴托克,她的解释太不靠谱了——哼,她以为她是谁?!"

"别再纠缠考津齐夫人,别再浪费时间了!"我告诉露露。

"你从来就不会站在我这一边,我也不想参加今晚的表演。我已经不再对这件事感兴趣了,是那个女人毁了这一切。你就让索菲娅自个儿去演奏吧!"露露说道。

最后,还是克里斯蒂娜将我们从差不多水深火热的窘况中拯救出来。

当我们到达老音乐学院时,笑容满面、热情洋溢的克里斯蒂娜跑过来迎接我们,她兴奋地拥抱了女孩子们,还分别送给她们一件小礼物,并说:"有你们俩来参加演出,我们开心极了!你们姐妹俩真是才华横溢呀!"之后,她又摇了摇头,举重若轻地提到考津齐夫人,说她不应该在表演的前一天纠正露露的指法。

"你太有才了!"她一个劲儿地夸奖露露,"这次的表演一定很精彩!"说完,她飞快地把两个女孩从我的身边带走了。她们去了后面的房间,在那儿，她要把表演的节目再检查一下。

直到最后一秒钟，我对她们的节目会演成啥样，心里一点儿底都没有。也不知道那天晚上应该让一个女儿单挑，还是两个女儿都上场。但不知怎的，奇迹发生了——露露终于摆脱了恶劣的情绪，姐妹俩在音乐会的表演竟然大获成功、极为轰动。热情豪放、慷慨宽厚的匈牙利人三次全场起立，把长时间雷鸣般的掌声，送给了这对"音乐神童小姐妹"。博物馆的馆长还说"随时欢迎你们再来这里演出"。演出后，我们和蒲甘夫妇、我的父母还有及时赶来观看的杰德的父亲和他的新太太哈里特，一起外出吃晚饭，好好地庆贺了一番。

这次匈牙利之行后，事情发生了微妙的变化。

对露露来说，与考津齐夫人发生冲突，对任性地发泄愤怒和无礼地挑战权威的体验，干扰了她对是非的判断力，也令她对中国人行为方式的态度，变得尖酸刻薄——做一个中国人，即意味着要逆来顺受，要接受考津齐夫人一类的人物，而她，压根儿就不愿意接受其中任何一部分。此外，她也体验了假如她不按照老师和妈妈的要求去做会产生什么样的后果，她发现天并不会塌下来，地球也照样转动。相反，是她赢得了"战争"。

而我的父母，即使他们曾经那么严格地训练过我，现在却对露露深表同情。

于我而言，我感觉有些环扣已经在松脱，就像巨轮启动了沉重的锚——我部分地失去了对露露的控制。

希望中国的女儿永远不要做出像露露那样的行为，希望中国的母亲不再允许发生这样的事情！

BATTLE HYMN
OF THE TIGER MOTHER

Part Three
第三部分

　　老虎有能力付出博大的爱，而且爱得过于强烈。它们也拥有领地感和占有欲。威风凛凛的至尊地位通常让老虎付出代价，那就是——与孤独为伴。

23 普希金

　　它喜欢将自己的肚子紧贴在冰凉的地板上，四肢向外伸展，仿佛有人将它从半空中扔下来，它就这样俯身朝下、四肢张开，像个短胳膊短腿儿的"大"字，毫不走样地"吧唧"一声降落到地面上。

可可和普希金——两条美丽雪白的狗狗

"哪一条狗是我们的？"杰德问道。

那是2008年的8月，杰德和我来到罗得岛。为了某些对每个人（包括我自己）来说都很神秘的理由，我坚持要养第二条狗，于是我们来到可可的老主人家里。

带着乡村纯朴之风、铺着木地板的屋子里，3条体格健壮、神气十足的萨摩耶犬在里面走来走去。我们得知，其中一对是新生小犬的父母，另外那条显得举止稳重、目光威严的6岁萨摩耶犬，则是它们的爷爷。大狗脚下有4条喧闹不止的小狗。它们看起来就像可爱的、会叫的、来回滚动的4团白棉球。

"哦，你们的小萨摩耶犬在那儿，"狗主人说，"就在楼梯下面。"

杰德和我回过头来，看到眼前的那个小家伙与其他的小狗大不一样，它显得更高、更瘦，身上的毛没有那么厚实，看起来也就不那么精美。它的后腿比前腿要长两英寸，于是站立时身体就呈现出某种尴尬的倾斜状。它有一对细细的、上挑的眼睛，竖立的耳朵形状有点儿古怪。与其他的小狗相比，它的尾巴更长、更丰满；或许因为它太重，要保持向上卷曲的形态比较困难，因此它索性就左摇右摆，活像拖着一条老鼠的大尾巴。

"你确信那是一条狗吗？"我满腹狐疑地问。这个问题其实并不像听起来那么荒谬。这个小生灵酷似一只小羊羔，而饲养人在自己的牧场也放养了很多羊。搞不好会有一只羊吃着草，走着走着就迷了路，混进了狗群呢！

"错不了！"饲养人确认。她得意地向我们眨了眨眼睛，然后说："你们就等着看好吧，它长大后会变成个'大美女'，它那对健壮的萨摩耶犬后腿，跟它奶奶真个是一模一样呀！"

我们把这条幼犬带回了家。虽然它是条母狗，我们还是为它取名叫"普希金"——简称"普希"（Push）。我们的家人和朋友前来看望它时，他们都为我们感到遗憾。从外形上看，这只小狗就像一只小兔，可走起路来却跌跌撞撞的。

我母亲有一次看到普希金摇晃着撞到了墙上和椅子腿儿上，她担忧地问："你能不能把它退回去呀？"

"我知道问题出在哪里了——它的眼睛可能是瞎的。"我说。我的"瞎说"提醒了杰德。有一天，他把普希金送到了兽医那里。兽医经过检查后确认，普希金的视力完全正常。

普希金一天天长大，站立时前低后高的倾斜姿态依然固我，下楼时经常摔跤。普希金的躯干很长，它好像无法完全控制自己的后半身，因此，走起路来如风摆杨柳。同时，它的身体又有着不可思议的柔软度。直到今天，它都喜欢将自己的肚子紧贴在冰凉的地板上，四肢向外伸展，仿佛有人将它从半空中扔下来，它就这样俯身朝下、四肢张开，像个短胳膊短腿儿的"大"字，毫不走样地降落到地面上。每当我们看到它这副滑稽的睡相，就会用一个象声词来称呼它——"吧唧"！

有一件事儿果然被饲养人说中了——普希金就是一只丑小鸭。短短一年之内，它就变成了一条令人眼前一亮的大狗。每次我们带它外出散步，那些开车的人总是不断地停下来，对普希金的纯美赞不绝口。与皮毛雪白、长着一对奇异猫眼的可可相比，普希金的身材更为高大（追溯复杂、古怪的血缘关系，可可实际上是普希金的侄孙女）。在普希金的身上，一些"冬眠"的肌肉显然已经"苏醒"并日趋健硕，因为现在它的尾巴高高地卷曲在后背上，活像一束巨大而张扬的羽毛。

在才能方面，普希金仍然处于未开化的低能状态。可可给人的印象就比较平淡，但是与普希金相比，它已经算得上是个天才了。也许因为普希金比可可更甜美、更温顺，它不能完成其他狗狗能够做到的事情。比如，它不会为人拿取东西，也不喜欢奔跑。它经常被卡在一个令人匪夷所思的地方——洗手盆的下面、浆果灌木丛中，或趴在浴缸边沿上不去也下不来，等着被别人"英雄救美"。

开始，我否认普希金的任何不正常，我耗费数小时试图教它做一些事情，但总是徒劳无功。更怪异的是，普希金似乎喜欢音乐。它最为惬意的时光，就是坐到索菲娅的钢琴旁边，在索菲娅的伴奏下引吭高歌（而在杰德看来——那简直就是引颈嗥叫）。

尽管普希金有这样那样的缺点，我们一家四口却十分喜爱它，其程度与喜欢可可不相上下。实际上，正是因为那些短处，才让普希金更加招人爱怜。

"哦……哦……哦，可怜的小家伙！瞧你多么可爱呀！"每当我们看到它纵身一跃，努力地想跳到什么高一点儿的地方，不幸却差了好大一截，我们都会赶忙跑到它身边如此这般地安慰一番。或者我们会说："啊哈……快来看呀，它看不见飞盘！它简直是太可爱了。"

最初，可可对它新来的姐妹百般提防，我们看到它小心翼翼地试探普希金。而普希金则恰恰相反，它显得比较木讷，其情感能够感知的范围十分有限，提高警惕和小心谨慎均不在它精神活动的"词典"中。它心满意足地跟着可可，总是一副和蔼可亲的模样，并避免参与一切需要灵活性的活动。

虽然普希金非常甜美可爱，对我们家来说，喂养第二条狗似乎毫无必要，没有人比我更清楚这一点了。养狗是一件麻烦而琐碎的工作。在我们家里，我承担了90%的责任，而其他三人的付出只占10%。每天清晨6点，我就起床给它们喂食，带它们外出散步，并一路尾随，打扫它们的粪便。我带它们去宠物店美容，去兽医那里看病。更让我忙碌到疯狂的是，我的第二本书刚刚出版。此外，我还担任着一门课程从头至尾的教学重任；要和孩子们一起练琴；不断地飞来飞去举办讲座。我常常想方设法地压缩旅程，将去华盛顿特区、芝加哥或迈阿密安排在一天完成。我不止一次在凌晨3点飞往加利福尼亚，去作一个午餐演讲。然后，再赶夜航班机回家。

"你到底想干吗呀？"朋友们会这样问我，"你已经给自己揽下了超负荷的事情，你为什么还要养第二条狗呢？"

我的朋友安妮想到一个便捷、通俗的解释。"我所有的朋友，"她说，"都在孩子们的青少年时期养狗。为了弥补孩子不在家时的空虚，狗就成为了孩子们的替代之物。"

安妮的说法十分有趣，因为中国人养育孩子与饲养狗狗完全不同。事实上，是截然相反的两码事。一方面，养狗是一项社会性的工作。在你外出遛狗时，你会碰到其他的狗主人，围绕宠物，你们有许多的话题要交流。与此相反，生活在美国的中国父母，在教育孩子时却逃不掉令人难以置信的孤独——你至少要尝试在西方的社会背景中培养和教育孩子，而你除了自己，没有人可以依靠。你不得不面对整个植根于英语教化、个人自主权、儿童发展理论，以及人权的普遍宣言的价值观体系。没有人可以与你进行推心置腹的谈话，甚至是与那些你喜欢的、尊敬的人在一起，也无法做到这一点。

例如，在索菲娅和露露还很幼小的时候，其他父母邀请她们其中的一个去参加孩子们的玩伴聚会，是我最为担忧的事情。为什么、为什么、为

　　什么，西方社会有如此令人头疼的习俗？一次，我试图向一位孩子的妈妈说明我的真实想法。我告诉她，露露要练小提琴，她没有富裕的时间去参加玩伴聚会，可这位妈妈一点儿也不理解。我只好求助于其他借口来争取西方人的谅解，比如：露露要去接受面试，进行身体的理疗，参加社区的活动。我有时会在其他母亲的脸上看到不屑的表情，随后，她们对我的态度立马就变得冷冰冰的，好像我自以为露露比她们的女儿要优秀许多。

　　这真是两种世界观的冲撞啊！

　　每当我婉言谢绝了一个玩伴聚会日的邀请，总还有另外一个建议紧随其后。"改到星期六怎么样？"而星期六对露露很重要，因为她星期日就要赶到纽约去上直子小姐的小提琴课。"那么，下下个星期五如何？"站在她们的立场上，西方妈妈就是无法理解，露露为什么每天下午都在忙碌，而且一年到头都是如此。

　　在养狗和教育孩子方面，还存在另外一个巨大的差异。狗的饲养比较容易，这项工作要求保持耐心、付出爱心，可能还要在初始阶段多花一些时间来训练它们。相比之下，中国人培养孩子却是一项我所能想到的最为艰巨的系统工程。它的艰难在于，有时候，你不得不接受这样的现实——你希望你所爱的人也能爱你，可他们却憎恨你；这种状况没有缓和的时候，事情也不会突然间就变得容易。可是，这还不算最难的。你想在美国社会按照中国人的方式教育孩子，你会遭遇各种稀奇古怪的事情。那是一场永远也无法结束的攻坚战，既要求你一周7天、一天24小时地履行承诺、保持愉快心情，又逼迫你足智多谋。你还得把自尊藏在心底，随时准备变幻作战方略，并充满创造的活力。

　　例如，去年我参加耶鲁法学院学生们的期末聚会，那是一项我很乐意加入的活动。"你对你的学生太好了！"索菲娅和露露常常对我说，"其实，他们压根儿就不知道真实的你究竟什么样。他们都认为你充满养育子女的母性又善于帮助他人。"

女儿们说得一点儿不错，我对待法律专业学生（尤其是那些有着严厉的亚洲父母的学生）的方式，与我对待自己孩子的方式迥然不同。

聚会在三楼的乒乓球室举行，而那里也正好是露露练习小提琴的地方。一个叫罗兰的学生，在那里发现了我留给露露的一些练习笔记。

"天哪，这怎么可能？"他一边翻阅那些笔记，一边露出难以置信的表情，"蔡教授，这些笔记难道是……是你写的吗？"

"哦，罗兰，请你把它放下好吗？不过，这确实是我写的。"我别无选择地承认，"我每天都把这些要点和说明留给我那练小提琴的女儿，当我不在这里的时候，这些提示可以帮助她更好地练琴。"

罗兰似乎并没有认真听我说。"哦，我的上帝——这还有好多呐！"他惊奇地说。是的，他发现了几十张指导练习的笔记，有的是打印的，有的是手写的，我忘记藏起来了。"我简直不敢相信，这真是太不可思议了！"

我不认为这有什么让人"不可思议"的，但是你可以作出自己的判断。

这里有三张我为露露写下的、未经编辑的日常练习笔记。别管那些古怪的标题，我这么写只是为了吸引露露的注意力。我得附带着说明一下，在第二篇笔记里，字母"m"代表"measure"（小节）——这就是说，我逐节地给她提示练习的方法。

松狮犬勒伯夫
设施一

只练55分钟!!

你好，露露!!!你做得很好。运弓时要轻一点儿!!轻点儿!!!!
再轻点儿!!!

阿波罗的使命：把琴夹好，保持正确的姿势，即使是在完成高难度的部分时也要坚持这个要求。

15分钟：练习音阶。手指轻落速起，抬高一点儿，注意运弓要轻一点儿，以拉出悦耳的声音。

15分钟：练习施拉迪克（Schradieck）的曲子。(1)训练手指的敏捷性，更加注意手指轻落速起、抬高一点儿的要领。(2)注意手的姿势，小指头要立于琴弦之上；用节拍器练习全曲；然后特别注意攻克难关，每段练25遍。然后再把全曲过一遍。

15分钟：克罗伊策（Kreutzer）8度音。选任何一个调性。先慢练—注意音准—练两遍。

今天的挑战：

10分钟：克罗伊策作品32号，借用节拍器的帮助来完成练习，要缓慢、轻轻地运弓；假如你能这样做，你就太棒了!

洛杉矶波波族麦克纳马拉——布鲁赫协奏曲

（1）把琴抬高！特别是在拉和弦的时候！（2）准确度——把注意力放在"小"音符上，声音要清晰、明亮；手指头要快速、敏捷（手指头要直立）。（3）要有旋律感，注意把握强弱——从慢弓开始，逐渐加快弓速。

重点训练：

第7页

从开始到第18~19小节：（1）用一半的压力以快弓拉和弦。手肘放低，小提琴要稳！（2）把注意力放在小音符上（da-da-dum），把它们拉清楚——手指头快速下打，然后放松。

第21小节：（1）拉三连音时，不要跳弓——练习25次！（2）把8分音符拉清楚——重点练习！手指下打后注意放松！

第23~26小节：拉和弦的时候只用一半的运弓压力，声音要清晰；拉短音的时候手指头要快。

第27~30小节：非常重要的是，这个旋律拉得太重，握小提琴的手就会往下掉、琴身就会下移！这是相当轻盈的和弦，要非常清楚和准确地表现出来。第二次旋律再现时可以将前面的要求表现得更加突出一点儿。

第32小节：手指头从高处往下打，然后马上放松。注意把琴夹紧。

第33小节：快弓，轻一点儿！拉和弦后把弓提起来！

第8页

第40小节：这个和弦你拉得太重了！用一半的运弓力度即可，把琴抬高！短音符要拉清楚。

第44小节：此处的和弦还需要轻拉，但声音要大一点儿——用快弓！

第44~45小节：抓弓的手和手腕都要注意放松。

第48~49小节：要把这两小节拉得活泼一点儿、快一点儿，手指头要轻、要立起来，然后放松！

第52小节：注意准确性！

第54~58小节：用越来越多长的弓法，逐渐增加激情！

第78小节：手指抬高！不要下压——保持手指的轻灵！

第82小节：渐强，弓子从慢到快！回收一点儿，然后大幅度地渐强！第一串音符像是泰勒·斯威夫特！第二串音符好似雷迪嘎嘎!!第三串音符则像是碧昂斯!!①

第87小节：顺着乐谱上音符上下起伏的方向来表现音乐。

---

① 泰勒·斯威夫特（Taylor Swift），美国年轻的当红乡村音乐女创作歌手；雷迪嘎嘎（Lady GaGa）意为狂热小姐，是2008年美国流行音乐新晋"舞后"，不仅有一流的声线，更是个前卫、另类的创作酷妹；碧昂斯（Beyonce），当今美国红得发紫的天才歌手、第46届格莱美5项大奖得者。作者用这些如雷贯耳的名人，来强调音乐"渐强"的感觉。——译者注

第9页

第115~116小节：先用少弓（即短弓），然后到高音A的时候，用很多弓（长弓）。要有方向感！

第131小节：安静（即拉轻一点儿）！

第136~145小节：要表现出音乐的弧线（强的时候多弓，弱的时候少弓），侧重音准，练50次。

第146~159小节：安静，但要清晰准确。

第156~158小节：稳步渐强。

第160~161小节：注意准确。

第10页

第180小节：练习开头。要有方向感，从慢弓到快弓；在高音B上，用很多弓。

第181~183小节：着重练习准确度——手指头要快、要轻！

第185小节：拉和弦时只用一半的弓速——轻一些！把小音符拉清楚（da-da-dum），手指头要快！

第193~195小节：练习换把——要换到准确的把位上！练50次。

第194小节：开始时小声，然后渐强。

第200小节：牢记准确的音符——重点练习30次。

第202小节：练习和弦——注意手的位置要精确，注意音准！

第204小节：手要轻，手腕要放松！

斯珀基精选——你好！溪流7
门德尔松！

无穷动曲[①]

第2页

开头：

•渐强时，音乐的激情也要跟上！

•还有，在三次同样音形时，把它们演奏得有所不同——或许最后一次稍微缓和一些。

•在第二行的最后一个小节，和声是不同的——这应该明确地表现出来。

第3行：把旋律拉出来，重复的音符小声一些，然后自然地减弱。

第4行：重要的音符一定要用更长的弓。

第5行：把不和谐的音拉出来。

第6行：太多"La"音了！没意思——把它们拉得轻一些，然后把其他音符拉响一点儿。

第7行：很长的一段8度音阶——开头小声一点儿，然后大幅度地渐强。

---

① 无穷动曲（Perpetual Mobile），一种快速行进的器乐曲，多以16分音符谱成，起句和收句相呼应，只要有兴致，可以首尾相连、永无止境地演奏下去，如同无穷的动力、不息的生命。——译者注

第3页

第5行：在有"f"记号^①的地方，几乎用全弓——要有兴奋感！然后渐弱到只有一点儿声音。

第6~7行：弱的地方小声一点儿，然后在强的地方突然爆发。

第8~9行：同样，先小声然后突然爆发！

第10行：把最高的两个音拉出来，不必在意低音。

门德尔松

开头：

• 小行板——稍快。

• 要非常平静和安祥，就像身边有几只酣睡的狗，别把它们吵醒了。

• 同样的旋律出现两次后，在第三次出现时稍稍明亮一些——稍稍放开点儿拉！

第4行：现在，稍转不安、紧张。或许，其中有只酣睡的狗狗似乎病了。

第5行：要把更大的能量释放在最高的那个音符上！然后慢慢地回到开始时的那种温和平静的意境中。

---

① "f"记号，即英文"forte"的缩写，是代表强音的符号。——译者注

中间部分：

这部分百分之百地拥有不同的特征，那就是：恐怖的特征！

非常快速地用弓！融入更多的力量！在某些地方要用全弓，注意变换弓速！！

最后3行：开始时少用点儿弓，逐渐地增加用弓——每次增长1.5英寸。

其中的第2行：由弱转强！把紧张的气氛表现出来！

第11页

第1行：要有激情，渐强至乐曲的高潮！！

我有数百张，也许数千张这样的笔记。它们悠久的历史，甚至可以追溯到女儿们还是小不点儿的时候。由于我对人的要求比较严苛，所以常常给女儿们留下一些提醒她们的小纸条。小纸条无处不在——我把它们放到枕头上、装进午饭盒中、夹在乐谱里。比如，上面会写着："妈妈虽然有一副坏脾气，但妈妈爱你！""你是妈妈骄傲和喜悦的源泉！"

而和狗狗在一起，你完全不需要为它做任何这样的事情。即使你做了，它们也不会明白，尤其是对我们家憨厚的普希金来说，就更无这种可能了。

我的狗狗什么都不会——这真让人感到宽慰呀！

我对它们没什么要求，也不会努力去塑造今天的它们或者操心它们的未来。我基本上相信它们自己的选择，总是期待着看到它们活蹦乱跳地围绕在我身旁。而且，我喜欢就那么静静地坐在那里看它们睡觉，想着狗狗是不是也会做梦……

这是一种多么平凡而超然的关系！

24 秀发DIY

露露用剪子"咔嚓"了自己的头发！而刚刚被她DIY的头发，有一边参差不齐地挂在下巴旁，另一边高高地夭折在耳朵之上，呈现出难看的锯齿状……

13岁的露露

(Peter Z. Mahakian)

中国人良性循环的理念和方法在露露身上不起作用，为什么会这样？我就是搞不明白，而一切事情又似乎在按照计划向前推进。我总是梦想着露露大踏步地走向成功——无论要付出多大的代价，我都不会犹豫。

经历了好几个月艰苦的准备，包括我们之间经常性的争吵、恐吓、大喊加尖叫，露露通过试演赢得了著名的耶鲁青年管弦乐队首席小提琴手的位置——尽管她只有12岁，比乐队大多数音乐家要年轻得多。她还荣获了康涅狄格州的"少年天才奖"，相关事迹被刊登在报纸上。

她在学校的学习成绩年年捧回全优，并赢得了学校法语和拉丁语朗诵的第一名。然而，这些成功并没有帮助她提升自信、感激父母、渴望更加投入地付出努力。恰恰相反，露露开始流露出反叛的情绪：不仅反感练琴，而且讨厌我曾经主张的一切事情，俨然摆出一副与我对着干的架势。

回忆往事，我感觉变化从露露六年级的时候就悄然开始了，而当时我对这一点还没有清醒的认识。露露最憎恨不过的事情，是我总是把她从校园生活里拽出来，进行额外的小提琴练习。我认为露露在学校的某些活动会浪费大量宝贵的时间，因此在一个星期中，我会好几次给老师写请假条，说露露有演奏会或将要参加试音，请求老师允许她在午饭时间或体育课期间离开学校。有时候，我能够将零零星星的午饭时间、两节课的课间休息，让孩子们学习敲打铃铛的音乐课，或为万圣节博览会小摊制作装饰物的美术课，拼凑成整整两个小时的小提琴练习时间。

我知道，露露很怕在学校见到我。每当我出现在那里，她的同学都会诧异地看着我。可她只有11岁，我还可以把我的意志强加给她。不过我确信，正是由于这些额外的小提琴训练，才使露露赢得了这么多音乐的荣誉。

说真话，我也实属不易。

　　我是耶鲁法学院的教授，也有许多要和学生们待在一起的工作时间。忽然间，我会借口要开会匆匆离去。我得像参加比赛一样开车冲到学校去接她，然后又以赛车的速度把她送到基旺老师的公寓；紧接着再飙车返回办公室，在那里，一大帮学生已等候我多时。半小时后，我又不得不找出理由去把露露送回学校。然后，我则以疯狂的速度，一路上在加油门的浑厚低音和踩刹车的尖利高音的"二重唱"中回到办公室；等待我的，是接下来长达3个小时的会议。而我之所以要不辞辛苦地把露露送到基旺老师那里，是因为在老师的监督下，练习会更有成效。我不认为露露会公然冒犯基旺，当然就不会与她发生冲突。再说，基旺也还没有成家，在她那里练琴不会给他人带来任何不便。

　　有一天下午，我放下露露，离开基旺家仅仅15分钟，就接到基旺打来的电话，她的声音听起来慌乱而沮丧。"露露不愿练琴，"她说，"你最好还是来把她接回去吧。"

　　我返回基旺的公寓，一个劲儿地向她道歉，含糊其辞地说露露可能太累了，因为她睡眠不足。结果，事实上露露不仅拒绝练习，她还粗鲁地对待基旺老师，和她顶嘴，并挑战她的指导。回到家后，我严厉地批评和教训了露露。

　　可是，随着时间的流逝，事情却变得越来越糟。

　　无论何时我到学校去接露露，她的脸上总是阴云密布。她常常与我抗争，说她不想离开学校。最后，好不容易把她送到基旺那里，她又时常拒绝下车。如果我好说歹说把她劝说到了基旺家（这时很可能只剩下20分钟练习时间了），她会拒绝练习，或故意搞怪，把小提琴拉得跑调或不投入丝毫情感，让琴声听起来空洞得像一杯乏味的白开水。她还会蓄意地激怒基旺，慢慢地惹恼她，然后再假装关切地连连问道："这是怎么啦？你没事儿吧？"

一次，基旺的法国男友亚伦正好在场，目击了一堂练习课。事后他说："假如我有一个女儿，我绝不会允许她做出如此无礼的行为。"

这真是一记响亮的耳光呀！

亚伦曾经非常喜欢露露，他是一个善于和人友好相处的人。他成长在一个开明和宽容的西方家庭，这种家庭的孩子从不逃学，他们也做许多自己感兴趣的事情。他对我教育孩子的方式和我女儿的行为举止持批评意见。

大约在同一时间，露露开始和我顶嘴；在我父母到访时，当着他们的面公开地不服管教。这在西方家庭里，恐怕不是什么大不了的事儿，但是在我们的家庭，却像是亵渎神灵一样不敬。事实上，这样的行为超出了我们能够容忍的界限，没人知道该怎么对付。我父亲悄悄地把我拉到一旁，私下里力劝我别让露露再练小提琴了。我母亲则坦率地告诉我："你不能再这样固执下去了，美儿！你对露露太严厉了——太过分了。你将来会后悔的！"母亲与露露是互通电子邮件的笔友，她们的关系很是亲密。

"为什么你现在这么说我？"我反驳说，"你过去不就是这样教育我的吗？"

"你不能再像你爸和我一样教育孩子了，"我母亲回答道，"因为时代已经变了。露露不是你，也不是索菲娅。她有她独特的个性，你不能强迫她。"

"我要坚持中国人教育孩子的方式，"我说，"中国人的方式更有效，我不在乎有没有人支持我，而你肯定是被你的西方朋友洗脑了。"

我母亲只是一个劲儿地摇头。"我一直在告诉你，我们很担心露露。"她说，"我从露露的眼神就知道有什么地方不对劲。"听了这句话，我感觉很受伤。

　　远离了良性循环，我们正在栽进恶性循环的深渊。露露13岁了，她变得更加疏离和愤懑。脸上总是浮现出冷淡的表情，"不"或者"我不在乎"，成了她挂在嘴边的口头禅。她不认同我对宝贵生命的看法、对时间的珍视。

　　"我为什么不能像别人那样和朋友到外面去玩儿？"她质问道，"为什么你这么反感逛商店？为什么我们不能在外面过夜？为什么每天我都得练琴、练琴，没完没了地练琴？"

　　"露露，别忘了你是首席小提琴手。"我回答，"这是管弦乐队给予你的巨大荣誉。你肩负着重任，整个乐队都指望着你的出类拔萃！"

　　露露的反应却极为令人愕然："我为什么会出生在这样的家庭？"

　　尽管露露的回答总是偏离我的期望，但奇怪的是，她实际上非常喜欢管弦乐队。她在那儿有许多朋友，成为领头的琴师让她开心至极，她与乐队指挥布鲁克斯先生很合得来。我曾经亲眼看见她在排练时和周围的人谈笑风生，一脸灿烂——或许是因为排练时我没有待在她的身边。

　　与此同时，杰德和我之间的不一致也与日俱增。私下里，他会生气地要我对自己多加克制，别再狂热而过分地对西方人和中国人的言行举止品头论足或一概而论。

　　"我知道你批评别人是为了帮他们一个大忙，促使他们翻然改进。"他略带讥讽口吻地说，"但是你有没有想过，你只是在令别人感觉糟糕？"而他最重磅的批判则是："你为什么总是在露露面前说索菲娅那些闪光的成就？你有没有考虑过露露会怎么想？你难道没有看见这样做的恶果吗？"

　　"我不想只是为了'保护露露的感情'就闭口不谈索菲娅应该得到的赞扬，"我极力地搜寻带着讽刺口吻的言辞，"这样露露才知道我认为她完全应该和姐姐一样棒，她不需要什么刻意的扶持。"

为了化解冲突，杰德除了偶尔向我提出意见之外，他总是在女儿面前义无反顾地支持我。从一开始，我们就确立了坚持统一战线的教育策略。即便有种种担忧，杰德也没有破坏我们之间的约定。相反，他尽了最大的努力来平衡我们的家庭关系——带领一家人骑自行车去旅行，教女儿们玩扑克牌、学游泳，为孩子们朗读科幻小说、莎士比亚和狄更斯的文学作品……

而露露的行为却令人匪夷所思：她公开地表现自己的反叛。她知道，在西方社会，中国人的教育方式天生就带有一种"关起门来"的私密性。假如在大庭广众之下进行，就会让孩子难堪，从而产生逼迫孩子违背父母意志的恶果；倘若你公开期望自己的孩子比别人的孩子强，或不允许自己的孩子应邀到别人家去过夜，其他孩子的父母就会对你大为不满，你的孩子也会为此付出代价。因此，美国移民的父母都学会了隐瞒他们教育孩子比较严厉的真相，他们知道在公开场合要表现得轻松愉快。比如拍拍孩子的后背，说："很不错嘛，伙计！"紧接着再来一句："注意团队精神哦！"

是的，在这个社会，没人想因为自己的格格不入而遭人唾弃。

这就是露露的叛逆策略如此聪明的原因。无论是在大街上、饭店里，或者是商店内，她都会高声地与我争吵。"别管我！我不喜欢你，走开！"听到一个女孩子这样嚷嚷，陌生人的回头率就急剧增长。我们邀请朋友共进晚餐，当他们关切地询问她："最近小提琴练得怎么样啦？"她会说："嗨，我总得练琴，是我妈逼着我练的，我有什么办法。"有一次，不知我说的什么话激怒了她，她就在一个停车场里尖叫着不肯下车，搞得惊天动地的，把警察也招来了。"这里发生了什么事情？"他们问道。

更为怪异的是，学校也成了露露与我对阵的一座不可侵犯的堡垒。在西方孩子的反叛期，他们的成绩会大受影响，偶尔还会在考试中不及格。可是，与半数处于反叛期的中国孩子一样，露露一直保持着全优的成绩；在学校给家长的报告卡上，各个科目的老师都会异口同声地称赞她"慷慨、友好，乐于帮助同学"的优秀品质。

"露露是一个天性快乐的孩子，"一位老师写道，"她有着敏锐的眼光、强烈的同情心，在同学中人缘很好。"

露露对此却有不同的看法，她声称："我没有朋友，没人喜欢我。"

"露露，你为什么这样说呢？"我关切地问道，"你这么风趣、漂亮，大家都喜欢你呀！"

"我很丑，"露露反驳说，"你什么也不明白。我怎么会有朋友呢？你任何事情都不让我做，我哪儿也去不了。都是你的错，你本身就是一个怪胎。"

露露拒绝帮助家里去遛狗，也不愿外出扔垃圾。只让索菲娅干家务活儿，这显然有失公允。可你怎么能够逼着一个5英尺高的大活人去做她压根儿就不想做的事情呢？这类问题并非中国家庭独有，我也没有解决的良方。因此，我知道我唯一能做的，就是针锋相对，毫不退让。

我说她作为女儿"很丢脸"，可她的回答却是："知道、知道，我耳朵都听出老茧了！"

我说她"吃得太多了"，她则说："别说了，你病态！"

我拉出艾米·蒋、艾米·王、艾米·刘和哈佛·黄（他们都是出生在美国的亚洲孩子）来进行比较，说他们没人会和自己的父母顶嘴。我问露露"我到底做错了什么"，是要求她不够严格，给予她太多，还是因为不允许她与那些只会带来恶劣影响的孩子混在一起？她的反应是——"你竟敢侮辱我的朋友？"

我告诉她，我正考虑从中国收养第三个孩子，在我要求她练小提琴时，她不会拒绝。没准儿除了小提琴、钢琴，还能摆弄一下大提琴哩！

当她发火后扔下我扬长而去时，我会冲她大声宣告："你要是满了18岁，我才不想管你呐，你完全可以去犯你想犯的所有错误。但是在你18岁之前，我是不会撒手的！"

"我希望你别再管我！"露露不止一次地嚷嚷道。

当我们的对抗进入比拼耐力之时，我们俩真是旗鼓相当啊！但我有我的优势，我是母亲，我有车钥匙、银行信用卡，以及在请假条上签字的权利，而这一切，都受到美国法律的保护。然而，我们之间的对抗却在不断翻新。

"我要理发。"一天，露露对我说。

我回答说："你对我说话如此无礼，还拒绝好好练习门德尔松的曲子。现在，你指望我能立刻钻进汽车，带你去任何你想去的地方吗？"

"为什么我要做每件事情都得求你？"露露愤愤不平地说。

那天晚上，我们母女俩大吵了一场，然后，露露把自己锁在闺房里。她拒绝出来，我在门外与她讲话，她也不答理。时间已经很晚了，我在书房里听到她一脚踢开了自己的房门。我赶忙跑过去，看见她坐在自己的床上，一副风平浪静的模样。

"我想我该上床睡觉了，"她用极为寻常的口吻波澜不惊地说道，"我已经做完了所有的家庭作业。"

可我却吃惊地看着她，无法听清她到底在说什么。

露露用剪子"咔嚓"了自己的头发！而刚刚被她DIY的头发，有一边参差不齐地挂在下巴旁，另一边高高地夭折在耳朵之上，呈现出难看的锯齿状……

心跳加速的我几乎马上就要大发雷霆了，可内心里有种力量（我想那是担忧）却让我欲言又止。

接下来是短暂而尴尬的停顿。

"露露……"我终于开口了。

"我喜欢短发。"她打断我的话。

我把目光转向一旁，我不忍心再看她。露露原本有一头令人羡慕的秀发：呈波浪形的、棕黑色的、中国—犹太特色的长发。可是现在……那一刻，我体内的某个部分只想对露露歇斯底里地尖叫，然后再把什么东西狠狠地砸过去；而另一个部分却想伸出双臂紧紧地抱着她，失声痛哭。

可我没有这么做，我平静地说："明天早晨醒来，我会在第一时间去预约一个美发沙龙，我们得找个高手来帮你修理一下。"

"好的。"露露耸了耸肩。

过了一会儿，杰德对我说："有些事儿恐怕得改变一下了，美儿，我们要有大麻烦了。"

听了杰德的话，那个夜晚我再次有一种想放声大哭的冲动。但是，我忍住了。"这没有什么大不了的，杰德。"我说，"别再没事儿找事儿了，放心吧，我能搞定这件事儿。"

25　光鲜与黑暗

和三妹美文在一起欢度的童年时光在我的记忆中光鲜无比。35年过去了，我们依然亲密无间。但是有一天我接到美文的电话，得知她被诊断出患有一种致命的白血病！

三妹美文和我（摄于20世纪80年代初）

在我从小丫头长成大姑娘的过程中，我最开心的事，莫过于和我的三妹美文在一起玩耍了。也许因为她比我小7岁，我们之间没有竞争和冲突。她的娇小可爱简直令人惊叹——亮晶晶的黑眼睛、闪耀着乌黑光泽的娃娃头、玫瑰花般含苞欲放的双唇。她的美丽总是吸引着陌生人的目光，她的照片甚至赢得了全美杰西潘尼摄影大赛①的奖项。因为我母亲总是忙于照顾我最小的妹妹美音和二妹美夏，于是，照看三妹美文的任务自然就非我莫属了。

我们在一起度过的那些童年时光在我的记忆中光鲜无比。我总是自信满满，善于发号施令，而美文则对大姐姐充满崇拜，因而我们实在是一对完美的搭档。我负责编排游戏、组织故事会，并教她玩抛石游戏、中国式的"跳房子"和荷兰式的双绳跳；玩过家家时，我扮演大厨和服务员，她是客人；做学校的游戏时，我是老师，而她和5只填充式缝制的小动物乖乖地坐在一起，成为我的学生（美文上我的课，学得很快哦）；为肌肉萎缩症患者筹集资金，我组织了麦当劳嘉年华聚会，她就负责掌控展位、收集资金。

35年过去了，美文和我依然亲密无间。我们俩是四姐妹中看起来长得最像的一对。而且，我们都从哈佛大学获得了两个学位（实际上，她是三个，她的学士、硕士和博士学位都是哈佛大学的）；我们都嫁给了美籍犹太人，并像父亲一样在大学里教书；我们都有两个孩子。

美文在斯坦福大学任教并管理着一个实验室。就在露露剪掉长发的几个月前，我接到美文的电话。可以说，这是我生命中迄今为止所接到的最不开心的电话。

---

① 杰西潘尼摄影大赛（JCPenney photo contest），由美国知名百货公司杰西潘尼为美眉们发起的摄影大赛。——译者注

她在电话里伤心地哭泣着……我得知她被诊断出患有一种致命的白血病!

不可能!我的脑子一片混乱。

难道,该死的白血病会再一次袭击我们这个幸运的家庭?

然而,这个不可能的事情却真实地发生了。美文在过去的几个月里一直感觉疲惫不堪、恶心、气短,后来她去了医院,血液化验给出了毋庸置疑的结果。而导致她罹患白血病的那种细胞突变,恰好是她的实验室正在研究的课题——这真是一种残忍的巧合!

"我可能活不了多长时间了,"她哭着对我说,"这对我儿子杰克意味着什么?幼小的女儿艾拉甚至还没有开始记事,我不会在她记忆中留下任何痕迹。"美文的儿子只有10岁,女儿年仅1岁。

"你得确切地让她知道我是她的母亲,你要答应我,美儿。我最好留下一些照片……"说到这里,她泣不成声。

我感到极为震惊,无法相信这是真的。美文10岁时的鲜活形象浮现在我脑海里,我就是无法将它与"白血病"这几个恐怖的字眼联系在一起。这样的事儿怎么会发生在我可爱的妹妹美文身上呢?我的父母要是得知这个不幸该会作何反应?他们怎么能够面对这样残酷的不幸——这简直会要了他们的命!

"医生到底是怎样说的,美文?"我听到自己以一种奇怪而沉静的声音问道。我强行让自己回归大姐应该保有的无懈可击之势。

美文没有回答。她说她得挂了,会再打电话给我的。

10分钟后,我收到她的电子邮件。她在邮件中这样写道:"美儿,抱歉,这个消息真的是非常、非常糟糕!我需要进行化疗,然后有可能会作骨髓移植，接着再做更多的化疗，存活的可能性极小……"

作为一位科学家，她的话当然不会错。

26   青春期反叛

我为杰德的50大寿张罗了生日聚会，露露断然拒绝为父亲写贺词。我使出浑身解数，想尽一切办法来威胁她、贿赂她、启发她、羞辱她，答应在写作时帮她出谋划策，向她发出最后通牒……结果，我的努力却一败涂地！

在露露自己动手剪掉头发的第二天，我带她去了一家美发店。一路上，我们在车里没有怎么说话。我的脑子里有许多想法，让我的神经像上了发条一样紧绷着。

"她怎么啦？"理发师问道。

"她自个儿剪的。"我解释说。我没有什么好隐瞒的，"在她的头发长长之前，你有什么办法让她好看一点儿吗？"

"哇——你为自己做了件实实在在的事情，宝贝儿。"女理发师说。她用惊异的眼光打量着露露，"你为什么要这么做呀？"

"哦，这主要是一种对抗我妈妈的青春期毁灭性行为。"我猜露露也许会这样说。她肯定掌握这样的词汇，并有着之所以这样做的自我意识。

可是露露却用愉悦的声音回答："我试着剪出层次来，可最终还是搞砸了。"

回到家后，我对露露说："露露，你知道妈妈爱你，妈妈所做的所有事情都是为了你，为了你的将来。"

我感觉自己的声音听起来有点儿做作，露露一定颇有同感，因为她以一种平淡的、麻木不仁的口气答道："那真是太好了。"

杰德的50大寿到了。我张罗了一个生日聚会，准备给他一个大大的惊喜。我邀请了他童年时代的老朋友，其他每个人生阶段的朋友也无一遗漏。我还要求他们每个人都得带来一个有关杰德的趣事。提前好几个星期，我就布置索菲娅和露露撰写给爸爸的生日贺词。

"不能随随便便地交差，"我要求说，"一定要寓意深刻，不能只是一些乏味的陈词滥调。"

索菲娅马上就动手去做。她像往常那样，全然没有向我请教或征询我的建议。而露露却说："我可不想写什么贺词。"

"你必须给爸爸写贺词。"我回答。

"像我这种年龄的人，没人会为别人敬酒，再献上什么贺词。"露露不以为然地说。

"那是因为他们没有家教。"我答道。

"你知道这样说有多么离谱吗？他们并不是没有家教。"露露说，然后又反问道，"什么是'没有家教'？"

"露露，你实在是不知好歹。我像你那么大时，马不停蹄地做事儿。我为妹妹们搭建了一座树屋，因为父亲要求我这么做。无论他说什么，我都会照办，这也是我为什么会使用电锯的原因。我还建了座蜂鸟屋；担当埃尔瑟利托报刊社的送报人，脖子上挂着一个重达50磅、塞满了报纸的布袋，步行5英里把报纸送到客户手中。可是看看你——你已经拥有了种种机会和特权，你从来就不用穿商标上有4根斜杠而不是3根斜杠的阿迪达斯冒牌货。可你连为父亲写个贺词这样的小事儿都不肯做，这太让人恶心了。"

"我不想写贺词。"露露依旧执拗地说。

我使出浑身解数，搜肠刮肚地想尽一切办法来威胁她、贿赂她、启发她、羞辱她，答应在写作时帮她出谋划策。我向她发出最后通牒，深知这是我们母女间一场关键的战役。

杰德的生日聚会到来时，索菲娅交上了一篇迷你版的杰作。脚蹬高跟鞋，身高只有5英尺6英寸高的16岁女孩，用她的聪明才智令众人刮目相看。她在生日贺词中完美地抓住了父亲生命中的闪光点，用轻松诙谐的笔法，表达了对父亲的赞美。后来，我的朋友亚历克西斯对我说："索菲娅的表现简直令人难以置信。"

我点着头赞同地说："她的贺词的确很棒。"

"是的，毫无疑问……但这并不是我想说的。"亚历克西斯说。"我不知道有谁能真正地了解索菲娅，她是一个非常有主见的人，总是努力去做那些为你们家光宗耀祖的事情，而露露则是个可爱迷人的女孩。"

"可爱迷人"？我现在一点儿也没有这种感觉。在索菲娅发表生日祝贺词的时候，露露站在姐姐身旁，殷勤地微笑着。她没有准备贺词，也拒绝哪怕是开口说上一个字。

我的努力一败涂地！这竟是我的第一次失利。经过了那么多家庭内部的矛盾冲突和纷争，我从来没有遭遇过失败——至少是在重要的问题上。

这种公然的违抗和不敬激怒了我。我的愤怒在内心里积聚，而我并没有将它们全部释放。"你为这个家庭、为你自己带来了耻辱，"我对露露说，"你难道要带着自己的错误度过自己的余生吗？"

露露反驳说："你就是一个喜欢炫耀的人。你已经有了一个对你唯命是从的女儿，为什么还需要加上我？"

现在，我感觉我们母女之间好似竖起了一堵墙。

在过去的日子里，我们曾野蛮地激战，但最后总能握手言欢。我们依偎在她的或我的床上，亲密地相拥，并模仿曾经令我们面红耳赤的争吵，咯咯地笑个不停。而我说话的口吻完全不像一个母亲，比如，"我很快就要死了"或"我不相信你如此爱我，爱到让我心疼"。而露露则会笑着说："妈咪！你太奇怪了！"

现在，露露在夜里不再进我的房间。她的愤怒不只是冲我发泄，也殃及杰德和索菲娅。越来越多的时间里，她把自己紧锁在闺房里。

别以为我没有努力去争取露露。在我不生气或没有与露露发生争吵的时候，我尽力做一切我能做的事情。

一次，我对露露说："嗨，露露！让我们改变一下自己的生活，做一些完全不同的有趣的事情吧——比如搞一次车库拍卖会①。"我们真的做了，净赚241.35美元。拍卖会的确很开心，但它并没有改变我们的生活。

另一次，我建议她去上电子小提琴课。她去了，而且似乎很喜欢。可在我为她预订第二次课程时，她却告诉我，"傻乎乎的，没劲透了"，随之也就放弃了。不久之后，我们又重新陷入相互的敌意中。

---

① 车库拍卖会（garage sale），在美国，人们常将家里不用的一些旧家具、衣物、小器具等旧货，在自家的车库或院子里进行清仓拍卖。——译者注

可是作为总是让对方感觉不爽的两个人，露露和我在一起度过了许多时光（尽管我不会真正地将它们看做美好时光）。下面就是我们平常的周末训练日程：

星期六：早晨8点30分，驾车1个小时去康涅狄格州诺沃克

参加管弦乐团3个小时的练习

再驾车1个小时回到纽黑文

做家庭作业

1~2个小时的小提琴练习

1个小时有趣的家庭活动（可选择的）

星期日：1~2个小时的小提琴练习

2个小时驾车去纽约城

1个小时上田中直子小姐的小提琴课

2个小时驾车返回纽黑文

做家庭作业

事后回想起来，这样的周末真够折磨人的。但换个角度来看，这些付出又是值得的。事实上，露露对小提琴是爱恨交加、欲罢不能。

有一次，她对我说："在我拉巴赫的曲子时，感觉自己就好像正走在旅行的路上，在我去过的第18个国家。"她告诉我，她是如此醉心于音乐超越历史的感觉。在田中直子一年两次的一场音乐演奏会上，我记得露露着迷于观众与门德尔松小提琴协奏曲的共鸣。后来，田中直子小姐对我说："露露

与其他小提琴手的区别，就在于她真正地感受并理解了音乐的内涵与魅力。你会发现她对小提琴的热爱。”

此时此刻，我心中有个“我”想为田中直子小姐擦亮眼睛，告诉她露露有时候憎恨小提琴；而另一个“我”却为她的“发现”欢欣鼓舞、重拾决心。

露露的“成年礼”临近了。我不是犹太人，但成年礼是杰德家族的习俗。在这个时刻，露露和我又出现了对立。我希望她在成年礼上演奏小提琴，而约瑟夫·阿赫龙的《希伯来旋律》是一首美丽而虔诚的乐曲。露露的老朋友莱克西推荐了它，杰德也赞同，可露露就是不愿意。

“拉小提琴？在我的成年礼上？这太可笑了，我不干！”露露惊疑地说，“这两件事儿完全就不搭调！你知道成年礼的含义吗？它不是一场独奏演出秀。”她还补充道：“我只想参加一个热热闹闹的聚会，得到许许多多的礼物。”

这个说法激怒了我。而多年来，露露听我义正词严地斥责过那些富家子弟的父母，他们花费数百万美元来操办孩子的成年礼，在聚会上跳沙龙舞①，或把聚会办成“甜蜜的16岁”狂欢。

事实上，露露对自己的犹太人身份有着强烈的认同感。不像索菲娅（或杰德），露露总是坚持遵从逾越节的规矩，在赎罪日不进食。她甚至比姐姐索菲娅更加重视成年礼，将它看做自己生命中的重要事件；她带着一种狂热，投入对部分希伯来律法和先知书的学习之中。

这一次，我不会再让露露牵着我的鼻子走。“如果你拒绝拉小提琴，”我以平静的口吻对她说，“那么，你爸爸和我就不会为你举办聚会。我们只

---

① 沙龙舞（cotillion），流行于19世纪的一种不断交换舞伴、穿插各种花样的轻快的交谊舞。——译者注

搞一个小型的典礼——毕竟，宗教的仪式是至关重要的。"

"你没有权利这么做！"露露愤怒地说，"这太不公平了，你并没有让索菲娅在她的成年礼上弹钢琴！"

"索菲娅没能做的事情而你做了，这对你有好处。"我说。

"你又不是犹太人，"露露反驳道，"你根本不知道你在说什么，而这件事与你毫不相干！"

在露露成年礼之前的6个星期，我送发了邀请信，但是我警告露露："如果你不演奏《希伯来旋律》，我就取消这次聚会。"

"你不能这么做。"露露轻蔑地说。

"那你就试一试，露露！看看我敢不敢这么做。"我口气强硬地说。

说真的，我并不知道谁会成为这次对弈的赢家。这也是一个高风险的策略，因为如果我输了，就将无路可退。

27　向白血病宣战

在美文住院之前，她坚持要为孩子们洗衣服，一洗就是满满两大筐。她仔仔细细地叠好儿子的衬衫、抚平女儿的围嘴和连裤衣，我在一旁看得目瞪口呆。

美文身患癌症的消息令父母痛不欲生。我心目中那两个最坚强的人，完全被痛苦击倒了。母亲一直在哭泣，她把自己关在家里，不接任何一个朋友打来的电话，甚至是心爱的外孙女打来的电话也不例外。父亲则不断地给我打电话，声音里充满令人心碎的哀伤。他一遍又一遍地问我，还有没有哪怕只是一线的希望……

在治疗方面，美文选择了波士顿的达纳-法伯/哈佛癌症治疗中心。我们得知，这所医院拥有全美最好的骨髓移植设备。而哈佛大学也是美文和丈夫接受学习和训练的地方，他们在那儿认识很多人。

美文的白血病如此迅速地改变了一切。

在她被确诊后的三天之内，美文锁上了在斯坦福大学的家门，举家迁往波士顿（她拒绝考虑把孩子们留在加利福尼亚由爷爷、奶奶照看的建议）。我们在朋友乔丹和亚历克西斯的帮助下，为他们在波士顿租到了一处房子，为杰克联系了学校，为艾拉找好了日托的幼儿园。

美文的白血病来势汹汹，达纳－法伯医院的大夫要她马上作骨髓移植。因为白血病患者没有存活的可能，除非进行骨髓移植。美文必须跨越两个巨大的障碍。首先，她得经受住高强度的化疗和放疗以缓解病情的恶化。其次，假如一切顺利，她还得幸运地找到配对的骨髓捐赠者。由于存在这样的障碍，成功的可能性很小，能够跨越两个障碍的概率微乎其微。即使是所有的努力都见效了，白血病患者接受骨髓移植后的生存也不容乐观，他们会面临更加严峻的考验。

住进波士顿的医院之前，美文还有两天时间。在她对孩子们说"再见"时，我就陪伴在她身边。她坚持要为孩子们洗衣服，一洗就是满满两大筐。第二天，再把杰克的衣服收拾整齐。当她仔仔细细地叠好儿子的衬衫、抚平女儿的围嘴和连裤衣，我在一旁看得目瞪口呆。

"我喜欢洗衣服。"她对我说。

在她离开家去住院之前，她把自己所有的珠宝和贵重物品都交给我代为保管。"万一我回不来了呢？"她说。

我开车送她去了医院。在我们等候填写住院登记表时，她一个劲儿地和我开玩笑。"别忘了给我买个好看的假发，我总是希望自己有一头美丽的秀发。"她还为占用了我大量的时间而一再向我表示歉意。

我们终于走进了她的病房。帘子的另一边，是一位面色如土的老太太。显然，她刚刚做完化疗。美文走进病房所做的第一件事，就是把家人的照片摆放在病榻旁。一张是艾拉的面部特写，一张是杰克3岁时的照片，另一张是他们一家四口在网球场拍摄的，照片上的每个人都笑得很灿烂。尽管美文看起来时不时地有些走神，但她总的来说显得平静而安然。

而两位亚洲和尼日利亚裔的实习医生则令人感到不安。他们向美文作了自我介绍，而让我感到愤怒的是，他们就像仅仅在扮演医生的角色，没有回答我们的任何问题。他们两次说错了美文所患白血病的种类，结果，美文不得不向他们解释病人住进医院的当天晚上应遵循的程序。我只能猜想：他们还是学生？难道我妹妹的性命就攥在这样的医学院学生的手中？

美文的反应则迥然不同。"我简直难以相信这是我待在这所大楼里的最后时光，我曾经在这里学习、实习，我是他们中的一分子，手术室和我好似刚刚认识的朋友。"她在实习医生离开后若有所思地说，声音中透着几分伤感。

最初几个星期的化疗进展顺利。就像我们在杰德的母亲弗洛伦斯患病后住院时看到的情形一样，化疗的影响日积月累。在刚开始化疗的那几天，美文感觉很好。事实上，比她的自我感觉更好的是，几个月来，大量的能量注入她的体内，因为医生定期为她输血以改善贫血的状况。在医院里，美文继续撰写学术论文（其中一篇在她住院期间就发表在《细胞》[①]医学期刊上），长途遥控她在斯坦福的生物医学实验室，通过互联网订购书籍、玩具，以及杰克和艾拉的冬装。

即便是在美文开始感受化疗的杀伤力后，她也从不抱怨，更别说默默承受将希克曼线插入胸腔、让化学毒素直接滴入主动脉这样痛苦的治疗，经历突然发作、令人战栗的高烧，接受数百次的注射，服用数不清的药片，

① 《细胞》（Cell），是美国细胞出版社（Cell Press）出版发行的极具学术权威的生物医学期刊。——译者注

忍受由于打吊针的反复穿刺给皮肤留下的百孔千疮。

美文持续不断地给我发来风趣幽默的邮件，有时会逗得我哈哈大笑。一次，她在邮件中写道："哇！我开始感到恶心。在我的体内，用化学武器装备起来的'军队'正在向前挺进……一切都在按计划进行。"另一次，她则说："我期盼抽血的医生今天上午能出现在我的病榻前，这正好能让我减轻体重。"抽血的医生告诉她血液的指标，然后说："你可以再喝清汤了。试试鸡汤，美味无比哦。"

当美文没有及时回复我的电话或邮件，我发现她不是病得很厉害，就是由于输入血小板而导致的过敏反应令组织产生肿胀、皮肤出现麻疹（这类情况会经常发生），或者因镇静止痛药导致的迟钝增加了令人恐怖的痛苦。然而，她的最新信息总是充满了轻松。对我日常向她问候的邮件，（"昨天晚上情况怎么样？"）她的回复是："你并不希望知道。情况不是太坏，也根本不可能太好。"或者是："哎哟，又是另一场高烧。"

同时我也看到：美文决心为自己的孩子而活下去。

在成长的过程中，美文是我们四姐妹中最能够集中精力做事儿的人，她总是能全力以赴。现在，她把自己全部的聪明才智和创造力都投入了与白血病的战斗中。她接受过医生的职业训练，对自己的疾病有着最尖端的医学知识。她仔细地核对用药的剂量，审阅自己的细胞遗传学监测报告，研究互联网上发布的临床实验。她喜欢自己的医生，拥有专业、先进的医学知识的她足以领会医生的经验、洞察力和良好的判断力；而她的医生以及所有的护士和年轻的实习医生也都喜欢她这样的病人。

有一次，一个医学博士生认出她就是来自斯坦福大学、在颇具权威性的科学期刊《自然》（Nature）上发表过两篇学术论文的美文博士，她高兴得就地转了个圈儿，并满怀敬畏地就一些专业的学术问题请求美文的指教。

为了在治疗期间保持健康的体形，美文强迫自己一天两次、每次走20分钟，即便是得自己一路高举着输液瓶。

2008年的那个秋冬之际，我常常去波士顿陪伴美文。每个周末，我们都全家出动——有时候，在露露和我结束田中直子小姐4个小时指导的学习之旅后，我们立即驾车两个小时赶往波士顿。化疗破坏了美文的免疫系统，医生不希望她接待客人，可美文却一点儿也不在乎，她只担心杰克和艾拉，她为我们能花时间来陪伴他们而感到开心。索菲娅很喜欢她的表妹艾拉，而露露与杰克成为了最要好的朋友。他们俩不仅脾性相投，而且外貌也很相似，人们甚至以为他们是一对亲兄妹哩！

当然，我们都为美文捏着一把汗，急于知道身患白血病的美文能否幸免于难。20天后，医生进行了关键的活组织检查，一个星期后得知了检查的结果。疗效并不好——应该说是情况不妙。美文的头发掉光了，皮肤也在脱落，并出现了所有可能发生的胃肠并发症状，可是病情并未得到缓解。医生告诉她，她还需要进行一个疗程的化疗。

"世界的末日尚未来临。"医生尽量带着乐观的口吻对美文说道。

可是，经过认真研究的我们都清楚地知道，如果下一个疗程依然无效，要想成功地进行骨髓移植的希望就会化为泡影。

这是她最后的机会了。

28 一袋大米

　　家里一片狼藉。只见一个大粗麻袋被撕成碎片，碎布和塑料袋满地都是，而可可和普希金正在室外的暴风雨中狂吠。就在那个时候，索菲娅一脸郁闷地走进厨房，手里还拿着一把笤帚……

成熟独立的索菲娅

一天晚上，我从学校回到家里，发现厨房的地毯上散落着一些大米。我刚刚给学生上完课，课后还和他们在一起工作了4个小时。我又累又紧张，打算在晚饭后再开车去波士顿。

家里一片狼藉。

只见一个大粗麻袋被撕成碎片，碎布和塑料袋满地都是，而可可和普希金正在室外的暴风雨中狂吠。我立刻知道发生了什么事情。

就在那个时候，索菲娅一脸郁闷地走进厨房，手里还拿着一把笤帚。

我忍不住对索菲娅发火了。"索菲娅，你怎么旧错重犯！食品储藏室的门敞开着，是你干的吗？我给你说过多少遍了，狗狗会对大米感兴趣！这下好了。整整50磅的一袋大米就这样被糟蹋了，我们的狗狗很可能就要死了。可你就是拿我的话当耳旁风，总是说，'噢，我实在是太抱歉了，不会再有第二次了，我太不像话了，杀了我吧！'可是你却毫无改变，你不在意别人，唯一关心的是躲开麻烦。对你这种不听劝告的行为我感到恶心——恶心死了！"

杰德经常指责我有一种言过其实的倾向：我习惯将严重的关乎道德的责难，强加到微不足道的小事儿上。可索菲娅的策略通常是不予反驳，她等待着暴风雨的平息。

然而这一次，索菲娅却没有保持沉默。"妈妈！我会打扫干净的，这样总该行了吧？你的反应就像是我抢了银行，你难道不知道我是一个好女儿吗？我认识的所有人成天都聚在一起寻欢作乐，他们酗酒，甚至吸毒。你知道我在做什么吗？我每天都从学校直接跑步回家，我一路奔跑，你知道这样做看起来有多么怪异吗？有一天我突然想到，'为什么我要这么做？为什么我要跑步回家？'这么做只是为了有更多的时间练习弹琴！你经常说做人要心存感激，可你要感激的应该是我。别再将你不能掌控露露的挫败感发泄在我的身上！"

索菲娅所言极是。

16年来，她让我感到骄傲，令我的生活如此轻松惬意。可是，有时候我知道做错了并开始厌恶自己，可内心却反而变得冷酷，言行更加过火。因此，我对索菲娅说："我从来没有要求你跑步回家——这么做看起来很愚蠢、很可笑。如果你想要吸毒，那就尽管去做。也许你会在戒毒所遇到一个好小伙。"

"我们这个家庭的相互关系真是荒谬可笑，"索菲娅抗议说，"我做了所有的工作，我对你几乎唯命是从，而我犯了一个错误，你就对我大喊大叫。露露从不听你的话，总是和你对着干，她顶嘴、扔东西，可你还买礼物哄着她。你到底是一个什么样的中国妈妈呀？"

索菲娅的话一针见血。说到这里，明确中国式教养的重点和孩子们因在家里排行有别而呈现的不同特点，也许正是时候。我有个学生名叫斯蒂芬妮，她最近告诉我一个有趣的故事。

斯蒂芬妮是韩国移民家庭的女儿，在家里排行老大。她上高中的时候，成绩全优，是学校的数学神童、音乐会的小小钢琴演奏家。她的妈妈总是吓唬她："如果你不做某某事，我就不让你去学校！"不去学校就意味着她会"缺课"——这令斯蒂芬妮极为恐怖。于是，她会对妈妈唯命是从，并千方百计地争取做得又快又好。可与此相反，当妈妈用同样的话来威胁斯蒂芬妮的小妹妹时，她妹妹的反应却是："太棒了！我就喜欢待在家里——我讨厌学校。"

虽然也有很多例外，但是这种老大乖巧能干、老二叛逆难管的模式，我发现在许多家庭，尤其是移民家庭里，的确是司空见惯。我只是在想，我可以通过坚定的意志和辛勤的工作，来应对露露的反叛。

"索菲娅，你知道我在露露身上遇到了麻烦。"我承认，"对你有效的教育方式，对露露却不起作用，而且其结果简直可以说是一塌糊涂。"

"哦……别担忧，妈。"索菲娅的声音忽然变得友善，她说，"这只是一个阶段性的问题。我在13岁的时候，情况也很糟糕，我曾经为此而痛苦，但是一切都会好起来的。"

我不知道索菲娅在13岁时会感到痛苦。回想一下，恐怕我母亲也不知道13岁的我内心深处的痛苦。与大多数亚洲的移民家庭一样，我们在家里也没有那种掏心窝子似的交谈。我母亲从不给我讲述关于青春期的知识，尤其是不会告诉我那些由7个字母组成，由P-u开头、y结尾的关于青春期生理的单词。我们从来不会在一起探讨生命的真相——只要想象一下那时与父母能够进行的谈话，我就感到寒心。

"索菲娅，"我说，"你在家里的情况跟我过去的处境很相像：排行老大，每个家庭成员都指望着依靠你，却没有人来为你分忧。能在家里扮演这样的角色是一种光荣，问题是西方社会的文化对此却并不认同。在迪士尼的电影里，'好女儿'总是感到精神崩溃，发现生活并不完全需要循规蹈矩、力争上游。然后，她们脱掉衣服奔向大海，或做一些类似的事情来放纵自己。可这只是迪士尼吸引那些从未赢得任何奖项的人的一种方式。获奖使你拥有更多的机会，这意味着你可以自由地进行选择，并不需要你飞身跳进大海。"

说完这段话，我不禁被自己的"演说"深深打动。尽管如此，我依然感到心痛。索菲娅怀抱沉重的课本从学校飞奔回家的镜头在我的脑海里闪现，我难过得几乎无法忍受。

　　"把笤帚给我，"我对索菲娅说，"你需要时间去练琴，让我来打扫吧！"

29 穿过绝望的迷雾

美文的第一个化疗疗程并没有成为一个无法苏醒的噩梦，第二个疗程或许还有机会弥补。可是现在，极为残酷的是我听不到来自她的消息，而时间却在一天天地悄然流逝。

我和妹妹美夏都在进行检测，争取成为美文的骨髓捐献者。

兄弟姐妹拥有最好的机会成为完美的匹配者，其概率大约为1/3。我指望我的血液能够合格，可事情并不像我想象的那样，我和美夏的血液指标与美文均不匹配。可笑的是，检查结果显示，我们俩倒是一对完美的匹配者，可我们却无法搭救美文。这就是说，美文现在不得不求助于国家骨髓捐献的登记系统，以找到与自己匹配的捐献者。

让我们沮丧不已的是，我们得知如果兄弟姐妹的骨髓无法匹配，从其他途径找到捐献者的概率则会大大下降，尤其是那些亚洲和非洲的后裔。互联网上，挣扎在死亡线上的病人寻找骨髓捐献者的诉求比比皆是。即便是能够找到一个匹配者，其过程也会长达好几个月——而美文或许并没有几个月的时间可以耐心地等候。

美文的第一个化疗疗程并没有成为一个无法苏醒的噩梦，第二个疗程或许还能弥补。可是现在，极为残酷的是我听不到来自她的消息，而时间却在一天天地悄然流逝。带着恐惧，我拨通了医院手术室的电话，可听到的常常是她的语音留言，或者她在应答时有些唐突地说："我现在不能说话，美儿。我争取以后再通话吧。"

化疗后导致死亡的主要原因是感染。类似感冒或流感的普通疾病，就可以轻而易举地杀死一个体内白细胞被化疗摧毁的癌症病人。美文的感染接踵而至。为了对抗感染，医生在治疗中采用了大量的抗生素，这导致了各种令人痛苦的副作用。当这些抗生素不起作用时，医生就尝试换用其他种类的抗生素。

美文无法进食和饮水已经好几个星期了，不得不通过静脉注射营养液来维持生命。她时常不是浑身冰凉就是周身发烫，在并发症和病危不断袭来的状态中，她常常在痛不欲生中挣扎，不得不使用镇静剂。

当第二个化疗疗程完成后，我们再一次提心吊胆地等待，期盼着听到好消息。我们了解到，假如美文白血病的恶化得到缓解，这就意味着健康的血液细胞开始滋生——特别是那些能够对抗细菌感染的中性白细胞，都是与死神对阵的精兵。

我知道，抽血化验是美文每天要做的第一件事情。于是在清晨6点，我就会坐在电脑前等候她的电子邮件，可美文却不再给我写邮件。我无法忍受等待的焦急时，就会给她发邮件。我只会得到简洁的答复，诸如："血液指标还没升高"或"奇迹尚未发生，失望至极"。很快，我就根本看不到她的电子邮件了。

我经常奇怪，那些接连进行语音留言的人，到底是怎么了。比如，你在哪里？我很担心你！给我打电话！他们不明白，人们不回电话显然是有一个理由。可是现在，我却焦急得不怕被人讨厌。美文结束化疗后的那个星期，我一次又一次地在早晨给她打电话，即便她从来不接电话。美文有来电显示，因此，她知道是我打来的电话。我不断地留言，就一些生活小事告诉她最新的信息，希望以愉快和活泼的情绪来感染她。

一天早晨，美文终于接了我的电话。她的声音听起来好像变了一个人，微弱得我几乎无法听清她在说什么。我问她感觉怎么样，她只是在电话的另一端叹息。然后她说："治疗没有效果，美儿。我要坚持不住了，没有希望了……没什么希望了……"她的声音越来越弱。

"别犯傻了，美文。等待血液指标的上升需要很长的时间，有时会是好几个月，这种情况完全正常。杰德对此进行了切实而透彻的研究，如果你有兴趣，我可以把这些数据发给你。另外，手术室的医务人员也告诉我，医生对你的情况相当乐观，再等一等好吗？"

美文没有回答，于是我继续鼓动。"露露简直是一个噩梦！"我试图用露露练小提琴或她跟我干仗的故事，来分散她的悲观情绪。

在美文生病之前，我们经常在一起交流教育孩子的看法，谈到我们不可能再像父母对待我们那样，将家长的权威用到我们的孩子身上。

而现在让我欣慰的是，在电话的那一端，美文笑了，然后她用较为正常的声音说："可怜的露露！她是一个多么可爱的女孩，美儿，你不应该对她如此严厉。"

在万圣节到来的时候，我们得知，医院为美文找到了一个完全匹配的华裔捐赠者。4天后，我收到了美文发来的电子邮件，她说："我有中性白

细胞了！指数是100，我需要达到500，有希望增加。"事实上，美文的中性
白细胞正在升高——虽然非常缓慢，但它们的确在上升。

　　11月初，美文被医院"释放"回家，以更好地恢复体力。距离骨髓移
植只有一个月时间了，可令人难以想象的是，她还需要进行一个疗程的化
疗（这个举足轻重、拥有重磅杀伤力的疗程要在一个特殊的无菌病房里进
行），以彻底清除病变的骨髓。这样，捐赠者健康的骨髓才能顺利地进行替
换。许多白血病患者都没有能够走出这个特殊的病房。

　　美文住在家里的那个月里，她似乎非常开心地享受着与家人在一起的
美好时光：给艾拉喂饭，带孩子们外出散步，静静地看着他们酣睡的可爱
模样。她最感兴趣的事情是观看儿子杰克打网球。

　　美文的骨髓移植在圣诞节前夜进行。我们的父母和我的全家都住在
波士顿的宾馆里，我们点中餐的外卖，和手术室的医务人员以及杰克和艾
拉一起打开圣诞的礼物。

30 《希伯来旋律》

"我不会在我的成年礼上演奏！我讨厌小提琴，我不拉了，放弃了！"露露在家里尖声叫喊的分贝高得无法测量……

2009，崭新的一年。而我们却并没有感觉到多少节日的气氛。

从波士顿回到纽黑文，全家人都疲惫不堪。要将节日的欢愉带给妈妈还躺在骨髓移植的重症监护病房的杰克和艾拉，是件非常困难的事情。而要安慰忧伤的父母，则更加痛苦不堪。

母亲始终在折磨自己，她不停地追问，为什么美文会得白血病？为什么？到底是为什么？我有几次回答她时很不耐烦，事后自我感觉也很糟。父亲则一遍又一遍地问我同样的医学问题，我求助于杰德，他耐心地解释了骨髓移植过程中的科学原理。我们对2009这个新年会带给我们什么，都充满了恐惧。

回到纽黑文，发现我们的家又黑又冷。在我们离家期间，一场史无前例的狂风挟带着肆无忌惮的暴风雪席卷了纽黑文，家里的一些窗户被吹破了，接着还发生了停电，一时间把我们置于冷冰冰的世界。

新学期到了，杰德和我都得为教学而作好准备。最为糟糕的是，露露即将进行三场小提琴音乐会的演奏（包括她的成年礼），演出时间日益逼近。

"又要重返战场了"，我严肃地想。

露露很少和我说话。她自剪头发是一种暴力的非难，尽管美发师使出浑身解数，它依然看起来太短并呈小锯齿状。只要看见它，我的心情指数便直线下降。

1月下旬，医院准许美文回家。开始时，她极度虚弱，上楼梯都会有问题。她依然极易感染，如果没有防毒面罩的保护，医生不允许她去饭店吃饭、去食品杂货店购物、去电影院看电影或去剧场看戏。我们都在虔诚地为她祈祷，期盼新鲜血液不会排斥她自己的身体。我们清楚地知道，在几个月之内，不管她是否会发生最严重的并发症，急性移植物抗宿主病都是潜在的致命灾难。

几个星期过去了，距露露的成年礼越来越近，露露和我进入了强化训练的阶段。与索菲娅的成年礼一样，我们一反传统，在自己的家里举办成年礼。杰德担当了主要的组织工作，而我则不断地游说露露，练习《希伯来旋律》中的先知书部分——尽管在成年礼上演奏希伯来的乐曲是犹太人的传统，可还是需要我这个严格要求的中国妈妈，才能保证露露成年礼的完美。

像往常一样，我们围绕小提琴展开了最为激烈的战斗。

"你没有听见我说的话吗？我要你上楼去练习《希伯来旋律》，现在就去！"我一定像打雷一般吼叫了无数次，"这首曲子并不太难，可是如果不练到难以置信的流畅，那你就会把这首曲子糟蹋了。"

"你想让自己变得平庸吗？"我在另外一个场合喊道，"这就是你想要的结果吗？"

露露常常发起激烈的反攻。"不是每个人的成年礼都要办得独特，我不想练习。"她还击道。或者她会说："我不会在我的成年礼上拉小提琴！你甭想改变我的想法。"还有就是："我讨厌小提琴，我不拉了，放弃了！"她在家里尖声叫喊的分贝高得无法测量。因此，直到露露成年礼举办的前一刻，我都不知道她是否会演奏《希伯来旋律》，尽管杰德已将它赫然地打印到节目单上。

结果——露露在她的成年礼演奏了《希伯来旋律》！

带着镇静和自信，她朗读了律法和先知书；她演奏的优美的《希伯来旋律》在房间里萦绕、回荡，它迷人的音调令宾朋们热泪盈眶，每一个人都被她对《希伯来旋律》发自内心深处的诠释而打动了。

在随后的招待会上，我看到露露在迎接宾客时容光焕发。"哦，天啊，露露，你简直就像是小提琴的克星，我的意思是——你太棒了！"我听到她的朋友这样对她说。

"她真是才华超群啊！"我的一个歌手朋友惊叹道，"她显然拥有一份来自上天的馈赠，一些无师自通的本事。"当我告诉她为了让露露坚持练习小提琴，我和她之间经历了怎样的战火硝烟，我的朋友说："你千万不能让她告别小提琴，如果有一天她放弃了，她会在自己的余生中后悔不已的。"

而露露在拉小提琴时经常出现的场景是，听众被她的琴声打动了，而她被自己演奏的音乐吸引了。可是当露露和我激烈对抗时，她坚持说她"讨厌小提琴"，这让我感到格外困惑和气恼，因为事实并不是这样。

"祝贺你，美儿。上帝知道，如果我有你这样的母亲，我也会……"

我的朋友、过去曾是个舞蹈演员的卡伦对我开玩笑说，"我也会出类拔萃的！"

"噢，不，卡伦，我可不希望成为任何人的母亲。"我摇摇头说，"在家里，我不得不经常大声嚷嚷、尖叫。我甚至不认为露露今天能演奏小提琴。实话实说吧，经历这个过程真的是伤痕累累啊！"

"但是你为女儿们付出了太多！"卡伦坚持认为，"你让她们认识到自己的才能，理解了走向卓越的价值。这是会让她们终身受益的东西呀！"

"也许是这样吧！"我口气犹疑地说，"我现在只是不再那么确信这一点了。"

露露的成年礼举办得非常成功，每个参加聚会的人都兴致勃勃。聚会的亮点，是美文和她的家人也来了。在过去出院后的5个月中，美文慢慢地恢复了体力。然而，她的免疫系统仍然比较脆弱，因此在聚会中，每当有人不小心咳嗽两声，我都十分惊恐。美文看起来比较消瘦，但很精神。她几乎是有些扬扬得意地带着小女儿艾拉四处玩耍。

那天夜晚，当所有的客人都离去了，我们尽力打扫了聚会的房间。然后，我躺在床上，想着露露会不会爬上来拥抱我，就像当年那个难忘而磨人的夜晚，在我们终于解决了"小白驴"钢琴曲的难题之后。

我等了很久，露露并没有来。于是我来到她的房间。

"今天你演奏了《希伯来旋律》，你感到快乐吗？"我问。

露露似乎很开心，但对我并不是很热情。"是的，妈妈。"她说，"你可以得到大家的赞扬了。"

"是的。"我尽力带着微笑说，"我为你感到骄傲，你今天的表现非常卓越。"

　　露露笑了，笑得很优雅。但她看起来也有些心不在焉，让我几乎不耐烦地想要走开。我还读出了她眼睛里的一些东西——它们似乎在说，我这个强势妈妈的日子已屈指可数了。

31　泪洒红场

莫斯科咖啡馆，"鱼子酱风波"陡起。我冲出咖啡馆拼命地奔跑，不知道要逃往何方。一个疯狂的46岁的女人，脚蹬一双凉鞋以百米冲刺般的速度在飞跑、在哭泣……

露露成年礼举办的两天后，我们动身去了俄罗斯。这是一次我期盼已久的假日旅行。在我还是个小女孩的时候，就听父母极力赞美过圣彼得堡。而杰德和我也希望能带女儿们到我们从来不曾涉足的地方去旅行。

陪伴美文刚刚度过了急性移植物抗宿主病的最险恶时期，在过去的整整10个月里，基本上没有休息过一天的我们，的确是需要一个假期。

俄罗斯之旅的第一站是莫斯科。杰德找到了一家位于市中心的很方便的宾馆。稍事休息后，我们就开始了对俄罗斯的初步体验。

我尽量让自己成为一只悠闲的"菜鸟"，傻傻的，但很自在。我这种状态最让女儿们感到舒适、开心。我努力抑制住自己平时对她们的穿着品头论足、对她们没完没了的口头禅唠唠叨叨的旧习。可是，有些事情注定要令我们的那一天变得坎坷。

在一个被人们称为银行的地方，我花了一个多小时，先后排了两次长队，以兑换手中的货币。之后，我们要参观的博物馆却到了闭馆的时间。

于是，我们决定去红场看看，从我们下榻的宾馆步行到那里并不太远。

红场的宽阔令人惊叹。从我们进入的大门到洋葱式圆顶的圣巴索大教堂的另一端入口，之间差不多能容纳三个足球场。我想，这不像时尚之都意大利的广场那样时髦或迷人，这个广场设计得雄伟庄严，令人充满敬畏。

露露和索菲娅一直在相互攻击，这让我感到恼怒。实际上令我不爽的是，她们俩已经长成个头与我相仿的青少年（索菲娅比我还要高出3英寸），再也不是可爱的小女孩了，应该懂事了。

"时光如梭。"我的老朋友们经常伤感地对我说，"不经意间，孩子们就长大了、离开家了。而你将会慢慢地变老，尽管你以为自己还像以前一样年轻。"

我从不相信朋友们的话，因为对我来说，有这种想法的人，他们的心态似乎已经在变"老"。由于我从日常生活中的每时每刻挤出了许多时间，我想我也许为自己赢得了更多宝贵的生命时光。而人们所说的"睡得少＝活得长"，则是一个纯粹的、数学的事实。

"那道长长的白墙后面，就是列宁的陵墓。"杰德告诉女儿们，"他的身体经过防腐处理后供游人参观，明天我们可以去看一看。"然后，杰德为孩子们简要地介绍了俄罗斯的历史和关于冷战的政治。

在红场漫步一会儿后，我们吃惊地碰到了少数美国人和不少中国人，他们看上去对我们完全漠不关心。我们在一家咖啡馆的露天桌子旁坐下来，这家咖啡馆与著名的口香糖百货商场（the GUM shopping mall）毗邻。口香糖百货商场建于19世纪，这座富丽堂皇、商铺林立的建筑占据了整个红场的东侧，正好与西侧堡垒般的克里姆林宫遥相呼应。

我们点了俄式煎饼和鱼子酱，这个有趣的尝试让我们开始度过莫斯科之旅的第一个夜晚。当服务员为我们呈上鱼子酱（这道30美元的菜肴被盛放在一个细小的容器里），露露说："哇，真恶心！"她一点儿也不想尝一尝。

"索菲娅，别一下拿得太多，给别人也留一点儿。"说完，我转向另一个女儿，"露露，你怎么就像个没有文化的野蛮人。试试鱼子酱吧，你可以在上面多放一点儿酸奶油。"

"这样就更糟了，"露露说，她做了个颤抖的手势，"别叫我野蛮人！"

"别毁了我们大家的假期，露露。"

"是你在让这个假期不愉快！"

我把鱼子酱朝露露面前推了推，我让她尝一粒鱼子——就一粒。

"为什么？"露露挑衅地问，"为什么你这么在意我吃不吃鱼子酱？你不能强迫我吃任何东西！"

我感觉自己的火气在上升。难道我就不能要求露露做一件小事情？"尝一粒鱼子，现在！"

"我不想吃。"露露说。

"现在就尝一粒，露露！"

"不！"

"美儿，"杰德开始出面缓和我们之间的剑拔弩张，"我们大家都累了，我们为什么不能只是……"

我打断他的话："你知道，要是我的父母在这里看到这番情景，他们会感到多么沮丧和羞耻。露露——你竟然在公共场所和我对着干？看看你的脸，你只是在伤害自己。我们现在在俄罗斯，你拒绝只是尝一尝这里的鱼子酱！你像一个野蛮人，如果你认为自己是一个叛逆的大人物，那你就完全是个凡夫俗子。没有任何独特之处，与一个无所事事的美国青春期少年相比，你只会更加平庸、更加普通、更加低等。你会无聊乏味，露露——没劲透了！"

"闭嘴！"露露生气地说。

"你胆敢对我说'闭嘴'，我是你的妈妈！"我压低声音，但还是有一些客人朝我们这边张望。"别再以粗暴的行为让你的姐姐印象深刻。"

"我恨你，我真的恨你！"露露说出这话可没有压低嗓门儿。现在，她声嘶力竭的喊叫让整个咖啡馆的客人都在盯着我们。

"你不爱我！"露露厉声地说，"你以为你爱我，可事实并不是这样。你每一秒钟都在让我的自我感觉一落千丈，你毁了我的生活，我无法忍受继续待在你的身边。这就是你想要的结果吗？"

愤怒的岩浆在我内心里积聚、膨胀。露露也看到了这个征兆，可她继续不顾一切地发泄着："你是个令人恐怖的妈妈，你是个自私自利的家伙，除了你自己，你谁也不关心。你是不是难以相信，你为我做了那么多，我却是多么的忘恩负义？你为我而做的一切，实际上都是为了你自己！"

我想，露露像我一样，也会强迫自己表现得残忍。"你是一个令人恐怖的女儿！"我大声地说。

"我知道，我不是你心中期待的那个女儿。我不是中国人！我也不想成为中国人。你为什么不让这个想法见鬼去？我讨厌小提琴，我憎恨我的生活，我恨你，我恨这个家！我现在就要把这个玻璃杯砸个粉碎！"

"你请便吧！"我回敬道。

露露从桌子上抓起一个玻璃杯狠狠地砸在地上。水和玻璃碎片四处飞溅，一些客人被惊得目瞪口呆。咖啡馆里所有的眼睛都齐刷刷地看过来，他们看到了这番怪诞的景象⋯⋯

过去，我曾经看不起那些无法掌控孩子的西方父母；现在，我却拥有这样一个最无礼、最粗鲁、最暴力、最失控的女儿！

露露气得浑身哆嗦，眼泪也快流下来了。"如果你不放过我，我就要砸掉更多的杯子！"她哭喊道。

我再也无法忍受，站起来便跑出了咖啡馆。我拼命地奔跑，不知道要逃往何方。一个疯狂的46岁的女人，脚蹬一双凉鞋以百米冲刺般的速度在飞跑、在哭泣⋯⋯我冲过了列宁的陵墓，从手握钢枪的卫兵身旁跑过，疑心他们会不会端起手中的枪，瞄准——射击。

然后，我停下了脚步。发现我已经来到了红场的尽头。

在那里，已无路可逃。

32　象征

小提琴象征着卓越、高雅和深邃。可是对露露来说，小提琴却伴随着"压抑"，她把这种"压抑"也传给了我。

　　每个家庭都拥有一些象征意义的东西：经常前往度假的位于乡村的一个湖，爷爷的勋章，安息日的晚餐。而在我们家里，小提琴则是一个象征之物。

　　于我而言，与购物中心、众所周知的可口可乐、青少年服饰和粗俗的消费主义相比，小提琴象征着卓越、高雅和深邃。与轻轻松松地听iPod不同，拉小提琴很难，它需要专注、精准和对音乐作出诠释。就拿小提琴本身来说，它打磨得平滑光亮的木质琴身、精雕细刻的琴头、用硬马鬃制作的琴弓、精美的琴桥和发音点，既精致、微妙，又难以驾驭。

　　在我眼里，小提琴象征着对等级、标准和专业技巧的尊敬。那些对这种尊敬知之甚深并能够传授他人的人，那些能够演绎小提琴的真谛并能够感染他人的人，那些像我这样送孩子去学习音乐的父母，对此也会秉持同样的看法。

音乐亦是书写历史的符号。中国人的音乐造诣还没有达到西方古典音乐的高度，中国乐坛还未能产生超越贝多芬第九交响曲的杰作，但是中国传统的音乐深深地植根于灿烂的华夏文明。与孔夫子有关的七弦琴至少已有 2 500 年的历史，它被尊为圣人的乐器；而唐朝的伟大诗人则令它余音缭绕、千古流芳。

最重要的是，小提琴象征着一种掌控的力量。它避免一代不如一代的堕落、解决兄弟姐妹因在家里的排行不同而导致的差异，它帮助人们把握自己的命运，引导孩子们找到始终奋发向上的途径。

为什么移民的第三代只能够弹弹吉他或敲敲鼓？为什么第二个孩子不出意料地在学校里不那么守规矩，也不太成功？与家里最大的孩子相比，他们为什么更容易被社会所同化？简而言之，超越这些现象，小提琴象征着中国养育模式的成功。

可是对露露来说，小提琴却伴随着"压抑"。

当我缓缓地穿过俄罗斯的红场，我意识到小提琴对我来说，也成为了一种压抑的象征。

我曾经坐在家门前思考露露与小提琴的关系。在最后一分钟，我第一次对强烈要求露露坚持练习小提琴的做法产生了怀疑。想想在数不清的时间和岁月中，我付出了多少努力，经历了多少争斗，体验了多少恼怒，又忍受了多少痛苦……这到底是为了什么？我同时也明白了对未来，我到底最为担心的又是什么。

我还想到，我此时此刻的焦虑一定与西方父母相似，这也是他们常常让孩子放弃高难度乐器练习的原因。你为什么要折磨自己并为难孩子呢？

这样做有何意义？假如孩子不喜欢甚至讨厌做某事，强迫她去做又有什么好处呢？然而，我同时也十分清楚，作为一个中国妈妈，我很难认同这样的思维方式。

可是现在，我回到了口香糖百货商场旁的咖啡馆，服务员和那里的客人甚至尴尬地避免直视我的眼睛。

"露露，"我说，"你赢了，战斗结束了，我们放弃你的小提琴练习吧！"

33 向"西"走

为了在星期六早晨能够去打网球，露露决定辞去管弦乐队首席小提琴手的职务。这个决定让我在每一秒钟都感到撕心裂肺的痛。

我的父亲（摄于20世纪70年代初）

我没有虚张声势。

过去，我总是与露露处于战争的边缘；但这一次，我是认真的。虽然我还不能确认我为什么会这样做。或许是因为我最终允许自己对露露无法动摇的力量作出让步，即便是我极为痛苦地不认同她的选择；也可能是因为美文，在那些令人绝望的日子里，看着她在死亡线上苦苦挣扎，认清对她来说什么是重要的，这一切令我们所有人都感到震撼。

也可能是我母亲促使我作出这样的决定。对我来说，她是一位典型的中国妈妈。长大后，在她的眼里，什么事情对她来说都觉得不够好。（比如，她会说："你说你得到了第一，但实际上你只是并列第一，是吗？"也就是说，即便对"第一"她也能挑出"毛病"来。）她常常和美音一起练钢琴，一天三小时，直到老师轻声地告诉她，这样练习会超过自己的极限，产生过度疲劳。甚至在我做了大学教授，邀请她参加我的某些讲座时，在座的每个人都说我做得很棒，她却总是作出令人痛苦的一语中的的评论。（"有时候，你太兴奋了，说话像打机关枪。试着保持冷静，你会做得更好。"）

是的，我的中国妈妈很久以前就警告过我，有些方法对露露不起作用。"每个孩子都是独特的，你得调整对露露的教育方法，就像我不得不学会调整对待美音的方式一样。你要作出改变，美儿。"母亲说。"看看你爸爸发生了什么变化。"她又补充道。

那么，关于我父亲，我想是该透彻地探讨一些相关的问题了。

我经常给杰德讲述我自己和其他华裔孩子的例子，它们最终证明中国孩子是如何看待父母在家里的权威的。尽管父母对他们有着近乎残酷的要求、口头的辱骂和对孩子内心渴望的漠视，可中国孩子最终对父母都充满了爱慕和尊敬，并希望在父母年老时照顾他们。杰德在开始时总是问我：

"你对自己的父亲怎么看，美儿？"而我从未给出过令他满意的回答。

我父亲在他的家庭里被看做不务正业的"坏小子"，他的母亲不喜欢他，待他也不够公正。在他的家里，将孩子们进行比较是件司空见惯的事，比较的结果当然对父亲不利。我父亲是六个兄弟姐妹中的老四，他总是吃亏。其他家庭成员对经商很感兴趣，而他却对科学知识和急速赛车情有独钟。8岁那年，他甚至自个儿折腾出了一个无线电台。与兄弟姐妹相比较，父亲是家里不守规矩、敢于冒险和桀骜不驯的孩子。说得婉转一点儿，他的母亲没有尊重他的选择，没有珍视他独特的个性，或者也未能关心他的自尊——这些所有的要点，都是西方教育经中的老生常谈。结果，我父亲讨厌他的家庭，因为它让他感到窒息和备受打击。后来，当他一有机会，便离开家走得远远的，再也没有回头。

我父亲的故事说明了什么，是我从来就不想思考的问题。父亲成长的个案，区别于中国的养育方式大获成功的普遍案例。这说明中国的养育方式并不总是拥有完美的结局，我父亲就是其中不完美的一个。他很少与他的母亲进行交谈，除了他感到愤怒的时候，他从未想起过自己的母亲。在我奶奶的晚年生活中，这个家庭在我父亲的心目中好像完全就不存在。

这让我想到，我不能失去露露，没有什么比这更重要了。

因此，我做了我能想到的最"西化"的事情：我给了她选择的自由。我告诉她，她可以根据自己的意愿放弃小提琴练习，然后做她自己喜欢的事情。比如在那个时段，她着迷于打网球。

一开始，露露以为这是我设下的一个圈套。因为多年来，我们俩在对立中斗智斗勇、大打精心策划的心理战，她自然对我的网开一面满腹狐疑。但是当她发现我是认真的，她的回答反而令我大吃一惊。

"我不想放弃，"她说，"我热爱小提琴，我绝对不会放弃它。"

"哎，拜托啦！"我摇着头说，"别让我们再次陷入对立的恶性循环。"

"我没打算放弃小提琴，"露露重复道，"我只是不想为此付出如此多的精力。在我的生活中，拉小提琴不是我的主要目标。是你为我选择了它，不是我自己。"

后来发生的事实证明，"不需要付出太多精力进行强化训练"是露露的基本要求，可是对我来说，却是令我心碎并意味深长的事情。

首先，为了在星期六的早晨能够去打网球，露露决定辞去管弦乐队首席小提琴手的职务。这个决定让我在每一秒钟都感到撕心裂肺的痛。看着露露在坦格尔伍德的音乐会上作为管弦乐队的首席小提琴手演奏了最后一首曲子，我几乎流下了热泪。

其次，露露决定不再在每个星期天到纽约去上小提琴课。这样，我们就不再去田中直子小姐的音乐室现场——那可是聆听朱利亚音乐学院名师指点的宝贵机会。这样的决定让我难以接受！

为了弥补这个巨大的损失，我在纽黑文为露露找到一个小提琴老师。经过长时间的商谈，我们最后达成协议，没有我的训导、没有定期给予指导的教练，露露将自己练习小提琴，每天坚持半个小时——我知道，要使露露保持高水平的小提琴技艺，这点儿时间远远不够。

在露露作出决定的最初几个星期，我在我们家房子的周围闲荡，就像一个失去工作、没有生活目标的可怜人。

最近在一次午餐时，我遇到了耶鲁大学教授伊丽莎白·亚历山大，她曾经在奥巴马的就职典礼上朗读她创作的诗歌。我告诉她，我非常钦佩她的工作。我们也进行了短暂的交谈。

然后她说："等一等——我想我知道你。你是不是有两个在社区音乐学校学习的女儿？你就是那两个令人难以置信的音乐天才的母亲？"

原来伊丽莎白也有两个孩子，比我的孩子小一点儿。他们同样参加社区音乐学校的训练，并曾经好几次听过索菲娅和露露的演奏。"你的女儿真是令人称奇呀！"她说。

要是在过去，我会谦虚地说："噢，她们其实还不够好。"然后，强烈希望她继续询问，这样，我就能向她介绍索菲娅和露露最新的艺术造诣。可是现在，我只是摇了摇头。

"她们依然在练习吗？"伊丽莎白继续问道，"我在社区音乐学校看不到她们的身影了。"

"我的大女儿仍然在练钢琴，"我回答道，"可我的小女儿——那个小提琴手，已不再认真地进行专业的练习了。"我说出的这句话好似一把尖刀直插我的心脏，"她宁愿去打网球。"即使她的网球水平在新英格兰能排到第10 000名，我想，那就是10 000名中的最后一名呀！

"噢，不！"伊丽莎白叹道，"这太可惜了！我记得她的天赋如此出众，她曾经激励了我的两个小家伙。"

"这是她自己的决定，"我说，"练小提琴要花的时间太多了。你知道，13岁青春期的孩子是什么样子。"我暗自思忖，我原来是位中国妈妈，现在也变成了西方妈妈，多么失败呀！

我咽下了我刚才想到的话。

我让露露按照自己的兴趣、迈出自己的步伐、作出自己的决定——去打网球。我记得她第一次申请参加美国网球协会新手锦标赛时，她回家时的心情好极了，显然受益于大量分泌的肾上腺素。

"你今天怎么样？"我问。

"噢，我输了——但这是我第一次参赛，我的比赛策略完全不对路。"

"比分是多少？"

"0比6，"露露说，"和我对阵的女孩真的很棒。"

我暗自在想，要是那个女孩很棒，她为什么还要参加新手锦标赛？可我却大声地说："比尔·克林顿最近告诉耶鲁大学的学生，你只能在你热爱的事情上做到出类拔萃。那么，你对网球的热爱将会让你受益无穷。"

可是在另一个方面，虽然你钟情于某些事情，可是假如你不去努力，"热爱"这种情感并不能保证你就一定会所向披靡、拥抱成功。要知道，大多数人都曾在自己热爱的事情上折戟沉沙！

34   故事的结局

在为大法官们演奏的宴会上，索菲娅的钢琴曲技惊四座；网球场上，
教练赞扬露露是那种"不付出110%的努力，就绝不会善罢甘休的小姑娘"。

网球场上的露露——那就是我的女儿
(Peter Z. Mahakian)

最近，我们在家里举办了一个正式的晚宴，招待来自世界各地最高法院的大法官。

作为一名耶鲁法学院的教授，最让人激动不已的事情是有机会与一些令人敬畏的人物会面——他们中不乏当今最伟大的法学家。10年以来，耶鲁的全球宪政研讨会吸引了来自世界几十个国家的杰出法官，包括来自美国最高法院的斯蒂芬·布雷耶法官和安东尼·肯尼迪法官。

为了活跃晚宴的气氛，我们邀请了索菲娅的钢琴教授杨伟毅，前来表演他为耶鲁著名的霍洛维茨钢琴系列而准备的部分节目。伟毅也慷慨地建议他的年轻学生索菲娅参加演出。为了能让演出生动有趣，老师和学生将同台表演一首二重奏——"和巴托"，该乐曲选自法国作曲家德布西的《娇小的套房》(*Petite Suite*)。

为此，我兴奋得难以自持并有些紧张。我和颜悦色地对索菲娅说："不要疏忽大意，你所有的努力都会体现在你的表演中。大法官们并不是到纽黑文来观看一个高中生的才艺表演的，如果你不是以超水平的发挥表现完美，就是我们对他们的大不敬。现在，去坐到钢琴前，别离开，好好练吧！"

我想，我当时的口吻俨然还是一位中国妈妈。

在接下来的几个星期里，我们就像重返卡内基音乐厅一样进行精心的准备，唯一不同寻常的是，索菲娅几乎都是独自进行练习。过去，我会让自己沉浸在她弹奏的音乐里——法国音乐大师圣桑作曲的《热情的快板》(*Allegro Appassionato*)和波兰音乐家肖邦创作的《即兴幻想曲》(*Fantaisie Impromptu*)……可是如今，索菲娅已经长大了，不再需要我的陪练了。她清楚地知道自己应该做什么，我只会偶尔从厨房里或楼梯上高声发表自己的评论。与此同时，杰德和我把所有的家具都搬出了客厅，只留下一架钢琴。

我卖力地擦洗地板，并租借了供50位宾客使用的椅子。

表演的那天晚上，索菲娅身穿一袭红色的长裙，显得格外娇艳。当她走上来向观众鞠躬致礼时，恐惧便一把抓住了我。实际上我在她演奏整个波洛内茨舞曲的过程中紧张得浑身冰凉；我无法真正地欣赏圣桑的乐曲，尽管索菲娅的演奏几乎是天衣无缝。这首曲子意味着纯粹的艺术享受，可紧张得无法感受它迷人魅力的我却一个劲儿地在想：索菲娅能将她的曲子弹奏得星光闪烁、清澈见底吗？她会不会因练习过度而导致双手疲劳无力？我不得不克制自己不要做出坐立不安、自哼自唱——这些听女孩们演奏一首高难度曲目时我的习惯性动作。

当听索菲娅演奏最后一首肖邦的《即兴幻想曲》时，一切都改变了。处于某种难以言表的原因，我的紧张状态悄然消失了，紧绷的神经松弛了，紧咬的牙关张开了——我用全部精力注意到，这首曲子真的属于她！

我看到，索菲娅站起来优雅地向听众鞠躬，呈上她鲜花般绚丽的笑靥。我想，那是我的女孩——幸福的女孩，是美妙的音乐让她沉浸在甜蜜的幸福中。

这一刻我忽然明白，她过去付出的一切都是值得的！

索菲娅赢得了听众三次热烈张扬的掌声。此后，法官们——包括许多过去被我顶礼膜拜的人物，都对索菲娅赞不绝口。一个说索菲娅的演奏让人感受到崇高，而他愿意坐下来听上一个通宵。另一个则坚持说索菲娅应该去追求专业的钢琴生涯，否则浪费了她的音乐天赋将是一种犯罪。

此外，令人惊讶的是，许多身为父母的法官，也向我提出了一些个性化的问题，包括："在培养孩子方面你有什么秘诀？你是否认为得益于亚洲家庭文化的熏陶，才培养出了如此优秀的音乐家？""请告诉我，索菲娅是因为热爱钢琴艺术而自己坚持练习，还是你强制性地要求她进行练习？而我从来不可能让我的孩子练琴超过15分钟。""你的另一个女儿情况怎么样？我听说她是个传奇般的小提琴手，我们下一次能听到她的演奏吗？"

我告诉他们："我正在努力地完成一本书，它回答了你们所有的问题。而我会在成书后送给你们。"

差不多就在索菲娅为法官们奉上精彩的钢琴演奏前后，我驾车一个小时，到康涅狄格州一个荒凉的网球场去接露露。

"猜猜我要告诉你什么消息，妈妈——我赢了！"露露欣然地说。

"赢了什么？"我问。

"这次的锦标赛呀。"露露答道。

"什么意思？"

"我赢了三场比赛，最后还打败了种子选手。她可是新英格兰的第60名，我简直不敢相信我能搞定她！"

露露的话让我大吃一惊。

我还是一个小姑娘的时候就开始打网球，不过常常是与家里人或学校的朋友在一起，只是为了好玩。长大后，我也试着参加过几次比赛，但很快就发现我无法适应比赛的压力。因此，打网球就成为一项家庭的活动。杰德和我让索菲娅和露露都参加了网球训练课，但我们从未对她们的网球造诣抱任何希望。

"你还是在打初级水平的比赛吗？"我问露露，"就是最低的水平？"

"是的。"她和颜悦色地说。自从我把选择的权利交给她自己，我们的关系就大大改善了。这样做给我带来的负面的痛苦，对她来说却似乎成了正面的收获，她变得更加耐心、更加友善。"我很快就要尝试高一级水平的比赛，我肯定要吃败仗，但是我想试一试，这样做一定很好玩。"

然后，我出乎意料地听到露露说："我很想念管弦乐队，真的！"

在接下来的6个星期里，露露又赢得了三场比赛的胜利。在最后的两场中，我亲临现场为她助阵。让我极为震惊的是，她在球场上东奔西跑，简直就像一团燃烧的火；她的击球是那样有力，她的注意力是那样集中；每一个球她都认真对待，从来不曾放弃！

露露的网球水平日益提升，她遭遇的比赛对手便越发强硬。在一次比赛中，她输给了一个块头比她大一倍的女孩。下场时，她仍然优雅地微笑着。回到车里，她对我说："下次我一定要打败她！现在，我的技术还不够好——但是，用不了多长时间……"然后，她问我能不能为她申请额外的网球训练课程。

在接下来的训练课上，我看到露露极为专注和执著地训练自己的反手球，这种态势我从来不曾见过。课后，她问我能不能给她多多"喂球"，这样她就可以反复练习了。于是，我们又增加了一个小时的训练。在开车回家的路上，我告诉她，我感觉她的反手球看起来已经大有改进。可她说："不，还不够好，还是很糟糕。我们明天能不能预订球场再练一练？"

"她提高球艺的心情如此迫切，"我暗暗在想，"如此……强烈。"

我与露露的网球教练进行了交流。"对露露来说，她已经不可能真的练成优秀的网球选手，是这样吗？我的意思是，她已经13岁了，或许晚了10年。"我还听说那些知名的网球学校差不多已经人满为患，连4岁的孩子也配备了专门的私人教练，"而且，她像我一样，个头也太矮了。"

"重要的是露露热爱网球这项运动，"教练的回答很"美国"，"此外，她有着令人难以置信的职业信条——我从未见过谁能像她这样提高得如此迅速。她的确是一个出众的孩子，你们夫妇俩一定在露露身上倾注了难以想象的心血。她是那种不付出110%的努力，就绝不会善罢甘休的小姑娘。而且，她总是那么乐观向上、彬彬有礼。"

"你一定是在开玩笑吧！"我嘴上这么说，可心里却像吃了蜜糖一样甜。

露露在网球场上的表现是不是体现了中国传统美德的良性循环？我过去让她练小提琴，是不是一个错误的选择？与保龄球相比，网球在社会上是非常高雅并受人尊重的体育项目。张德培就是著名的华裔网球选手。

我也开始热身准备了。

我进一步熟悉了美国网球协会的诸多规则、程序和全国排名系统，拜访教练，并给我们所在地区最好的网球训练中心打电话。

一天，露露无意中听到我在打电话。"你在干什么？"她问道。当我向她解释我正在作一个小小的研究，她突然生气了。"不，妈妈……不！"她激动地说，"请不要像毁了小提琴一样毁了我的网球。"

这么说的确很伤人，我不想再与她争论。

第二天，我想再试一试。"露露，在马萨诸塞州有一个地方……"

"不，妈妈……请别再为我操这个心。"露露说，"我自己可以搞定这些事，我不想把你牵扯进来。"

"露露，我们需要为你的实力找到突破的渠道……"

"妈妈，我自己会这样做的。我仰望你，听你的说教已经多达100万次了，我不希望你控制我的生活。"

我凝视着眼前的露露，想起了一些往事。

人人都说露露长得很像我，我很高兴听到这话，可是露露却极力否认。她3岁那年，站在寒冬的室外倔犟地不肯低头的情景，仿佛浮现在我的眼前。"好一个不屈不挠的女孩！"我想。而且直到今天，她一点儿也没有改变。

然而，不管她在哪里，她最终都能为你带来惊喜。

"好吧，露露，我接受你的建议。"我说，"看看妈妈是多么通情达理，要在这个世界上走向成功，你总得作出调整。这正是我擅长的事情，你应该向我学习。"

可是我并不是真的打算放弃。虽然我的行动策略要进行一些重大的修改，但我依然身处战场。我有了新的认同感和开放的心态。有一天，露露告诉我，以后她练小提琴的时间可能会更少了，因为她想花时间投入一些她更感兴趣的事情，比如写作和"即兴表演"。

我没有为她的想法感到讶异，而是表现出支持的、向前看的态度。从长远来看，虽然即兴表演似乎不那么"中国"，并与古典音乐背道而驰，但露露可以进行滑稽表演秀的模仿，它的确也是一门技能。我同时也心存念想，希望露露不会远离她热爱的音乐。期盼将来的某一天，她会回到属于她的小提琴的世界——这一天也许不会太遥远。

那段时间的每个周末，我都驾车送露露去网球赛场，在那儿看她打球。最近，她又作为初中唯一的学生参加了高中篮球队。由于露露坚持不需要我发表建议或批评，我就适当地客串了一把间谍，并展开了游击战。我暗地里向露露的教练灌输一些想法，给教练发送短信：既提问题，也提建议。然后将短信及时删除，这样露露就不会发现了。

有时在露露最无防备的时候，比如早餐时或晚上我对她说"晚安"前，我会突然大喊"在凌空扣杀时多一点儿旋转"或者"发上旋球时右脚不要移动"！而露露立刻会用双手蒙住自己的耳朵来表示反感，我们也许会"短兵相接"，争辩一番，但我会说出我的看法。

我心如明镜的是，她知道我的话句句在理。

尾 声

全家福（2010年）

老虎活力四射、大胆鲁莽，即使身处危险也浑然不觉。

但它们善于积累经验、获得新的能量和强大的实力。

(Peter Z. Mahakian)

这本书的写作始于 2009 年 6 月 29 日。那一天，我们从俄罗斯返回纽黑文。那时候，我并不知道我为什么要写这本书，或这本书将如何结尾。然而，即便在写作时我常常会有作家忽然文思枯竭的通病，但这一次，我的所思所想却如潺潺流淌的泉水，一路叮咚……

本书第一部分和第二部分的写作我只用了 8 个星期的时间，第三部分却写得很痛苦。本书的每一页，我都请杰德和女儿们分享。

"让我们一起来写这本书。"我对索菲娅和露露说。

"不，我们不能。"她们异口同声地说，"妈妈，这是你的书，不是我们的。"

露露甚至还贸然地加上一句："我敢肯定，无论如何，这本书写的都是你。"

可是随着时间的流逝，女孩们读到的篇章越多，她们的贡献就越多。事实上，写作的过程充满了自我的剖析和诊疗——这个西方的概念，还是她们提醒我的。

漫长的岁月中，我遗忘了许多事情，有好的，也有坏的，孩子们和杰德帮助我唤起了那些尘封的记忆。为了把所有的片段拼接在一起，我整理了年代久远的电子邮件、文档、音乐演出的节目单和相册。在这个过程中，杰德和我常常沉浸在浓浓的怀旧之情中难以释怀。

仿佛就在昨天，索菲娅还只是一个小小的婴孩；可今天，她还有一年就要走进大学的校门了。而索菲娅和露露则发现，她们曾经是多么美丽可爱的小女孩！

别误会我的意思：写这本书其实一点儿也不容易。在我们家，没有什么事可以与"容易"比肩而行、称兄道弟。我不得不写下无数的草稿、反

复修改，以化解女孩们的反对。关于杰德，我不能写得太多，因为他还有
另外一本书要撰写，那才真正是他自己的故事秀。一些部分在让索菲娅和
露露双双都满意前，我不得不重写了差不多20遍。有好几次，姐妹俩中的
一个在阅读了一个章节的文字后，会突然间流着泪摔门而去。或者，我会
得到她们一个简短的评论："这段好棒啊，妈，好玩死了。""我就是不知道
你在说什么，这肯定说的不是我们家的生活。"

"哦，不！"有一次露露大哭道，"难道我应该是傻了吧唧的普希金？
而索菲娅是什么都一学就会的聪明的可可？"我说可可并不聪明，也不是
学什么会什么。我向女孩们保证，不会再用狗狗来比喻她们了。

"那么，养狗狗的目的是什么？"索菲娅问得很有逻辑性，"它们为什
么要出现在书里？"

"我也不知道，"我承认，"可我知道在我们家里，它们很重要。因为狗
肉也是中国人餐桌上的佳肴，中国妈妈在美国养狗，本来就不大对劲。"

还有一次，露露抱怨："我觉得你夸大了索菲娅和我的不同，以使这本
书读起来更有趣味。你让我看起来就像一个典型的、叛逆的美国青少年，
而我与这种形象甚至毫不沾边。"与此同时，索菲娅则抗议道："我认为你
对露露的毛病轻描淡写，让她看起来好似一个天使。"

自然，两个女孩都感觉这本书好像亏欠了她们。

"你应该明确地将这本书献给露露，"有一次，索菲娅故显大度地说，"她
显然是该书的女主角，栩栩如生、华丽耀眼。而我是乏味透顶的那一个，
读者会喝倒彩的。"

从露露那里，我们则听到："也许你应该给自己的书取名为'完美女孩
与食肉恶魔'，或者是'为什么中国家庭的老大更优秀'，这难道不是这本

书的全部内容吗？"

夏日的时光悄然流逝，而女孩们对我的烦扰依然不肯消停。

"这本书你打算如何结尾呀？妈妈，它会是一个欢乐的圆满结局吗？"

我的回答差不多总是："这取决于你们俩呀！不过，我估计它的结尾很可能是悲剧式的。"

好几个月过去了，可我还是没有考虑好怎样为这本书收尾。一天，我突然跑过去向女儿们宣布："我想好结尾了！我即将完成这本书。"

女儿们非常兴奋。"那么，你的结尾是什么样子的？"索菲娅问道，"你要表现的重点是什么？"

"我决定采取一种混合的方法，"我说，"孩子在18岁前，按照中国的方法为他们构筑自信，并认识走向卓越的价值；18岁后再采用西方的方法，让每一个个体找到属于他们自己的路。我想这样可以两全其美。"

"等等……要到18岁？"索菲娅惊讶地问道，"这不是一种混合的方法，那是将中国式的养育方法贯穿孩子整个的童年和青少年！"

"我认为你说得过于严重了，索菲娅。"

不过，我回头还是东修修、西补补地进行了修改。终于，有一天——确切地说，是昨天，我问女孩们："你们认为这本书该怎样收尾？"

"这么说吧，"索菲娅说，"在这本书里，你是想对读者说真话，还是只想讲述一个好听的故事？"

"当然是说真话。"我答道。

"这就太难了，因为真实的事情一直处于变化之中。"索菲娅说。

"不会的，"我说，"我的记忆力很好，记得很多真实发生的事情。"

"那你为什么还要不断地修改书的结尾呢？"索菲娅又问。

"因为她不知道她到底想说什么。"露露自作聪明地来了个抢答。

"完完全全地描述真实是不可能的，"索菲娅说，"你遗漏了太多的事实，这就是说，没有人能真正地了解全部的事实真相。例如，人人都会以为我对中国的养育方式逆来顺受，可我并不是这样。我伴随它前行，只是出于我自己的选择。"

"在你很小的时候肯定不是这样。"露露反驳说，"年幼的时候，妈妈从来就不给我们选择的机会。如果不是这样，你会愿意连续练琴五六个小时吗？"

"选择……我不知道，假如一切都归结为……"我说，"西方家庭的教育观念相信要给孩子选择的权利；中国家庭的教育方式则截然不同。我过去常常和婆婆逗乐，说要给你爸爸一次选择去上小提琴课的权利。当然，他的选择是不去。但是现在，露露，我想如果当初我没有强行要求你去朱利亚音乐学院试音，或每天练好几个小时小提琴，谁知道情况会是什么样呢？也许你依然喜欢小提琴，或者我让你选择自己喜欢的乐器，或者什么乐器你都不会喜欢。毕竟，对你没有选择学练小提琴的爸爸来说，他今天的情况也还不错。"

"我知道你要说这太显老套，"露露说，"但我还是要说，我很高兴你坚持让我去练习小提琴，我一直都酷爱小提琴；我甚至也为你让我练习指数题而开心，当然还包括每天花两个小时学习中文。"

"真的？"我问道，"现在回过头来思考这些问题，我认为这些选择真的很棒，即便是几乎所有的人都担心你和索菲娅会在妈妈的'强权政治'下造成永久性的心理损伤。你知道，关于什么对孩子好、什么不好，那些西方父母同样也有自己的'路线方针'。我对这些情况想得越多，就越不相信他们真的作出了什么选择。他们只是做了一些人人都在做的事情，他们也不会对任何事情问一问'为什么'，这应该是西方人最擅长的事情了。他们只是一直在反复强调，'你得给孩子们追求最爱的自由'。而孩子们的'最爱'，很可能就是一头扎进Facebook，一连10个小时泡在那里，完全是在浪费时间，或者是随心所欲地吃进大量令人恶心的垃圾食品！我一直在说，这个国家正在直线式下降！难怪西方的父母在老年时被赶进养老院！你们俩最好不要把我塞进一处这样的地方，我也不想在我还没有断气时被拔掉输氧管。"

"别激动，妈妈。"露露说。

"当孩子们做什么事情失败了，西方父母不是告诉他们要更加努力，他们所做的第一件事情是提起诉讼！"

"你到底在说谁呀？"索菲娅问道。

"我并不想在政治上对那些显然无聊乏味，而且并不是植根于历史的西方社会的规范品头论足。但无论如何我想知道，孩子们的'玩伴聚会'起源何在？你认为我们美国的开国元勋在孩提时代可曾参加过'在别人家过夜'的活动？其实，我倒认为美国的开国元勋拥有中国人的价值观。"

"我不想打断你，妈妈，但是……"

"本·富兰克林说过——'如果你热爱生命，那就永远不要浪费时间。'托马斯·杰斐逊说——'我是幸运的忠实信徒，我越是努力地工作，拥有的幸运就越多。'亚历山大·汉密尔顿还说——'不要成为悲观主义者。'这些闪光的言论与中国人的思维方式完全一致。"

"妈妈，假如开国元勋以这样的方式来思维，那么，那就是美国的思维方式呀！"索菲娅说，"此外，我认为你或许是在断章取义。"

"那你去查一查呀！"我对她说。

我妹妹美文的身体状况现在大有改善。生活对她来说，毫无疑问是艰难的。她依然尚未走出困境，但她是一个英雄，气度非凡地承受了一切痛苦和不幸。她昼夜不停地投入自己的研究工作，一篇接一篇地撰写学术论文，同时尽量抽出时间和孩子们待在一起。

我禁不住时常在想，从美文的疾病我们应当悟出某些人生哲理。生命是如此短暂，如此脆弱。毫无疑问，我们每个人都应当抓住每一次呼吸、每一个短暂的瞬间，去体验更多、得到更多。这是不是意味着我们要拥有最充实、最丰满的生命呢？

我们每个人都不可能长生不老。那么，我们会以什么样的方式走完自己的生命之路呢？

我刚刚告诉杰德，我想再养一条狗。

致 谢

我的母亲和父亲——没人能比他们更相信我。对他们，我怀着深深的钦佩和感激。

我要向许多人道谢：

索菲娅和露露——给予我快乐的源泉、令我骄傲的作品，我生命中的喜悦。

我那些与众不同的姐妹——美夏、美文和美音。

特别是我的丈夫杰德·鲁宾费尔德（Jed Rubenfeld）。25年来，他阅读了我写下的所有文字。得益于他的仁慈和天才，我的幸运令人难以置信。

下列亲爱的朋友们，我向你们独立的见解、无价的支持表示诚挚的感谢！

亚历克西斯·康斯坦特（Alexis Contant）、乔丹·斯莫利尔（Jordan Smoller）、西尔维亚（Sylvia）、沃尔特·奥斯特尔（Walter Austerer）、苏珊（Susan）、保罗·菲德勒（Paul Fiedler）、马里纳·圣地利（Marina Santilli）、安妮·戴利（Anne Dailey）、安妮·托夫勒米尔（Anne Tofflemire）、莎拉·比尔斯顿（Sarah Bilston）、丹尼尔·马科维特斯（Daniel Markovits）、凯瑟琳·布朗－多拉托（Kathleen Brown-Dorato）、以及亚历克斯·多拉托（Alex Dorato）。同时，我也要感谢伊丽莎白·亚

265

历山大（Elizabeth Alexander）、巴巴拉·罗森（Barbara Rosen）、埃米莉·贝兹伦（Emily Bazelon），以及安妮·维特（Annie Witt）的慷慨鼓励。

我要感谢的人当然还包括社区音乐学校的米歇尔·津盖尔（Michelle Zingale）、卡尔·舒加特（Carl Shugart）、菲奥娜·默里（Fiona Murray）、乔迪·罗特斯切（Jody Rowitsch）、亚历克西斯·津盖尔（Alexis Zingale），以及霍英英（Ying Ying Huo）、黄玉亭（Yu-ting Huang）、南希·靳（Nancy Jin）、基旺·纳姆（Kiwon Nahm）和亚历山德拉·纽曼（Alexandra Newman）；还有杰出的田中直子（Naoko Tanaka）和阿尔迈塔·瓦莫斯（Almita Vamos）；尤其是我的好朋友、无与伦比的杨伟毅（Wei-Yi Yang）。是你们把对音乐的爱，深深地种在了索菲娅和露露的心里！

感谢索菲娅和露露在福特学校的优秀、聪慧和富有爱心的老师们，尤其是朱迪·卡思伯森（Judy Cuthbertson）和克利夫·萨林（Cliff Sahlin）。

感谢在网球训练场上给予露露指导和帮助的亚历克斯·多拉托（Alex Dorato）、克里斯蒂安·阿普尔曼（Christian Appleman）和斯塔查·方塞卡（Stacia Fonseca）。

感谢我的学生杰奎琳·埃塞（Jacqueline Esai）、罗南·法罗（Ronan Farrow）、休·古安（Sue Guan）、斯蒂芬妮·李（Stephanie Lee）、吉姆·利戈坦伯格（Jim Ligtenberg）、贾斯廷·罗（Justin Lo）、彼得·麦克里戈特（Peter McElligott）、卢克·诺里斯（Luke Norris）、阿米莉亚·罗尔斯（Amelia Rawls）、娜比哈·赛义德（Nabiha Syed），以及叶琳娜·泰特尔鲍姆（Elina Tetelbaum）。

最后，我还要衷心感谢我所能找到的最好的出版经纪人、令人称奇的蒂娜·班尼特（Tina Bennett），我的编辑和出版人、天才而卓越的安·戈多弗（Ann Godoff）以及帮我更好地完善这本书的赵芳和孙子谏。

慢养：给孩子一个好性格

黑幼龙　全家合著

中信出版社2009年6月出版

　　华文卡内基创办人黑幼龙夫妇及黑家四个孩子联手创作。最好读的育儿经历，最励志的成长故事，最温暖的家庭情感，马英九、金韵蓉倾力推荐。

　　孩子长大后，最怀念父母的不是汽车、房子、财产，甚至不是念最好的学校。他们最怀念父母的是，父母帮助他们培养了好性格。本书以"华文卡内基之父"黑幼龙四个性格各异的子女的生动成长经历，讲述了孩子的"好性格"是怎样"慢养"出来的。

　　发自内心的自信，良好的人际沟通，是父母送给孩子最好的礼物。作为父母，最应该做的就是认识到孩子的唯一和独特，以耐心和包容，陪伴他们慢慢长大。

慢养2：给青少年一个好性格

黑幼龙　著

中信出版社2010年10月出版

　　继《慢养：给孩子一个好性格》之后，黑幼龙先生又一力作。书中引入卡内基经典原则，通过自信、抗压、热忱、沟通、人际关系、影响力6个篇章，辅以卡内基青少年班学员的真实成长案例，为父母及青少年厘清思路，找到提高情商、性格塑造的关键入口！书中案例真实呈现了青少年性格形成过程中可喜的变化，从不知所措的困惑，到有能力解决问题，而这一切变化都得益于卡内基所倡导的6种能力。每一个孩子都应该在青少年时期储备这样的能力，未来，他们才有机会赢得人生！

妈妈学校：合格妈妈的4堂必修课

[韩]徐亨淑　著

金吉文　译

中信出版社 2010年11月出版

　　我们每一个人都会怀着本能的爱，做自然的母亲。但一种成熟的母爱，必须经过培育才能发展起来。做妈妈是要靠后天的努力才能获得的一项技能，作为孩子的第一任老师，妈妈应该做更多的"职业"准备和培训。

妈妈学校：爱是慢半拍

[韩]徐亨淑　著

董小娇　译

中信出版社　2010年12月出版

　　想教出优秀的孩子，就要先成为一位好妈妈。学做好妈妈就像学做菜一样。熟悉了做妈妈的方法，教育孩子也会变得轻松。

　　妈妈的角色，不是干涉者，而是要学会在爱里等待，懂得包容，给孩子更多的支持与理解，与其勉强去改变孩子，不如先将自己塑造成孩子们成长中最需要的妈妈。

How to Build Wooden Gates *and* Picket Fences

How to Build Wooden Gates *and* Picket Fences

100 Classic Designs

Kevin Geist

STACKPOLE
BOOKS

Published by
STACKPOLE BOOKS
5067 Ritter Road
Mechanicsburg, PA 17055

Printed in the United States of America

10 9 8 7 6 5 4 3 2 1

First Edition

Plates on pages 13, 14, 15, and 204 are from *Early Illustrations and Views
of American Architecture* (Dover Publications, Inc., 1971).
Plates on pages 196–203, 205–207, and 214 are from *Combined Book of
Sash, Doors, Blinds* (Rand, McNally & Company, 1898).
Plates on pages 209 and 210 are from *Victorian Domestic Architecture
Plans and Details* (Dover Publications, 1987).
Plates on pages 211 and 212 are from *Architecture* (S. Bailey and Eager, 1868).
The plate on page 208 is from *Woodward's National Architect* (Geo. E.
Woodward, 1869).
The plate on page 213 is from *Pallister's New Cottage Homes and Details*
(Pallister, Pallister & Co., 1887).

Cover design by Kathleen D. Peters

Cover illustrations by Kevin Geist

Library of Congress Cataloging-in-Publication Data

Geist, Kevin.
    How to build wooden gates and picket fences : 100 classic designs
    Kevin Geist. — 1st ed.
      P.   cm.
    Includes index.
    ISBN 0-8117-3006-9
     1. Fences—Design and construction—Amateurs' manuals.
    2. Gates—Design and construction—Amateurs' manuals. I. Title.
TH4965.G45   1994   93-46302
717—dc20   CIP

*To my mother, Marilyn, with thanks for seeding me with the
inspiration to write this book*

*To my friend Tani Dean with thanks for reviewing and editing
the manuscript*

*To my wife, Mary, with special thanks for assisting me with the
photographs and editing and for her tireless support and patient
waiting through the process of creating this book*

Contents

Introduction

When I was looking for a book to help me construct a fence for my home, I found a number that told me how to make a fence. I wanted to see dozens of patterns that I could choose from, however, and only a few books contained more than a handful of picket- or grid-style fence patterns.

This book includes one hundred fence patterns from the eighteenth, nineteenth, and twentieth centuries. Each design has a brief description and a ratings section that will help you determine the level of privacy, security, and environmental buffering the fence will provide, as well as the ease of cutting and assembly. Many of the designs in this book are *very easy* and *easy*. If you want a more elaborate fence, designs with a *moderate* difficulty rating may take a little more time to cut or construct, but they should not be too difficult for even a first-time fence builder.

This book also guides you through the general construction steps for making decorative posts, gates, and each style of fence featured. In the Construction Techniques chapter, you will find out how to make beautiful fence accents like decoratively sawn pickets, ornamental rosettes, and finials to grace post tops.

Once you have selected a design, you may want to enlarge the pattern yourself. The simplest and most inexpensive way to alter the size of a pattern is to use a photocopier. Newer machines include a feature that reduces or enlarges. On some machines, the process might take two or more steps; just enlarge the enlargement until you get the size you want.

An alternative is to get a photomechanical transfer (PMT) made at a local printing shop. This photographic method can provide exact enlargement without any effort on your part, but does involve some expense. You could also use a drawing tool called a pantograph or the grid and dot-to-dot method frequently used by woodworkers.

If you do not wish to make the pattern yourself, traceable picket and finial patterns are available for sawn baluster and picket fence designs. See page 217 to order.

Making a Fence

Choosing a Beautiful and Functional Fence

EVERY ASPECT OF SELECTING YOUR FENCE SHOULD BE A THOUGHTFUL PROCESS. EVERYONE who constructs a fence will receive more than one blessing or malediction from it. Forethought and education will maximize your satisfaction and minimize your regrets.

FUNCTIONS

Give careful thought to *why* you want a fence. Write down the benefits you could receive from having a fence, and rank them by importance to you. Review the list a week later

Well-designed fences provide functional services and lend beauty to the homes they embrace.

Even a simple fence can enhance a home's appearance.

and see if you feel the ranking should be changed. Consider whether the following benefits are of high, moderate, or low importance to you.

Appearance

A fence can enhance a property's appearance by creating a sense of balance and stability. A house that may appear adrift in a sea of grass is given the appearance of being harbored and secured when contained by a fence. Homes that are close to the sidewalk appear to have more land associated with them when a fence separates them from the street. The fence may complement the structures on the property, possibly by using some of the architectural details in its own design. It harmonizes with the landscaping in some settings, serving as a backdrop for a bed of tulips or a support for climbing clematis or roses.

It enchants the eye with its rhythmic repetitions and symmetrical appearance. Moldings, rosettes, finials, and other detail work on the fence hold the viewer's attention and accentuate the simple repetition.

Boundaries

A fence benefits a property by marking its boundaries. Visually, it can create a sense of definition, showing which areas are inside and which are outside the property compound.

Fence barriers can also be used to separate the property into sections; for example, fenced areas might distinguish the rose garden, the dog run, and the area of the backyard used for the family's recreation.

The fence boundary also helps you control how people pass by your house. A fence can deter passers-by from deviating off the sidewalk and cutting across the corner of your yard. The fence openings will help visitors recognize the preferred methods of approach to your home.

Security

Undoubtedly, security was the primary reason the first fences were built. These fences protected the tribe, flock, and crops from predators, both animal and human. Early American pioneers built palisade fortresses that were crude, large-scale picket fences. These fences were a formidable barrier, and their sharp-pointed tops were difficult to climb and straddle.

Through the colonial, Early American, and Victorian periods, security fencing became more beautiful and more subtle. As rural areas became increasingly urbanized, the cruder branch-and-sapling fences were replaced by elegantly scrolling wrought iron and uniformly sculptured wood picket fencing.

These beautiful fences employed the same pointed tops to discourage climbing; how-

Fences clearly identify property boundaries and demonstrate preferred methods of approach.

ever, the height was reduced and spacing was placed between the pickets, making these fences easier to see over and through. This changed the security formula. Now would-be intruders could see into the yard, but homeowners and neighbors could also see them.

Good fencing was especially useful in town. Fences kept children in the courtyard, away from the dangers of bustling carriages and livestock on the way to market. They were also used to restrain and protect pets.

Almost any fence will increase your property's security. Even a small, easy-to-straddle fence suggests boundary limits. It states that you do not grant access to your property beyond the fence line, letting all intruders know that they are trespassing.

But to protect pets and children or to deter intruders, only certain types of fencing will function appropriately. It is virtually impossible to restrict cats. Most dogs, however, can be contained by a well-designed fence. Fencing to restrain pets must have the appropriate strength, density, and height to prevent the animals from breaking down, squeezing through, or leaping over the fence. Generally, the greater the height of the fence, the greater the security it will provide.

Fencing to protect children has the same density and height requirements as fencing for pets. But since children have the ability to climb, they are able to scale some types of fences, like post and rail, quite easily. Effective fencing for protecting children and securing against intruders must provide no toeholds. Horizontally placed infill, such as post

Fences have been used to provide protection for children and pets for hundreds of years.

Privacy fences act as screens for outdoor living areas.

and rail or horizontal spaced board fencing, acts as ladder rungs and facilitates climbing. Vertically placed board, picket, or pale fences are difficult to climb, especially if the pickets are attached to support stringers that are placed wide side to the infill and narrow side up.

Privacy

Have you ever been working in your garden and heard a passer-by point out the ripe tomato you missed? Has a neighbor ever left his lawn unmown the very weekend you were entertaining out-of-town guests? Doubtless you have, at least on occasion, had the desire for a privacy fence. We like to view our yards as our personal place where we can get a breath of fresh air, just muddle around, or coddle our loved ones.

Privacy fences can block out unsightly views and limit others' view to your personal outdoor living areas. To achieve a high degree of privacy, the fence must block visibility to the yard. An effective privacy fence is usually 6 feet high with tightly fit infill. Lattice and spaced pickets usually make poor privacy fences because they allow moderate visibility through the fence.

Privacy fences have a tendency to be bland in appearance, but you can compensate for this with the following techniques:

• Alternate boards of two or three different widths or heights.

• Decoratively cut board tops with designs that are simple and yet very appealing to the eye.

• Employ two shades of stain or paint to make an appealing contrast.

• Dress the area with shrubbery and flowering plants. The tall fencing will provide a beautiful backdrop.

A privacy fence may affect your property in several ways. It can significantly reduce the amount of sun that reaches the ground, thus limiting the types of plants that will thrive at the base of the fence.

Privacy fences, with their typically high walls, can give the yard a cramped, boxed-in look. This problem is not as noticeable in a large yard, but small yards will appear even smaller when surrounded by a high, solid fence. Additionally, privacy fences have large surfaces that will require up to four times more stain or paint than the average picket fence.

It is not usually necessary to surround your home and yard within a walled fortress. Your fence may be high on the sides where you need more privacy and lower on the sides where privacy is not an issue. Using this approach will allow you to deal with your privacy trouble spots without boxing in your entire yard and blocking out attractive views. If the transition between fence heights is a problem, consider planting trees and shrubs to camouflage that area.

A tall solid infill fence can buffer noise from an adjacent street.

Be well aware that many areas have zoning laws that apply to fence construction. These laws usually require fences to be less than 3 feet, 6 inches on the street side of a property and less than 6 feet high on all other sides of the property. Before constructing any fence, it is a good idea to discuss your plans with your local zoning code officer.

Buffering

For people living near heavily traveled roads, busy factories, or any other noisy, bustling area, noise pollution can cause great distress, especially when one is trying to enjoy an afternoon in the yard. Though a thick, high fence or wall may help buffer the noise, it is often difficult to create a fence that will eliminate or significantly reduce the noise level.

Even if a solid fence will not eliminate the noise, however, it may still reduce your distress. In addition to buffering the noise, it will hide the source of the noise from your view. Often the sight of the noise-causing menace can increase your disdain for the noise itself.

A fence may also serve as a buffer from snow or wind. Snow can present some difficulties. Solid fences generally tend to hold snow. If the fence holds the snow from drifting onto your driveway, this can be desirable. If a significant amount of snow drifts against the fence, however, some sections could topple. Also, fences buried under snow for long periods will decay more rapidly, since prolonged exposure to moisture speeds the decaying process. Spaced fencing will allow the wind to blow the snow through the fence and reduce this problem.

Total wind control is virtually impossible with a fence, although a spaced picket or solid wood fence will supply some wind buffering if it is not located too far from the area to be protected.

Keep in mind when building a fence that solid fences will allow only very limited sunlight on one or both sides of the fence. This may significantly limit your choice of plants that will grow along the fence.

STYLE

Selecting a fence design is surely the most enjoyable aspect of the planning process. If a primary reason for building a fence is to enhance the beauty of a home, it is important to pay special attention to this step.

While deciding on a style, consult your list and ranking of the reasons why you need the fence. As you see styles that appeal to you, you will be able to rate their abilities to

Ornamental posts give these two basic fences additional appeal.

meet your needs. All the fence designs in this book are rated. If you see a design you like that does not meet all your needs, think of ways you may be able to alter the design.

The style you choose should blend with your house and grounds, complementing the home's overall appearance and function. Perhaps, for example, you can incorporate some architectural details of your house into the fence design.

Your style should also be in accordance with your local building codes. If it is not, you will need to do one of two things—either apply for a variance giving you permission to build the fence as you want, or alter your design to meet the local coding requirements. Many municipalities have rules that restrict the height of fences.

Post Decoration

Posts can range in decoration from a simple bevel-cut top to lavish posts, adorned with raised panels, chamfered edges, molded caps and bases, and ornate finials.

Ornate posts can be created by attaching moldings to basic 4×4 or 6×6 posts. If you want ornate posts, space them evenly along the length of the fence. If the spacing is not

Use double-door gates where wide entranceways are necessary.

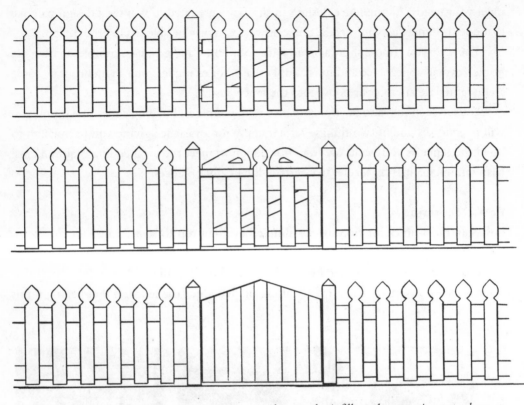

Hidden gates imitate the infill, accenting gates complement the infill, and contrasting gates bear little or no resemblance to the infill; yet all three styles handsomely adorn these fences.

even, the decorated post will draw attention to the irregularity and detract from the fence's beauty rather than adding to it.

An alternative to having every post decorated is to place ornate posts just at gates and corners and leave all the intermediate posts simple. If your intermediate posts are unevenly spaced, this helps draw attention away from the simple posts and toward the ornate posts. Another plus to this approach is that you have very few posts to decorate, while still giving your fence lovely accent pieces.

Gate Design

Gate openings must provide adequate passage for people. Small gates are usually at least 3 feet wide. Gates wider than 5 feet need extra support or should be divided into double-door gates. A double-door gate has one door that is opened frequently and one that remains stationary and is opened only when large items must pass through. Cane bolts, sold at hardware stores, can be used to hold the stationary side of the gate in place.

There are not many rules about choosing a style of gate for your fence. Gates can be designed to blend in with, contrast with, or accent the fence.

Hidden Gates. The overall fence pattern is incorporated into the hidden gate. Often this is done for security reasons: The gate opening is camouflaged and difficult to identify. Others are designed in this fashion to continue the flow of the fence rhythm, enhancing its aesthetic beauty. This approach is also useful in situations where unevenly sized or spaced gates are necessary for functional reasons.

Contrasting Gates. A contrasting gate can beautify a fence while serving a functional purpose: It leads visitors to the entrance by drawing attention to itself. But you do not want a contrasting gate that conflicts with your fence. Experiment by making a scale drawing of the gate with the fence. Or if you would like to reuse an existing gate, try standing it next to the fence. If the combination is appealing to you, hang the gate; if not, design a more complementary gate.

Accenting Gates. Accenting gates borrow features from the fence's overall design yet contain details that make the gate stand out from the fence. These gates have a special beauty because they combine elements that are both similar and dissimilar to the overall fence, showing the designer's ability to artfully blend the components to produce a masterful centerpiece. Accenting gates borrow a significant benefit from each of the other gate styles. Like contrasting gates, they draw attention to themselves, allowing visitors to easily find the acceptable entrances, but like hidden gates, they incorporate details from the fence in their design and form a unifying link between two separate sections of the fence.

Siting the Fence and Gates

❧

EXACTLY WHERE ON THE PROPERTY DO YOU WANT TO PLACE THE FENCE?

An assist to planning the fence perimeter will be an aerial view, or plan view, of your property. The plan view should show existing buildings and structures, such as the house, garage, sheds, patios, decks, gazebos, walkways, and any other permanent structures, as well as significant trees and shrubs. All these items will affect where you can place your fence. You may elect to remove or alter some of them to accommodate the fence.

Once you have a complete physical aerial view of your property, you should next sketch paths of all your traffic routes and areas of activity. Visual inspection of these paths will help you determine where you want to put the fence and where you need gates.

LOCATING THE POSTS

You will need posts at every corner your fence will turn and additional posts flanking each gate. Your posts must be able to adequately support the gate's infill. Post sizes and spacing can vary greatly depending on the density, thickness, and height of the infill. The space between your posts must not be too great, or stringers will easily sway when pressed against.

Post spacing is also important for aesthetic reasons. Posts spaced at even distances add visual appeal to the fence because of their rhythmic high points, while unevenly spaced posts will detract from a fence's appearance. A fence complemented by evenly spaced posts is as enchanting to the eye as a melody complemented by a steady beat is to the ear.

Unfortunately, if you have a number of gates along the same fence wall, you may be forced to have posts unevenly spaced. If this is the case, you do not want to make ornate intermediate posts; highly decorated posts will draw attention to themselves and make the uneven spacing more obvious. Choose simple posts or hide your posts behind the infill. If

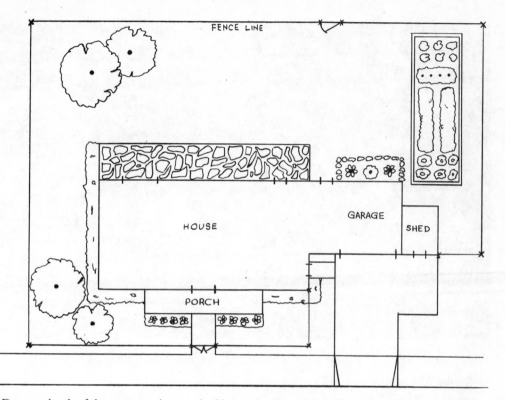

Draw a sketch of the property showing buildings, shrubs, and significant features. A sketch will help you plan where to place the fence, posts, and gates.

your fence will need to be attractive from both sides, or if your design requires integrated posts, try using double posts.

Double posts placed at gates, corners, or gates and corners can be used to take up the slack when numerous gates or odd fence stretches require uneven post placement. Draw your post placement on paper to help you visualize the best locations for your double posts.

Fence posts can be placed in front of or behind the fence infill, or with infill in between the posts. Here are some guidelines to help you determine the better choices for you.

Placing posts behind the fence is usually the fastest, easiest way to make an attractive fence. This method allows for stringers to be placed either between or in front of the posts. When the infill is attached, it partially or fully conceals the posts from view. This is helpful if post spacing is uneven. The uneven posts, however, will still be visible from the back side of the fence.

Fences in which the infill runs between the posts will reveal the entire post. If the post

Fence posts can be placed in front of the infill (above), in between the infill (below), or hidden behind the infill (right).

spacing is even, this is usually the most attractive choice. The rhythmic break in the fence pattern will catch the eye and enchant passers-by.

Placing posts in front of the infill is a third alternative. This is the least common way of making a fence. Here, what would normally be considered the back side of the fence is the front. Displaying the stringers in front of the infill can be especially charming, however, if the stringers are molded, as with a shaper or router.

SETTING THE POSTS

Start by hammering a stake at the location for each corner post. Stretch a line between each corner stake, making the line taut. If the distance is too great to keep the line taut, sink a temporary stake between the corner stakes and use it to help stretch the line.

Next, measure along the line and plant a stake for each intermediate post hole. Then dig holes with at least a 12-inch diameter at each stake location.

Depth

The general rule for minimum post depth is at least one-fourth of the post's total length or 2 feet deep, whichever is greater. This means a 6-foot-high fence would use, at the

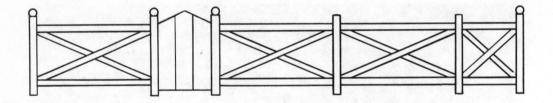

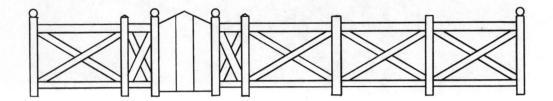

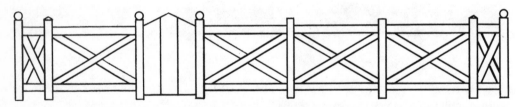

Rather than ending a stretch of fence in an odd-length section, use double posts (two posts placed closely together) to accent your gates or corner posts and make all other fence sections of equal length.

very shortest, 8-foot posts sunk 2 feet. But even a 4-foot-high fence should still use posts that are sunk at least 2 feet deep.

If the posts are longer than you need them to be, sink the extra length under the ground. The added depth will help make the posts more secure.

Foundations

Posts can be set in an earth and gravel foundation, a solid concrete and gravel foundation, or a foundation that uses layers of these elements. Generally speaking, the more concrete used, the sturdier the post foundation. Gate posts and corner posts should usually be set using at least some concrete, since these posts receive extra stress and heavy use.

All posts should be set with the bottom 6 inches of the post nestled in 1 foot of gravel. The gravel is used to ensure drainage away from the bottom of the post, thus inhibiting decay. Gravel and earth should be added slowly and then tamped thoroughly to remove

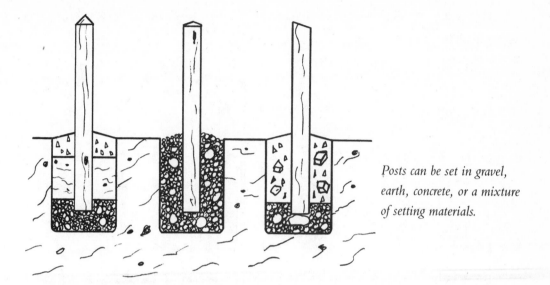

Posts can be set in gravel, earth, concrete, or a mixture of setting materials.

any air pockets. If rubble is used to extend concrete, the concrete-rubble mixture also should be tamped to remove air pockets.

Alignment

Set corner posts first. Use two spirit levels placed on adjacent sides of the post. One person should hold the post level while the other adds and tamps the gravel and earth and then pours the concrete. Bracing the posts with pieces of 2×4 may be necessary to keep the posts level while the concrete is setting.

Use two spirit levels placed on adjacent sides of the post to help keep posts plumb while setting.

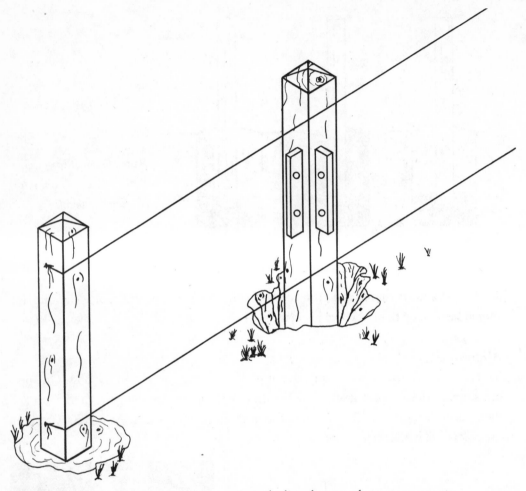

Position post flush with, but not pressing against, the lines between the two corner posts.

When corner posts are set, hammer two nails 1 inch deep into the outer sides of each post, one near the top of the post, the other near the bottom. Tie a line to the top nail. Pull the line around the side of the post; attach the line to the top nail on the far side of the second corner post. Make certain the line is tight. Do the same for the bottom nail.

Begin setting intermediate posts. Position the posts so that they are just flush with, but not pressing, the lines between the two corner posts. Use two spirit levels to help you adjust the posts to plumb. Add footing matter and tamp thoroughly. Stake the posts to keep them plumb if necessary as the concrete sets.

THE GATES

Where do I put them? How many will I need? How wide should they be? Should they all look exactly the same? Will single- or double-door gates work better for me? These are a few of the questions all gate builders should ask themselves before starting construction.

The primary reason for a gate is to allow passage into or outside a fenced area. While this statement may seem obvious, many fence builders do not give enough serious thought to the present and future traffic patterns of the residence.

Gates should be strategically placed, sized, and constructed to allow easy, unhindered traffic to and from the residence. Even if you use only the front door now, consider the possibility that one day you may use the side door as well, and you may want a gate close to that door too. It is much easier to design several gates into the fence from the start than to add one or two after posts have been set or the fence completed.

Once you have decided upon your gate's design, size, location, swing direction, and material, it is time to actually begin making the gate. If you are not using a preplanned gate pattern, I suggest you make a scale drawing of your gate and the adjoining fence. From this drawing you will be able to see how the fence, posts, and gate will look together. You will also be able to calculate the size of each piece of lumber to be used in the gate.

Location of gate hardware should also be shown on the scale drawing. This will help you evaluate which locations look and function better for hinges and latches. You may find that in this process you erase and redraw several details of the gate; do not let this frustrate you. It is much better to find out if the gate will not look good or function well at this stage. Another sheet of paper and a new pencil are far less expensive than more lumber and new hinges.

All gates have a frame. The most basic frame, simple to construct, is the Z frame. It gets its name from the three structural members used to support the gate's infill—two horizontal and one diagonal. The bottom of the diagonal member must meet the horizontal member near the bottom hinge. That means that the top of the diagonal member always extends away from the hinged side of the gate. This design helps to shift more of the gate's weight to the bottom hinge and the bottom of the supporting post.

Another kind of frame is the perimeter frame. Two verticals and two horizontals form the perimeter of the rectangle. A fifth diagonal member is often added; it is attached on the bottom hinge side and extends diagonally across the gate to the top of the latched side. As you can tell by its description, the diagonal member forms a Z in the perimeter frame and helps to provide the same type of support as in the basic Z frame.

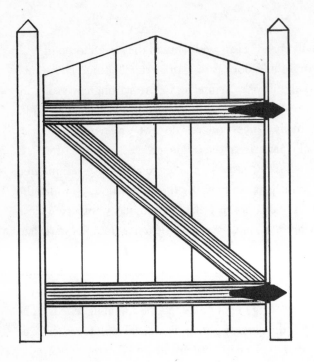

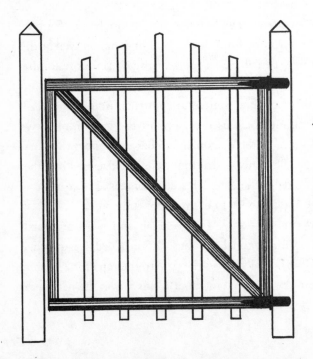

*The Z-frame gate can be used when the
gate infill is sturdy and capable of
supplying vertical support to the gate.
The perimeter frame gate can be used
when the gate infill is frail, because
it does not require the infill for its
vertical support.*

Half lap, rabbet, and basic butt joints can be used when making the perimeter of the gate. Though butt joints are the easiest to construct, they offer the least structural support. If you use the butt joint, you can add L mending plates for a stronger connection.

GATE CONSTRUCTION

Now that you have an overall understanding of how gates are constructed and how they function, here are the step-by-step procedures for building a gate.

1. Measure the opening. Measure at two places, along the top and along the bottom of the fence. Your overall gate size should be the distance between your posts, minus the clearance for your hinges and opening swing, usually ½ to ¾ inch. Clearance is needed to keep the gate from catching on the posts as it swings open. Some hardware may require additional clearance. Smaller hinges and hinges mounted on the outer face of the post

Basic steps for building a simple gate:

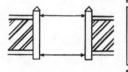

1. Measure the opening.   *2. Cut the frame parts.*   *3. Assemble the frame.*   *4. Add the diagonal brace.*   *5. Add the infill.*

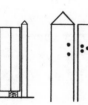 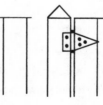   

6. Check the fit.   *7. Drill holes for hardware.*   *8. Hang the gate.*   *9. Add detail pieces.*   *10. Apply finish.*

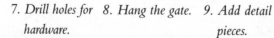

often require little clearance, but larger hinges, especially screw hook and strap or screw hook and eye styles, can require ¾ inch clearance and even more in some cases.

2. Cut the frame parts. Cut the stock to the necessary lengths, and prepare and cut the joints if you are planning to use special joints. Cut cross members to overlay the upright members, to keep water from entering the joints.

3. Assemble the joints. Assemble the perimeter of the frame into a rectangle. Continually check and adjust to maintain squareness as you attach the pieces to one another. You can use nails, screws, or bolts to connect the gate perimeter pieces. Bolts or screws will provide a more permanent and secure fit, making your gate stronger and more stable. Once the frame is assembled, you can make a final check for squareness. Measure both diagonal stretches across the gate; if the measurements are the same, the gate is square.

4. Add the diagonal brace. Lay your diagonal brace and place the frame on top of the brace. Place 2×4 blocks under the unsupported corners to hold the frame level. With a pencil, mark the lines where you will cut the diagonal member. When sawing your diagonal member, do not cut on the line, but cut immediately next to it on the outer side. This will ensure a snug fit. Toenail the diagonal support in place.

5. Add the infill. Lay the frame down so that you can add the infill. Make certain that the diagonal brace bottom will be on the hinge side of the gate.

6. Check the fit. Use scrap boards or bricks to prop the gate to its correct height in the gate opening. Have a helper balance the gate while you check the fit. Take your hinges and gate latch, and mark their locations on the posts and gate.

7. Fasten hardware. Install hinges with the longest screws or bolts that will not poke through the far side of your post and gate lumber. Attach the hinges and latch mechanism on the gate first. Refit the gate to make certain that the post hinge markings match up with the hinges already attached to the gate.

8. Hang the gate. Drill pilot holes in the post for gate hinge screws or bolts. Attach the gate and check its swing for post clearance and maximum opening distance. Mark the latch catch position on the post, and install the latch mechanism onto the post.

9. Add detail pieces. Add finer aesthetic details as desired.

10. Apply finish. Finish with an appropriate treatment of wood sealer or paint.

FENCING A SLOPE

Most of us do not have perfectly flat yards on barren square lots. Many yards have trees, boulders, slopes, curves, dips, and mounds—all obstacles that the fence builder must ingeniously overcome.

Trees in the fence line must be handled carefully. Attaching your fence to a tree can make it susceptible to disease. If the tree does not become diseased and die, it will continue to grow and expand, and as it does, it will distort and pull at your fence. Your fence should stop short of the tree to allow the tree to live and grow.

Fencing a slope is probably the most common obstacle fence builders need to hurdle. If the terrain is particularly uneven, the sharp horizontal lines of a baseboard will draw attention to the unevenness of the land. There are several approaches to fencing a slope, each with advantages and drawbacks.

Stepped Infill and Frame

Stepped frame fences have stringers hung perpendicular to the posts. In that sense, the construction of this type of fence is the same as that of a basic fence. It differs, however, in that the ends of the stringers on the uphill side of the fence section are closer to the earth than the ends on the downhill side. This type of construction has the appearance of steps, thus the term stepped frame. Such fences look best and are most practical on gradual slopes. On steep slopes, there will be huge, triangular gaps between the fence bottom and the ground. Such gaps can appear unsightly and reduce the fence's ability to provide privacy and security.

Stepped frames are usually the best choice for geometric grid, panel, and lattice fences. They also work well for picket, grape stake, and spindle fences.

Sloping Frameworks

Sloping framework fences have stringers hung parallel to the earth. This type of fence is well suited to traverse either gradual or steep slopes. Each stringer must be cut at an angle so that it fits the post snugly.

Nail-on infill, such as pickets, is easily applied to the sloped frame, but infill that is inserted in the frame is not as easily used if the grade is steep. Conventional-sized lattice and panels may not be available to fit using only one piece between each section. Geometric grid patterns will need some alterations on the slope, but if well designed, such alterations will greatly increase the beauty of the fence and display the designer's creativity and adaptability. (See design 73.)

Stepped Frame with Sloping Infill

The stepped frame, in which stringers are placed perpendicular to the posts, is easier to construct than the sloping frame, because stringers do not need to be miter cut to fit each section. It is also stronger, because the length of the perpendicular stringers is shorter than that of a stringer placed parallel to the earth. As mentioned before, stepped frames leave large triangular voids along the bottom of the fence. To cover these voids, the infill is extended below the stringers on the bottom side of the slope and above the stringers on the top side.

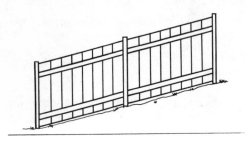

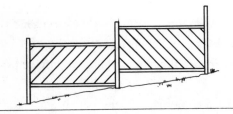

To fence a hillside you can use a sloping frame with sloping infill, a stepped frame with stepped infill, or a stepped frame with sloping infill.

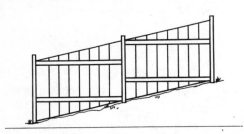

Tools and Materials

WILL YOU BUILD THE FENCE YOURSELF OR HIRE A CONTRACTOR? COST WILL BE A BIG consideration, but there is no harm in checking out the option of hiring out the work. Contractors can quote you estimates over the phone from the information you give them.

Accurately describe the fence's dimensions, the terrain it will traverse, the number of gates it will need, and the general style of infill you want used. All these items should be easy to explain over the phone, and the contractor should be able to give you a rough estimate or a high-low range. Also inquire as to what types of materials, such as woods, fasteners, and hinges, would be used. Ask whether the contractor would be willing to do a portion of the task and allow you to do the rest.

If you decide to have the work done, have several contractors come to the site to discuss locations of posts and gates, materials, a time frame for completion, and the method of payment. When you choose one of these contractors, get all of these details written in your contract so that there will be no disputing what your final decisions were for each aspect of the fence.

Many people decide to perform certain portions of the fence project themselves. Most common is finishing the fence with the desired paint or stain. Still others enjoy cutting the pickets and hanging the stringers but would be glad to pay someone else to dig the post holes and align the posts. Each aspect must be clearly defined as to job function and completion time, since one party will be depending on the other party to finish its portion to specification by a completion date.

TOOLS FOR DOING IT YOURSELF
The basics of fence construction can be understood and applied by just about anyone. The structural frames for fences vary little. Creating infill is usually a matter of cutting

repetitive pieces. Hanging gates requires patience and care but is not technically difficult. Confidence, ability to work hard, and a good assistant for certain phases of the project will provide the weekend carpenter with all he needs to complete the project.

If you decide to build the fence yourself, you will want to be able to safely and effectively operate some power tools. Before operating any piece of machinery you buy or borrow, always read and understand the owner's manual. Heed all safety recommendations, such as wearing eye protectors. This book will briefly discuss some of the most common power tools used in fence construction, but it is not intended to cover the general safety and operation of power tools.

Circular Saw and Table Saw

The circular saw is probably the most commonly used power tool in constructing a fence. Since a large area of its blade can be exposed, it has the potential to be one of the more dangerous power tools. Always operate a circular saw with extreme care.

The circular saw has much practical use in cutting stringers, posts, and other members to length. It can also be used to create decorative chamfers and to miter post tops.

The table saw has a round blade like the circular saw, but rather than being a handheld tool, it is mounted on a table. If you have access to a table saw, you will be able to make beautiful raised panel appliqués and beveled post caps.

Band Saw, Jigsaw, and Scroll Saw

The band saw cuts curves that would be impossible to make with the wide, flat blade of the circular saw. This allows you to make a variety of scrolling cuts—very useful in creating decorative pickets, post tops, and gate scrolls. The band saw can make beautiful fretwork even in thick lumber such as 2× and 4× material.

Jigsaws and scroll saws also allow you to make scrolling cuts. These saws can make interior cutouts, which are not possible on a band saw. The advantage a band saw has over the jigsaw and scroll saw is that it can cut thicker wood faster and with greater ease.

Router

The router is another useful tool for making decorative moldings and fretwork for your fence. Routers can be used to make decorative moldings on baseboards, raised panels to incorporate in the infill or on posts, and decorative post tops. They also can allow you to cut out scrolling patterns with greater accuracy and speed than a band saw.

To make decorative moldings, such as the molding on a baseboard, you use a decorative cutting bit with a bearing guide. This bearing guide rides along the bottom portion of the workpiece while cutting the upper portion with the decorative design.

Special pattern bits are available for cutting out patterns with a router. To make scrollwork with a router, you need a template. Trace the pattern onto a piece of pressed hardboard and cut it out using a band saw (cardboard templates do not give the router bit's guide bearing the firm surface it requires for a clean cut). Strict attention to the cutting line is imperative while cutting out the template from which every picket or scroll bracket will be made. The guide bearing of the pattern bit will ride along the template edge while cutting through the workpiece.

Templates are nailed or screwed to the workpiece. With the router mounted on a router table, the workpiece is fed into the router bit until the guide bearing and template contact. The workpiece is fed through the router while keeping the template against the pattern bit's guide bearing. After going all the way around the template, the picket or scroll bracket is completely cut out. The template can also be clamped to the workpiece on a workbench. The hand-held router can then be traced around the edge of the template to cut out the design.

Using a router and template is easiest when making thinner pickets. If your pickets are thicker than ¾ inch, you will probably find them easier to cut on a band saw.

Router bits are available made of all high-speed steel or carbide-tipped. Carbide-tipped router bits are more expensive than other kinds, but they will last much longer and produce output that requires little or no sanding.

Drills and Drill Presses

You will need a drill to make holes for gate hinge screws and bolts. Drills can have other uses, as well. Many times a single dimple or combinations of holes in a picket and gate add to the appearance. Do not neglect to use the drill as a decorating and constructing tool.

MATERIALS

When choosing the types of lumber to construct your fence, give consideration to the style of your fence and what type of lumber will be easiest and most economical to use to achieve the fence you want. If you want your fence to last a lifetime, the cheapest lumber may not be the most economical.

In addition to lumber dimensions, consider the lumber treatments and species of wood that are available.

Types of Lumber

Redwood and cedar lumber have natural insect-repelling properties that make them attractive for fence construction. The price for these two types of lumber is often rather high, however.

An alternative is to use pressure-treated lumber. This lumber is pressure-cooked with chemicals to make it resistant to insects and decay. A commonly reported drawback to pressure-treated lumber is that it is more prone to twisting and cracking.

Other lumber, such as oak, spruce, or fir, can also be used, but it will be more liable to decay. An economical option may be to use naturally resistant wood or pressure-treated lumber for posts, which must come in contact with the ground, and other lumber for the infill, which is above the ground.

Naturally resistant wood can be allowed to weather naturally, but other woods should be treated with some type of finish to prevent cracking and extend their useful life.

Picket fences are often made from 1× or ¾-inch stock. If the pickets will be relief sculptured, 2× material may be used. You can then cut relief work up to ¾-inch deep on one side, and the board will still maintain adequate strength to be a sturdy picket.

Lattice and plywood panels come in 4×8-foot sections. Pressure-treated lattice and exterior-grade plywood are available and should be used when constructing a fence. You can buy lattice slats or cut them from 2× material if you want to construct your own lattice with a different pattern.

Gridwork patterns are often constructed from 2×4 material. This material tends to give the fence strong architectural characteristics—an attractive feature of the geometric grid-style fence.

Turned spindles should be made from a suitable turning stock of wood that is well seasoned and free of splits. Turning is probably the most time-consuming method of making fence infill and is not practical for long stretches of fence. Faux turnings and relief-cut pickets have the appearance of turned spindles but are much faster and easier to cut.

Calculating Quantities

Just how many posts, stringers, baseboards, pickets, post caps, post urns, nails, bags of concrete, hinges, latches, and stringer hangers will you need? Don't panic—we will handle each of these items one at a time. If you have a plan drawing of your fence, this task will not be very difficult.

Posts. Count the number of posts marked on your plan drawing. This is the number of posts you will need.

Determine the height above the ground you want the posts to be and the depth below the ground you need the posts to be, and add these two figures together. This number is the length you need for each post.

Concrete. Count the number of fence posts you have on your plan. Assume one bag of premix concrete for each post hole. If you want extra-sturdy posts, use one and a half bags per hole; if you are building a light-duty fence, use two-thirds of a bag per hole.

Stringers. Take the number of posts and multiply this number by the number of stringers you will have between two posts—probably two stringers. This gives you the total number of stringers you will need. Some of these stringers may be different lengths, and the distance between gate posts will probably be different than distances between other posts. Group the sections by length and figure how many stringers you need for each.

Baseboards. Follow the same procedure used to calculate stringers. Multiply the number of posts by the number of baseboards you will have between two posts: one if the baseboard is on only one side of the fence, and two if the baseboard is on both the inside and outside of the fence. If your posts are not evenly spaced, calculate the number of odd-size baseboards in each length group.

Infill. To calculate most infill, pickets, grape stakes, plain boards, and grid patterns, determine the amount of lumber necessary to complete one section, then multiply those lumber needs by the number of sections. Again, if you have several section lengths, you must perform this exercise for each group.

If you use additional moldings for posts or appliqués, you will need to estimate those lumber dimensions as well. Finally, allow for some spoilage, cutting errors, lumber defects, and last-minute changes that may require additional lumber. You may want to purchase 10 percent more lumber than you expect to use if picking up the extra lumber on an as-needed basis will be inconvenient.

Nails and Screws

For your fence to last a long time, you need to choose nails that will resist rust or not rust at all.

Nails that resist rust are galvanized or coated with a rustproof material. Galvanized nails are covered with a rustproof surface by an electroplating process. Often the coating is very thin and becomes damaged when the nails are installed; the nails then will begin to rust wherever this damage has occurred.

Nails that are dipped in a rust-resistant metal have a thicker coating than galvanized nails. They are less likely to flake or chip during installation and will last for many years.

The cost of these nails is somewhat higher than that of galvanized nails, but their performance is well worth the price.

Still better than galvanized or coated nails are nails made of stainless steel or aluminum. Damage caused to these nails during installation or by many years of use will not affect their rust-resistance. These nails cost far more than the coated nails, however, which often precludes them from being used in many large projects.

The nails you choose will need to last the lifetime of your fence. Determine how long you want your fence to last and choose your nails accordingly.

Latches and Hinges

There are a number of latches and locks available for keeping gates secured in the open or closed position. Choose those with the ability to stand up to the use and abuse they will receive. If you do not need your gate to latch closed, you may still want to add a simple handle you can use to pull the gate open.

When choosing hinges, keep in mind that the most important factor is their ability to

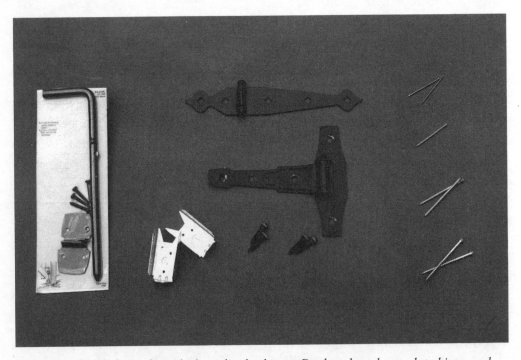

To make a durable fence, choose high-quality hardware. Purchase large heavy-duty hinges and extra-long bolts to make a strong, long-lasting gate. Use nails and screws that resist rust.

provide a firm grasp to both the gate and the post. Do not be afraid to use a hefty set of hinges. Dainty is not "in" when it comes to gate hinges—a gate that sags on bent hinges will be a constant irritant each time it is opened.

Many hinges are available with a spring mechanism that allows the gate to be self-closing. Use them where appropriate. This feature is very handy for gates that are opened frequently.

Choose appropriate bolts or screws to use with your hinges. Small bolts or screws can be pulled out of the post or gate after only a modest amount of activity. Use hinges secured with very large bolts or several moderately large bolts. Long, thick bolts will grasp the post and gate firmly, ensuring a lengthy service life for your gate.

By now you should have the information you need to choose a beautiful, functional fence. As you review the patterns in this book, keep in mind your priorities and consider the ability of each fence to meet them. The fence must meet not only your high standards, but also those of your local coding authority. Always apply for a fence construction permit and any variances you may need. Plan the location of your fence, its perimeter, post placements, and gate locations carefully. Use quality tools, hardware, and materials that will enable your fence to serve beautifully for many, many years.

Construction Steps

THIS CHAPTER GIVES AN OVERVIEW OF THE STEPS NECESSARY TO COMPLETE THE INDIVIDUAL components of your fence. Reviewing the steps to build fence sections, gates, and ornate posts will help you put these tasks into perspective. You will find these steps useful as you design, assemble, and erect the pieces of your fence.

ORNATE POSTS

For ornate corner posts, use 4×4 or 6×6 posts encased in 2× materials. This technique makes your corner posts both beautiful and extremely durable. Decorative posts encased in thinner lumber will provide a high-quality look years after construction. Actual 6×6 and 8×8 posts can be used, but they usually crack and split more readily than posts encased in thinner lumber. Use post lumber that is thoroughly dry; wet lumber may twist and distort over time.

It is usually easier to encase and decorate the posts first, then set them. But if you prefer, set the posts first and come back to this step when you are ready to encase and decorate them. For assistance on encasing posts and making post decorations, see the next chapter.

Construction of Ornate Posts
1. Encase the decorative posts.
2. Create decorative grooves, chamfers, and rosettes if applicable to post pattern.
3. Cut and apply decorative panels if applicable to post pattern.
4. Cut and apply desired post cap and decorative cove molding below cap if desired.
5. Cut and apply decorative pedestal if desired.
6. Turn finial on a lathe or cut out on a band saw.
7. Drill a hole in the center of the pedestal, going through the cap and into the post itself. Drill a hole in the bottom of the finial at center about 3 inches deep. Screw a threaded steel

dowel rod through the pedestal and cap and into the post, and screw the finial on top. Use extra nails or screws to keep the finial securely in place.

8. Apply base molding. You may want to apply base molding to the corner posts and the rest of the fence at the same time.

GATES

Your gates will receive heavy use. Their constant opening and closing will test how well you constructed them. In constructing your gates, use extra concrete and the best posts to reduce the chance that your posts will lean or break; select the best lumber and the sturdiest hardware to ensure that they will be beautiful and low-maintenance gates.

Construction of Gates

1. Measure the opening. Allow enough clearance for hinges and latches to open the gate without sticking or binding. (Most hinges require at least ½ to ¾ inch.)

2. Cut the frame parts. Cut the top, bottom, and two side members of the frame from 2×4 lumber.

3. Assemble the frame.

4. Add the diagonal brace for a stronger gate.

5. Add the infill. *Either* use the fence infill material across the gate frame to make a hidden gate, *or* use boards and a center picket flanked by two decorative scroll brackets to make a complementing gate. (See the next chapter for assistance in making decorative gates. Add the scroll brackets after the gate is installed.)

6. Check the fit. Use blocks to hold the gate at the height you want it to be when installed.

7. Drill holes for the hinges.

8. Hang the gate. Be sure to use the biggest gate bolts available that will not protrude out of the back side of your lumber. Gates receive heavy use and require maximum-strength materials for a long, maintenance-free life.

9. Add the scroll brackets. Drill holes from the underside of the top frame member. Use hefty screws for a good hold. Add handles, latches, stops, or any other finishing details.

10. Apply protective finish.

NAIL-ON INFILL FENCES

These fences include board, pale, privacy, simple picket, and sawn picket fencing. Nail-on infill, as its name implies, is nailed onto the fence frame. Nail-on infill can be tall boards that are tightly fit to form a solid wall or privacy fence, or it can be short, slender pales with spacing placed between them to form a decorative yet effective security fence.

Nail-on infill is probably the easiest type of infill to apply to the fence frame. For this reason, most fencing that will enclose a lengthy perimeter will be made with this type of infill.

Construction

Posts

1. Cut to desired length, allowing for below-ground length. (Example: 4 feet, 2 inches above ground + 3 feet below ground = 7 feet, 2 inches total length.)

2. Decorate posts to your taste—simply, moderately, or extravagantly. Cut pointed tops for simple decoration, cut and attach decorative cap and finial to make the post more exciting, or create elaborate corner posts with numerous details. (See the next chapter for help making post decorations. See the "Construction of Ornate Posts" section of this chapter for construction steps for ornate posts.)

3. Set the posts. (The following is one of several commonly used settings; for more options, see "Setting the Posts" in "Siting the Fence and Gates.")

• Dig a hole 3 feet, 6 inches deep.

• Fill the hole with 6 inches of gravel to allow drainage. (Good drainage prevents premature post decay.)

• Nestle post in gravel. Add a small amount of earth and tamp firmly.

• Use a partner to hold the post plumb while you add and tamp small amounts of earth, concrete, or both. Using concrete provides a more solid footing for your posts.

Pickets

1. Cut pickets to desired length.

2. Cut ornamental picket tops, and body design if applicable. (See the next chapter for ideas on how to cut picket tops.)

3. Construct the fence. (Of the several commonly used infill construction methods, the following is the one I prefer.)

• Use metal stringer hangers to suspend stringers between posts. If the span between posts is greater than 8 feet, use three stringers between each set of posts for extra strength.

• Use a spacer when nailing on pickets. Cut a board to the width you want between your pickets, and use this board when nailing pickets to the stringers to provide even spacing. Tight spacing provides better security for smaller pets.

• Use 6d or 8d nails to provide a strong hold but without protruding from the back side of your stringers.

4. Add the baseboard. (See the next chapter for help making decorative baseboards.)

• Use a router to cut a decorative edge on your baseboard.

• Nail your baseboards at each post, using 16d nails.

• Nail pickets to the baseboard for added strength. Use 6d or 8d nails.

Gates

Once the fence is completed, build and hang the gates. See the "Construction of Gates" section of this chapter for steps for building gates. (See the next chapter for details on making gate decorations.)

GRID AND PANEL FENCES

The beauty of a grid and panel fence is determined not by how ornate its pattern is, but rather by how well its pattern is planned. The pattern should fit neatly between the posts of the fence. Each section between posts should be symmetrically balanced.

Unlike most pale, picket, and board fences, grid and panel fences almost always have their infill inset in the frame rather than nailed onto the frame.

Also unlike most picket fences, grid and panel fences are very sensitive to changes in height and width. For this reason, it is important for you to make a scale drawing of a section of fence. You will use this drawing to determine the exact post spacing necessary to achieve a fence that is balanced in appearance.

Construction

Posts

1. Cut to desired length, allowing for below-ground length. (Example: 4 feet, 2 inches above ground + 3 feet below ground = 7 feet, 2 inches total length.)

2. Decorate posts to your taste—simply, moderately, or extravagantly. Cut pointed tops for simple decoration, cut and attach decorative cap and finial to make the post more exciting, or create elaborate corner posts with numerous details. (See the next chapter for help making post decorations. See the "Construction of Ornate Posts" section of this chapter for construction steps for ornate posts.)

3. Set the posts. (The following is one of several commonly used settings; for more options, see "Setting the Posts" in "Siting the Fence and Gates.")

• Dig a hole 3 feet, 6 inches deep.

• Fill the hole with 6 inches of gravel to allow drainage. (Good drainage prevents premature post decay.)

• Nestle post in gravel. Add a small amount of earth and tamp firmly.

• Use a partner to hold the post plumb while you add and tamp small amounts of earth, concrete, or both. Using concrete provides a more solid footing for your posts.

Infill

1. Cut panel inserts (if applicable to design).

• Cut panels from 1× material or exterior-grade plywood.

• Use a drill press, jigsaw, or scroll saw to decorate panels with cutout designs.

2. Cut grid components.

• Measure and cut grid components to necessary lengths. Use 2× lumber for grid components.

• Cut channels in grid components to hold panel inserts, where applicable to design.

3. Construct fence. (Of the several commonly used infill construction methods, the following is the one I prefer.)

• Assemble the fence section on a flat surface.

• Use 12d nails where possible. Use smaller nails where 12d nails will protrude from the back side of your lumber.

• Use metal hangers to suspend stringers between posts, *or,* for top stringers, cut the post top flat and overlap the stringers on the post tops.

4. Add the baseboard. (See the next chapter for help making decorative baseboards.)

• Use a router to cut a decorative edge on your baseboard.

• Nail your baseboards at each post, using 16d nails.

• Nail pickets or other infill component to the baseboard for added strength. Use 6d or any other size nails that will not protrude out of your baseboard.

Gates

Once the fence is completed, build and hang the gates. See the "Construction of Gates" section of this chapter for steps for building gates. (See the next chapter for details on making gate decorations.)

BALUSTRADE FENCES

Fences made with balustrade infill are among the most formal of all fence styles. They are usually accented by decoratively molded top and bottom rails and ornate baseboards. Balusters with round ends can be inserted in holes that are drilled into the stringers. Square-topped balusters and sawn balusters are often inserted into channels to hold them in place on the top stringer. Sometimes the bottom stringer is sloped to one side or beveled on two sides, like a gabled roof, to encourage water drainage. The baluster bottoms are then angled or notched to fit the bottom stringer.

Construction

Posts

1. Cut to desired length, allowing for below-ground length. (Example: 4 feet, 2 inches above ground + 3 feet below ground = 7 feet, 2 inches total length.)

2. Decorate posts to your taste—simply, moderately, or extravagantly. Cut pointed tops for simple decoration, cut and attach decorative cap and finial to make the post more exciting, or create elaborate corner posts with numerous details. (See the next chapter for help making post decorations. See the "Construction of Ornate Posts" section of this chapter for construction steps for ornate posts.)

3. Set the posts. (The following is one of several commonly used settings; for more options, see "Setting the Posts" in "Siting the Fence and Gates.")

• Dig a hole 3 feet, 6 inches deep.

• Fill the hole with 6 inches of gravel to allow drainage. (Good drainage prevents premature post decay.)

• Nestle post in gravel. Add a small amount of earth and tamp firmly.

• Use a partner to hold the post plumb while you add and tamp small amounts of earth, concrete, or both. Using concrete provides a more solid footing for your posts.

Balusters

1. Cut balusters to desired length.

2. For sawn balusters, cut ornamental baluster body using a band saw. For turned balusters, turn balusters using a lathe or purchase turned balusters from a lumberyard. (See the next chapter for ideas on cutting sawn pickets.)

3. Construct the fence. (Of the several commonly used infill construction methods, the following is the one I prefer.)

• Cut a channel in the underside of the top stringer in which to insert the balusters.

• Drill pilot holes through the bottom of the bottom stringer at the center of each baluster.

• Assemble and nail the balusters in the channels of the stringers. Toenail the balusters to the top stringer. Sink the nails through the pilot holes in the bottom stringer and into the center of each baluster. If balusters tend to crack, predrill nail holes in the baluster tops and bottoms.

• Use metal hangers to suspend stringers between posts, *or,* for top stringers, cut the post top flat and overlap the stringers on the post tops.

4. Add the baseboard. (See the next chapter for help making decorative baseboards.)

• Use a router to cut a decorative edge on your baseboard.

• Nail your baseboards at each post, using 16d nails.

• Nail pickets to the baseboard for added strength. Use 6d or 8d nails.

Gates

Once the fence is completed, build and hang the gates. See the "Construction of Gates" section of this chapter for steps for building gates. (See the next chapter for details on making gate decorations.)

COMBINATION FENCES

Combination fences use two or more styles of infill to form the fence design. These fences are usually more decorative and their construction is more complex.

Generally, a fence can combine pales, pickets, and broad boards without significantly increasing the construction complexity. The assembly of these three types of infill is basically the same, because all three are typically nailed onto the stringers.

The infill of grid and panel and balustrade fences, on the other hand, is often inset in the frame. Thus, fences that combine a baluster or grid and panel design with pales, pickets, or boards are usually the most time-consuming, because they require the assembly of two or more types of infill.

Construction Techniques

SOME FENCES THAT SEEM DETAILED AND complicated are actually easy to make if you take just one step at a time. This pictured guide will guide you through making detail features like panel appliqués, inlaid rosettes, decorative veining, and chamfering. Once you review each step, and maybe practice your technique on a scrap piece of wood, you will feel confident that you can make these detailed accents.

POINTED AND BEVELED TOPS FOR POSTS, PALES, AND PICKETS
Tool required: circular saw or table saw

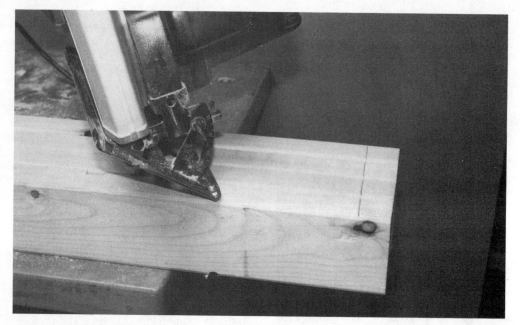

1. Adjust the blade to desired angle. If using a circular saw, clamp several members and strike a guide line across them. Follow this line with the saw blade. With a table saw, use a sliding miter guide to feed the workpiece into the blade.

2. For pickets, flip the pickets one-half turn and repeat this action on the opposite side. For post and pales, flip the post or pale one-quarter turn and repeat this action until all four sides have been cut.

3. Completed picket tops.

DECORATIVELY MOLDED PALES
Tools required: router and router table with sliding guide

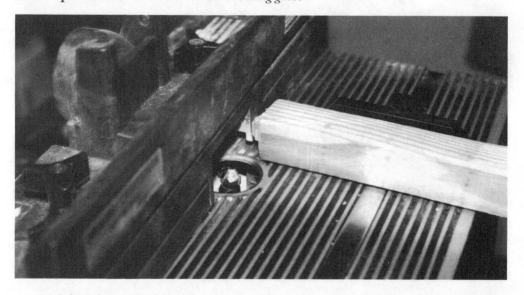

1. Select decorative bit and mount it in the router. Mount the router on the router table. Use a sliding guide to feed the pale into the router bit. Flip the pale one-quarter turn and repeat this action until all four sides are shaped.

2. Completed pale tops made with a router and router table.

PARALLEL VEINING AND GROOVING

Tools required: router and router guide with parallel attachment

1. Mark the start and stop points on the posts or boards to be veined. Fit the router with the parallel guide attachment and the veining bit. Adjust the guide until the proper width is achieved. Align the start mark to the router edge.

2. Engage the router and steadily sink the cutter into the wood. Move the router along, keeping the parallel guide pressed firmly against the workpiece. Continue until you reach the stop mark.

3. Finished post with veining.

PERPENDICULAR VEINING AND GROOVING
Tool required: *router or circular saw*

1. Clamp or attach a straight edge over several boards. The straight edge should be parallel to the desired groove. Fit the router with a grooving or veining bit. Guide the router along the straight edge to achieve a groove that is parallel to the straight edge. If using a circular saw, adjust the blade to make a shallow cut, about ⅛ inch deep.

2. Completed groove made using a router.

3. Completed veins made using a circular saw.

CREATING A DURABLE TEMPLATE FOR USE WITH A ROUTER

Tools required: router, pattern bit, and template. To make the template you may need a piece of hardboard, drill press, scroll saw, jigsaw, or band saw to cut out the original pattern.

Suggestions: Use a router and pattern bit if cutting pickets from stock less than ¾ inches thick. If the thickness is greater than ¾ inches it may be faster to cut the pickets on a band saw or scroll saw.

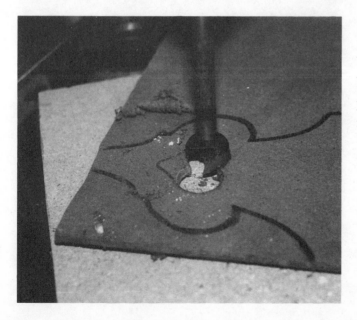

1. Trace the desired pattern onto a piece of hardboard and cut it out using a band saw, scroll saw, and drill press. Use a drill press to make perfectly round holes.

2. Use a scroll saw to make interior cuts.

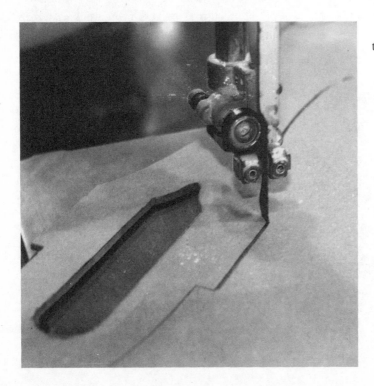

3. Use a band saw
to make exterior cuts.

4. Clamp or nail the hardboard pattern to the board that will be used to make the picket; cut out the picket design. Keep the pattern bit bearing pressed against the hardboard pattern while you feed the router around the pattern.

5. For interior cuts, drill a hole large enough for the pattern bit to fit through easily, engage the router, and begin working the bit toward the pattern edge. Guide the bit around the edge of the pattern to cut out the design.

6. Two finished picket tops: the thinner one was cut with a router and pattern, the thicker one with a drill press to make the heart rounds, a scroll saw to make the heart point, and a band saw to cut the outer edges.

MOLDED EDGES
Tool required: router

1. Select a decorative bit that has a bearing guide.

2. Guide the router along the work material, keeping the bit bearing guide firmly against the work material.

CUTTING A CONSTANT DEPTH CHAMFER
Tool required: router with chamfer bit

1. Set the stop points. Use clamps as shown or pencil lines to mark the starting and ending points for the chamfer.

2. Guide the router from start point to end point to form the chamfer.

CUTTING A GRADUALLY DEEPENING CHAMFER

Tool required: circular saw

1. Draw the chamfer on the post or post casing.

2. Cut the chamfer. Adjust the blade of your circular saw to a 45-degree angle. Secure the board or post in a vise or with clamps and cut one angle of the chamfer. Flip the board or post one-quarter turn and cut the other angle of the chamfer.

3. Since the circular saw blade is round, it will not completely cut the chamfer. Use a hand saw to finish the cut.

4. Plane and sand the chamfer to the desired smoothness.

DECORATIVE GATE SCROLLS AND PEDIMENTS

Tool required: band saw or scroll saw

1. Trace the pattern onto the desired stock and cut out the scroll or pediment. Most styles of scrolls and pediments are strongest if made from 2× material.

2. Attach the scrolls or pediment to the top member of the gate frame, using long screws for a good hold. For a more formal look, set the scrolls on a base plate fastened to the top member or the frame.

3. Finished gate featuring two scrolls on two base plates.

ENCASING DECORATIVE POSTS

Tool required: circular saw

Posts may be encased, either before or after they are set, to reduce the chance of splitting and cracking, which can detract from their appearance. Encasing posts gives them a stronger, more noticeable character.

The following set of equations tells you how to make encased posts for four different sizes.

One 5½-inch square post = one 3½-inch square post encased in two 1-by-3½-inch boards and two 1-by-5½-inch boards

One 6½-inch square post = one 3½-inch square post encased in two 1½-by-3½-inch boards and two 1½-by-6½-inch boards

One 7½-inch square post = one 5½-inch square post encased in two 1-by-5½-inch boards and two 1-by-7½-inch boards

One 8½-inch square post = one 5½-inch square post encased in two 1½-by-5½-inch boards and two 1½-by-8½-inch boards

1. Cut the encasing lumber to the desired length and width. Encase only the above-ground portion of your post. Attach the casing to the post. Use 16d nails near the top and the bottom of each casing member. These nails will be covered by decorative baseboard and cap molding in the later steps.

2. Make rosettes, veins, chamfers, and other casing decorations.

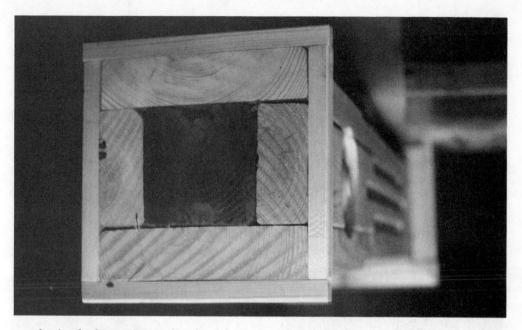

3. Apply decorative appliqués such as raised panels, baseboard moldings, and post cap moldings. This top view of an encased post displays the post cap molding.

4. Apply the cap, pedestal, and finial.

MAKING POST CAPS

Tools required: table saw or circular saw and router

1. Cut the boards into squares, using a table saw, radial arm saw, or circular saw.

2. Cut the top bevel on the cap. Use a router and panel-raising bit to make the top bevel. For a longer bevel cut, use a table saw with sliding guide.

3. Mold the underside edge of the post cap. Use a router to make a decorative edge on the bottom of the cap. (Optional)

4. Drill a hole through the center of the cap to allow a dowel screw to hold the post, cap, pediment, and finial firmly together.

MAKING THREE-DIMENSIONAL FINIALS

Tool required: band saw

1. Trace the finial pattern onto two adjacent sides of a 4×4 or 6×6 piece of lumber.

2. Cut the two outer edges first. Cut slowly and accurately.

3. Cut the two inner, adjacent edges of the pattern. Cut a little on one side, then turn to the adjacent side and cut a little on that side. Continue alternating sides until the finial is cut out on both sides. If you cut out one adjacent side completely, you will cut off the drawn pieces of your pattern, making it difficult to cut the last side.

4. Cut off the excess from the base and attach the finial to the post.

MAKING DECORATIVE ROSETTE INLAYS

Tool required: router with trammel guide attachment

1. Select the location for the rosette inlay and mark the center with an X. Drill a ⁵⁄₁₆-inch hole or use a nail to make a hole at the center of the rosette for the trammel guide pin to rest inside.

2. Fit the router with a decorative bit and trammel guide. Place the guide pin in the hole and pivot the router around the guide pin. (Change bits, change pivot arm length, or change the depth to create a variety of designs.)

3. This decorative rosette was completed using two bits.

4. Completed rosette.

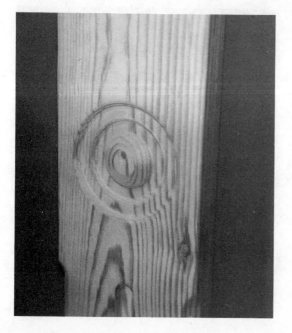

MAKING PANEL APPLIQUÉS

Tools required: *router and table saw or circular saw*

1. Cut panels to desired size and shape, using a table saw or circular saw. Use a router with panel molding bit to create a decorative edge on the panel.

2. Use a rubberized router mat to work on small pieces; it shouldn't be necessary to clamp them down.

3. A completed post with raised panel appliqués.

Designs

Simple Picket Fences

DESIGN 1: CARDINAL GOTHIC PICKET FENCE

Surprisingly beautiful, these gently arching Gothic pickets add dignity and charm to any style of architecture while rendering a substantial degree of security. The picket design is perfect for accenting vaulted windows and arched detailing common to many periods and styles of architecture, including modern housing. The rounded design of these simple pickets gives this fence a friendly feel while still making it difficult to climb and uncomfortable to sit on.

The pickets are quite easy to make using a band saw, and the matching post is almost as easy to make as the pickets themselves. This style is hard to surpass for ease of fabrication and durability of design. You can add variety to this fence by alternating the picket height or gracefully scalloping the picket height between posts.

DESIGN 2: SERRATED PICKET FENCE

These concave pointed pickets have their own unique character, which lends charm and grace to the homes they embrace. The concave slopes of the picket points gently flow away from the picket center, giving this fence an interesting nautical appeal. The picket design is perfect for accenting vaulted windows and arched detailing common to many periods and styles of architecture, including modern housing. The sharp points make this fence uninviting to climb and unthinkable to sit on.

The pickets are a breeze to cut using a band saw, and the matching post is almost as easy to make as the pickets themselves. This style is hard to surpass for ease of fabrication and durability of design. Alternating or scalloping the picket height would add variety to the fence and make the design appear more elaborate.

Fence: 3 feet, 8 inches high.
Posts: 4 feet, 1 inch high.
High security: The rounded pickets are difficult to straddle and uncomfortable to sit on.
Low privacy: The pickets are below eye level and spaced, thus allowing easy visibility over and through the fence.
Low buffering: This fence filters little sun and wind.
Construction. Fence, very easy. Posts, very easy.

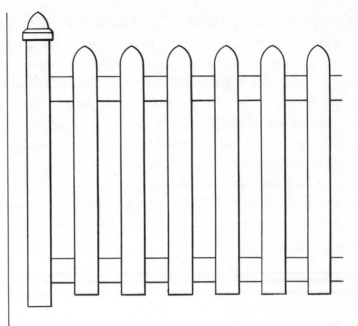

Fence: 3 feet, 8 inches high.
Posts: 4 feet, 1 inch high.
High security: The pointed pickets are difficult to straddle and uncomfortable to sit on.
Low privacy: The pickets are below eye level and spaced, thus allowing easy visibility over and through the fence.
Low buffering: This fence filters little sun and wind.
Construction: Fence, very easy. Posts, very easy.

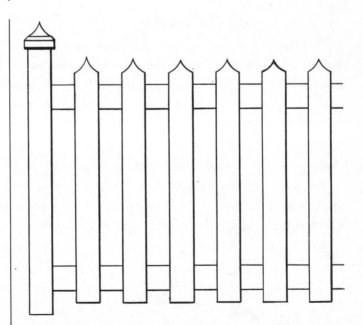

DESIGN 3: DIAMOND HEAD PICKET FENCE

This fence style, with its strong character, provides elegance and maximum security for minimal effort. This picket design was very popular in the eighteenth century for its attractive appearance, ease of fabrication, and utilitarian function. Fences very similar to this one can be seen in the restored colonial capital city of Williamsburg, Virginia. The piercing diamond-headed pickets are both attractive to passers-by and intimidating to would-be fence sitters. The fence's simplistic styling makes it versatile, able to enhance both traditional and contemporary architecture.

The pickets can be cut using a circular saw, a band saw, or both. The matching post is a three-dimensional complement to the two-dimensional picket design. As illustrated, this fence is perfect for a country cottage. To give this fence a more formal image, suitable for a larger estate or urban home, add a decoratively molded baseboard.

DESIGN 4: WHISTLE STOP PICKET FENCE

Cute, simple, and charming, this fence is easy to construct and is durable. These picket tops have an unusually low pitch for a picket fence, which are usually known for their piercing pointed heads. The blunt points of this style make it an excellent counterpart for the low profiles of ranch, split-level, and many other homes with a shallow-pitched roof.

The blunt-headed pickets are supported by a stout neck, which makes it unlikely that the heads will ever break off. Use a circular saw or band saw to make the pointed top and a drill press for the concave cut neck. The matching post is a three-dimensional complement to the two-dimensional picket design. The post finial can be made easily using a band saw. As illustrated, this fence is perfect for a quaint country home. It can be given a more formal appearance by adding a decoratively molded baseboard.

Fence: 3 feet, 9 inches high.
Posts: 4 feet, 3 inches high.
High security: The pointed pickets are difficult to straddle and uncomfortable to sit on.
Low privacy: The pickets are low and spaced, thus allowing easy visibility over and through the fence.
Low buffering: This fence filters little sun and wind.
Construction: Fence, very easy. Posts, very easy.

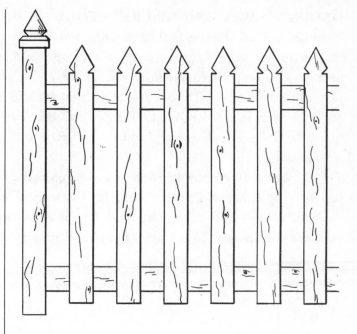

Fence: 3 feet, 9 inches high.
Posts: 4 feet, 4 inches high.
High security: Even though blunted, the picket tops are difficult to straddle and uncomfortable to sit on.
Low privacy: The pickets are low and spaced, thus allowing easy visibility over and through the fence.
Low buffering: This fence filters little sun and wind.
Construction: Fence, very easy. Posts, very easy.

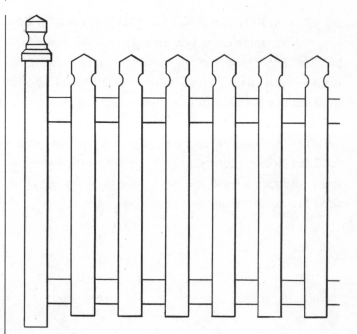

DESIGN 5: SAWN FINIAL PICKET FENCE

Victorian emphasis is strong in this impressive and effective picket fence. This elegantly fashioned picket design is a perfect companion to the slender urban housing that was commonly built in the nineteenth century. The spiring spear-headed pickets are supported by a gracefully curving neck. The design is intimidating to climb. Sitting on this picket fence is out of the question, even for the bravest fence sitters. Even though the fence has a Victorian flavor, the design is rudimentary enough to allow it to adapt to many other types of architecture.

The curves of this picket design are easy to cut on a band saw. If cutting several of these pickets, using a router and pattern could speed the cutting process. The complementary post finial is very easy to cut on a band saw. This fence as illustrated is ideal for small and moderate-sized homes. To make this fence more suitable for a stately residence, add a decoratively molded baseboard.

DESIGN 6: ROUND AND GOTHIC PICKET FENCE

The shorter, rounded pickets give this easy-to-make fence a country feel, while the pointier Gothic pickets add dignity and increase security. Although this fence features no sharp-pointed pickets, it is still uncomfortable to sit on and difficult to straddle. This fence is obviously well suited for Gothic-inspired architecture, but with its elementary nature it will look good with any type of home.

These pickets can easily be cut with a band saw or a router and pattern. The post finial can either be turned or be made with a band saw. This design is very easy to construct, and the picket style is among the most durable. To make this fence more formal, add a decoratively chamfered baseboard.

Fence: 4 feet high.
Posts: 4 feet, 4 inches high.
High security: The pointed pickets are intimidating to straddle and unthinkable to sit on.
Low privacy: The pickets are low and spaced, thus allowing easy visibility over and through the fence.
Low buffering: This fence filters little sun and wind.
Construction: Fence, very easy. Posts, very easy.

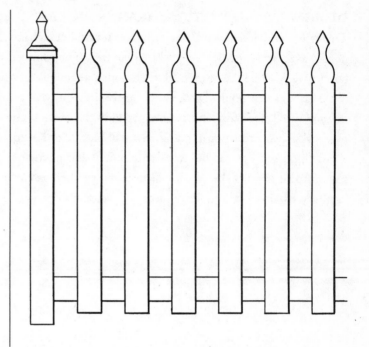

Fence: 3 feet, 8 inches high.
Posts: 4 feet, 3 inches high.
High security: The rounded pickets are difficult to straddle and uncomfortable to sit on.
Low privacy: The pickets are below eye level and spaced, thus allowing easy visibility over and through the fence.
Low buffering: This fence filters little sun and wind.
Construction: Fence, very easy. Posts, very easy.

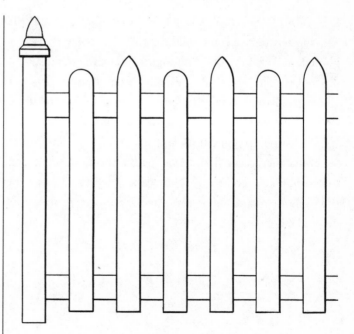

DESIGN 7: SWEET LITTLE HEARTS PICKET FENCE

This whimsical design is full of charm and sentimental character. Double-humped picket heads are accentuated by delicate heart cutouts. The rounded picket tops give the fence a country feel, while the heart cutouts demonstrate the maker's craftsmanship. Although this fence has no sharp-pointed pickets, it is uncomfortable to sit on and difficult to straddle. This design is well suited for country cottages and small town homes with a country flavor. The fence is easy to construct and doubtless will be a neighborhood eye catcher.

The picket tops can be made with a drill and jigsaw or, if making several pickets, a router and pattern. The post's ball finial can either be turned or be purchased from a lumberyard. To make this fence more formal, add a decoratively molded or beveled baseboard.

DESIGN 8: SERRATED SCALLOPED PICKET FENCE

The most attractive roses will look twice as lovely cascading over this fence. The sloping, pointed pickets alternate with slightly concave cut pickets for a brisk rhythm. The sharply pointed pickets tell would-be fence sitters that they would be more comfortable sitting elsewhere. Even though this fence has an idiosyncratic style, its overall simplicity allows it to blend with almost any setting and any type of residential architecture.

The sloping, pointed pickets are easy to cut on a band saw, and the concave pickets are even easier to cut. This fence style is among the easiest and quickest of all fence designs to assemble and construct. The post's acorn finial can either be turned or be purchased from a lumberyard. To give this fence a more traditional appearance, add a decoratively molded baseboard.

Fence: 3 feet, 8 inches high.
Posts: 4 feet, 3 inches high.
High security: The rounded picket tops are awkward to climb and bothersome to sit on.
Low privacy: The pickets are low and spaced, thus allowing easy visibility over and through the fence.
Low buffering: This fence screens little sun and wind.
Construction: Fence, very easy. Posts, very easy.

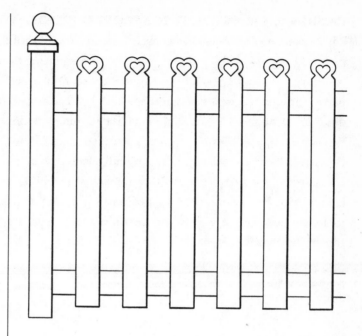

Fence: 3 feet, 9 inches high.
Posts: 4 feet, 3 inches high.
High security: The higher-pointed pickets catch appendages and clothing of fence climbers.
Low privacy: The pickets are low and spaced, thus allowing easy visibility over and through the fence.
Low buffering: This fence screens little sun and wind.
Construction: Fence, very easy. Posts, very easy.

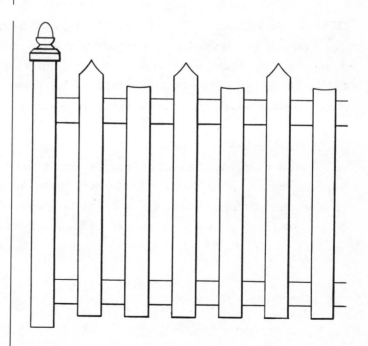

DESIGN 9: ORB-TIPPED SCALLOPED PICKET FENCE

This picket fence is a delightful complement for a traditional European-style garden, with posies among the pickets and lush, flowering vines gracing the posts. These contemporary ball-tipped pickets have gently sloping necks that flow over the adjacent concave-topped picket and into the next ball-tipped picket. The ball-tipped pickets will make the fence quite an uncomfortable seat. This fence is charming yet sophisticated and can be used to dress up a simple home or handsomely accent a more stately abode.

The ball-tipped pickets can be cut with a band saw or a router and pattern. The concave pickets are very easy to cut on a band saw. Assembly and construction of this fence are fast and easy. For the post's ball-topped finial, you can purchase a turned ball and attach it to a sawn pedestal. To give this fence a more traditional appearance, add a decoratively molded baseboard.

DESIGN 10: SCALLOPED CLOVER PICKET FENCE

This whimsical fence has clover-topped pickets with gently sloping necks whose lines flow down to the two adjacent pickets and into the next clover-topped picket. These pickets, although appearing quite friendly, make the fence uncomfortable for sitting. The clover-topped pickets mimic the fence posts and give the fence a rhythmic feel. This design is ideal for cozy country cottages and informal homes and will make the perfect backdrop for a quaint country garden.

The clover-topped pickets can be cut on a band saw or by using a router and pattern. The intermediate concave-sloped pickets are very easy to cut on a band saw. Assembly and construction of this fence are fast and easy. The post's ornamental finial can either be turned or be cut on a band saw. A decoratively molded baseboard will add strength of character to this fence.

Fence: 3 feet, 9 inches high.
Posts: 4 feet, 2 inches high.
High security: The higher
ball-tipped pickets catch
appendages and clothing of
fence climbers.
Low privacy: The pickets
are low and spaced, thus
allowing easy visibility over
and through the fence.
Low buffering: This fence
screens little sun and wind.
Construction: Fence, very
easy. Posts, very easy.

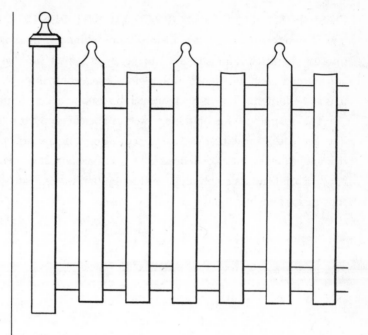

Fence: 4 feet high.
Posts: 4 feet, 2 inches high.
High security: The higher
clover-topped pickets catch
appendages and clothing of
fence climbers.
Low privacy: The pickets
are low and spaced, thus
allowing easy visibility over
and through the fence.
Low buffering: This fence
screens little sun and wind.
Construction: Fence, very
easy. Posts, very easy.

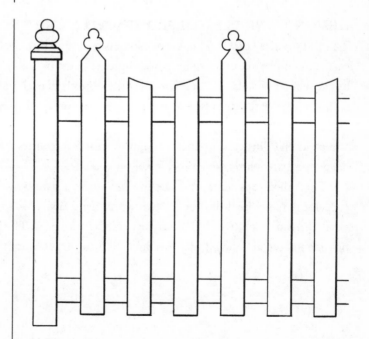

DESIGN 11: HANDLE-TOPPED PICKET FENCE

This design features whimsical handle- or bowling-pin-like tops, which give this fence an unusual character. The gate has a picket as its center finial and two decorative brackets adorning its crest. The fence infill is closely spaced, making the fence ideal for restricting pets and children. This simple fence can be used to accent almost any home.

The ornamental tops on these pickets can be cut with a band saw or a router and pattern. The decorative scroll brackets can be cut using a jigsaw or a scroll saw. Cut the brackets' decorative circles with a drill press. The post's ornamental finial can either be turned or be cut on a band saw. Assembly and construction of this design are simple, and these sawn picket tops are extremely durable.

DESIGN 12: NIPPLE-TOPPED SPACED PICKET FENCE

This rudimentary picket fence is handsomely accented by a decorative gate. In this design, small circles ornament a simple pointed picket pattern. The massive posts are contrasted by the slender pickets. The semicircles at the bottom of each picket make the fence appear delicate. The gate features a picket as its center finial, flanked by two decorative gate scrolls. The close spacing of the pickets in this fence makes it ideal for restricting small pets and children. This easy-to-make design is great for country houses and bungalows. The decorative baseboard adds a more stately appearance.

The balled tops on the pickets can be cut on a band saw. The decorative semicircle cutouts can either be drilled or be sawn with a band saw. The ornamental gate scrolls can be sawn, and the decorative cutouts can be made with a jigsaw. The posts are decorated with an ornamental cap and sawn finial. Assembly and construction of this design are quite simple.

Fence: 3 feet, 8 inches high.
Posts: 4 feet, 4 inches high.
Very high security: Tightly spaced infill protects small pets and children. The jagged fence line make this fence unattractive to climb.
Low privacy: The pickets are low and spaced, thus allowing visibility over and through the fence.
Low buffering: This fence screens some sun and wind.
Construction: Fence, very easy. Posts, very easy.

Fence: 3 feet, 11 inches high.
Posts: 4 feet, 5 inches high.
High security: Closely spaced infill protects small pets and children. The picket tops make this fence unattractive to climb.
Low privacy: The pickets are low and spaced, allowing some visibility.
Low buffering: This fence screens little sun and wind.
Construction: Fence, very easy. Posts, easy.

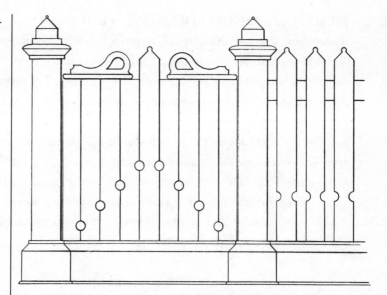

DESIGN 13: V-GROOVE PICKET FENCE

This design has many outstanding qualities. It is versatile and can enhance both vintage and contemporary architecture: As shown it looks just right for a bungalow, but with the addition of a decorative baseboard it will become more formal. This fence provides a reasonable measure of security while still allowing passers-by to look in and admire your house and flower beds.

The gate shown uses a single picket as the center finial, with scrolls flanking the finial.

DESIGN 14: WINGED DIAMOND FENCE

This formidable-looking design has distinctive folk accents, reminiscent of the German Victorian accents popular in the latter half of the nineteenth century. The gate pediment mimics the winged diamond theme of the basic fence. The virtually solid infill of this fence makes it ideal for restricting small pets and children. This design is perfect for country-style farmhouses and yards.

The pointed tops on the pickets can be cut with a band saw, a table saw, or a circular saw. The decorative diamond and winged designs can either be stenciled or be cut out using a band saw. The ornamental gate pediment can be sawn and the decorative cane scrolls veined or appliquéd. The post's ornamental finial can either be turned or be cut on a band saw. Assembly and construction of this design are simple, and the durable style of infill makes this fence very long lasting.

Fence: 3 feet, 10 inches high.
Posts: 4 feet, 2 inches high.
High security: The tightly spaced, pointed pickets are difficult to straddle and very sturdy.
Low privacy: The pickets are low and allow easy visibility over the fence.
Low buffering: This fence blocks some sun and snow.
Construction: Fence, easy. Posts, easy.

Fence: 3 feet, 9 inches high.
Posts: 4 feet, 3 inches high.
Very high security: Solid infill protects small pets and children. Unattractive to climb because of the jagged fence line.
Moderate privacy: The picket height is low but the fence is practically solid, blocking some visibility. This fence can be made higher if more privacy is desired.
Marginal buffering: This fence screens some sun and wind.
Construction: Fence, moderate difficulty. Posts, very easy.

DESIGN 15: NIPPLE-TOPPED PICKET FENCE

This rudimentary picket fence is handsomely accented by a decorative gate. In this design, small circles ornament a simple pointed picket pattern. The silhouette of the fence line mimics a once-common running trim style. A jagged edge separated by circles was a favorite in Victorian times for its appearance and ease of cutting. The gate pediment adds a highlight to the simple fence infill. The virtually solid infill in this fence makes it ideal for restricting small pets and children. This easy-to-make design is great for country houses and bungalows. To give this fence a more formal appearance, add a decorative baseboard.

The balled tops on the pickets can be cut on a band saw. The decorative semicircle cutouts can either be drilled or be sawn with a band saw. The ornamental gate pediment can be sawn and the decorative feathers can be veined or stenciled. The post's ornamental finial can either be turned or be cut on a band saw. Assembly and construction of this design are quite simple, and this infill style is extremely durable.

DESIGN 16: CHERRY PICKET FENCE

The raised pickets of this whimsical design have decorative cherries hanging from their bases. The arching necks supporting the picket heads give the fence a regal appearance. Several decorative lines and configurations embellish the picket body; this highly decorated appearance can be created by stenciling, grooving, applying moldings, or a combination of these techniques. This interpretation of late Victorian architectural detailing can be simplified by omitting the ornate veining, thus creating a streamlined picket appropriate for many types of housing. The baseboard adds a sophisticated finishing touch to the fence and post.

This picket style is suitable to construct of either 1× or 2× material. Using 2× material for pickets will produce a stronger, more substantial looking fence. Cut picket tops using a band saw. If cutting numerous picket tops, use a router and pattern to speed the process. Create decorative veining on pickets using a router and pattern. Use half-round molding to accent the upper portion of the post. The decorative finial can either be turned or be cut on a band saw.

Fence: 3 feet, 10 inches high.
Posts: 4 feet, 2 inches high.
Very high security: Solid infill protects small pets and children. Unattractive to climb because of the jagged fence line.
Moderate privacy: The picket height is low but the fence is practically solid, blocking some visibility. This fence can be made higher if more privacy is desired.
Marginal buffering: This fence screens some sun and wind.
Construction: Fence, very easy. Posts, very easy.

Fence: 4 feet, 1 inch high.
Posts: 4 feet, 5 inches high.
High security: Closer spacing of picket infill will better protect small pets and children. The pickets tops make this fence unattractive to climb.
Low privacy: The pickets are low and spaced, thus allowing visibility over and through the fence.
Low buffering: This fence screens little sun and wind.
Construction: Fence, advanced difficulty. Posts, moderate difficulty.

DESIGN 17: SCALLOPED FENCE WITH IMITATION POST

This is a conventional pale fence with both variety and character. From the stately corner post, with its decorative orb and raised panel and rosette appliqués, the fence's scalloped design rises and falls rhythmically. A sloping picket line crests at a center pointed picket, then dips and crests again at a broad-width picket cut in an imitation post style. The combination of scallops and imitation posts is surprisingly easy to construct and gives this fence a cosmopolitan appearance. This design is ideal for almost any house, from Cape Cods and rural cottages to country chateaus.

The pointed pickets are a breeze to cut using a band saw, and the sloping pickets are twice as easy to cut. The imitation post can be cut using a band saw. If making several imitation posts, use a router and a pattern to speed the cutting process. Assembly and construction of this fence are fast and easy. The post's ornamental finial can be cut using a band saw or turned on a lathe. The beveled cap can be made using a table saw or with a router and panel raising bit. The decoratively molded baseboard adds character to this fence.

DESIGN 18: SWEET HEART CHAPEL PICKET FENCE

The elegant picket top of this intricate, ornate fence is decorated with upside-down swirling hearts, which give this fence a country Victorian charm. Numerous decorative lines and configurations embellish the picket body; this highly decorated appearance can be created by stenciling, grooving, applying moldings, or a combination of these techniques. This interpretation of late-nineteenth-century architectural detailing can be simplified by omitting the ornate veining, thus creating a simple arrow-topped picket appropriate for a broad range of architectural styles. A molded baseboard accents both the fence and post.

This picket style is suitable to construct of either 1× or 2× material. Using 2× material for pickets will produce a stronger, more substantial looking fence. Cut picket tops using a band saw. Create decorative veining on pickets using a router and pattern. Make decorative chamfers in the ornate corner posts. The roofed post top mimics the vintage towers and turrets commonly found on homes of the past century. You can substitute a cap, a finial top, or both for the ornate corner posts.

Fence: 3 feet, 7 inches high.
Posts: 3 feet, 11 inches high.
High security: The pointed pales catch appendages and clothing of fence climbers.
Low privacy: The pickets are low and spaced, thus allowing easy visibility over and through the fence.
Low buffering: This fence screens little sun and wind.
Construction: Fence, easy. Posts, moderate difficulty.

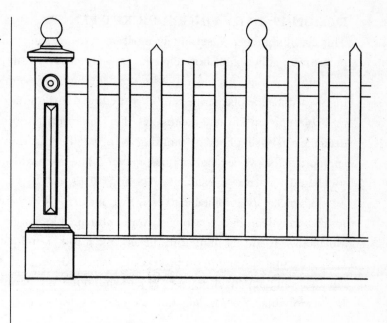

Fence: 3 feet, 10 inches high.
Posts: 4 feet, 5 inches high.
High security: Closer spacing of picket infill will better protect small pets and children. The picket tops make this fence unattractive to climb.
Low privacy: The pickets are low and spaced, thus allowing visibility over and through the fence.
Low buffering: This fence screens little sun and wind.
Construction: Fence, advanced difficulty. Posts, advanced difficulty.

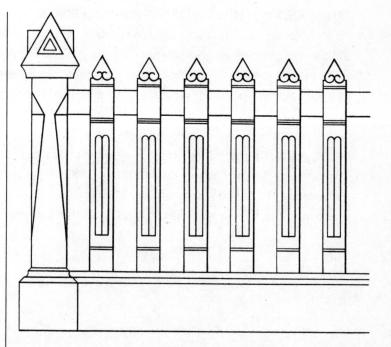

DESIGN 19: LADY FINGER PICKET FENCE

This charming fence is extremely intricate yet surprisingly durable. The broad-necked picket tops, although elaborately cut, have no narrow weak points, so these pickets are very strong. Numerous decorative lines and configurations embellish the picket body; this highly decorated appearance can be created by stenciling, grooving, applying moldings, or a combination of these techniques. This interpretation of late Victorian architectural detailing can be simplified by omitting the ornate veining, thus creating a simplified picket appropriate for a wide range of housing types. The baseboard adds a sophisticated finishing touch to the fence and post.

This picket style is suitable to construct of either 1× or 2× material. Using 2× material for pickets will produce a stronger, more substantial looking fence. Cut picket tops using a band saw. If cutting numerous pickets, use a router and pattern to speed the process. Create decorative veining on pickets and ornate corner posts using a router and pattern. An interesting way to relate your fence to your house is to create a post top that mimics the house's roof line. You can substitute a cap, a finial top, or both for the ornate corner posts.

DESIGN 20: SIMPLE ADAM'S APPLE FENCE

The picket design of this classic-style fence was made available during the nineteenth century in a Victorian architectural-details pattern book published by Rand, McNally and Company. The simplistic styling of this fence makes it appropriate for many traditional and contemporary housing types. The picket features a sharply pointed arrowhead top supported by a potbelly neck. The accent post has an elegantly molded post cap and a decorative molded base with a raised panel and rosette appliqué.

Construct these pickets using 1×4s. Cut picket tops using a band saw. If cutting numerous pickets, use a router and pattern to speed the process. The post finial can either be turned or be cut on a band saw. See "Construction Techniques" for help with making decorative finials, pedestals, caps, rosettes, and other post decorations.

Fence: 3 feet, 11 inches high.
Posts: 4 feet, 4 inches high.
High security: Closer spacing of picket infill will better protect small pets and children. The picket tops make this fence unattractive to climb.
Low privacy: The pickets are low and spaced, thus allowing visibility over and through the fence.
Low buffering: This fence screens little sun and wind.
Construction: Fence, advanced difficulty. Posts, advanced difficulty.

Fence: 3 feet, 8 inches high.
Posts: 4 feet, 2 inches high.
High security: The pointed pickets are difficult to straddle and uncomfortable to sit on.
Low privacy: The pickets are low and allow easy visibility over the fence.
Low buffering: This fence filters some sun and snow.
Construction: Fence, easy. Posts, moderate difficulty.

DESIGN 21: ORNATE CLASSICAL FENCE

This elegant fence is one of a few designs that can enhance a wide variety of contemporary and period homes, including Queen Anne, East Lake, Italianate, Gothic, and many other Victorian styles, as well as colonial, Georgian, and Cape Cod. The picket pattern is somewhat more ornate than the preceding pattern. The picket features a sharply pointed top supported by a decorative neck. The posts and gate depicted are relatively simple to assemble.

Construct these pickets using 1×4s. Cut picket tops using a band saw. If cutting numerous pickets, use a router and pattern to speed the process. See "Construction Techniques" for help with making decorative finials, pedestals, caps, rosettes, scrolls, and other post and gate decorations.

DESIGN 22: SHOOTING HEART PICKET FENCE

This whimsical border fence adds Victorian hearts to the traditional alternating-height pale fence. The pickets are easy to cut, and the heart scrolls and teardrops can be etched or stenciled. The high baseboard and close infill make this fence ideal for restraining pets and children. The accenting post is easy to make, including the sawn heart medallion and post toppers.

Construct these pickets using 1×4s. Cut picket tops using a band saw. If cutting numerous pickets, use a router and pattern to speed the process. See "Construction Techniques" for help with making decorative finials, pedestals, caps, and other post decorations.

Fence: 3 feet, 11 inches high.
Posts: 4 feet, 5 inches high.
High security: The pointed
pickets are difficult to straddle
and uncomfortable to sit on.
Low privacy: The pickets
are low and allow easy
visibility over the fence.
Low buffering: This fence
filters some sun and snow.
Construction: Fence,
easy. Posts, moderate
difficulty.

Fence: 3 feet, 10 inches high.
Posts: 4 feet, 3 inches high.
High security: The pointed
pickets are difficult to straddle
and uncomfortable to sit on.
Low privacy: The pickets
are low and allow easy
visibility over the fence.
Low buffering: This fence
filters some sun and snow.
Construction: Fence,
moderate difficulty. Posts,
easy.

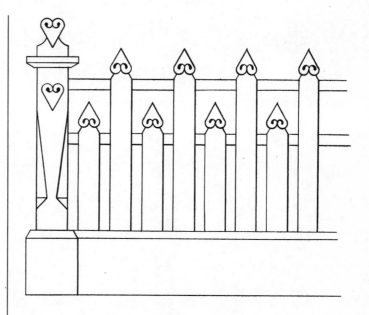

DESIGN 23: TRUMPET-TOPPED VICTORIAN PICKET FENCE

This simplistic fence has a strong Victorian flavor. Nippled trumpets sit atop a straight body picket. The complementary gate uses a modified picket as its center finial. The flanking decorative scroll brackets can be carved or stenciled with the slender cornucopia design. The windows in the gate mimic the center finial, while still providing contrast. Accenting posts use a combination of flat and dimensional ornamentation.

Construct these pickets using 1×4s. Cut picket tops using a band saw. If cutting numerous pickets, use a router and pattern to speed the process. See "Construction Techniques" for help with making decorative finials, pedestals, caps, and other post decorations.

Fence: 4 feet, 4 inches high.
Posts: 4 feet, 6 inches high.
High security: The pointed pickets are difficult to straddle and uncomfortable to sit on.
Low privacy: The pickets are low and allow easy visibility over the fence.
Low buffering: This fence filters some sun and snow.
Construction: Fence, easy. Posts, moderate difficulty.

Board Fences—Partial
and Full Privacy

DESIGN 24: COUNTRY MOON BOARD FENCE

Setting half-moon crested boards are overlapped by tall sentinel pickets to create contrast in this striking Victorian country fence. This design makes a wonderful privacy and security fence; the fence height can be increased to provide added privacy and security without sacrificing beauty. The irregular line of the fence top makes it cumbersome to climb. The board-on-board style allows minimal visibility while permitting some air flow through the fence. The feathered crescent design on every other board can be stenciled or carved. The ornamental post is simple in style but provides a handsome accent to the pickets, while the baseboard adds a sophisticated touch.

The fence infill can be made from 1× stock. Both types of boards in this fence can be cut with a band saw or a router and pattern. The pointed pickets could also be cut on a table saw. For more privacy, allow overlap between pickets and boards.

DESIGN 25: FLAT ARROW FENCE

This design is plain and simple but attention-grabbing. Broad, skyward-pointing arrow boards rise in contrast to narrow, plunging arrow cutouts. To increase the privacy value of this fence, eliminate the spacing between the boards. This fence is excellent for restraining children and pets because of its narrow spacing and limited toeholds. The illustration depicts one method of altering the fence to accommodate a hillside or a set of steps. The accent post is decorated by a beveled top and chamfered neck. This fence is well suited for rustic country-style homes, especially if the boards are rough-sawn lumber.

This board infill should be constructed using 1× material, which should be adequately durable for most residential use. Cut the board tops using a band saw. If cutting numerous boards, use a router and pattern to speed the process. To reduce waste wood and cutting time, space boards 1 to 2 inches apart instead of ripping them to form the plunging arrow shaft. The point of the plunging arrow will be sacrificed, but the reduction in time and materials may justify this for you.

Fence: 3 feet, 11 inches high.
Posts: 4 feet, 4 inches high.
High security: The pointed picket tops make this fence unattractive to climb.
High privacy: The infill design is dense, allowing very limited visibility through the fence. The fence easily lends itself to added height.
Moderate buffering: This fence blocks sun and hinders wind.
Construction: Fence, easy. Posts, very easy.

Fence: 3 feet, 10 inches high.
Posts: 4 feet high.
High security: The close spacing of the board infill makes this an excellent fence for small children and pets.
Moderate privacy: The picket boards can be made high enough for privacy, but the spacing between the boards would need to be eliminated to render complete privacy.
Moderate buffering: This fence blocks sun and filters wind.
Construction: Fence, moderate difficulty. Posts, very easy.

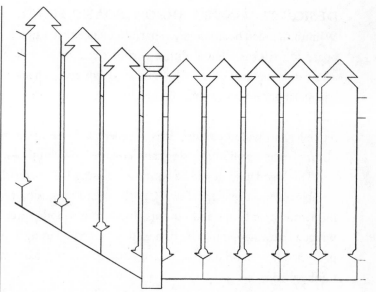

DESIGN 26: PIGTAIL HEARTS FENCE

This is a rudimentary, extremely versatile design with country charm. Each board has half-heart cutouts that pair up with the cutouts on the neighboring boards to form a whimsical offset heart design. The boards are topped with upside-down hearts that have Victorian-style pigtail scrollwork. To increase the privacy value of this fence, eliminate the heart cutouts in the middle of the fence or replace them with heart appliqués. With this change, this fence would also be excellent for restraining children. The illustration depicts one method of altering the fence to accommodate a hillside or a set of steps. The accent post is decorated by a two-dimensional heart finial that complements the fence infill. This fence is well suited for country homes or small town homes with a country flair.

This board infill should be constructed using 1× material, which should be adequately durable for most residential use. Cut the board tops using a band saw. If cutting numerous boards, use a router and pattern to speed the process. The pigtails on the posts and boards can be stenciled or etched into the wood using a router with veining bit and pattern.

DESIGN 27: WINGED ARROW BOARD FENCE

Whimsical broad boards form a charming fence that is quick to construct. Each semicircle board top is ornamented with a cutout circle or a circle appliqué. A graceful winged arrow design embellishes each board. A decorative urn accents the simple post style. The triangular accent boards may be heightened to increase security or omitted if you would like to simplify the fence. For added privacy, the board spacing may be eliminated. As this fence has no wide openings, it is excellent for restraining pets and small children. This cheery fence is well suited for quaint cottages and country-style farmhouses.

This board infill should be constructed using 1×8 material, which should be adequately durable for most residential use. Cut the board tops using a band saw or jigsaw. If cutting numerous board tops and cutouts, use a router and pattern to speed the process. The winged arrow design may be stenciled or be etched using a router with straight cut bit and pattern. The urn on the post can be turned, cut on a band saw, or purchased from a local lumberyard.

Fence: 3 feet, 7 inches high.
Posts: 4 feet high.
High Security: The close spacing of the board infill makes this an excellent fence for small children and pets.
Moderate to high privacy: The picket boards can be made high enough for privacy, but the cutouts between the boards would need to be eliminated to render complete privacy.
Moderate buffering: This fence blocks some sun and filters wind.
Construction: Fence, moderate difficulty. Posts, easy.

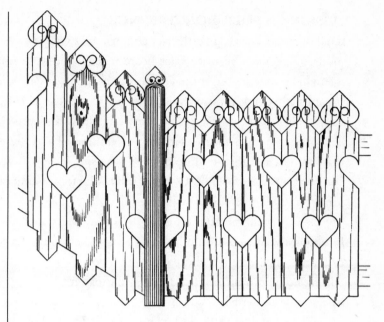

Fence: 3 feet, 7 inches high.
Posts: 4 feet, 5 inches high.
High security: The close spacing of the board infill makes this an excellent fence for restraining small children and pets.
Moderate to high privacy: For added privacy, the board height can easily be increased and the spacing between the boards eliminated.
Moderate buffering: This fence blocks some sun and filters wind.
Construction: Fence, moderate difficulty. Posts, easy.

DESIGN 28: FOLK BOARD FENCE

Circle-topped boards give this fence a friendly country charm while still providing a moderate degree of security. Each board is decorated with three circle cutouts: At the top is a round donut design, at the center is a circle cutout decorated with a molded edge and ornamental veining, and at the bottom is a semicircle with a circle cutout. The rounded board bottoms may be omitted to provide increased security for pets and small children. The spacing between the boards can be eliminated and the circles can be etched rather than cut out to provide more privacy. The simple post is accented by a ball finial that complements the circles in the board infill. The folk styling of this fence makes it perfect for a country farmhouse or farmette.

Construct the board infill using 1×8 material, which should be adequately durable for most residential use. Cut the board tops and bottoms using a band saw or jigsaw. Use a drill press, jigsaw, router and pattern, or a combination thereof to cut out the circles. If cutting numerous boards, use a router and pattern to speed the process. The decorative design may be stenciled, but etching the design into the wood will make it permanent. Use a router with straight cut bit and pattern. The ball on the post can be turned, cut on a band saw, or purchased from a local lumberyard.

DESIGN 29: VICTORIAN BOARD-ON-BOARD FENCE

Circle-topped boards give this fence a friendly country charm while still providing a high degree of security. Tall, drilled-hole pickets alternate with short, stenciled pickets. The stencils illustrated here give the fence a Victorian flavor, but other stencils can be used or they can be omitted entirely. This design is very adaptable, and the fence looks great either short or tall. For the front yard, it can be a low, charming picket fence that allows you to view the activities of the street and permits passers-by to enjoy your flower beds. For the backyard, increased height can provide more privacy. The detailed nature of these pickets, the corner posts, and the decorative baseboard make this fence suitable for the most sophisticated town houses, but it is informal enough to grace cozy country cottages.

Construct the board infill using 1×6 material, which should be adequately durable for most residential use. Cut the board tops using a band saw or jigsaw. Use a drill press, jigsaw, router and pattern, or a combination thereof to cut out the circles. The decorative design may be stenciled, but etching the design into the wood will make it permanent. Use a router with straight cut bit and pattern. The urn on the corner post can be turned, cut on a band saw, or purchased from a local lumberyard. The decorative panel on the corner post body can be created with molding or by applying a raised panel appliqué.

Fence: 4 feet, 1 inch high.
Posts: 4 feet, 3 inches high.
Moderate security: This fence can be made more secure for restraining small pets by omitting the rounded bottoms and adding a baseboard.
Moderate to high privacy: For added privacy, the board height can easily be increased and the spacing between the boards and decorative circle cutouts eliminated.
Moderate buffering: This fence blocks some sun and filters some wind.
Construction: Fence, moderate difficulty. Posts, easy.

Fence: 3 feet, 11 inches high.
Posts: 4 feet, 3 inches high.
High security: Even though the tops of these pickets are rounded, they will still catch clothing and appendages, making climbing difficult.
Moderate to high privacy: For added privacy, the board height can easily be increased. To maximize privacy, place all pickets on one side of the stringers instead of alternating from front to back.
Moderate buffering: This fence blocks some sun and filters some wind.
Construction: Fence, moderate difficulty. Posts, moderate difficulty.

DESIGN 30: PLEASANTLY PLUMP COUNTRY HEARTS FENCE

This broad-boarded fence with chubby, upside-down hearts has a friendly appearance while still inhibiting fence climbers and sitters. For added security and privacy, the fence height can be increased and the heart cutouts between boards may be changed to heart appliqués. This design is very adaptable, and the fence looks great either short or tall. For the front yard, it can be a low, charming picket fence that allows you to view the activities of the street and permits passers-by to enjoy your flower beds. For the backyard, increased height can provide more privacy. This style is ideal for a Victorian country farmhouse.

Construct the board infill using 1×8 material, which should be adequately durable for most residential use. Use a band saw, jigsaw, router and pattern, or a combination thereof to cut out the board tops, bottoms, and midsection hearts. Use a router with veining bit and pattern to decorate the post body with the simple design depicted.

DESIGN 31: RURAL GOTHIC BOARD FENCE

Elements of country charm and Victorian Gothic combine in this infill design, which was featured in an 1873 Victorian architectural-details pattern book. Victorian Gothic arches top each board, and between the boards are sawn Gothic windows. The chamfered post, beveled rail, and baseboard contrast with the arching cuts of the fence infill. For additional privacy and security, the fence can be made higher. This fence is excellent for restraining pets and children. It is ideal for quaint country churchyards and Gothic-inspired homes.

Construct the board infill using 1×8 material, which should be adequately durable for most residential use. Use a band saw, jigsaw, router and pattern, or a combination thereof to cut out the board tops and midsection designs. The deep chamfers depicted can be made using a circular saw with some skill and patience. For quick-to-cut, shallower chamfers, use a router with chamfer bit.

Fence: 3 feet, 11 inches high.

Posts: 4 feet, 2 inches high.

Moderate to high security: This fence can be made more secure for restraining small pets by adding a decorative baseboard.

Moderate to high privacy: For added privacy, the board height can easily be increased and the heart cutouts eliminated or replaced with heart appliqués.

Moderate buffering: This fence blocks some sun and filters some wind.

Construction: Fence, moderate difficulty. Posts, easy.

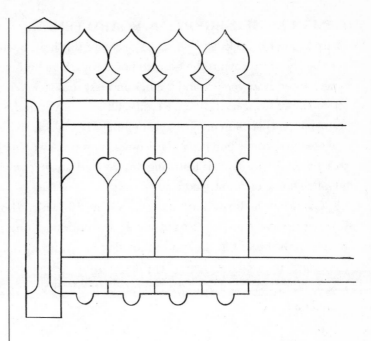

Fence: 3 feet, 6 inches high.

Posts: 3 feet, 9 inches high.

High security: Pointed tops and tightly spaced infill are perfect for keeping pets and children in and unwanted intruders out.

Moderate to high privacy: For added privacy, the board height can easily be increased and the window cutouts eliminated.

Moderate buffering: This fence blocks some sun and filters some wind.

Construction: Fence, easy. Posts, moderate difficulty.

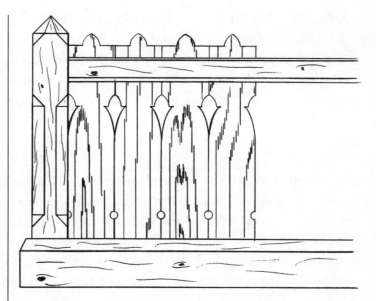

DESIGN 32: NEO-EGYPTIAN BOARD FENCE

Sharp triangular peaks and windows decorate this bold board fence. An obelisk-styled post boldly complements the pointed board tops. The flush, molded baseboard gives the fence a smooth appearance and is quick and easy to install. With its narrow lower windows and no inner stringers, this fence is difficult to climb from the inside and thus is good for restraining small children. This style of infill was available in the late 1800s and frequently was used to decorate porches and balconies. This fence would be an excellent complement to a vintage Victorian villa featuring this fretwork style; it would also add a nice accent to a Gothic home or country cottage.

Construct the board infill using 1×8 material, which should be adequately durable for most residential use. Use a band saw, jigsaw, router and pattern, or a combination thereof to cut out the board tops and midsection designs. If cutting numerous boards, use a router and pattern to speed the process. The deep chamfers depicted can be made using a circular saw with some skill and patience. For quick-to-cut, shallower chamfers, use a router with chamfer bit.

DESIGN 33: SCALLOPED BOARD FENCE

This whimsical design was inspired by porch and balcony fretwork in Cummings and Miller's Victorian architectural-details pattern books. A scalloped wave top gives the fence a nautical flair, making it a great accent for waterside cottages. The strong post and bold stringer style add character. This charming board fence with small windows is superb for restraining small pets and children, and it adapts well to increased height, making it an excellent security fence. For a more formal appearance, the lower stringer may be replaced or overlaid with a baseboard.

Construct the board infill using 1×8 material, which should be adequately durable for most residential use. Use a band saw, jigsaw, router and pattern, or a combination thereof to cut out the board tops and midsection designs. If cutting numerous boards, use a router and pattern to speed the process. The deep chamfers depicted can be made using a band saw and a circular saw with some skill and patience. For quick-to-cut, shallower chamfers, use a router with chamfer bit. The beveled rails can be made with a circular saw or table saw.

Fence: 3 feet, 8 inches high.
Posts: 4 feet, 1 inch high.
High security: Pointed tops and tightly spaced infill are perfect for keeping pets and children in and unwanted intruders out.
Moderate to high privacy: For added privacy, the board height can easily be increased and the window cutouts eliminated.
Moderate buffering: This fence blocks some sun and filters some wind.
Construction: Fence, moderate difficulty. Posts, moderate difficulty.

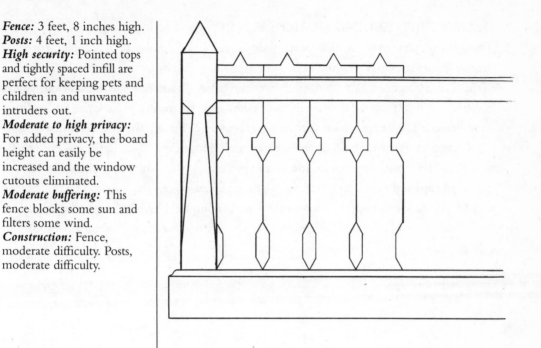

Fence: 3 feet, 5 inches high.
Posts: 3 feet, 8 inches high.
High security: Pointed tops and tightly spaced infill are perfect for keeping pets and children in and unwanted intruders out.
Moderate to high privacy: For added privacy, the board height can easily be increased and the window cutouts eliminated.
Moderate buffering: This fence blocks some sun and filters some wind.
Construction: Fence, easy. Posts, advanced difficulty.

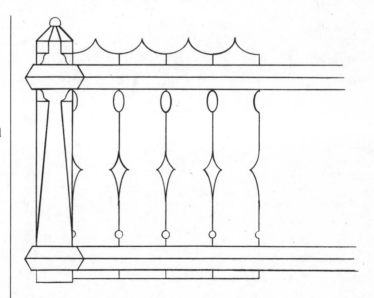

DESIGN 34: BLEEDING HEARTS FENCE

The intricate pattern of this Victorian-style fence can be handsomely complemented by delicate flowering vines weaving in and out of the bleeding heart windows. The crisp lines of the accent post contrast with the curves of the fence. To increase the fence's security and durability, you can reduce the size of the bleeding heart cutouts or back the fence with a lattice screen. This design makes a charming accent fence for any Victorian country cottage.

Construct the board infill using 1×8 material. (For increased strength, you can use 2× material.) Use a band saw, jigsaw, router and pattern, or a combination thereof to cut out the board tops and midsection designs. Use a table saw to cut the post cap and to cut the post to length. Use a band saw to cut the panel appliqué. The beveled baseboard can be made with a circular saw or table saw. The post is easy to cut and assemble, and turned balls can be purchased at most lumberyards.

Fence: 4 feet, 1 inch high.
Posts: 4 feet, 7 inches high.
Moderate security: Large decorative openings will enable small pets to slip through the fence.
Low privacy: The infill is quite open, with numerous large windows that allow visibility into the yard.
Low buffering: This fence filters some sun and a little wind.
Construction: Fence, advanced difficulty. Posts, moderate difficulty.

Sawn Picket Fences

DESIGN 35: TAPERED WHISTLE-TOP FENCE

This fence's narrow pickets are among the easiest full body sawn pickets to cut, with just six straight cuts and four concave arcs per picket. The sharp, arrowhead points are attractive and very effective at deterring fence sitters. The elegantly tapered body gives the illusion of greater height. The post finial of ball and spire stands in sharp contrast to the overall fence. This fence will enhance any home with a similarly pitched gable or hip roof line.

Construct the board infill using 1×4 material. (For increased strength, you can use ¾×4 material.) Use a drill press to make semicircle cutouts. Use a band saw or table saw to make the straight cuts. The deep chamfers on the post depicted can be made with a circular saw, but you may find it easier to add smaller decorative chamfers using a router with chamfer bit. The beveled baseboard can be made with a circular saw or table saw. The decorative finial can either be turned or be cut on a band saw.

DESIGN 36: OVER-UNDER CIRCLES FENCE

This is a charming Victorian picket fence with a friendlier appearance than a typical pointed-top picket fence. These slender pickets with sawn beaded middles are similar to porch turnings, while the picket top ensemble reflects one of the more common Victorian running trims. The strong oversized post with raised panel appliqué lends stability to the fence's appearance. This fence is both elegant and functional and can grace a variety of homes, especially those with similar architectural detailing.

Construct the board infill using 1×8 material. (For increased strength, you can use ¾×6 material.) Use a band saw or a router with pattern to cut the decorative tops and picket bodies. The oversized decorative post cap can be made by layering the post cap with multiple reducing pedestals until the last pedestal comes to a point. Cut out the panel appliqué on a band saw and use a router with panel raising bit to create the decorative edge. The ball to place on the top of the post cap may be purchased at a lumberyard. The beveled baseboard can be made with a circular saw or table saw.

Fence: 3 feet, 4 inches high.
Posts: 4 feet, 4 inches high.
High security: The closely spaced pickets make it difficult for most pets and children to squeeze through this fence.
Low privacy: The infill design is open, allowing virtually unhampered visibility into the yard.
Low buffering: This fence filters very little sun and wind.
Construction: Fence, moderate difficulty. Posts, moderate difficulty.

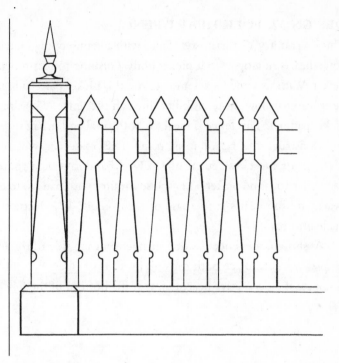

Fence: 3 feet, 4 inches high.
Posts: 4 feet, 4 inches high.
High security: The closely spaced pickets make it difficult for most pets and children to squeeze through this fence.
Low privacy: The infill design is open, allowing virtually unhampered visibility into the yard.
Low buffering: This fence filters very little sun and wind.
Construction: Fence, moderate difficulty. Posts, advanced difficulty.

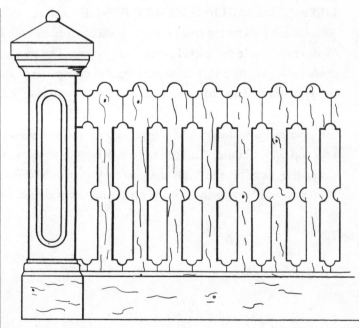

DESIGN 37: FOLK HEART FENCE

This is a country Victorian-style fence with a Pennsylvania Dutch accent. Whimsical upside-down hearts sit atop a stout picket body. Gushing fountain hearts adorn the belly of each picket. With its wide angles and curves, this picket pattern is easy to cut. The pickets can be spaced to allow more visibility through the fence. The simple post topper mimics the picket pattern. This fence is ideal for both rural and urban use.

Construct the board infill using 1×8 material, which should provide adequate strength for most residential uses. Use a band saw or a router with pattern to cut the decorative tops and picket bodies. Use a router with pattern to etch the decorative fountain hearts and the hearts at the base of each board. The decorative post finial can easily be made on a band saw.

As shown, the fence has one stringer on each side of the infill. To make construction simpler, you can place both top and bottom stringers behind the infill, and you can also eliminate the decorative heart points at the bottom of the fence.

DESIGN 38: SMILING HEART FENCE

This cheerful Victorian fence features pickets adorned with decoratively stenciled hearts. Wide curves make this picket pattern easy to cut. The gate is ornamented with an upside-down heart pediment that displays a stenciled vine pattern. Joker hearts are stenciled on the solid gate body. This charming fence can give country-style homes an even friendlier feel.

Construct the board infill using 1×8 material, which should provide adequate strength for most residential uses. Use a band saw or a router with pattern to cut the decorative tops and picket bodies. You can use a router with straight cut bit and pattern to etch the decorative swirls in the heart designs, or you can create a stencil and paint them. The heart post finial can easily be made on a band saw and decorated with a stencil or etchings.

Fence: 3 feet, 4 inches high.
Posts: 4 feet, 4 inches high.
High security: The closely spaced pickets make it difficult for most pets and children to squeeze through this fence.
Low privacy: The infill height is low, allowing visibility over the fence.
Low buffering: This fence filters some sun and wind.
Construction: Fence, advanced difficulty. Posts, easy.

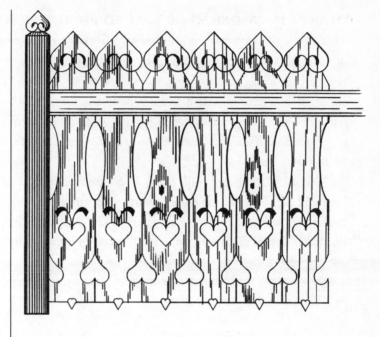

Fence: 3 feet, 11 inches high.
Posts: 4 feet, 5 inches high.
Moderate security: Spacing the pickets more closely would improve the security for small pets.
Low privacy: The infill height is low, allowing visibility over the fence.
Low buffering: This fence filters some sun and wind.
Construction: Fence, advanced difficulty. Posts, easy.

DESIGN 39: GOOSE NECK SPACED PICKET FENCE

This formal picket pattern with elongated necks complements the gingerbread fretwork of many Victorian homes. This fence is quite open in design, allowing you to easily see beyond your fence and allowing passers-by to enjoy your flower beds. Although the pickets are ornately sawn, the actual fence is basic and easy to assemble. The accenting post is enhanced by a lone diamond appliqué and an urn with an unusual egg shape. Pickets are placed flush with the post fronts, eliminating the need to cut and apply additional moldings to the post bases.

Construct the board infill using 1×6 material. (For increased strength, you can use ¾×6 material.) Use a band saw or a router with pattern to cut the decorative tops and picket bodies. Saw the post appliqué using a scroll saw or jigsaw. The post urn can be turned, cut on a band saw, or purchased from a mill house or lumberyard.

DESIGN 40: CLOVER TOP PICKET FENCE

Traditional Victorian sawn picket bodies are topped by clovers on stout, very durable necks. Molded stringers accent both the post and fence. The post is ornamented with additional trim, baseboard, panel, and medallion appliqués, as well as a beveled post cap and pedestal-supported ball finial. This design is an excellent choice for restorationists who want a fence with authentic Victorian flavor while still maintaining a high degree of strength and durability.

Construct the board infill using 1×6 material. (For increased strength, you can use ¾×6 material.) Use a band saw or a router with pattern to cut the decorative tops and picket bodies. See "Construction Techniques" for help with making decorative rosettes, panels, and other post decorations. The decorative ball finial can be turned or purchased from a lumberyard.

Fence: 3 feet, 11 inches high.
Posts: 4 feet, 7 inches high.
Moderate security: Spacing the pickets more closely would improve the security for small pets.
Low privacy: The infill height is low, allowing visibility over the fence.
Low buffering: This fence filters little sun and wind.
Construction: Fence, moderate difficulty. Posts, easy.

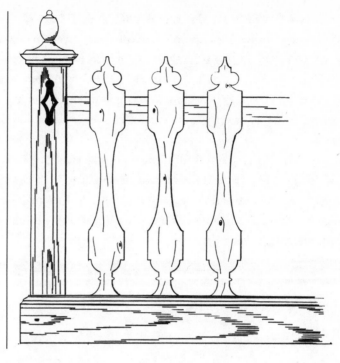

Fence: 4 feet, 1 inch high.
Posts: 4 feet, 7 inches high.
Moderate security: Spacing the pickets more closely would improve the security for small pets. The clover-topped pickets make sitting on this fence undesirable.
Low privacy: The infill design is low and spaced, allowing visibility over and through the fence.
Low buffering: This fence filters little sun and wind.
Construction: Fence, moderate difficulty. Posts, moderate difficulty.

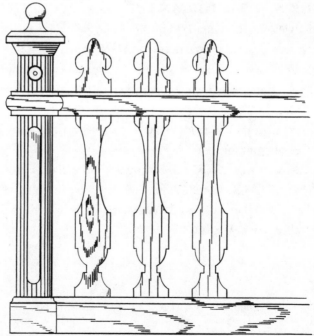

DESIGN 41: FLEUR DE LIS PICKET FENCE

These graceful sawn Victorian pickets with decorative heart cutouts display a French country flair. These charming pickets are surprisingly easy to cut. The elegant picket tops are supported by delicate curved necks. This fence design should not be used where it will receive heavy abuse or the thin necks may snap. The simple accent post with oversized post cap is excellent for corners or for flanking a main gate. This fence beautifully accents French country-style homes.

Construct the board infill using 1×6 material. (For increased strength, you can use ¾×6 material.) Use a band saw or a router with pattern to cut the decorative tops and picket bodies. See "Construction Techniques" for help with making decorative rosettes, panels, and other post decorations. The oversized post cap can be created by layering multiple pedestals atop the post cap.

DESIGN 42: VICTORIAN PEDESTAL PICKET FENCE

This style and others similar to it were made available in the late 1800s in numerous Victorian architectural-details pattern books. Here, vintage-style Victorian pedestal pickets stand beautifully beside either lavish or basic accent posts. A raised panel accent post is capped by a sawn finial that resembles the picket tops. While this fence with its accent posts is one of the more time-consuming styles to cut and construct, the beauty of the finished piece is worth the effort. This fence creates a charming trim for any bric-a-brac adorned Victorian cottage or mansion.

Construct the board infill using 1×6 material. (For increased strength, you can use ¾×6 material.) Use a band saw or a router with pattern to cut the decorative tops and picket bodies. See "Construction Techniques" for help with making decorative panels, finials, and other post decorations.

Fence: 3 feet, 6 inches high.
Posts: 4 feet, 6 inches high.
High security: Closely spaced pickets provide security for pets and children. The fleur-de-lis-topped pickets make sitting on this fence unthinkable.
Low privacy: The infill height is low, allowing visibility over the fence.
Low buffering: This fence filters little sun and wind.
Construction: Fence, moderate difficulty. Posts, moderate difficulty.

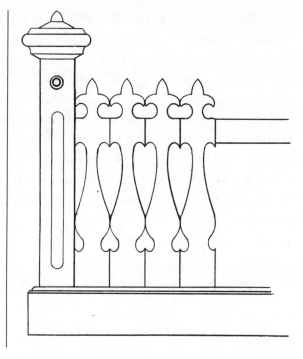

Fence: 3 feet, 6 inches high.
Posts: 4 feet, 2 inches high.
Moderate security: Open areas at picket bottoms could allow some smaller pets to squeeze through.
Low privacy: The infill design is low and spaced, allowing visibility over and through the fence.
Low buffering: This fence filters little sun and wind.
Construction: Fence, moderate difficulty. Posts, advanced difficulty.

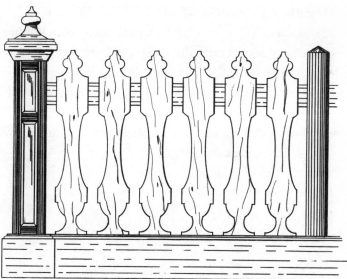

DESIGN 43: BIRDHOUSE PICKET FENCE

This attractive fence is very ornate, with its sawn edges and decorative cutouts. The picket tops resemble gable-roofed birdhouses with little drilled doors. Siamese diamonds grace the middle of the fence. The picket infill is fully sawn and is fascinating to look at and through. This design is suitable for restraining children and discouraging people from sitting on your fence. The post finial reflects the pitch and flavor of the picket tops. You can adapt the pitch of these points to reflect the roof line of your house.

Construct the board infill using 1×6 material. (For increased strength, you can use ¾×6 material.) Use a band saw or a router with pattern to cut the decorative tops and picket bodies. See "Construction Techniques" for help with making decorative veining, finials, and other post decorations.

DESIGN 44: SCALLOPED BOARD FENCE

Semicircle tops grace this broad picket-style design. Simple miter-cut accent posts and beveled baseboard make this fence quick and easy to cut and assemble. The fence may be made higher for added security. This durable fence is a good choice for heavy-use areas.

Construct the board infill using 1×8 material, which should provide adequate strength for most residential needs. Use a band saw or a router with pattern to cut the decorative tops and picket bodies. See "Construction Techniques" for helpful hints on making the corner post more decorative.

Fence: 3 feet, 9 inches high.
Posts: 4 feet, 3 inches high.
Moderate security: Open areas at picket bottoms could allow some smaller pets to squeeze through.
Low privacy: The infill design is low and spaced, allowing visibility over and through the fence.
Low buffering: This fence filters little sun and wind.
Construction: Fence, advanced difficulty. Posts, moderate difficulty.

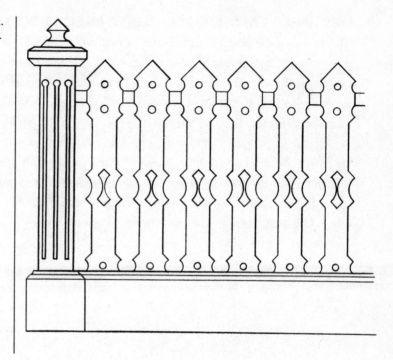

Fence: 3 feet, 11 inches high.
Posts: 4 feet, 3 inches high.
Moderate security: Open areas at picket bottoms could allow some smaller pets to squeeze through.
Low privacy: The infill design is low and spaced, allowing visibility over and through the fence.
Low buffering: This fence filters some sun and wind.
Construction: Fence, moderate difficulty. Posts, very easy.

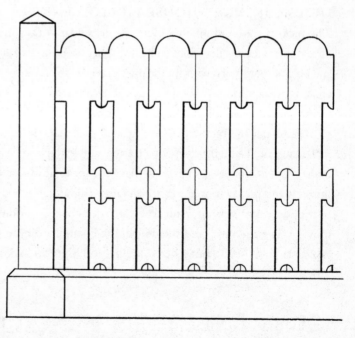

DESIGN 45: BALL-TOPPED CHAMFERED PICKET FENCE

This is one of the simplest and quickest to cut of all the full body sawn picket styles. The decorative medallions can be painted carved, or appliquéd onto each picket, or they can be omitted to further simplify the design. The handsome, multilayered, ornamental post is especially complementary to a turreted Victorian manor, although this fence can enhance both modern and period architecture.

Construct the picket infill using 1×6 material, which should provide adequate strength for most residential needs. Use a band saw or a router with pattern to cut the decorative tops and picket bodies. The ornate beauty of the multilayered post body is not very difficult to create, but the hipped roof post cap will present a challenge. See "Construction Techniques" for some helpful hints on making decorative corner posts.

DESIGN 46: WREN HOUSE PICKET FENCE

The pickets are handsomely sawn with inner and outer incisions. The spacing between pickets forms a propeller design. The strong accent post, ornamented with overstated moldings and bold accents, borrows from the picket style. Gabled picket tops feature drilled center holes creating the appearance of birdhouses. This attractive picket combination is especially flattering to Victorian homes with similar sawn balustrades on their porches and balconies.

Construct the picket infill using 1×6 material. (For increased strength, you can use ¾×6 material.) Use a band saw or a router with pattern to cut the decorative tops and picket bodies. Use a scroll saw or jigsaw to make the spear-head-shaped cutouts. The round decorations on the picket tops are easy to craft using a drill press. The ornate, multichamfered post body is not very difficult to create; the curved middle indentation can be sawn on most larger band saws, and the deepening chamfers can be sawn using a circular saw. See "Construction Techniques" for some helpful hints on making decorative corner posts.

Fence: 3 feet, 8 inches high.
Posts: 4 feet, 5 inches high.
Moderate security: Open
areas at picket bottoms
could allow some smaller
pets to squeeze through.
Low privacy: The infill
design is low and spaced,
thus allowing visibility over
and through the fence.
Low buffering: This fence
filters some sun and wind.
Construction: Fence,
advanced difficulty. Posts,
advanced difficulty.

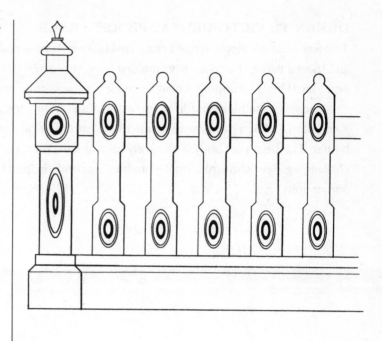

Fence: 4 feet, 3 inches high.
Posts: 4 feet, 8 inches high.
Moderate security: Open
areas at picket bottoms
could allow some smaller
pets to squeeze through.
Low privacy: The infill
design is low and spaced,
thus allowing visibility over
and through the fence.
Low buffering: This fence
filters little sun and wind.
Construction: Fence,
advanced difficulty. Posts,
advanced difficulty.

DESIGN 47: VICTORIENTAL PICKET FENCE

This fence features nipple-topped chamfered body-style pickets along with accent posts with an Oriental flavor. The posts have molded bases, recessed full body panels, and pagodalike post caps. This is a stunning accent fence for Oriental-influenced homes.

Construct the picket infill using 1×6 material. (For increased strength, you can use ¾×6 material.) Use a band saw or a router with pattern to cut the decorative tops and picket bodies. The large post body is relatively easy to construct, but the oversized cap is more challenging. See "Construction Techniques" for some helpful hints on making decorative corner posts.

DESIGN 48: HIGH VICTORIAN GINGERBREAD GOTHIC FENCE

This Gothic Victorian picket fence is graced by numerous curvaceous arches and angular cuts. The strongly styled accent post features a full-body elliptical molding decoration and balled post cap. This is one of the most splendid accent fences for any Gothic-inspired Victorian home, small or grandiose.

Construct the picket infill using 1×8 material, which should provide adequate strength for most residential uses. Use a band saw or a router with pattern to cut the decorative tops and picket bodies. The large post is relatively easy to construct. Use the table saw method to create the decorative post cap. See "Construction Techniques" for some helpful hints on making decorative corner posts.

Fence: 3 feet, 4 inches high.
Posts: 4 feet, 1 inch high.
Moderate security: Open areas at picket bottoms could allow some smaller pets to squeeze through.
Low privacy: The infill design is low and spaced, thus allowing visibility over and through the fence.
Low buffering: This fence filters little sun and wind.
Construction: Fence, moderate difficulty. Posts, advanced difficulty.

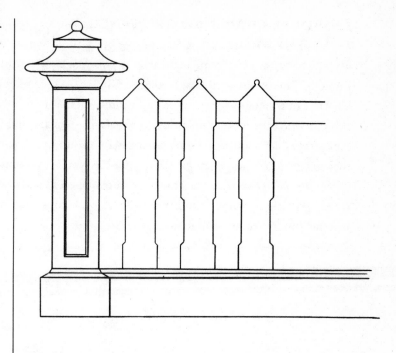

Fence: 3 feet, 10 inches high.
Posts: 4 feet, 7 inches high.
High security: Open areas at picket bottoms are quite narrow, making it difficult for even a small pet to squeeze through.
Low privacy: The low infill design and numerous cutouts allow visibility over and through the fence.
Low buffering: This fence filters some sun and wind.
Construction. Fence, moderate difficulty. Posts, moderate difficulty.

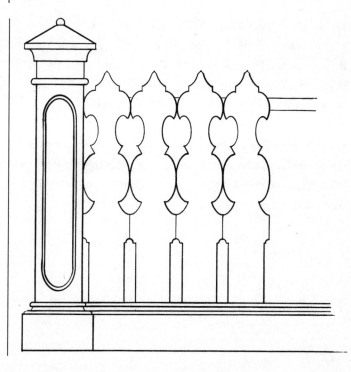

DESIGN 49: CHAPEL GOTHIC FENCE

Gothic arches abound in this fanciful design. Gothic windows are cut in the center of each picket and between pickets, making this fence especially charming to look at and through. The ornamental post features a Gothic panel appliqué and a rounded post cap. This design is suitable for any Gothic-inspired Victorian home or chapel.

Construct the picket infill using 1×8 material, which should provide adequate strength for most residential needs. Use a band saw or a router with pattern to cut the decorative tops and picket bodies. Use a jigsaw to make the window cutouts. The ornate corner post is relatively easy to construct. Saw the panel appliqué on a band saw. Stack multiple pediments on the post cap to achieve the layered effect. See "Construction Techniques" for help on making caps, moldings, and other post decorations.

DESIGN 50: PEEK-A-BOO PICKET FENCE

Rudimentary nipple-topped pickets are heightened by a solitary vertical line divided by a drilled circle. The easy-to-make posts imitate the picket design. You can use a simple baseboard, like the one shown, or a more elaborate one. Simple styling makes this fence appropriate for most settings and housing styles.

Construct the picket infill using 1×6 or 1×8 material, which should provide adequate strength for most residential needs. Use a band saw or a router with pattern to cut the decorative tops and picket bodies. The decorative circle cutout can be made on a drill press. Use a router with a parallel guide to make the long vein in each picket. The corner post is easy to construct.

Fence: 3 feet, 6 inches high.
Posts: 4 feet, 3 inches high.
High security: Open areas at picket bottoms are quite narrow, making it difficult for even a small pet to squeeze through.
Low privacy: The infill height is low, thus allowing visibility over the fence.
Low buffering: This fence filters some sun and wind.
Construction: Fence, advanced difficulty. Posts, moderate difficulty.

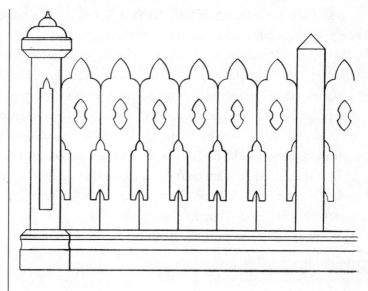

Fence: 3 feet, 8 inches high.
Posts: 4 feet high.
High security: Open areas at picket bottoms are quite narrow, making it difficult for even a small pet to squeeze through.
Low privacy: The infill height is low, thus allowing visibility over the fence.
Low buffering: This fence filters some sun and wind.
Construction: Fence, advanced difficulty. Posts, very easy.

DESIGN 51: STORYBOOK GINGERBREAD FENCE

These pickets are among the most fanciful and whimsically styled. The spade tops sit on an oversized Adam's-apple neck featuring a doughnut-hole cutout. The gradually slendering picket body flows into a similarly shaped doughnut-hole potbelly, which is supported by a trumpet base. The gate mimics the decorative pediment used over the windows and doors of numerous late-nineteenth-century dwellings. The posts are ornamented with numerous moldings and crowned with urn finials. This full body sculptured design will superbly complement any gingerbread-adorned home, be it a small country cottage or a big city mansion.

Construct the picket infill using 1×6 material. (For increased strength, you can use ¾×6 material.) Use a band saw or a router with pattern to cut the decorative tops and picket bodies. The decorative circle cutouts can easily be made using a drill press. The gate posts feature deep chamfers that can be made using a band saw and a circular saw. The post cap and base moldings are relatively easy to make and assemble. The decorative urns can be sawn, turned, or purchased from a mill house. See "Construction Techniques" for help on making caps, moldings, and other post decorations.

DESIGN 52: ALPINE GOTHIC FENCE

These German-inspired pickets have classic Gothic styling with a lighthearted twist. The picket style gives the illusion of melting ice or snow, making the fence charming in winter. The handsome accent post features a full body, raised panel, and oversized post cap. Ornamentally molded baseboard further enhances the fence. This fence beautifully complements chalet-type homes.

Construct the picket infill using 1×10 material. (For increased strength, you can use 2×10 material.) Use a band saw or a router with pattern to cut the decorative tops and picket bodies (use router and pattern only if using 1× material). The decorative cutouts can be made using a router and pattern or a jigsaw. The corner post features an oversized cap, which can be made by layering multiple pedestals on a post cap. The full body raised panel can be created using a table saw. See "Construction Techniques" for help on making caps, moldings, and other post decorations.

Fence: 3 feet, 6 inches high.
Posts: 4 feet, 3 inches high.
High security: Open areas at picket bottoms are quite narrow, making it difficult for even a small pet to squeeze through.
Low privacy: The infill height is low, thus allowing visibility over the fence.
Low buffering: This fence filters some sun and wind.
Construction: Fence, moderate difficulty. Posts, advanced difficulty.

Fence: 3 feet, 10 inches high.
Posts: 4 feet, 6 inches high.
High security: Pointed pickets are uninviting to fence sitters and climbers.
Low privacy: The infill design is low and spaced, thus allowing visibility over and through the fence.
Low buffering: This fence filters little sun and wind.
Construction: Fence, advanced difficulty. Posts, moderate difficulty.

DESIGN 53: SALMON PICKET FENCE

These pickets give the impression of a school of fish. This is one of the easiest full body sawn picket designs to make; only six straight lines need to be cut on the outer edges of the pickets. The circular, triangular, and pentagonal shapes that decorate each picket may be cut out, stenciled, or appliquéd. The accent post closely imitates the picket's silhouette. This nautical design is ideal for seaside cottages and small vacation homes.

Construct the picket infill using 1×8 material. (For increased strength, you can use 2×8 material.) Use a band saw or a router with pattern to cut the decorative tops and picket bodies (use router and pattern only if using 1× material). The decorative cutouts can be made using a router and pattern or a jigsaw. The corner post features a tapered body, which can be made by encasing a 4×4 post in a diagonally split 2× casing. See "Construction Techniques" for help on making caps, moldings, and other post decorations.

DESIGN 54: POTBELLY PICKET FENCE

Sawn balustrade pickets are crowned with amiable ball toppers. The rounded potbelly near the base of the pickets mimics the design of the old-fashioned potbelly stove. The simple post body is ornamented with engraved circles and elongated keyholes. Decoratively molded railings and baseboards accent the fence and posts. This fence is excellent for any home featuring heavy balustrade work.

Construct the picket infill using 1×6 material. (For increased strength, you can use ¾×6 material.) Use a band saw or a router with pattern to cut the decorative tops and picket bodies (use router and pattern only if using 1× material). The corner post features a veined body and multilevel post cap. See "Construction Techniques" for help on making caps, moldings, and other post decorations.

Fence: 4 feet, 2 inches high.
Posts: 4 feet, 5 inches high.
High security: Pointed pickets are uninviting to fence sitters and climbers.
Low privacy: The infill design is low and spaced, thus allowing visibility over and through the fence.
Low buffering: This fence filters little sun and wind.
Construction: Fence, advanced difficulty. Posts, advanced difficulty.

Fence: 3 feet, 11 inches high.
Posts: 4 feet high.
Moderate security: Large, open spacing at picket base could allow small pets to slip through.
Low privacy: The infill design is low and spaced, thus allowing visibility over and through the fence.
Low buffering: This fence filters little sun and wind.
Construction: Fence, moderate difficulty. Posts, moderate difficulty.

DESIGN 55: TRUMPET-TOPPED PICKET FENCE

This original design incorporates a miniature trumpet shape at the top of the picket. The body of the picket is chamfered for extra styling. The post is a forceful adaptation of the picket style. The chamfered post complements the pickets in the infill, and the shallow urn finial bears a strong resemblance to the picket tops. The chamfered post cap and baseboard add the finishing touches. With its simple styling, this picket fence is appropriate for many types of architecture.

Construct the picket infill using 1×6 material. (For increased strength, you can use ¾×6 material.) Use a band saw or a router with pattern to cut the decorative tops (use router and pattern only if using 1× material). Use a router with a chamfer bit to make the decorative chamfers on the sides of each picket. The corner post features a chamfered body and ornate urn finial. See "Construction Techniques" for help on making caps, moldings, and other post decorations.

DESIGN 56: MEDALLIONED BALUSTRADE PICKET FENCE

Sawn balustrade pickets are topped by Turkish-style crowns and ornamented by medallion appliqués. The accent post is enhanced by thin molding strips that lend height and refinement, and a basic post cap and ball add the crowning touch. Molded rails and baseboards adorn the fence and posts. This picket design will complement any vintage or contemporary home.

Construct the picket infill using 1×6 material. (For increased strength, you can use ¾×6 material.) Use a band saw or a router with pattern to cut the decorative tops and picket bodies (use router and pattern only if using 1× material). The decorative vertical strips on the ornamental post can be appliquéd or etched using a router and parallel guide. See "Construction Techniques" for help on making caps, moldings, and other post decorations.

Fence: 3 feet, 10 inches high.
Posts: 4 feet, 7 inches high.
High security: Pointed picket tops are unattractive to climb or sit on.
Low privacy: The infill design is low and spaced, thus allowing visibility over and through the fence.
Low buffering: This fence filters little sun and wind.
Construction: Fence, moderate difficulty. Posts, moderate difficulty.

Fence: 4 feet, 1 inch high.
Posts: 4 feet, 3 inches high.
High security: Pointed picket tops are unattractive to climb or sit on.
Low privacy: The infill design is low and spaced, thus allowing visibility over and through the fence.
Low buffering: This fence filters little sun and wind.
Construction: Fence, advanced difficulty. Posts, moderate difficulty.

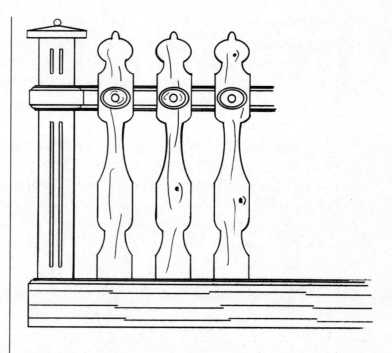

DESIGN 57: PROPELLER PICKET FENCE

This picket features an arrowhead top resting on a symmetric propeller-style body. The bold arrowhead toppers are a strong deterrent to fence climbers. Molded railings and baseboards accent both fence and posts. The post top is miter cut with rounded edging. Oval medallions and raised panel appliqués add the finishing touches to this handsome fence and post combination. This fence makes a beautiful complement to houses with porches or balconies with similar balustrade fretwork.

Construct the picket infill using 1×6 material. (For increased strength, you can use ¾×6 material.) Use a band saw or a router with pattern to cut the decorative tops and picket bodies (use router and pattern only if using 1× material). The decorative round cutout can be made with a drill press. The triangle cutouts can be made with a jigsaw or a router and pattern with a panel cutting bit. See "Construction Techniques" for help on making panel appliqués, moldings, and other post decorations.

DESIGN 58: SPADE-TOPPED PICKET FENCE

This charming Victorian design is a decorative version of the traditional Gothic fence. Numerous cutouts in each picket give the fence a lacy appearance. The slender posts adorned with moldings, appliqués, and spade toppers complement the infill pattern. The use of three stringers between posts makes this fence more durable than if it were constructed using just two stringers. This timeless design is appropriate for any type of home.

Construct the picket infill using 1×4 material. (For increased strength, you can use ¾×4 material.) Use a band saw or a router with pattern to cut the decorative tops and concave picket bodies (use router and pattern only if using 1× material). The decorative round cutout can be made with a drill press. The triangle cutouts can be made with a jigsaw or a router and pattern with a panel cutting bit. See "Construction Techniques" for help on making panel appliqués, moldings, and other post decorations.

Fence: 3 feet, 10 inches high.
Posts: 4 feet, 2 inches high.
High security: Pointed picket tops are unattractive to climb or sit on.
Low privacy: The infill design is low and spaced, thus allowing visibility over and through the fence.
Low buffering: This fence filters little sun and wind.
Construction: Fence, advanced difficulty. Posts, moderate difficulty.

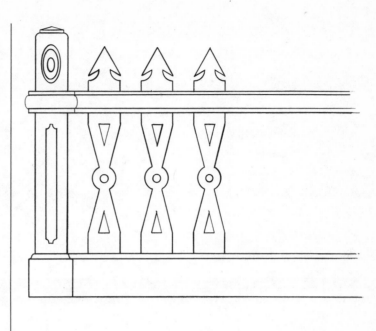

Fence: 4 feet, 3 inches high.
Posts: 4 feet, 3 inches high.
High security: Pointed picket tops are unattractive to climb or sit on.
Low privacy: The infill design is low and spaced, thus allowing visibility over and through the fence.
Low buffering: This fence filters little sun and wind.
Construction: Fence, advanced difficulty. Posts, moderate difficulty.

Balustrade Fences

DESIGN 59: NEO-CLASSIC FENCE

This Victorian sawn baluster shows neo-classic influence. This pattern was popular in the late nineteenth century and was featured in many pattern books of the period. The accent post is enhanced by a detailed topper, cap, medallion, and moldings. Pyramid-fashioned base molding gives the fence and posts an impression of strength and stability. This fence is an outstanding choice for homes ornamented by heavy balustrade work.

Construct the baluster infill using 1×6 material. (For increased strength, you can use ¾×6 material.) Use a band saw or a router with pattern bit and pattern to cut the decorative baluster bodies (use router and pattern only if using 1× material). The decorative cutouts can be made using a drill press and either a jigsaw or a router with pattern bit and pattern. See "Construction Techniques" for help on making the cap, pedestal, finial, rosettes, moldings, and other post decorations.

DESIGN 60: RUNNING GINGERBREAD FENCE

Charming and simple, this basic balustrade fence is exquisitely accented by fretwork inserts between each window. The post, with its simple mitered top, is very easy to make. Delicately molded top rail and baseboard complete this delightful fence, which is perfect for a Victorian rose garden or patio.

Construct the baluster infill using 2×4 material. Cut the inserts between each baluster from 1×6 material. Use a band saw or a router with pattern bit and pattern to cut the decorative baluster inserts (use router and pattern only if using 1× material). Cut channels in the top and bottom of each baluster to hold the inserts, or nail the inserts into place.

Fence: 3 feet, 2 inches high.
Posts: 4 feet, 2 inches high.
Moderate security: The infill is dense enough to restrain many types of pets, but the smooth rail top facilitates climbing and sitting.
Low privacy: The infill design is low and spaced, thus allowing visibility over and through the fence.
Low buffering: This fence filters little sun and wind.
Construction: Fence, advanced difficulty. Posts, moderate difficulty.

Fence: 3 feet, 6 inches high.
Posts: 4 feet high.
Low security: The smooth rail top facilitates climbing and sitting.
Low privacy: The infill design is low and spaced, thus allowing visibility over and through the fence.
Low buffering: This fence filters little sun and wind.
Construction: Fence, moderate difficulty. Posts, very easy.

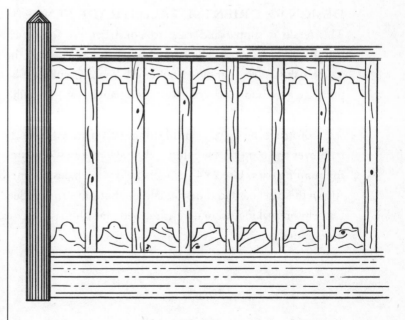

DESIGN 61: COLUMNED BALUSTRADE FENCE

In this simple yet refined fence design, tall, slender balusters are topped by decorative drilled circles and separated by semicircle arches. Bevel-cut rail and baseboard are complemented by an oversized beveled post cap. The post body is decorated with a long, full body recessed panel and a centered obelisk appliqué. Contemporary or classic, large or small, virtually every house will look magnificent framed by this fence.

Construct the baluster infill using 2×2 material. Use 2×4 material for the running trim over the top of each baluster. Use a drill press to make the decorative semicircle and circle cutouts in the running trim. Use dowel screws or rods to connect the balusters to the running trim. Use 2×4 stringers below the balusters and on top of the running trim. Attach the baseboard to the posts and the bottom stringer. See "Construction Techniques" for help on making the cap, pedestal, finial, rosettes, moldings, and other post decorations.

DESIGN 62: ORIENTAL BALUSTRADE FENCE

This fence is simple and easy to construct yet sophisticated displaying column-like balustrades that support elliptic archways. Fluted cuts add the appearance of more height to the balustrades. A molded rail and baseboard enhance both the fence and posts. The posts are accented by decorative raised panels, oval medallion appliqués, and a post cap and ball.

Construct the baluster infill using 2×2 material. Use 2×4 material for the running trim over the top of each baluster. Use dowel screws or rods to connect the balusters to the running trim. Use 2×4 stringers below the balusters and on top of the running trim. Attach the baseboard to the posts and the bottom stringer. See "Construction Techniques" for help on making decorative caps, pedestals, finials, rosettes, moldings, and other post decorations.

Fence: 3 feet, 5 inches high.
Posts: 4 feet high.
Moderate security: The infill is dense enough to restrain many types of pets, but the smooth rail top facilitates climbing and sitting.
Low privacy: The infill design is low and spaced, thus allowing visibility over and through the fence.
Low buffering: This fence filters little sun and wind.
Construction: Fence, moderate difficulty. Posts, moderate difficulty.

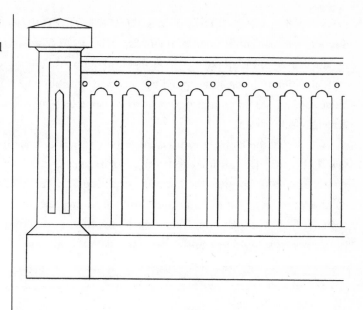

Fence: 3 feet, 4 inches high.
Posts: 4 feet high.
Moderate security: The infill is dense enough to restrain many types of pets, but the smooth rail top facilitates climbing and sitting.
Low privacy: The infill design is low and spaced, thus allowing visibility over and through the fence.
Low buffering: This fence filters little sun and wind.
Construction: Fence, advanced difficulty. Posts, advanced difficulty.

DESIGN 63: NEO-IONIAN BALUSTRADE FENCE

Simplified Ionian columns support circular arches in an aristocratic style. The infill is accented by a delicately molded rail and a bevel-cut baseboard. The post is adorned with an ornamental panel molding and topped by decoratively ribbed ball. Its classic styling makes the fence appropriate for contemporary as well as vintage homes. It's an ideal fence for an exotic Grecian-style garden.

Construct the baluster infill using 2×6 material. Cut the baluster design using a band saw. Use 2×6 material for the running trim over the top of each baluster. Use dowel screws or rods to connect the balusters to the running trim. Use 2×4 stringers below the balusters and on top of the running trim. Attach the baseboard to the posts and the bottom stringer. See "Construction Techniques" for help on making decorative caps, pedestals, finials, rosettes, moldings, and other post decorations.

DESIGN 64: GOTHIC FRET DESIGN FENCE

This skillfully ornate fence features dual balustrades that narrow into one to form an intriguing design. Gothic four-leaf-clover windows and tall, arching windows between balustrades give the fence an ecclesiastical effect. The decorative accent post is ornamented with moldings that match the fence rail and baseboard and a panel appliqué. This fence is the perfect companion for Gothic-style homes and religious structures.

Construct the baluster infill using 2×2 material. Angle-cut the left baluster and join it to the right baluster. Use 2×8 material for the running trim over the top of each baluster. Make the clover windows in the running trim with a drill press. Connect the balusters to the running trim with dowel screws or rods. Use 2×4 stringers below the balusters and on top of the running trim. Attach the baseboard to the posts and the bottom stringer. See "Construction Techniques" for help on making decorative caps, pedestals, finials, rosettes, moldings, and other post decorations.

Fence: 3 feet, 4 inches high.
Posts: 4 feet high.
Moderate security: The infill is dense enough to restrain many types of pets, but the smooth rail top facilitates climbing and sitting.
Low privacy: The infill design is low and spaced, thus allowing visibility over and through the fence.
Low buffering: This fence filters little sun and wind.
Construction: Fence, advanced difficulty. Posts, moderate difficulty.

Fence: 3 feet, 9 inches high.
Posts: 4 feet, 1 inch high.
Moderate security: The infill is dense enough to restrain many types of pets, but the smooth rail top facilitates climbing and sitting.
Low privacy: The infill design is low and spaced, thus allowing visibility over and through the fence.
Low buffering: This fence filters little sun and wind.
Construction: Fence, advanced difficulty. Posts, moderate difficulty.

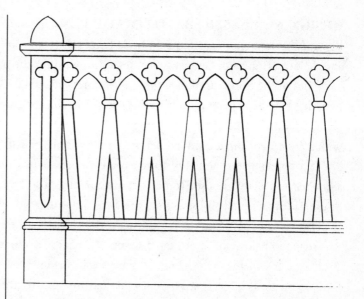

DESIGN 65: MOCK OVERSIZED BEADED FENCE

Victorian architecture is known for its beaded porticos and archways. This fence uses this motif with alternating rows of beads. The accent post is decorated with appliqué moldings and crowned with a large turned ball finial. The fence pieces are surprisingly easy to cut and assemble. This fence will enhance the beauty of any beaded Victorian manor.

Construct the baluster infill using 2×2 or 2×4 material. Use 1×4 material to make the bead appliqués. Nail or screw the bead appliqués to the baluster infill. Use 2×4 stringers below and above the balusters. Nail the stringers to the balusters. Attach the baseboard to the posts and the bottom stringer. See "Construction Techniques" for help on making decorative caps, pedestals, finials, rosettes, moldings, and other post decorations.

DESIGN 66: CLASSIC BALUSTRADE FENCE

Elegant and luxurious, turned balustrade fences were and still are among the most costly and the most beautiful. Fence balustrades fashioned after the balustrades of the verandas or balconies of the house itself give the most impressive effect. This fence may be simplified by using a "mock turning" relief cut picket. The accent post is ornamented by delicate panel molding, molded rail and baseboard, and a tall urn finial. This fence blends nicely with any home featuring similar balustrade work in its porches and balconies.

If you want to use actual turnings, you can turn them yourself or purchase them from a lumberyard or mill house. To make mock turnings, use 2×4 material and cut the profile of the balusters on a band saw, then use a router with grooving bit or a circular saw with the blade set to cut ⅛ inch deep to simulate the veins of a three-dimensional turning. Nail 2×4 stringers below and above the balusters. Attach the decorative finials over each baluster. Attach the baseboard to the posts and the bottom stringer. See "Construction Techniques" for help on making decorative caps, pedestals, finials, rosettes, moldings, and other post decorations.

Fence: 3 feet, 11 inches high.
Posts: 4 feet, 4 inches high.
Moderate security: The infill is dense enough to restrain many types of pets, but the smooth rail top facilitates climbing and sitting.
Low privacy: The infill design is low and spaced, thus allowing visibility over and through the fence.
Low buffering: This fence filters little sun and wind.
Construction: Fence, advanced difficulty. Posts, moderate difficulty.

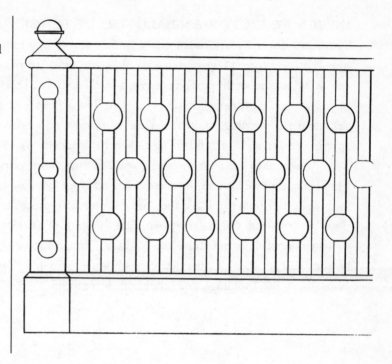

Fence: 3 feet, 10 inches high.
Posts: 4 feet, 3 inches high.
High security: Unlike most baluster fences, this design includes finials over each baluster, making fence climbing tricky.
Low privacy: The infill design is low and spaced, thus allowing visibility over and through the fence.
Low buffering: This fence filters little sun and wind.
Construction: Fence, advanced difficulty. Posts, moderate difficulty.

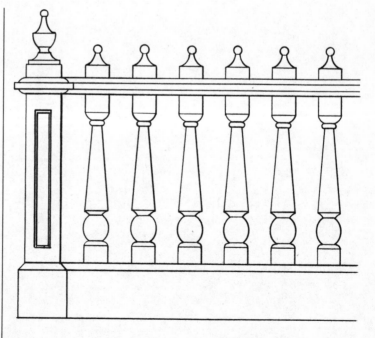

DESIGN 67: VICTORIAN BALUSTRADE FENCE

This fence displays magnificent craftsmanship and styling inspired by designs of the late nineteenth century. Long stretches of elaborate fence turnings once demonstrated the wealth and stability of the property owner, and still do today. This fence may also be simplified by using a "mock turning" relief cut picket. The accent post depicted is ornamented by delicate panel molding, molded cap and baseboard, and a decorative finial. This fence is appropriate for any home featuring similar balustrade work in its porches and balconies.

If you want to use actual turnings, you can turn them yourself or purchase them from a lumberyard or mill house. To make mock turnings, use 2×4 material and cut the profile of the balusters on a band saw, then use a router with grooving bit or a circular saw with the blade set to cut ⅛ inch deep to simulate the veins of a three-dimensional turning. Nail 2×4 stringers below and above the balusters. Attach the baseboard to the posts and the bottom stringer. See "Construction Techniques" for help on making decorative caps, pedestals, finials, moldings, and other post decorations.

Fence: 3 feet, 10 inches high.
Posts: 4 feet, 3 inches high.
Moderate security: The infill is tightly spaced, but the smooth rail top facilitates easy climbing.
Low privacy: The infill design is low and spaced, thus allowing visibility over and through the fence.
Low buffering: This fence filters little sun and wind.
Construction: Fence, advanced difficulty. Posts, moderate difficulty.

Grid and Panel Fences

DESIGN 68: FIVE-CIRCLE WHIRL-WHEEL GRID FENCE

This fence's strong architectural aspects and bold styling are attention grabbing. This durable style of infill was popularized in part by the Palliser brothers, whose architectural-details pattern books, published between 1876 and 1908, featured numerous piazzas and balconies with this eye-catching whirl-wheel design. The fence infill is primarily made of 2×4 material with accenting panel inserts. Molded baseboard adorns both the fence and post. The post finial is a bold ribbed ball with a delicate nipple ball top. Although this design is well suited for late Victorian homes, it also looks attractive with many modern housing styles.

See "Construction Steps" for help on constructing grid and panel fences.

DESIGN 69: DOUBLE WHIRL-WHEEL BULL'S-EYE FENCE

Symmetry is the hallmark of this strongly styled fence. A single hole drilled into a center panel draws the eyes to the middle of the fence. The infill and posts are easy to cut and assemble. This design works well in front of structures with defined perpendicular architectural details.

Construct the basic grid infill using 2×4 material; this can be decoratively veined with either a circular saw or a router. Make channels in the infill to hold the panel inserts, which are constructed from 1× material. Cut out or etch the designs in the panel inserts using a router and pattern. See "Construction Steps" for help on constructing grid and panel fences.

Fence: 3 feet, 6 inches high.
Posts: 4 feet, 2 inches high.
Low security: The smooth rail top is easy to straddle. To discourage would-be fence sitters, a running trim can be added along the top rail.
Low privacy: The infill is low and allows easy visibility over the fence.
Low buffering: This fence filters little sun and wind.
Construction: Fence, moderate difficulty. Posts, moderate difficulty.

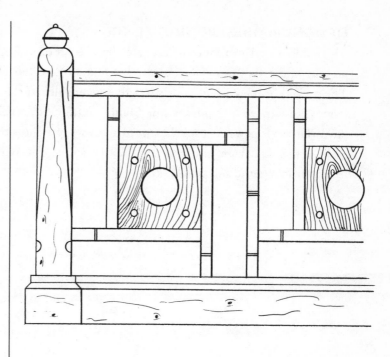

Fence: 3 feet, 6 inches high.
Posts: 4 feet, 5 inches high.
Low security: The smooth rail top is easy to straddle. To discourage would-be fence sitters, a running trim can be added along the top rail.
Low privacy: The infill is low and allows easy visibility over the fence.
Low buffering: This fence filters little sun and wind.
Construction: Fence, moderate difficulty. Posts, moderate difficulty.

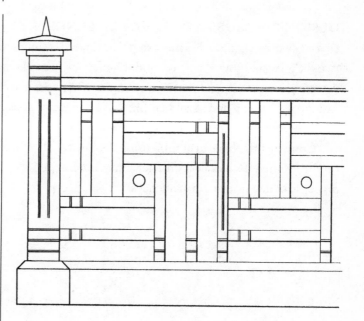

DESIGN 70: OBELISK GRID FENCE

This boldly styled grid pattern is accented by a center obelisk. Grid styles such as this were popular in the 1800s and were featured in numerous architectural-details pattern books. The broad chamfered post adds strength and stability to the overall appearance of this fence. The stout post cap is crowned with a mushroom finial, which can be turned or sawn. This style of fence is suitable for many types of architecture with strong lines.

Construct the basic grid infill using 2×4 material. See "Construction Steps" for help on constructing grid and panel fences.

DESIGN 71: CROSS-YOUR-HEART FENCE

Gracefully overlapping arches meet atop slant-braced columns forming a hidden heart design. A tightly crossed lower portion and 12-inch-high baseboard make this fence ideal for deterring small dogs from entering or exiting. The post is accented by an inlaid medallion and top with a cap and small ball finial. The graceful appearance of this fence makes it excellent for a cozy country cottage or bungalow.

Construct the basic grid infill using 2×4 material. The top arches forming the hearts can be omitted if a simpler, stronger fence is desired. See "Construction Steps" for help on constructing grid and panel fences.

Fence: 3 feet, 7 inches high.
Posts: 4 feet, 5 inches high.
Low security: The smooth
rail top is easy to straddle. To
discourage would-be fence
sitters, a running trim can
be added along the top rail.
Low privacy: The infill is
low and allows easy
visibility over the fence.
Low buffering: This fence
filters little sun and wind.
Construction: Fence,
moderate difficulty. Posts,
moderate difficulty.

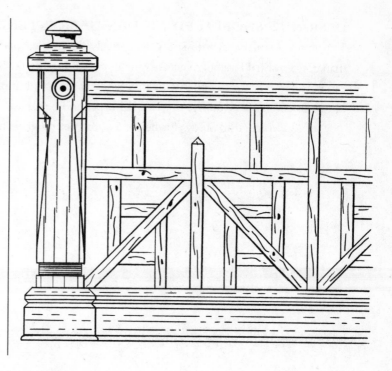

Fence: 3 feet, 8 inches high.
Posts: 4 feet, 2 inches high.
Moderate security: The
tightly spaced infill near the
bottom will restrain many
types of small pets, but the
fence's many diagonal and
horizontal members will
facilitate fence climbing.
Low privacy: The infill is
low and allows easy
visibility over the fence.
Low buffering: This fence
filters little sun and wind.
Construction: Fence,
moderate difficulty. Posts,
moderate difficulty.

DESIGN 72: SHOELACED HIDDEN HEARTS FENCE

This quick-to-make lacy design is deceptively fast and easy to cut. Running trim rather than conventional baseboard accents the curves along the fence bottom. The post topper can be created using a band saw or purchased through a lumberyard. The nautical flavor of this fence makes it suitable for seaside homes and cottages.

See "Construction Steps" for help on constructing grid and panel fences.

DESIGN 73: RISING-SUN PANEL INSERT FENCE

Classic gridwork is accented by decorative panel inserts. The open airy design gives a friendly feel while still providing a clear boundary marker. This charming style can be adapted to sloping terrain as shown in this illustration. The simple designs in this fence make it appropriate for most types of housing.

Construct the basic grid infill using 2×4 material. Make channels in the infill to hold the panel inserts, which are constructed from 1× material. Cut out or etch the designs in the panel inserts using a router and pattern. See "Construction Steps" for help on constructing grid and panel fences.

Fence: 3 feet, 4 inches high.
Posts: 4 feet, 2 inches high.
Moderate security. The tightly spaced infill near the bottom will restrain many types of small pets, but the fence's many diagonal and horizontal members will facilitate fence climbing.
Low privacy. The infill is low and allows easy visibility over the fence.
Low buffering. This fence filters little sun and wind.
Construction. Fence, moderate difficulty. Posts, easy.

Fence: 3 feet, 2 inches high.
Posts: 4 feet, 2 inches high.
Moderate security: The tightly spaced infill near the bottom will restrain many types of small pets, but the smooth rail top facilitates fence climbing and sitting.
Low privacy: The infill is low and allows easy visibility over the fence.
Low buffering: This fence filters little sun and wind.
Construction: Fence, moderate difficulty. Posts, easy.

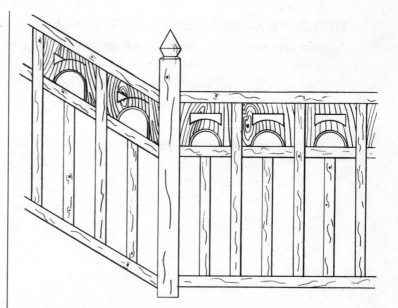

DESIGN 74: VICTORIAN H GRID FENCE

Strong, bold, and easy to construct, this grid design with an open, friendly feel uses relatively little lumber. The bold, oversized ornamental post lends strength and character to the simple appearance of the infill. The post is accented by layers of molding and a full body panel appliqué. A turned ball finial may be purchased or ordered via a lumberyard or mill house. This is an excellent garden fence, perfect for supporting climbing vines and roses.

Construct the basic grid infill using 2×4 material. See "Construction Steps" for help on constructing grid and panel fences.

DESIGN 75: GRID BASKET-WEAVE FENCE

A woven appearance makes this fence intriguing, and a molded rail and baseboard add style and power. The oversized post is decorated with a long, full body panel made from panel molding and a stout, bold-looking miter-cut post topper. This is an excellent garden fence for supporting flowering vines and climbing roses.

Construct the basic grid infill using 2×4 material. See "Construction Steps" for help on constructing grid and panel fences.

Fence: 3 feet, 9 inches high.
Posts: 4 feet, 5 inches high.
Low security: The smooth rail top facilitates fence climbing and sitting.
Low privacy: The infill is low and open, thus allowing easy visibility over and through the fence.
Low buffering: This fence filters little sun and wind.
Construction: Fence, easy. Posts, moderate difficulty.

Fence: 3 feet, 8 inches high.
Posts: 4 feet, 6 inches high.
Low security: The smooth rail top facilitates fence climbing and sitting.
Low privacy: The infill is low and open, thus allowing easy visibility over and through the fence.
Low buffering: This fence filters little sun and wind.
Construction: Fence, advanced difficulty. Posts, moderate difficulty.

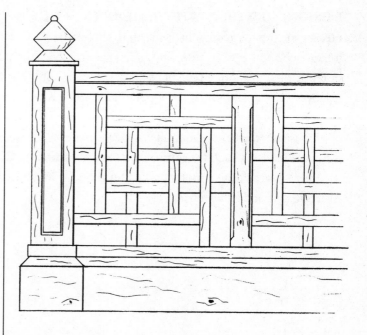

DESIGN 76: VICTORIAN GRID V SPAN FENCE

Strong and bold, this is a sturdy perimeter fence. All 2× lumber helps to make this fence both inexpensive to construct and durable. Upright 2×4s extend from the baseboard, bisecting the fence's center rail and butting against the rail top. Each rectangular grid in the lower half of the fence is divided by a single chamfered picket, and each upper grid is divided by a diagonally placed 2×4. The powerful accent post is adorned with a medallion and baseboard appliqué and topped by a mushroom-domed finial. The sturdy build of this fence makes it a good match for country homes.

Construct the basic grid infill using 2×4 material. See "Construction Steps" for help on constructing grid and panel fences.

DESIGN 77: WHIRL-WHEEL HEARTS FENCE

Heart panel inserts add country charm to this classic Victorian grid design. Whirl wheels mirror one another to create an intriguing pattern. The cutout heart panels may be omitted or replaced with another type of panel to suit your taste. The accent post is simple, with a narrow post cap and miter-cut topper. This fence is quick to cut, easy to assemble and construct, and adds a charming accent to any country-style home.

Construct the basic grid infill using 2×4 material. Make channels in the infill to hold the panel inserts, which are constructed from 1× material. Cut out or etch the designs in the panel inserts using a router and pattern. See "Construction Steps" for help on constructing grid and panel fences.

Fence: 3 feet, 6 inches high.
Posts: 4 feet, 1 inch high.
Moderate security: The tightly spaced infill at the bottom will restrain many small pets, but the smooth rail top facilitates fence climbing and sitting.
Low privacy: The infill is low and open, thus allowing easy visibility over and through the fence.
Low buffering: This fence filters little sun and wind.
Construction: Fence, moderate difficulty. Posts, moderate difficulty.

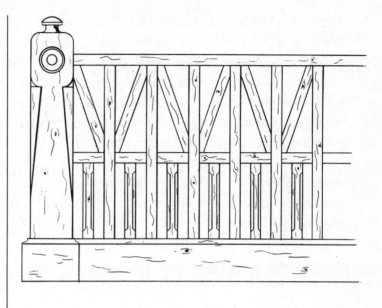

Fence: 3 feet, 6 inches high.
Posts: 4 feet, 2 inches high.
Low security: The smooth rail top facilitates fence climbing and sitting.
Low privacy: The infill is low and open, thus allowing easy visibility over and through the fence.
Low buffering: This fence filters little sun and wind.
Construction: Fence, advanced difficulty. Posts, easy.

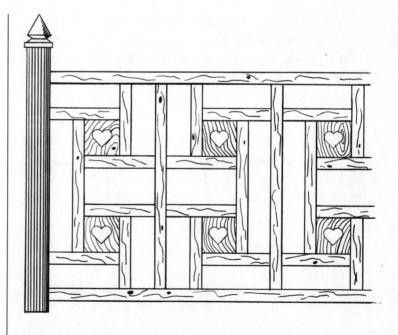

DESIGN 78: TRIPLE WHIRL-WHEEL GRID FENCE

Strong, powerful architectural lines give this fence an appearance of strength and stability. Boldly chamfered post and baseboard accentuate the fence's strong character. The center panel with circular cutout may be omitted or replaced by any style desired. Closely spaced infill makes this fence ideal for restraining small dogs and other pets. The basic pieces are very easy to cut and quick to assemble. The straight lines of this fence make it appropriate for many vintage and contemporary homes.

Construct the basic grid infill using 2×4 material. Make channels in the infill to hold the panel inserts, which are constructed from 1× material. Cut out or etch the designs in the panel inserts using a router and pattern. See "Construction Steps" for help on constructing grid and panel fences.

DESIGN 79: EASTLAKE ELONGATED TEE

Basic styling makes this fence practical, affordable, versatile, and beautiful. Fencing long stretches is fast work, and there is very little waste wood. The accent post displays a mitered top with chamfer-grooved neck and base. An oversized medallion adorns the center of the gate. The gate pediment is simple and complements the gate body and the overall fence. This design looks great in the town or country, with big homes or small.

Construct the basic grid infill using 2×4 material. See "Construction Steps" for help on constructing grid and panel fences and gate pediments.

Fence: 3 feet, 8 inches high.
Posts: 4 feet, 4 inches high.
Moderate security: The tightly spaced infill will restrain most small dogs, but the smooth rail top facilitates fence climbing and sitting.
Low privacy: The infill is low and open, thus allowing easy visibility over and through the fence.
Low buffering: This fence filters little sun and wind.
Construction: Fence, advanced difficulty. Posts, moderate difficulty.

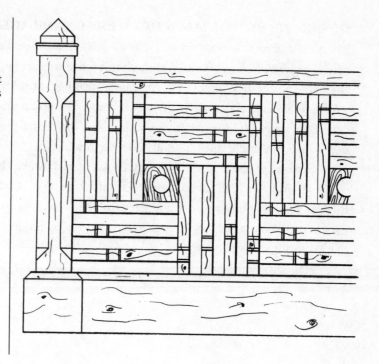

Fence: 3 feet, 2 inches high.
Posts: 3 feet, 9 inches high.
Low security: The smooth rail top facilitates fence climbing and sitting.
Low privacy: The infill is low and open, thus allowing easy visibility over and through the fence.
Low buffering: This fence filters little sun and wind.
Construction: Fence, very easy. Posts, easy.

DESIGN 80: VICTORIAN BRIC-A-BRAC COLLAGE FENCE

The panels, scrolls, and appliqués of this fence are borrowed from the gingerbread that adorns many Victorian houses. Although this fence appears quite ornate, the preparation, assembly, and construction of all its parts are surprisingly easy. Minor variations can be made to include architectural details of your own house. The post is simple yet has an eye-catching decorative topper. The gate infill is a variation of the overall fence design. This fence goes well with any home featuring similar architectural details.

Construct the basic grid infill using 2×4 material. Make channels in the infill to hold the panel inserts, which are constructed from 1× material. Cut out or etch the designs in the panel inserts using a router and pattern. See "Construction Steps" for help on constructing grid and panel fences, and "Construction Techniques" for help on making decorative scrolls and appliqués.

DESIGN 81: VICTORIAN KALEIDOSCOPE FENCE

Mirroring pairs of Victorian bric-a-brac adorn this classically styled late Victorian fence. Variations of arch supports, oval panels, balustrades, and roof cresting combine to form this curiously designed fence. Running trim adds height to the infill and discourages would-be fence sitters. The decorative accent post matches the eccentric nature of the fence infill. This fence blends well with any home featuring similar architectural details.

Construct the basic grid infill using 2×4 material. Make channels in the infill to hold the panel inserts, which are constructed from 1× material. Cut out or etch the designs in the panel inserts using a drill press, a router and pattern, or both. See "Construction Steps" for help on constructing grid and panel fences.

Fence: 3 feet, 6 inches high.
Posts: 4 feet, 2 inches high.
Low security: The smooth rail top facilitates fence climbing and sitting.
Low privacy: The infill is low and open, thus allowing easy visibility over and through the fence.
Low buffering: This fence filters little sun and wind.
Construction: Fence, advanced difficulty. Posts, easy.

Fence: 3 feet, 10 inches high.
Posts: 4 feet, 2 inches high.
Moderate security: The jagged running trim makes fence climbing difficult, but large gaps in the infill may allow pets or children to squeeze through.
Low privacy: The infill is low and open, thus allowing easy visibility over and through the fence.
Low buffering: This fence filters little sun and wind.
Construction: Fence, advanced difficulty. Posts, advanced difficulty.

DESIGN 82: VICTORIAN CROSS BRACE FENCE

This Victorian fence is quick and easy to make and interesting to view. Gracefully arching Y supports are decorated by two drilled circles. The powerful decorative post is accented with decorative etchings, a medallion appliqué, and a button post finial. In this example, the arched brackets were designed and cut to imitate the home's support brackets.

Construct the basic grid infill using 2×4 material. Drill holes in Y supports using a drill press. See "Construction Steps" for help on constructing grid and panel fences.

DESIGN 83: COUNTRY MORNING GOTHIC FENCE

This stunning fence combines ecclesiastical elegance and friendly country charm. For a more open look and feel, the rounded pickets in the center of each Gothic window may be eliminated. The decorative post is ornamented with an elongated keyhole panel appliqué and an urn finial, which may be turned, cut on a band saw, or purchased from a mill house. This fence makes a magnificent accent for any structure with Gothic windows or fretwork.

Construct the basic grid infill using 2×4 material. Make channels in the infill to hold the panel inserts that form the tops of the Gothic windows. Cut the panel inserts from 1× material using a band saw. See "Construction Steps" for help on constructing grid and panel fences, and "Construction Techniques" for help on making ornate corner posts.

Fence: 3 feet, 8 inches high.
Posts: 4 feet, 1 inch high.
Low security: The smooth top rail facilitates fence climbing, and large gaps in the infill may allow pets or children to squeeze through.
Low privacy: The infill is low and open, thus allowing easy visibility over and through the fence.
Low buffering: This fence filters little sun and wind.
Construction: Fence, moderate difficulty. Posts, advanced difficulty.

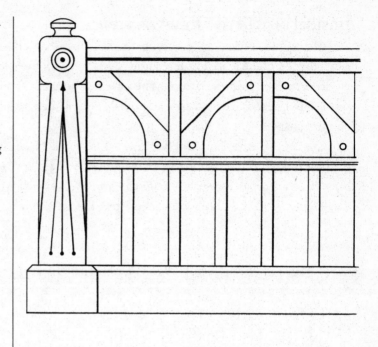

Fence: 3 feet, 6 inches high.
Posts: 4 feet, 6 inches high.
Moderate security: The smooth rail top is inviting to climb or sit on, but the tightly spaced infill makes squeezing through this fence difficult.
Low privacy: The infill is low and open, thus allowing easy visibility over and through the fence.
Low buffering: This fence filters little sun and wind.
Construction: Fence, advanced difficulty. Posts, moderate difficulty.

DESIGN 84: GOTHIC REVIVAL FENCE

Slender, pointed pickets are inset in majestically peaked Gothic windows. Running trim along the top of the fence features cutout windows with molded edging that creates a halo effect over each window separation. The adjoining post is of simple design with a small acorn finial. This impressive design can handsomely complement many big city churches or small country chapels.

Construct the basic grid infill using 2×4 material. Make channels in the infill to hold the panel inserts that form the tops of the Gothic windows. Cut the panel inserts from 1× material using a band saw. See "Construction Steps" for help on constructing grid and panel fences, and "Construction Techniques" for help on making ornate corner posts.

DESIGN 85: NEO-GOTHIC VICTORIAN FENCE

This delightful rail-topped fence has an open, neighborly appeal. Each infill section has window cresting with a decorative molded edge. Pales in the center of each window help prevent animals and children from getting through the fence. Decoratively molded rail and baseboard add a touch of class. The accent post is decorated with veining and a large medallion and has an oversized post cap with a half-ball finial. This fence is well suited to homes and churches featuring Victorian and Gothic architectural details.

Construct the basic grid infill using 2×4 material. Make channels in the infill to hold the panel inserts that form the tops of the Gothic windows. Cut the panel inserts from 1× material using a band saw. See "Construction Steps" for help on constructing grid and panel fences, and "Construction Techniques" for help on making ornate corner posts.

Fence: 3 feet, 6 inches high.
Posts: 4 feet, 2 inches high.
Moderate security: The smooth rail top is inviting to climb or sit on, but the tightly spaced infill makes squeezing through this fence difficult.
Low privacy: The infill is low and open, thus allowing easy visibility over and through the fence.
Low buffering: This fence filters little sun and wind.
Construction: Fence, advanced difficulty. Posts, very easy.

Fence: 3 feet, 8 inches high.
Posts: 4 feet, 4 inches high.
Moderate security: The smooth rail top is inviting to climb or sit on, but the tightly spaced infill makes squeezing through this fence difficult.
Low privacy: The infill is low and open, thus allowing easy visibility over and through the fence.
Low buffering: This fence filters little sun and wind.
Construction: Fence, advanced difficulty. Posts, moderate difficulty.

DESIGN 86: GOTHIC PINWHEEL FENCE

This is a striking style with an interesting triangular design. Molded rail and baseboard enhance the fence infill, which is surprisingly quick and easy to cut and assemble. The decorative accent post features a full body appliqué panel, molded post cap, and a unique post finial. This fence is an excellent complement to many Gothic structures.

Construct the basic grid infill using 2×4 material. Build the basic triangle frame, then add the ornamental brackets to make the three-leaf Gothic window. See "Construction Steps" for help on constructing grid and panel fences, and "Construction Techniques" for help on making ornate corner posts.

DESIGN 87: COLONIAL CROSSED FENCE

This basic crossed fence with boxlike infill supports was a common style in the eighteenth century. Simple straight cuts made it easier for craftsmen to construct this fence in the days before power tools. The large, simple post complements this colonial-style fence. This design is more useful as a boundary fence than for restraining small animals and children. This fence is suitable for colonial and country-style homes.

Construct the basic grid infill using 2×4 material. Assemble the basic crossed infill, then add the finer boxed infill. See "Construction Steps" for help on constructing grid and panel fences, and "Construction Techniques" for help on making ornate corner posts.

Fence: 3 feet, 6 inches high.
Posts: 4 feet, 5 inches high.
Low security: The smooth rail top is inviting to climb or sit on.
Low privacy: The infill is low and open, thus allowing easy visibility over and through the fence.
Low buffering: This fence filters little sun and wind.
Construction: Fence, advanced difficulty. Posts, moderate difficulty.

Fence: 3 feet, 2 inches high.
Posts: 3 feet, 7 inches high.
Low security: The smooth rail top is inviting to climb or sit on.
Low privacy: The infill is low and open, thus allowing easy visibility over and through the fence.
Low buffering: This fence filters little sun and wind.
Construction: Fence, easy. Posts, easy.

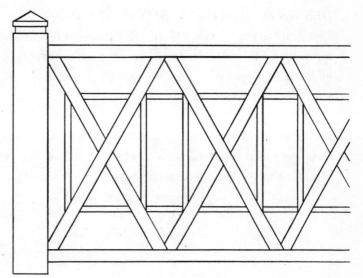

DESIGN 88: HALO FENCE

This magnificently ornate fence displays a variety of decorations that demonstrate the skill of its maker. Propeller-style pickets are crested with circular toppers haloed by circular panel cutouts. The 2×4s separating and framing each picket add to the fence's strong appearance, add variety to the pattern, and reduce the number of sawn pickets necessary. Each picket is highlighted by a simple rosette. The post is ornamented by a decorative fleur appliqué, lower body veining, and a molded cap and finial. This fence is suitable for country or city Victorian homes.

Construct the basic grid infill using 2×4 material. Cut the pickets from 1×4 lumber and make the haloed panels from exterior-grade plywood. Mortise the horizontal 2×4 infill to insert the pickets. Cut channels in the 2×4s to hold the haloed panel inserts. See "Construction Steps" for help on constructing grid and panel fences, and "Construction Techniques" for help on making ornate corner posts.

DESIGN 89: GOTHIC INSPIRATION FENCE

This is an elegant Victorian Gothic design with a row of keyhole windows above a row of recessed raised panels. Handsome corner posts are decoratively chamfered, adorned with moldings and rosettes, and crowned with an urn finial. This fence is magnificent for a Victorian cottage or Gothic chapel.

Construct the basic grid infill using 2×4 material. Use 1× material for the keyhole windows and the raised panel inserts. Use a table saw or a router with panel raising bit to make the raised panel inserts. Cut channels in the 2×4s to hold the panel inserts. See "Construction Steps" for help on constructing grid and panel fences, and "Construction Techniques" for help on making ornate corner posts.

Fence: 3 feet, 9 inches high.
Posts: 4 feet, 4 inches high.
Low security: The smooth rail top is inviting to climb or sit on.
Low privacy: The infill is low and open, thus allowing easy visibility over and through the fence.
Low buffering: This fence filters little sun and wind.
Construction: Fence, advanced difficulty. Posts, advanced difficulty.

Fence: 3 feet, 9 inches high.
Posts: 4 feet, 4 inches high.
Low security: The smooth rail top is inviting to climb or sit on.
Low privacy: The infill is low and open, thus allowing easy visibility over and through the fence.
Low buffering: This fence filters little sun and wind.
Construction: Fence, advanced difficulty. Posts, moderate difficulty.

DESIGN 90: CATHEDRAL PANEL FENCE

Beautiful arching panels are the focal point of this magnificent fence. Heavy molding throughout the fence infill and on the posts gives this design a lavish appearance. The light latticework on the top section of the fence can also be made using dowel rods, or even rope for a more nautical flavor. This stately fence is suitable for any formal home.

Construct the basic grid infill using 2× material. Use 1× material for the raised panel inserts. Use a router with panel raising bit to make the raised panel inserts. Cut channels in the 2× material to hold the panel inserts. See "Construction Steps" for help on constructing grid and panel fences, and "Construction Techniques" for help on making ornate corner posts.

Fence: 3 feet, 8 inches high.
Posts: 4 feet, 2 inches high.
Moderate security: The
smooth rail top is inviting
to climb or sit on, but
the high solid infill portion
is good for restraining
most small dogs.
Low privacy: The infill is
low, thus allowing easy
visibility over the fence.
Low buffering: This fence
blocks little sun and wind.
Construction: Fence,
advanced difficulty. Posts,
advanced difficulty.

Pale Fences

DESIGN 91: CLASSIC ALTERNATING-PICKET FENCE

In this beautiful, easy-to-make design, twin slender, pointed pales are separated by broad pickets with circle tops. The simple post combines the pitch of the pales with the circle tops of the pickets. This versatile fence will enhance any home style and looks attractive at any height.

Construct the infill using 1×2s for the pales and 1×6s for the pickets. Use a band saw for both picket and pale tops. When assembling the infill, use an extra pale as a spacer. See "Construction Techniques" for help and ideas on making ornate corner posts.

DESIGN 92: DIAMOND-TOPPED PALE FENCE

Simple, slender, and refined, this exquisite pale design was popular in the eighteenth century and is both beautiful and functional. The delicate diamond-point tops are easy to cut and quite effective in deterring would-be fence sitters. The simple, stout post has a miter-cut top that is a three-dimensional version of the pale tops. Although this fence design was popular in the colonial era, the simplicity of its design allows it to accent almost any type of housing.

Construct the infill using 1×2s or 2×2s for the pales. Saw the pale tops using a band saw or table saw. When assembling the infill, use an extra pale as a spacer. See "Construction Techniques" for help and ideas on making ornate corner posts.

Fence: 3 feet, 6 inches high.
Posts: 3 feet, 9 inches high.
High security: The pointed pale tops and tight spacing of the infill make this an ideal security fence for children and pets.
Low privacy: The infill is low and open, thus allowing easy visibility over and through the fence.
Low buffering: This fence filters little sun and wind.
Construction: Fence, very easy. Posts, very easy.

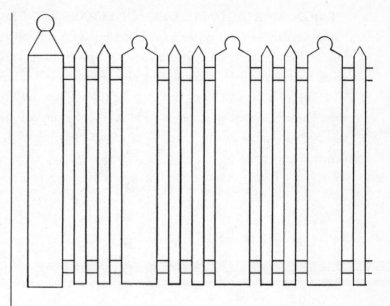

Fence: 3 feet, 4 inches high.
Posts: 3 feet, 11 inches high.
High security: The pointed tops and tight spacing of the infill make this an ideal security fence for children and pets.
Low privacy: The infill is low and open, thus allowing easy visibility over and through the fence.
Low buffering: This fence filters little sun and wind.
Construction: Fence, very easy. Posts, very easy.

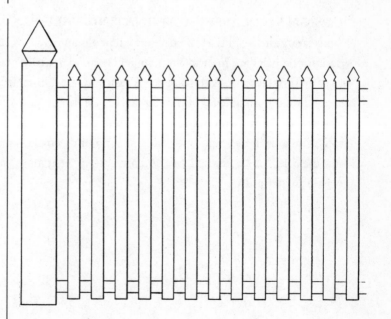

DESIGN 93: DIAGONAL DIAMOND PALE FENCE

In this charming variation of a basic fence style, diamond-topped pales are diagonally inset in the stringers. The picket tops are simple to cut, and this fence is easy and fast to install, as well as durable. This design goes well with both modern and period architecture.

Construct the infill using 2×2s for the pales. Use a band saw or table saw for the pale tops. Use a drill press with mortising attachment to make square holes in the stringers so that the pales can be inserted. See "Construction Techniques" for help and ideas on making ornate corner posts.

DESIGN 94: CLASSIC ALTERNATING-PALE FENCE

Alternating the heights of the pales in a fence is an easy way to vary a simple style. In this design, the pales are inset in the stringers to render a more formal appearance. The pale tops are simple to cut, and this fence is easy and fast to install, as well as durable. This basic fence design is suitable for almost any style of home.

Construct the infill using 2×2s for the pales. Use a band saw or table saw for the pale tops. Use a drill press with mortising attachment to make square holes in the stringers so that the pales can be inserted. See "Construction Techniques" for help and ideas on making ornate corner posts.

Fence: 3 feet, 4 inches high.
Posts: 3 feet, 11 inches high.
High security: The pointed tops and tight spacing of the infill make this an ideal security fence for children and pets.
Low privacy: The infill is low and open, thus allowing easy visibility over and through the fence.
Low buffering: This fence filters little sun and wind.
Construction: Fence, moderate difficulty. Posts, very easy.

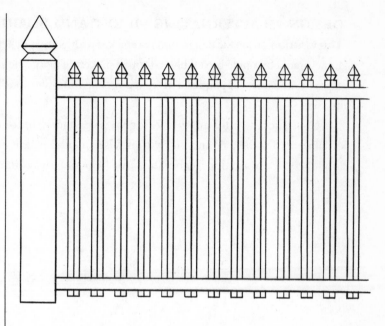

Fence: 3 feet, 7 inches high.
Posts: 4 feet, 5 inches high.
High security: The pointed tops and tight spacing of the infill make this an ideal security fence for children and pets.
Low privacy: The infill is low and open, thus allowing easy visibility over and through the fence.
Low buffering: This fence filters little sun and wind.
Construction: Fence, moderate difficulty. Posts, moderate difficulty.

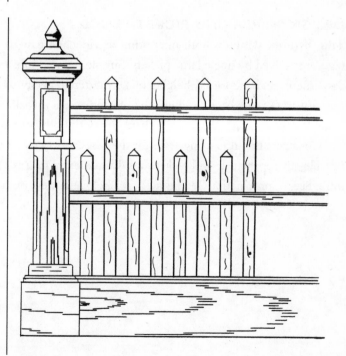

DESIGN 95: ALTERNATING PICKET AND BOARD FENCE

This variation on a basic design uses two picket widths and pitches. Trios of thin, pointed pales are separated by single broad, blunt-topped pickets. The simple post is topped with a mitered cap and medallion appliqué. This fence is charming with both contemporary and period houses.

Construct the infill using 1×2s for the pales and 1×6s for the pickets. Use a band saw or table saw for the pale and picket tops. Use an extra pale as a spacer when nailing on the infill. See "Construction Techniques" for help and ideas on making ornate corner posts.

DESIGN 96: PEAKING PICKET FENCE

This rhythmic design is both interesting to view and easy to construct. Trios of slender pales are flanked by single large pickets. Simple pointed tops make these pales and pickets easy to cut, and the varied heights make the fence tricky to climb. The strongly styled post features ornate base molding, chamfering, and a medallion appliqué. The post cap is a simple mitered top. This fence is charming with both contemporary and period houses.

Construct the infill using 1×2s for the pales and 1×6s for the pickets. Use a band saw or table saw for the pale and picket tops. Use an extra pale as a spacer when nailing on the infill. See "Construction Techniques" for help and ideas on making ornate corner posts.

Fence: 3 feet, 4 inches high.
Posts: 3 feet, 8 inches high.
High security: The pointed tops and tight spacing of the infill make this an ideal security fence for children and pets.
Low privacy: The infill is low and open, thus allowing easy visibility over and through the fence.
Low buffering: This fence filters little sun and wind.
Construction: Fence, very easy. Posts, easy.

Fence: 3 feet, 4 inches high.
Posts: 3 feet, 8 inches high.
High security: The pointed tops and tight spacing of the infill make this an ideal security fence for children and pets.
Low privacy: The infill is low and open, thus allowing easy visibility over and through the fence.
Low buffering: This fence filters little sun and wind.
Construction: Fence, easy. Posts, moderate difficulty.

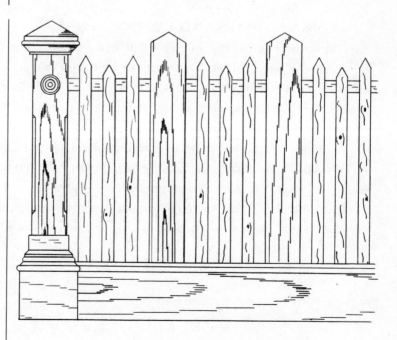

DESIGN 97: WINDOWED BOARD FENCE

Narrow pales alternate with broad, arch-topped boards to form a pleasing repetition. The accent post is ornamented with a full body panel appliqué and a molded Gothic post finial. This infill style is relatively easy to cut and assemble. The fence is adaptable to shorter or taller heights. The windows in the board centers may be omitted to increase privacy and security. This fence design is suitable for country or town Victorian homes and churches.

Construct the infill using 2×2s for the pales and 1×8s for the boards. Use a band saw for the pale and board tops. Cut out the decorative windows using a router and pattern. Use an extra pale as a spacer when nailing on the infill. See "Construction Techniques" for help and ideas on making ornate corner posts.

DESIGN 98: PALES AND LATTICE FENCE

This fence features a fanciful colonial pattern created with simple miter-topped pales and diagonally placed lattice. The miter-cut tops and chamfered molding are easy to make. Although this simple style was popular in eighteenth-century America, it will nicely accent most Victorian and contemporary homes. This fence is beautiful standing by itself or dressed with lush vegetation and flowering vines.

Construct the infill using 2×2s for the pales and lattice slats for the diagonal members. Use a band saw or table saw for the pale tops. Use a drill press with mortising attachment to make square holes in the stringers so that the pales can be inserted. Diagonally nail the lattice slats to the pales. Attach moldings below the top stringer if desired. See "Construction Techniques" for help and ideas on making ornate corner posts.

Fence: 3 feet, 8 inches high.
Posts: 4 feet, 3 inches high.
High security: The pointed tops and tight spacing of the infill make this an ideal security fence for children and pets.
Low privacy: The infill is low and open, thus allowing easy visibility over and through the fence.
Low buffering: This fence filters little sun and wind.
Construction: Fence, moderate difficulty. Posts, moderate difficulty.

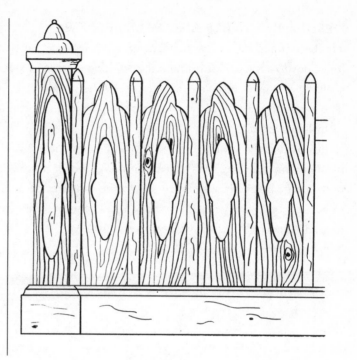

Fence: 3 feet, 8 inches high.
Posts: 4 feet, 3 inches high.
High security: The pointed tops and tight spacing of the infill make this an ideal security fence for children and pets.
Low privacy: The infill is low and open, thus allowing easy visibility over and through the fence.
Low buffering: This fence filters little sun and wind.
Construction: Fence, moderate difficulty. Posts, easy.

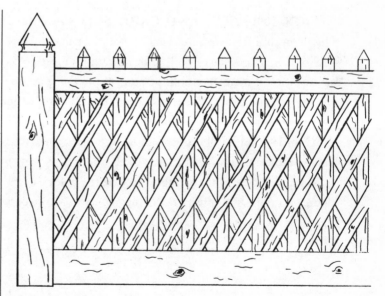

DESIGN 99: PANELS AND PALES FENCE

This beautiful fence features slender, pointed pales and a raised-panel midsection. The solid lower portion is ideal for restraining small dogs. Spaced pales on the top section increase visibility and give the fence an open feel. The simple post with mitered top and broad base is easy to make and complements the pale infill. This fence is a good match for any formal-style home.

Construct the infill using 2×2s for the pales and 1×12s for the panel inserts. Use a band saw or table saw for the pale tops. Use a drill press with mortising attachment to make square holes in the stringers so that the pales can be inserted. To create the panel inserts, use a table saw or router with panel raising bit. See "Contruction Techniques" for help and ideas on making ornate corner posts.

DESIGN 100: PALES AND CARD SUIT PANELS FENCE

This whimsical fence features slender, pointed pales and card suit panel inserts. The dense infill of this design makes it ideal for restraining most pets and children. Spaced pales on the top section increase visibility and give the fence an open feel. The simple post with mitered top and broad base is easy to make and complements the pale infill. This fence style is especially suited to whimsical country cottages.

Construct the infill using 2×2s for the pales and 1×12s for the panel inserts. Use a band saw or table saw for the pale tops. Use a drill press with mortising attachment to make square holes in the stringers so that the pales can be inserted. Make the card suit cutouts on the panel inserts with a jigsaw. See "Construction Techniques" for help and ideas on making ornate corner posts.

Fence: 3 feet, 11 inches high.
Posts: 4 feet, 1 inch high.
High security: The pointed tops and dense infill pattern make this fence ideal for restraining small pets.
Low privacy: The infill is low and open, thus allowing easy visibility over and through the fence.
Low buffering: This fence filters some sun and wind.
Construction: Fence, advanced difficulty. Posts, easy.

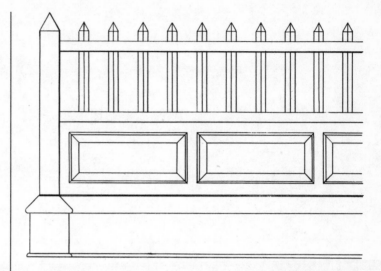

Fence: 3 feet, 9 inches high.
Posts: 4 feet, 3 inches high.
High security: The pointed tops discourage would-be fence sitters and climbers.
Low privacy: The infill is low and open, thus allowing easy visibility over and through the fence.
Low buffering: This fence filters some sun and wind.
Construction: Fence, advanced difficulty. Posts, easy.

Historical Fences

IN THE LATE NINETEENTH CENTURY, HOME PLAN BOOKS WERE MUCH DIFFERENT THAN they are today. In addition to showing the home's floorplan and an artistic sketch of the home's exterior, they showed numerous architectural details that could be used in the home's construction. Included were detailed drawings of newel posts, porch posts, balustrades, spandrels, brackets, and even picket fence sections. Extracts from several of these Victorian pattern books are included for helpful ideas on adorning your own picket fence.

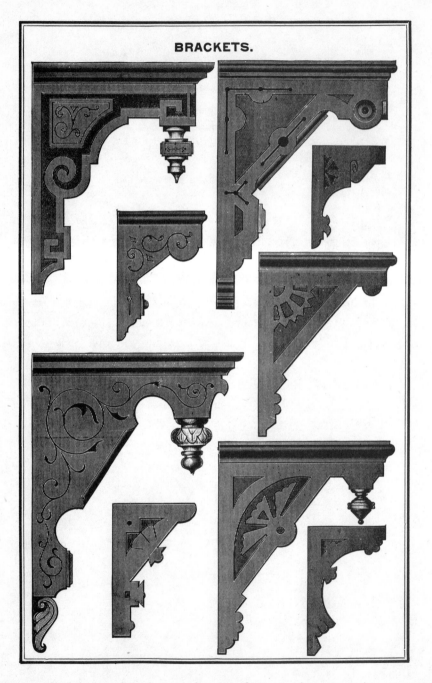

BRACKETS.

These decorative brackets, intended to support the eaves of Victorian homes, can also ornament fences and gates. Many of them can be turned sideways or upside-down to make decorative gate scrolls.

BRACKETS.

BRACKETS.

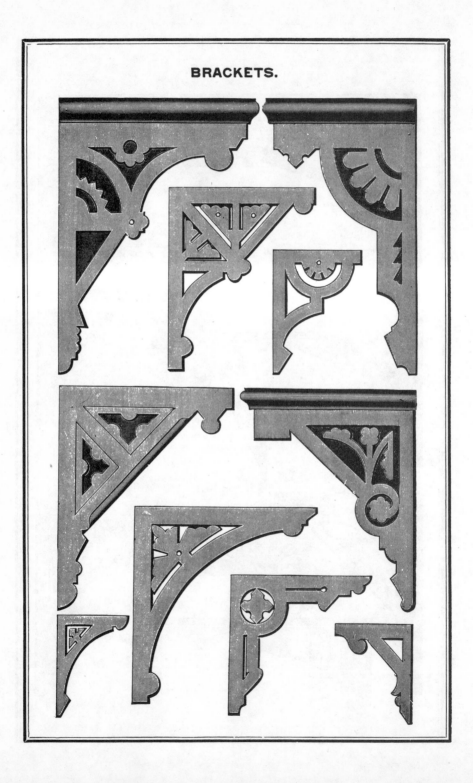

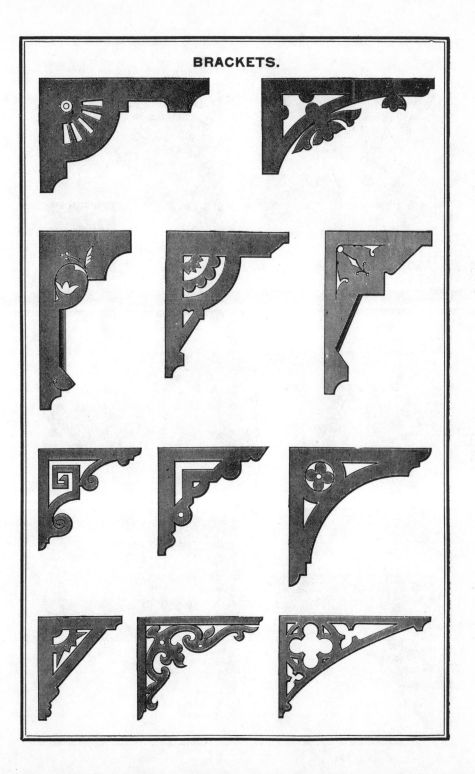

BRACKETS.

BRACKETS.

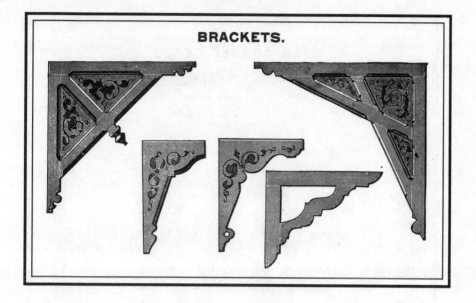

To make gate pediments, turn the brackets sideways or upside-down and mirror the bracket image from the right side to the left side.

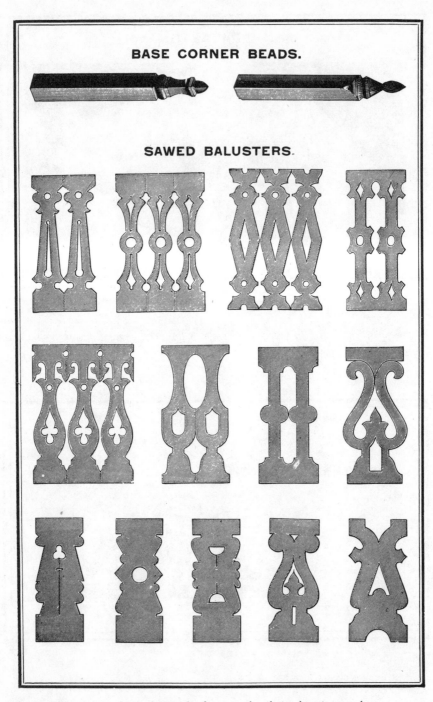

Sawn balusters were commonly used to make fences and rails in the nineteenth century.

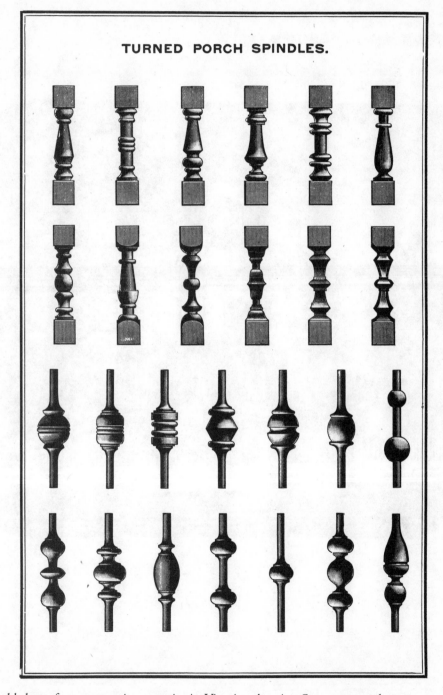

Turned baluster fences were quite expensive in Victorian America. See next page also.

NEWEL POSTS.

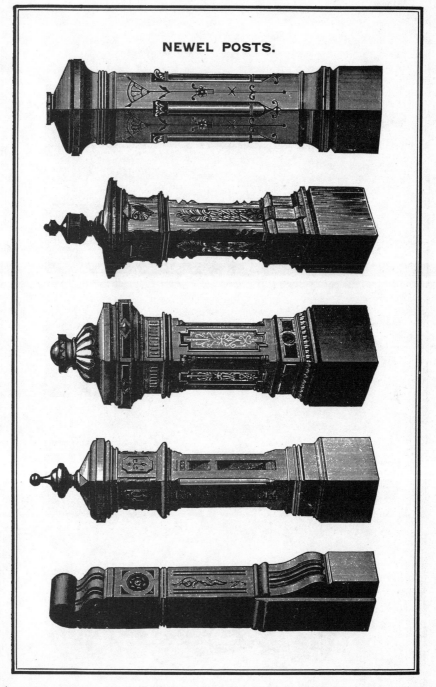

These decorative posts are typical of architectural details of the late 1800s. See next two pages also.

NEWEL POSTS.

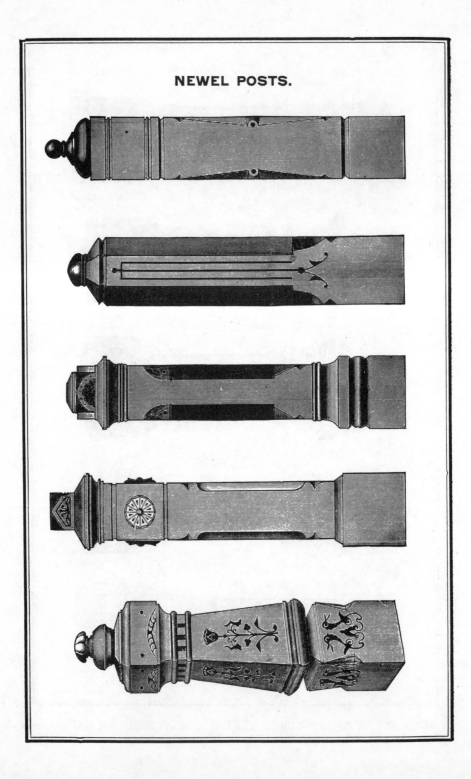

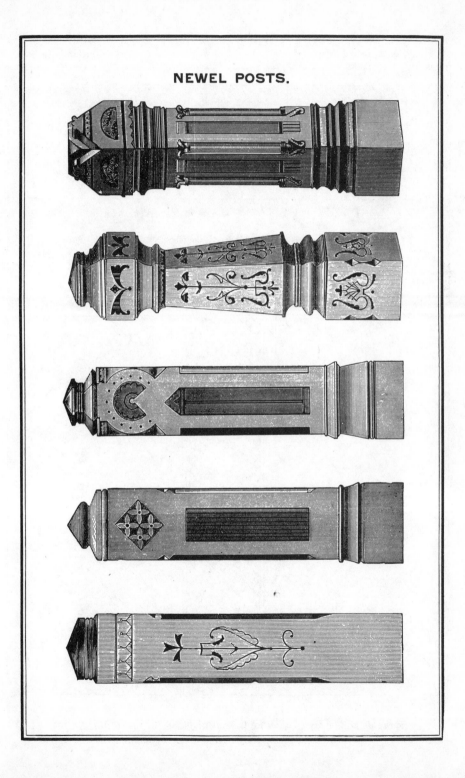

NEWEL POSTS.

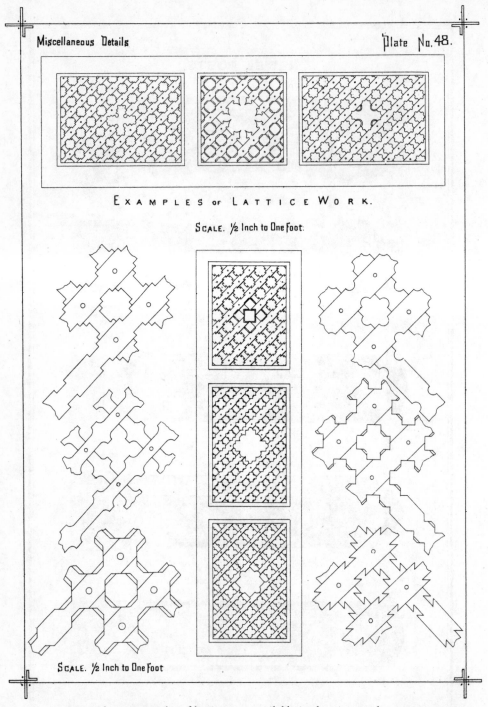

EXAMPLES OF LATTICE WORK.

SCALE. ½ Inch to One Foot.

SCALE. ½ Inch to One Foot

Many decorative styles of lattice were available in the nineteenth century.

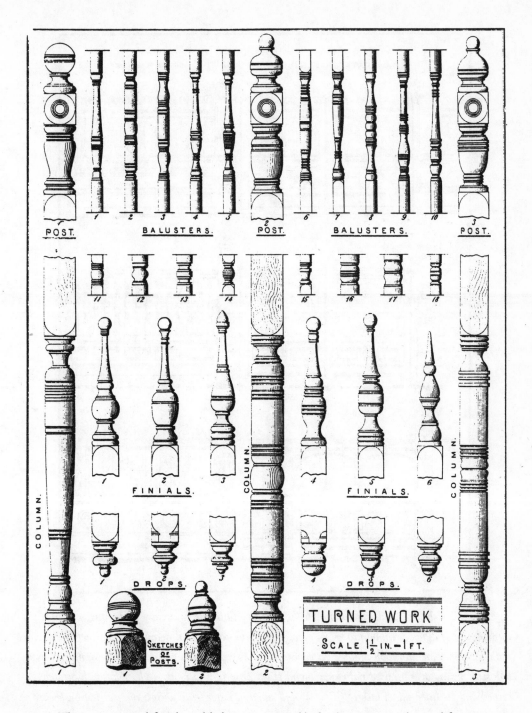

These ornamental finials and balusters are suitable for decorating porches and fences.

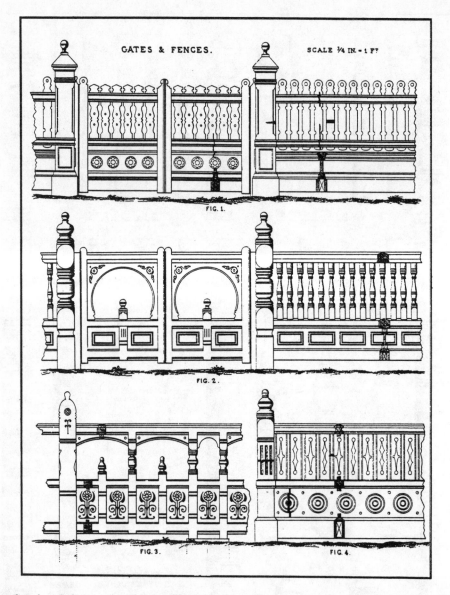

GATES & FENCES.   SCALE ¾ IN. = 1 FT

FIG. 1.

FIG. 2.

FIG. 3.   FIG. 4.

These four lavish fence styles of the nineteenth century illustrate a variety of designs achieved through use of different combinations of gate, fence, and ornamental detail: sawn picket fence with a double-door gate and high molded baseboard (Fig. 1); combination fence with decoratively sawn balusters resting over a raised panel baseboard (Fig. 2); grid and panel-style fence with ornately carved and stenciled panel inserts (Fig. 3); and sawn baluster fence with a rosette-clad baseboard (Fig. 4).

This fence plate from a mid-nineteenth-century architectural-details pattern book displays a selection of ornamental fence styles. Figs. 1, 2, and 3 are sawn picket fences. Figs. 4 and 7 feature two ornamental sawn baluster fences; Fig. 7 also displays an ornamental sawn running trim across its top rail. Fig. 5 features a grid-style fence with oversized post and ball. Fig. 6, the most lavish and costly fence, is highlighted by six-inch round balusters that are both turned and carved. The decorative post features a hipped roof cap with gabled dormers on all four sides.

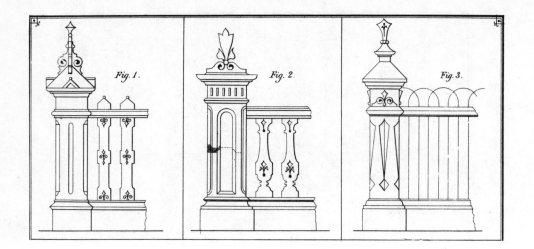

These three ornamental fences from an 1873 architectural-details pattern book all have wood-encased posts with decorative finishes: sawn and stenciled picket fence (Fig. 1); sawn balustrade fence (Fig. 2); wrought iron fence (Fig. 3).

PALLISER'S NEW COTTAGE HOMES AND DETAILS.

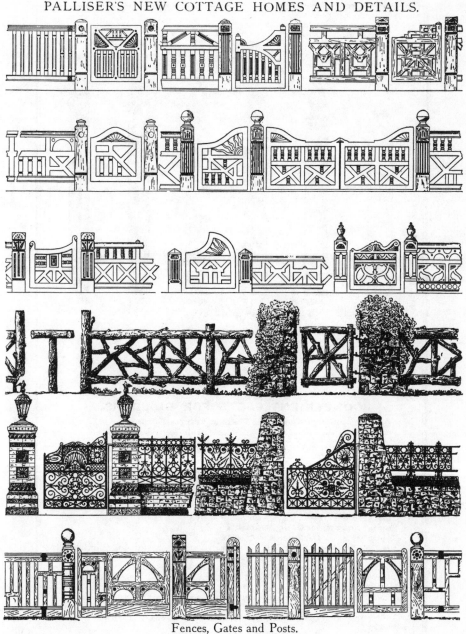

Fences, Gates and Posts.

These fence designs disseminated by the Palliser brothers in the late 1800s through the turn of the century include a number of grid-style fences.

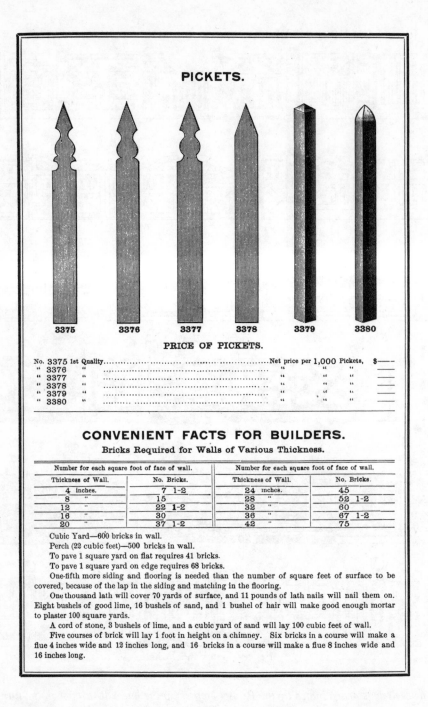

PICKETS.

| 3375 | 3376 | 3377 | 3378 | 3379 | 3380 |

PRICE OF PICKETS.

No. 3375 1st Quality...Net price per 1,000 Pickets, $———
" 3376 " .... " " " ———
" 3377 " .... " " " ———
" 3378 " .... " " " ———
" 3379 " .... " " " ———
" 3380 " .... " " " ———

CONVENIENT FACTS FOR BUILDERS.

Bricks Required for Walls of Various Thickness.

Number for each square foot of face of wall.		Number for each square foot of face of wall.	
Thickness of Wall.	No. Bricks.	Thickness of Wall.	No. Bricks.
4 inches.	7 1-2	24 inches.	45
8 "	15	28 "	52 1-2
12 "	22 1-2	32 "	60
16 "	30	36 "	67 1-2
20 "	37 1-2	42 "	75

Cubic Yard—600 bricks in wall.

Perch (22 cubic feet)—500 bricks in wall.

To pave 1 square yard on flat requires 41 bricks.

To pave 1 square yard on edge requires 68 bricks.

One-fifth more siding and flooring is needed than the number of square feet of surface to be covered, because of the lap in the siding and matching in the flooring.

One thousand lath will cover 70 yards of surface, and 11 pounds of lath nails will nail them on. Eight bushels of good lime, 16 bushels of sand, and 1 bushel of hair will make good enough mortar to plaster 100 square yards.

A cord of stone, 3 bushels of lime, and a cubic yard of sand will lay 100 cubic feet of wall.

Five courses of brick will lay 1 foot in height on a chimney. Six bricks in a course will make a flue 4 inches wide and 12 inches long, and 16 bricks in a course will make a flue 8 inches wide and 16 inches long.

This plate displays some of the basic picket patterns available in the nineteenth century.

Glossary

Accenting gate. A gate that uses the fence infill pattern but with some variations to make the gate stand out from the fence.

Ball. A round orb used to decorate post tops.

Balustrade. An ornamental upright post or picket giving support to a rail.

Baseboard. Boarding that lines the wall of a fence, just above ground level.

Bevel. An angle other than a right angle between two lines or surfaces, cut or slanted obliquely.

Board. 1. Any thin slab of lumber. 2. A broad picket used as fence infill.

Chamfer. A bevel on the edge of a board or other solid, usually 45 degrees.

Combination fence. A fence using more than one type of infill.

Complementing gate. See *accenting gate.*

Contrasting gate. A gate that bears little or no resemblance to the fence infill.

Finial. A crowning ornament, such as the tip of a spire or cap on a shaft.

Grid and panel. A network of rails and inset boards used as fence infill.

Hidden gate. A gate that uses the fence infill pattern, making the gate difficult to differentiate from the fence.

Infill. The material used to "fill in" the fence between the posts.

Intermediate post. A post between two terminal posts.

Pale. 1. A thin or square picket. 2. A narrow picket used as fence infill.

Pedestal. A supporting base used to support a finial and act as a connector to a larger post cap.

Pediment. A decorative member that extends across the top of a gate.

Picket. 1. Used generally, any upright member of fence infill. 2. Used specifically, an upright member of fence infill that is wider than a pale and narrower than a board.

Post cap. A top or cover placed on a post.

Post casing. Thinner lumber overlaying a post to provide a decorative or more substantial appearance.

Rosette. A design or ornament in circular, roselike form.

Scroll bracket. A decorative member used to ornament a gate top. Usually used in pairs to flank a decorative centerpiece.

Stringer. A structural member that spans two posts to support the fence infill.

Stringer hanger. A metal bracket used to connect a stringer to a post.

Terminal post. An end, corner, or gate post.

Urn. A vase with a base used to decorate post tops.

Ordering Picket and Finial Patterns

PICKET FENCES ARE BEAUTIFUL WHETHER THEY ARE DECORATED WITH SIMPLE POINTED tops or ornately scrolling designs. Even the most lavish sawn pickets are quite easy to cut; they just take more time than the simpler styles.

The most difficult part of making a picket fence is creating the original pattern from which every picket will be cut. You can order the picket and finial patterns displayed in this book by using the order form listed below. The order form lists each pattern by number and indicates (with an X) if a picket and/or finial pattern is available for that fence design.

These paper patterns are full-sized, suitable for tracing onto cardboard or hardboard to be used as templates. The price is $9.95 per pattern set. Pennsylvania residents must add 6% sales tax. Please allow 3 to 6 weeks for delivery.

Send your order to the following address:

Geist Designs

P. O. Box 169

Middletown, PA 17057

Pattern No.	Finial	Picket(s)
_____ 001	X	X
_____ 002	X	X
_____ 003	X	X
_____ 004	X	X
_____ 005	X	X
_____ 006	X	X
_____ 007	X	X
_____ 008	X	X
_____ 009	X	X
_____ 010	X	X

Pattern No.	Finial	Picket(s)
_____ 011	X	X
_____ 012	—	X
_____ 013	X	X
_____ 014	X	X
_____ 015	X	X
_____ 016	X	X
_____ 017	X	X
_____ 018	—	X
_____ 019	—	X
_____ 020	X	X
_____ 021	X	X
_____ 022	X	X
_____ 023	X	X
_____ 024	X	X
_____ 025	X	X
_____ 026	X	X
_____ 027	X	X
_____ 028	X	X
_____ 029	X	X
_____ 030	—	X
_____ 031	—	X
_____ 032	—	X
_____ 033	—	X
_____ 034	X	X
_____ 035	X	X
_____ 036	X	X
_____ 037	X	X
_____ 038	X	X
_____ 039	X	X
_____ 040	X	X
_____ 041	—	X
_____ 042	X	X
_____ 043	X	X
_____ 044	—	X
_____ 045	X	X
_____ 046	X	X

Pattern No.	Finial	Picket(s)
_____ 047	—	X
_____ 048	—	X
_____ 049	X	X
_____ 050	—	X
_____ 051	X	X
_____ 052	—	X
_____ 053	—	X
_____ 054	—	X
_____ 055	X	X
_____ 056	—	X
_____ 057	—	X
_____ 058	X	X
_____ 059	X	X
_____ 060	—	—
_____ 061	—	—
_____ 062	—	—
_____ 063	—	—
_____ 064	—	—
_____ 065	—	—
_____ 066	X	X
_____ 067	X	X
_____ 068	—	—
_____ 069	—	—
_____ 070	—	—
_____ 071	—	—
_____ 072	—	—
_____ 073	X	—
_____ 074	—	—
_____ 075	—	—
_____ 076	—	—
_____ 077	X	—
_____ 078	—	—
_____ 079	X	—
_____ 080	X	—
_____ 081	—	—
_____ 082	—	—

_____ 083	X	—
_____ 084	X	—
_____ 085	—	—
_____ 086	X	—
_____ 087	—	—
_____ 088	X	X
_____ 089	X	—
_____ 090	X	—
_____ 091	X	X
_____ 092	X	X
_____ 093	X	X
_____ 094	X	X
_____ 095	—	X
_____ 096	—	X
_____ 097	X	X
_____ 098	X	—
_____ 099	—	—
_____ 100	—	—

▪ Metric Conversions ▪

INCHES TO MILLIMETRES

IN.	MM	IN.	MM
1	25.4	51	1295.4
2	50.8	52	1320.8
3	76.2	53	1346.2
4	101.6	54	1371.6
5	127.0	55	1397.0
6	152.4	56	1422.4
7	177.8	57	1447.8
8	203.2	58	1473.2
9	228.6	59	1498.6
10	254.0	60	1524.0
11	279.4	61	1549.4
12	304.8	62	1574.8
13	330.2	63	1600.2
14	355.6	64	1625.6
15	381.0	65	1651.0
16	406.4	66	1676.4
17	431.8	67	1701.8
18	457.2	68	1727.2
19	482.6	69	1752.6
20	508.0	70	1778.0
21	533.4	71	1803.4
22	558.8	72	1828.8
23	584.2	73	1854.2
24	609.6	74	1879.6
25	635.0	75	1905.0
26	660.4	76	1930.4
27	685.8	77	1955.8
28	711.2	78	1981.2
29	736.6	79	2006.6
30	762.0	80	2032.0
31	787.4	81	2057.4
32	812.8	82	2082.8
33	838.2	83	2108.2
34	863.6	84	2133.6
35	889.0	85	2159.0
36	914.4	86	2184.4
37	939.8	87	2209.8
38	965.2	88	2235.2
39	990.6	89	2260.6
40	1016.0	90	2286.0
41	1041.4	91	2311.4
42	1066.8	92	2336.8
43	1092.2	93	2362.2
44	1117.6	94	2387.6
45	1143.0	95	2413.0
46	1168.4	96	2438.4
47	1193.8	97	2463.8
48	1219.2	98	2489.2
49	1244.6	99	2514.6
50	1270.0	100	2540.0

The above table is exact on the basis: 1 in. = 25.4 mm

U.S. TO METRIC
1 inch = 2.540 centimetres
1 foot = .305 metre
1 yard = .914 metre
1 mile = 1.609 kilometres

METRIC TO U.S.
1 millimetre = .039 inch
1 centimetre = .394 inch
1 metre = 3.281 feet or 1.094 yards
1 kilometre = .621 mile

INCH-METRIC EQUIVALENTS

FRACTION	DECIMAL EQUIVALENT		FRACTION	DECIMAL EQUIVALENT	
	CUSTOMARY (IN.)	METRIC (MM)		CUSTOMARY (IN.)	METRIC (MM)
	1/64 —.015	0.3969		33/64 —.515	13.0969
1/32 —.031		0.7938	17/32 —.531		13.4938
	3/64 —.046	1.1906		35/64 —.546	13.8906
1/16 —.062		1.5875	9/16 —.562		14.2875
	5/64 —.078	1.9844		37/64 —.578	14.6844
3/32 —.093		2.3813	19/32 —.593		15.0813
	7/64 —.109	2.7781		39/64 —.609	15.4781
1/8 —.125		3.1750	5/8 —.625		15.8750
	9/64 —.140	3.5719		41/64 —.640	16.2719
5/32 —.156		3.9688	21/32 —.656		16.6688
	11/64 —.171	4.3656		43/64 —.671	17.0656
3/16 —.187		4.7625	11/16 —.687		17.4625
	13/64 —.203	5.1594		45/64 —.703	17.8594
7/32 —.218		5.5563	23/32 —.718		18.2563
	15/64 —.234	5.9531		47/64 —.734	18.6531
1/4 —.250		6.3500	3/4 —.750		19.0500
	17/64 —.265	6.7469		49/64 —.765	19.4469
9/32 —.281		7.1438	25/32 —.781		19.8438
	19/64 —.296	7.5406		51/64 —.796	20.2406
5/16 —.312		7.9375	13/16 —.812		20.6375
	21/64 —.328	8.3384		53/64 —.828	21.0344
11/32 —.343		8.7313	27/32 —.843		21.4313
	23/64 —.359	9.1281		55/64 —.859	21.8281
3/8 —.375		9.5250	7/8 —.875		22.2250
	25/64 —.390	9.9219		57/64 —.890	22.6219
13/32 —.406		10.3188	29/32 —.906		23.0188
	27/64 —.421	10.7156		59/64 —.921	23.4156
7/16 —.437		11.1125	15/16 —.937		23.8125
	29/64 —.453	11.5094		61/64 —.953	24.2094
15/32 —.468		11.9063	31/32 —.968		24.6063
	31/64 —.484	12.3031		63/64 —.984	25.0031
1/2 —.500		12.7000	1 —1.000		25.4000